HIERARCHY, UNITY, AND IMITATION

Society of Biblical Literature

Academia Biblica

Steven L. McKenzie,
Hebrew Bible/Old Testament Editor

Sharon H. Ringe,
New Testament Editor

Number 24

HIERARCHY, UNITY, AND IMITATION
A Feminist Rhetorical Analysis of
Power Dynamics in
Paul's Letter to the Philippians

HIERARCHY, UNITY, AND IMITATION
A Feminist Rhetorical Analysis of
Power Dynamics in
Paul's Letter to the Philippians

Joseph A. Marchal

Society of Biblical Literature
Atlanta

HIERARCHY, UNITY, AND IMITATION
A Feminist Rhetorical Analysis of Power Dynamics in Paul's Letter to the Philippians

Copyright © 2006 by the Society of Biblical Literature

All rights reserved. No part of this work may be reproduced or transmitted in any form or by any means, electronic or mechanical, including photocopying and recording, or by means of any information storage or retrieval system, except as may be expressly permitted by the 1976 Copyright Act or in writing from the publisher. Requests for permission should be addressed in writing to the Rights and Permissions Office, Society of Biblical Literature, 825 Houston Mill Road, Atlanta, GA 30329, USA.

Library of Congress Cataloging-in-Publication Data

Marchal, Joseph A.
  Hierarchy, unity, and imitation : a feminist rhetorical analysis of power dynamics in Paul's letter to the Philippians / by Joseph A. Marchal.
    p. cm. — (Society of Biblical Literature Acdemia Biblica ; no. 24)
  Includes bibliographical references and index.
  ISBN-13: 978-1-58983-243-5 (pbk. : alk. paper)
  ISBN-10: 1-58983-243-4 (pbk. : alk. paper)
  1. Bible. N.T. Philippians—Feminist criticism. 2. Rhetorical criticism. 3. Feminist theology. I. Title.

BS2705.52.M36 2006
227'.606082—dc22   2006028596

Printed in the United States of America
on acid-free paper

Contents

Acknowledgements vii

I. Introduction 1
   A. Context, Purpose, and Procedure 1
   B. Rhetorical Approaches 3
   C. Further Reflections on Feminist Rhetorical Approaches 11
   D. Preliminary Issues in the Study of Philippians 16

Part One: Setting the Stage

II. Critical Overview of Scholarship on Prominent Images
    in Philippians 23
   A. Prominent Imagery in Philippians 24
      1. Friendship Imagery 24
      2. Military Imagery 29
   B. Feminist Assessment 34
      1. Reconsidering Friendship Imagery 35
      2. Reconsidering Military Imagery 50
      3. Reconsidering the Connections between
           Friendship and Military Imagery 64
   C. Cues from This Debate for the Rest of the Study 70

III. Situating the Rhetorics of Philippians 73
   A. Women's Participation in Cults at Philippi 73
      Excursus: Imitation of Women in Cultic Life 81
   B. Women's Participation in the Early Jesus Movement
      at Philippi 83
   C. Unity Rhetorics in Ancient Civic Speeches 91
   D. Colonial Status and Military Situation of Philippi 99

Part Two: How Philippians Implements These Rhetorics

IV. Evolving Rhetoric: The Interaction of Arguments As They Develop (Section-By-Section Analysis)	115
A. 1:1–11	119
B. 1:12–26	123
C. 1:27–2:4	128
D. 2:5–18	133
E. 2:19–30	138
F. 3:1–11	141
G. 3:12–21	143
H. 4:1–9	147
I. 4:10–23	152
J. Summary of the Argumentative Techniques	154
V. Prevailing Rhetoric: The Major Arguments	157
A. Arguments by Dissociation	158
B. Quasi-Logical Arguments	166
C. Arguments Based on the Structure of Reality	173
D. Arguments Establishing the Structure of Reality	180
E. Summary, Implications, and Suggestions	191
VI. Conclusions	203
A. A Different Understanding of the Letter to the Philippians	204
B. Implications Concerning Previous Scholarship	206
C. Usefulness for Feminist and Liberation Interpretations	207
Appendix: Outline of Argumentative Techniques in Philippians	213
Bibliography	217
Index of Ancient Sources	249
Index of Modern Authors	257

Acknowledgements

Just as the rhetoric of Paul's letter to the Philippians cannot be understood in isolation from the rhetorics of his and our times, it is hard to imagine this project coming to this particular form without the help and support of a number of good people.

First and foremost, as this project represents one version of my 2004 dissertation from the Graduate Theological Union, I must acknowledge the work of my dissertation committee: Drs. Antoinette Clark Wire, Mary Ann Tolbert and Elisabeth Schüssler Fiorenza. Their gracious, frank, and responsive efforts have made the work of this study possible in at least two tangible ways. I could not have completed such a daunting task without their working *with* me in the past months and years, giving generously of their time and energy. In an even larger way, though, it is their work *before* my efforts here that have prepared the way for vital feminist interpretations of biblical literature. I count myself fortunate to live in a time when three feminist pioneers could be assembled for this committee. In ways more intangible and variegated, Anne, Mary, and Elisabeth have modeled for a great many how to be engaged scholars, posing urgent questions, thirsting for justice and equality, and struggling in movements for change. It is hard to imagine my own place as a student, teacher, and scholar outside of such continuing efforts. I hope that one might see their distinct effects on the work contained herein.

By their nature dissertations are conceived, developed, and written in many, small, seemingly insignificant moments. This is the difficulty and the potential drudgery of our task. Yet, I was regularly encouraged and seriously considered in nearly all of these moments by my capable coordinator. In Anne Wire, I had a precise intellect, curious questioner, thorough reader, and tireless advisor. Over countless meetings, phone calls, and emails, Anne demonstrated an extraordinary level of patience, good humor, and acumen. Her pointed observations and comprehensive vision provoked my best efforts, while assuring me of their relevance. Anne's attention to detail and care for the conception of the whole as we worked through multiple drafts and revisions have considerably improved the contents of this study. Thus, considerable credit for the completion and improvement of this project is due to Dr. Wire's diligent efforts, even as ultimately the responsibilities for any of its shortcoming are mine.

As a student in biblical studies at the GTU, I received encouragement from many faculty, students, and staff. I am grateful for support in key phases of my studies from J. David Hester Amador, John C. Endres, Herman Waetjen, and Gregory Tatum. My particular interest in Philippians was initially stoked by a doctoral seminar led by Edgar Krentz. My enthusiasm was bolstered by the thoughtful responses to my paper for that seminar by both Dr. Krentz and Uriah Yong-Hwan Kim. Uriah's attentiveness in that instance demonstrates the wider collegiality I experienced among my peers in graduate studies, from the GTU and elsewhere. I would be remiss, then, if I did not also acknowledge Sung-Eun Lee, Peggy Vernieu, and Sean Burke. I am especially grateful for the careful and caring collegiality of three comrades who studied with me over these years and commented upon large sections of this project: Avaren Ipsen, Paul Fullmer, and Yong-Sung Ahn. Our monthly meetings over coffee discussing our work and the world are the stuff that keeps a scholar sane in this particularly insane time in which we are living. Speaking of sanity, Bob Buller's acceptance of this manuscript kept mine intact, while Leigh Andersen's patient help oversaw its maintenance.

Since there is no better way to learn than in our attempts to teach, the conception of my work has often been calibrated by my experiences teaching introductory students at the Church Divinity School of the Pacific, Pacific School of Religion, St. Mary's College of California, Colby College, and Austin College. The particularities of my approach have been developed in the context of my seminar on feminism, rhetoric, and Paul at the GTU, Colby, and Austin. Thanks go to the innumerable colleagues, students, and friends from these disparate locales, who in their own way made this possible.

There are also those who have stood by me over the years with a constancy and tenacity deserving of words greater than "friend," either in its contemporary or ancient usage. Thanks cannot be written for Tascha, Danielle, Curt, Steen, Anjuli, Molly, or Chad, but I have tried anyway. Thanks and praise to my siblings, Rachel, Sarah, Chris and (most of all) Mary, who love and understand me in the only way they can, as they scratch their heads at the preposterous and strange things I say and do.

Finally, my parents Andrea Brophy and William G. Marchal encouraged this path upon which I find myself. For as long as I can remember, they have encouraged me to read just one more book, ask when I have questions, and wonder how things might be affecting others. These activities have found a happy home in the course of this project. They also constitute what (if anything) is important about what I am trying to do. Though this was perhaps unwitting on their part, I am nonetheless abundantly grateful, as I cannot imagine acting or thinking in any other way. It is for this and many other reasons that I dedicate this book to them.

Chapter I

Introduction

A. Context, Purpose, and Procedure

We are living in a time that is simultaneously fascinating and treacherous for a rhetorician. For many this period has heightened our consciousness and sharpened our focus upon the interconnected specters of sexism, homophobia, racism, classism, militarism, and colonialism. Daily casualty reports for both civilians and soldiers mix with arguments over who are true "friends" and allies. Citizens are exhorted to stand united and remain loyal to prescribed authorities. Civil liberties have been curtailed for the sake of our safety and the "common good." The situation demands that I engage these complex rhetorics, resist their oppressive dynamics, and seek strategies for a productive response.

But what does an interpretation of Paul's letter to the Philippians have to do with this context? If we pause long enough to contemplate the rhetorical dynamics that appear in Philippians, we find that they connect in uncommon ways with our current situation. Some of the images implemented in the letter reflect Greco-Roman expectations about friendship and the military. Paul's arguments focus on the topic of unity, depicting his potential opponents in distinct ways. Exhortations to obedience are linked to claims about citizenship and a common identity. For the first audience of this letter, the community at Philippi, the realities of empire and the accompanying hierarchies of gender, class, status, and ethnicity are grimly familiar.

Given these aspects of the rhetorical exchange behind Philippians, how can I ensure that my own process for interpreting this letter matters? Since there is a great deal to confront both in this letter and in our world, this study adopts a critical stance vis-à-vis the rhetorics of the Bible and biblical interpretation. This stance is also an outgrowth of my feminist beliefs, since "at the very least, feminism, like other liberation movements, attempts a critique of the oppressive structures of society."[1] The place of my project within the feminist movement, then, will help to explain the choice of particular subjects and approaches. While this study will point to pathways for further research on several subjects, it will particularly focus on the critical issues of gender and of colonial and military status. To accomplish this analysis, the letter will be approached as a piece of rhetoric. Paul made a series of arguments in Philippians, and the interpretations of this letter have been used as arguments ever since. Thus, my critical task involves a feminist rhetorical interpretation of biblical literature and of biblical scholarship. The aim of this dual inquiry will be to produce an interpretation useful to my main communities of accountability: feminists both within and outside the academy as well as all people—past, present and future—struggling under pyramidal structures of domination.

After a further review of relevant developments for rhetoric, feminism, and the letter to the Philippians (Chapter I.B–D), this feminist rhetorical analysis develops according to the following plan. The core of the study begins by reconsidering the contexts of Philippians' interpretation (Part One). First, I examine the previous scholarship on the prominent imagery in the letter (Chapter II). This overview not only highlights some of the letter's significant images, but it also evaluates how interpreters have not considered the power dynamics that potentially inhere in both friendship and military images. Through this overview I seek to demonstrate the need for my project while providing cues for the analysis to follow. Next I situate the letter further in terms of its ancient context (Chapter III), namely in light of the roles of women in Philippi, the use of unity concepts in civic speeches, and the status of Philippi as a Roman colony.

Having set the stage by examining the contexts for the letter and its interpretation, this project turns to a more concentrated analysis of the argumentation of Philippians (Part Two). I approach the letter's rhetorics from two different vantage points. First, I consider Paul's evolving rhetoric in Philippians, assessing the argumentative techniques in the order that they appear in the letter (Chapter IV). This shows how the various arguments build upon and interact with each other. Appreciating how the argumentation develops facilitates the reading of the *function* of these rhetorics. Second, I discuss the letter's prevailing rhetoric by grouping the key arguments together according to type (Chapter V). This categorization allows me to discern what is most characteristic about the letter's rhetorics. Approaching the argumentation in these two different ways makes it possible to consider the implications of Philippians and venture suggestions about the potential audience at Philippi.

---

[1] Mary Ann Tolbert, "Defining the Problem: The Bible and Feminist Hermeneutics," *Semeia* 28 (1983): 115. For more on feminist approaches and definitions, see Chapter I.C and III.B below.

INTRODUCTION 3

This study concludes with observations about Philippians, scholarly interpretations, and the relevance of this study's approach for those communities concerned with power relations (Chapter VI). This feminist rhetorical analysis can broaden the boundaries of biblical interpretation and open further avenues of exploration, rather than limit the scope of our considerations or close down conversations.

First I will situate my own feminist rhetorical analysis of Philippians through a review of the most relevant developments in the study of rhetoric, feminism, and Paul's letter to the Philippians.

B. RHETORICAL APPROACHES

Though it was a subject of study in Greco-Roman antiquity and played a large role in centuries of education and interpretation, rhetoric has only recently enjoyed a resurgence through a variety of approaches.[2] Rehearsing the history of the development, practice, minimization, and more recent momentum in rhetorical studies as a whole is not the main task of this introduction.[3] Rather, it is important to place this study in its context in terms of these rhetorical approaches. Only since the late 1960s and 1970s has rhetorical criticism of the

---

[2] There are a number of introductory texts for the history of rhetoric and the accompanying development of rhetorical criticism of the Bible. The observations of this particular overview of rhetoric and rhetorical biblical interpretation draw primarily from the following sources: Antoinette Clark Wire, *The Corinthian Women Prophets: A Reconstruction Through Paul's Rhetoric* (Minneapolis: Fortress, 1990), 1–11, 197–201; Duane F. Watson and Alan J. Hauser, "Notes on History and Method," in *Rhetorical Criticism of the Bible: A Comprehensive Bibliography with Notes on History and Method* (Biblical Interpretation Series 4; Leiden: Brill, 1994), 101–125; Elisabeth Schüssler Fiorenza, *Rhetoric and Ethic: The Politics of Biblical Studies* (Minneapolis: Fortress, 1999); J. David Hester Amador, *Academic Constraints in Rhetorical Criticism of the New Testament: An Introduction to a Rhetoric of Power* (JSNTSup 174; Sheffield: Sheffield Academic Press, 1999), 11–124; Watson, "Rhetorical Criticism, New Testament," in *Dictionary of Biblical Interpretation* (2 vols.; ed. John H. Hayes; Nashville: Abingdon Press, 1999), 2: 399–402; David S. Cunningham, "Rhetoric," in *Handbook of Postmodern Biblical Interpretation* (ed. A. K. M. Adam; St. Louis: Chalice Press, 2000), 220–226.

[3] For such a history, see Wilhelm Wuellner, *Hermeneutics and Rhetorics: From "Truth and Method" to Truth and Power* (Scriptura Special Issue S3; Stellenbosch, RSA: Centre for Hermeneutical Studies, 1989); Thomas H. Conley, *Rhetoric in the European Tradition* (Chicago: University of Chicago Press, 1990); Patricia Bizzell and Bruce Herzberg, eds., *The Rhetorical Tradition: Readings from Classical Times to the Present* (Boston: Bedford Books of St. Martin's Press, 1990); George A. Kennedy, *Classical Rhetoric and Its Christian and Secular Tradition from Ancient to Modern Times* (2nd ed., rev.; Chapel Hill: University of North Carolina Press, 1999); and Sonja K. Foss, Karen A. Foss, and Robert Trapp, *Contemporary Perspectives on Rhetoric* (3rd ed.; Prospect Heights, Ill.: Waveland Press, 2002), 1–18.

Bible been revived and become recognizable as a field of study. This revival in rhetorical approaches to biblical interpretation was initiated by the efforts of James Muilenberg, Hans Dieter Betz, and Wilhelm Wuellner, among others.[4] To some degree each of these scholars called for or practiced a shift in approach to rhetorical interpretation of biblical materials. Yet, in terms of offering a codified methodology for rhetorical criticism, classical scholar George A. Kennedy was first in introducing an oft-applied and criticized five step process.[5]

Betz and Kennedy's initial forays into rhetorical criticism drew biblical scholars into the study of Greco-Roman treatises and handbooks on rhetoric, from Aristotle through Quintillian.[6] However, both rhetorical and feminist rhetorical interpreters have noted at least three major shortcomings for these initial rhetorical analyses based on ancient models. First, the *rigidity* of the application of ancient categories in terms of identifying arrangement, *topoi*,

---

[4] James Muilenberg, "After Form Criticism What?" *JBL* 88 (1969): 1–18; Hans D. Betz, "The Literary Composition and Function of Paul's Letter to the Galatians," *NTS* 21 (1975): 353–379; *Galatians: A Commentary on Paul's Letters to the Churches in Galatia* (Hermeneia; Philadelphia: Fortress Press, 1979); and *2 Corinthians 8 and 9: A Commentary on Two Administrative Letters of the Apostle Paul* (Hermeneia; Philadelphia: Fortress Press, 1985); Wilhelm Wuellner, "Paul's Rhetoric of Argumentation in Romans: An Alternative to the Donfried-Karris Debate over Romans," *CBQ* 38 (1976): 330–351; "Greek Rhetoric and Pauline Argumentation," in *Early Christian Literature and the Classical Intellectual Tradition: In Honorem Robert M. Grant* (ed. William R. Schoedel and Robert L. Wilkin; Théologique historique 53; Paris: Beauchesne, 1979), 177–188; "Where Is Rhetorical Criticism Taking Us?" *CBQ* 49 (1987): 448–63; *Hermeneutics and Rhetorics*; "Biblical Exegesis in the Light of the History and Historicity of Rhetoric and the Nature of the Rhetoric of Religion," in *Rhetoric and the New Testament: Essays from the 1992 Heidelberg Conference* (ed. Stanley E. Porter and Thomas H. Olbricht; JSNTSup 90; Sheffield: Sheffield Academic Press, 1993), 492–512; and "Rhetorical Criticism in Biblical Studies" *Jian Dao: A Journal of Bible and Theology* 4 (1995): 73–96.

[5] George A. Kennedy, *New Testament Interpretation through Rhetorical Criticism* (Studies in Religion; Chapel Hill: University of North Carolina Press, 1984). See also Kennedy, *A New History of Classical Rhetoric* (Princeton, N.J.: Princeton University Press, 1994), a revision and abridging of previous work: *The Art of Persuasion in Greece* (Princeton, N.J.: Princeton University Press, 1963); *The Art of Rhetoric in the Roman World* (A History of Rhetoric 2; Princeton, N.J.: Princeton University Press, 1963); and *Greek Rhetoric under Christian Emperors* (A History of Rhetoric 3; Princeton, N.J.: Princeton University Press, 1983).

[6] See Wire, *The Corinthian Women Prophets*, 197–198; Watson and Hauser, "Notes," 109–112; Hester Amador, *Academic Constraints*, 25–36; Watson, "Rhetorical Criticism," 400; Cunningham, "Rhetoric," 224. For an example of Kennedy's method in action, see the subsequent work of Watson: *Invention, Arrangement, and Style: Rhetorical Criticism of Jude and 2 Peter* (SBLDS 104; Atlanta: Scholars Press, 1988); "A Rhetorical Analysis of Philippians and Its Implications for the Unity Question," *NovT* 30:1 (1988): 57–88; and "1 Corinthians 10:23–11:1 in the Light of Greco-Roman Rhetoric: The Role of Rhetorical Questions," *JBL* 108 (1989): 301–318, among others.

and/or style tests the limits of the rhetorical approach.[7] How stringently can we imagine biblical writers like Paul of Tarsus adhering to the handbooks? If Paul did so, must we argue that Paul received a rhetorical education? How formal would this education have been? This line of questioning involves the second significant shortcoming of many of these initial rhetorical analyses, the persistent focus on the *historical* approach.[8] The application of Kennedy's or Betz's approaches is primarily deployed in order to help the scholar get to the historical context of the letter or gospel. Rhetorical criticism becomes just another tool in the belt of the biblical scholar as historian. Because of this lingering emphasis on historical issues, rhetorical criticism's process of identifying formal rhetorical aspects in order to gain access to the historical context has bypassed its own potential effectiveness in biblical studies. This leads us to the third and final shortcoming of these initial approaches: many failed to explicate the *relevance* of their rhetorical analyses. Beyond identifying and naming the genre, arrangement, or style of the material, there is little examination of how the material functions effectively *as* rhetoric.[9] Not only do these analyses pass over the "how" of rhetoric, but they have also neglected the "why" of the rhetorical act. To what end does the letter make its argument?[10] Why did it select the means it did? These questions get to the heart of the function of rhetoric, where concerns about power are most evident.[11]

---

[7] See Wire, *The Corinthian Women Prophets*, 3–4, 197–198; Watson and Hauser, "Notes," 111–112; Schüssler Fiorenza, *Rhetoric*, 86, 88, 131; Hester Amador, *Academic Constraints*, 26–27; Watson, "Rhetorical Criticism," 400–401; Cunningham, "Rhetoric," 224–226. Hester Amador labels this tendency as part of both the "antiquarian turn" and the "synthesist turn" in rhetorical methodology. See here also Margaret M. Mitchell, *Paul and the Rhetoric of Reconciliation: An Exegetical Investigation of the Language and Composition of 1 Corinthians* (HUT 28; Louisville, Ky.: Westminster/John Knox, 1991), 8–11.

[8] For these kinds of questions, see Watson and Hauser, "Notes," 123–125. For the critique of the "historical hermeneutic turn," see Hester Amador, *Academic Constraints*, 31–46. See here also Schüssler Fiorenza, *Rhetoric*, 31–55, 83–102. In particular, Hester Amador cites the evaluation of David Jasper, in Jasper, "Reflections on the London Conference on the Rhetorical Analysis of Scripture," in *The Rhetorical Analysis of Scripture: Essays from the 1995 London Conference* (ed. Stanley Porter and Thomas Olbricht; JSNTSup 146; Sheffield: Sheffield Academic Press, 1997), 476–482.

[9] See Wire, *The Corinthian Women Prophets*, 10; Watson and Hauser, "Notes," 113; Hester Amador, *Academic Constraints*, 27.

[10] See, for example, Hester Amador, *Academic Constraints*, 56; Cunningham, "Rhetoric," 224–225. For similar observations on the utility of rhetorical interpretations and interpretations, in general, of biblical literature, see Tolbert, *Sowing the Gospel: Mark's World in Literary-Historical Perspective* (Minneapolis: Fortress Press, 1989), 13, 106–107.

[11] Hester Amador characterizes the shortcoming of this kind of rhetorical criticism, since it is "a criticism which often avoids judgment or critique concerning the text's rhetorical power or performance. In other words, biblical rhetorical interpretation

Scholars implementing rhetorical approaches to biblical literature respond to these questions in different ways. For a significant group of rhetorical critics, the concerns over analytic rigidity can be answered by expanding the approaches through a combination with sociological or social world methodologies.[12] Though these combinations can take many forms,[13] the most prominent example is currently the development of socio-rhetorical criticism by Vernon Robbins.[14] Robbins' articulation of multiple "textures" for interpretation seeks to combine literary, rhetorical, sociohistorical, ideological, theological,

---

becomes a criticism that is often arrested before it fulfills its *critical* task." See Hester Amador, *Academic Constraints*, 31. For more on this critical task, see Schüssler Fiorenza, *Rhetoric*, 26–30, 58–67, 79–81, 95–102, 123–128; Hester Amador, *Academic Constraints*, 86–94; and the following section on feminist rhetorical approaches (Chapter I.C) below.

[12] On this development, see Wire, *The Corinthian Women Prophets*, 197; Schüssler Fiorenza, *Rhetoric*, 86–90; Watson, "Rhetorical Criticism," 402.

[13] See, for example, some of the more sociologically oriented work of Jerome H. Neyrey and Bruce J. Malina: Malina and Neyrey, *Portraits of Paul: An Archaeology of Ancient Personality* (Louisville, Ky.: Westminster John Knox, 1996); Malina, "Rhetorical Criticism and Social-Scientific Criticism: Why Won't Romanticism Leave Us Alone?" in *Rhetoric, Scripture, and Theology: Essays from the 1994 Pretoria Conference* (ed. Stanley E. Porter and Thomas H. Olbricht; JSNTSup 131; Sheffield: Sheffield University Press, 1996), 72–101; Neyrey, *Honor and Shame in the Gospel of Matthew* (Louisville, Ky.: Westminster John Knox, 1998).

[14] Vernon K. Robbins, *Exploring the Texture of Texts: A Guide to Socio-Rhetorical Interpretation* (Harrisburg, Penn.: Trinity Press International, 1996); Burton Mack, *Rhetoric and the New Testament* (GBS New Testament Series; Minneapolis: Fortress Press, 1990). Robbins' influence is made evident by: 1.) the proceedings of the Rhetoric and New Testament section of the Society of Biblical Literature, 2.) the application of socio-rhetorical criticism in the monographs: David A. DeSilva, *The Hope of Glory: Honor Discourse and New Testament Interpretation* (Collegeville, Minn.: Liturgical Press, 1999); DeSilva, *Perseverance in Gratitude: A Socio-Rhetorical Commentary on the Epistle to the Hebrews* (Grand Rapids, Mich.: Eerdmans, 2000); Wesley H. Wachob, *The Voice of Jesus in the Social Rhetoric of James* (SNTSMS 106; Cambridge: Cambridge University Press, 2000); and Jack N. Lightstone, *Mishnah and the Social Formation of the Early Rabbinic Guild: A Socio-Rhetorical Approach* (Studies in Christianity and Judaism/Études sur le christianisme et le judaïsme 11; Waterloo, Ont.: Wilfrid Laurier University Press, 2002); and 3.) a recent Festschrift in his honor, *Fabrics of Discourse: Essays in Honor of Vernon K. Robbins* (ed. David Gowler, L. Gregory Bloomquist, and Duane Watson; Harrisburg, Penn.: Trinity Press International, 2003). Duane Watson signaled his own disciplinary shift to this approach in 1999 by noting that the "future is glimpsed in the development of socio-rhetorical criticism." See Watson, "Rhetorical Criticism," 402. See also Watson, "Why We Need Socio-Rhetorical Commentary and What It Might Look Like," in *Rhetorical Criticism and the Bible* (ed. Stanley E. Porter and Dennis L. Stamps; JSNTSup 195; London: Sheffield Academic Press, 2002), 129–157.

INTRODUCTION   7

and broadly comparative approaches under the umbrella of his method.[15] Since Aristotle's genres seem an improper fit for Second Testament literature, Robbins has mapped out "a rhetorical version of form critical categories"[16] as a part of his socio-rhetorical program.[17]

This study's feminist rhetorical analysis does not follow Robbins' model for several reasons. The divisions of the socio-rhetorical program isolate and subsume feminist inquiry within "ideological texture," as if feminist modes of analysis should not have an impact on literary, sociocultural, or theological interpretation.[18] As a result, socio-rhetorical critics often fail to evaluate the social-scientific methods they use, ignoring the feminist critiques of a number of the models in use.[19] Finally, rather than clarifying a relevant rhetorical approach, the sheer expansiveness of socio-rhetorical criticism manages to muddle an analysis of Paul's arguments *as* arguments.[20]

The approach of socio-rhetorical criticism is not the only development beyond the initial rhetorical analyses based on ancient models. Some scholars simply continue in the direction of classical studies, investigating unexamined

---

[15] See, for example, the introduction and organization of Robbins' *Exploring the Texture*.

[16] Thomas H. Olbricht, "Introduction," in *Rhetorical Argumentation in Biblical Texts: Essays from the Lund 2000 Conference* (Emory Studies in Early Christianity; ed. Anders Eriksson, Olbricht, and Walter Übelacker; Harrisburg, Penn.: Trinity Press International, 2002), 1.

[17]See Robbins, "Argumentative Textures in Socio-Rhetorical Interpretation," in *Rhetorical Argumentation*, 27–65.

[18] Schüssler Fiorenza, *Rhetoric*, 87. See, for example, Robbins, *Exploring the Texture*, 2–4, 95–119. Oddly enough, at least half of the entries in the Robbins' Festschrift focus primarily upon an analysis of ideological texture. See the articles by John S. Kloppenborg, Gowler, Bloomquist, Charles A. Wanamaker, Russell B. Sisson, Wachob, and Willi Braun in *Fabrics*, 64–88, 89–125, 165–193, 194–221, 242–263, 264–280, and 317–332.

[19] See Tolbert, "Social, Sociological, and Anthropological Methods," in *Searching the Scriptures: A Feminist Introduction* Vol. 1 (ed. E. Schüssler Fiorenza; New York: Crossroad, 1993), 255–271; Schüssler Fiorenza, *Rhetoric*, 87–88; Schüssler Fiorenza, *Wisdom Ways: Introducing Feminist Biblical Interpretation* (Maryknoll, N.Y.: Orbis, 2001), 102–134. Robbins later characterizes Schüssler Fiorenza's approach as one of "oppositional rhetoric," thus misunderstanding the purpose of her illustrative assessment of his work and avoiding the concerns raised about the social-scientific models he uses. See Robbins, "The Rhetorical Full-Turn in Biblical Interpretation: Reconfiguring Rhetorical-Political Analysis," in *Rhetorical Criticism and the Bible* (2002), 48–60. One response to Robbins' mischaracterization can be found in Esther Fuchs, "Men in Biblical Feminist Scholarship," *JFSR* 19:2 (2003): 93–114.

[20] See the third shortcoming about relevance detailed above, as well as Schüssler Fiorenza, *Rhetoric*, 86–90; Hester Amador, *Academic Constraints*, 128–207. The assembling of virtually all the current approaches of biblical interpretation under the banner of one approach (socio-rhetorical criticism) could also be viewed as an imperialistic gesture.

aspects of these theories[21] or casting a broader net than Aristotle or Quintillian.[22] Other scholars address the concerns over the rigid limits of early analyses by embracing the historical axis of interpretation. Interpreters like Margaret M. Mitchell and Stanley Stowers argue that finding more appropriate analogues for Pauline letters is an essential aspect of rhetorical criticism.[23] In her analysis of 1 Corinthians, Mitchell emphasizes that "actual speeches and letters from antiquity must be consulted,"[24] while Stowers notes the role of diatribe, *prosōpopoeia*, and protreptic in Romans.[25]

In an effort to address all three of the shortcomings noted above and maintain the *critical* task of a feminist rhetorical analysis, this study like many others turns to scholarship in modern rhetoric.[26] Wilhelm Wuellner's influence upon rhetorical criticism is most frequently cited in these approaches, as he was one of the first to recommend more contemporary developments in rhetoric to biblical scholars.[27] In this context Wuellner opposed a "rhetoric restrained" where scholarship is reduced to "listing and labeling the rhetorical figures of

---

[21] See, for example, several of the entries in *Handbook of Classical Rhetoric in the Hellenistic Period, 330 B.C.–A.D. 400* (ed. Stanley E. Porter; Leiden: Brill, 1997); as well as a recent collection on arguments from emotion (*pathos*): *Paul and* Pathos (SBLSymS 16; ed. Thomas H. Olbricht and Jerry L. Sumney; Atlanta: Society of Biblical Literature, 2001).

[22] One well-received monograph considers the Sophistic tradition in the context of Acts and Paul's letters: Mark D. Given, *Paul's True Rhetoric: Ambiguity, Cunning, and Deception in Greece and Rome* (Emory Studies in Early Christianity; Harrisburg, Penn.: Trinity Press International, 2001).

[23] Mitchell, *Paul and the Rhetoric of Reconciliation*; *The Heavenly Trumpet: John Chrysostom and the Art of Pauline Interpretation* (HUT 40; Tübingen: Mohr Siebeck, 2000); Stanley K. Stowers, *The Diatribe and Paul's Letter to the Romans* (SBLDS 57; Chico, Calif.: Scholars Press, 1981); *A Rereading of Romans: Justice, Jews, and Gentiles* (New Haven: Yale University Press, 1994).

[24] Mitchell, *Paul*, 6. In keeping with the concerns outlined above, Mitchell also notes that early approaches were prone to "mechanistic analysis." See Mitchell, *Paul*, 9. For an assessment of Mitchell's approach, see Schüssler Fiorenza, *Rhetoric*, 86

[25] Stowers, *Diatribe*; *A Rereading*, 16–21, 97–107, 264–272, 326

[26] Wire, *The Corinthian Women Prophets*, 1–11, 198–199; Watson and Hauser, "Notes," 112–115; Hester Amador, *Academic Constraints*, 48–124; Schüssler Fiorenza, *Rhetoric*, 87–88; Watson, "Rhetorical Criticism," 400–401. Watson once summarized the state of rhetorical criticism primarily in terms of the split between Greco-Roman rhetoric and modern rhetoric. See Watson, "Rhetorical Criticism," 400.

[27] Watson and Hauser, "Notes," 114; Hester Amador, *Academic Constraints*, 87–112; Schüssler Fiorenza, *Rhetoric*, 90; Watson, "Rhetorical Criticism," 400–401. Again, one measure of the impact of Wuellner on rhetorical critics in biblical studies (and beyond) is the recent Festschrift, *Rhetorics and Hermeneutics: Wilhelm Wuellner and His Influence* (ed. James D. Hester and J. David Hester; Emory Studies in Early Christianity 9; New York: T & T Clark International, 2004).

speech and figures of thought."[28] Limiting rhetorical analysis to the study of style is simply repeating the history of its minimization in the Western academy. However, if one conceives of rhetoric as examining the argumentation of a rhetorical act, then rhetoric becomes untethered, more than just a process for identifying and classifying the form of the rhetorical expression.[29] So conceived, rhetorical criticism of the Bible can avoid some of its recent shortcomings.

However, Wuellner's perspective on modern rhetoric is only one of the contributing aspects to this study's feminist rhetorical analysis. Parallel to all of these developments in the discipline of rhetoric in biblical studies, feminist interpreters have implemented and even pioneered rhetorical approaches to biblical literature. Yet, it is difficult to integrate many of these contributions into a coherent narrative for the evolution of rhetorical criticism since so many of the practitioners ignored the concurrent efforts of feminist scholars. As far back as the 1970s, Phyllis Trible did significant work integrating feminist perspectives with an analysis of biblical rhetoric.[30] As the first woman president of the Society of Biblical Literature in 1987, Elisabeth Schüssler Fiorenza delivered a presidential address focused upon the rhetoric of biblical scholarship.[31] Antoinette Clark Wire, Elizabeth A. Castelli, and Schüssler Fiorenza have engaged in significant feminist rhetorical analysis of Pauline letters.[32] Still, few of the insights presented by feminists are recognized by malestream rhetorical criticism, while most, if not all, feminist rhetorical work is excluded in summaries of the field.[33]

---

[28] Wuellner, "Where," 450–451. It should be noted that Wuellner's first forays into rhetorical criticism were, like Betz's work, focused more on the ancient models as synthesized and presented by Heinrich Lausberg in his *Handbuch der literarischen Rhetorik* (2 vols.; repr.; Stuttgart: Franz Steiner, 1990).
[29] For the characterization of this kind of rhetorical analysis as "mechanistic," see Mitchell, *Paul*, 9; Hester Amador, *Academic Constraints*, 48–57.
[30] Phyllis Trible, *God and the Rhetoric of Sexuality* (Overtures to Biblical Theology; Philadelphia: Fortress Press, 1978). Though Trible was a student of Muilenburg, many of his followers neglected or obscured her rhetorical work.
[31] Schüssler Fiorenza, "The Ethics of Biblical Interpretation: Decentering Biblical Scholarship," *JBL* 107:1 (1988): 3–17; repr. in Schüssler Fiorenza, *Rhetoric*, 17–30.
[32] Schüssler Fiorenza, "Rhetorical Situation and Historical Reconstruction in 1 Corinthians," *NTS* 33 (1987): 386–403; "The Rhetoricity of Historical Knowledge: Pauline Discourse and Its Contextualizations," in *Religious Propaganda and Missionary Competition in the New Testament World: Essays Honoring Dieter Georgi* (ed. Lukas Bormann, Kelly Del Tredici, Angela Standhartinger; Leiden: Brill, 1994), 443–470; repr. in Schüssler Fiorenza, *Rhetoric*, 105–128, 129–148; Wire, *The Corinthian Women Prophets* (1990); Elizabeth A. Castelli, *Imitating Paul: A Discourse of Power* (Literary Currents in Biblical Interpretation; Louisville, Ky.: Westminster/John Knox Press, 1991). See also Schüssler Fiorenza, *Rhetoric*, 149–194.
[33] See, for example, Watson's doubled omission of feminist rhetorical approaches in Watson and Hauser, "Notes" (1994) and "Rhetorical Criticism" (1999).

This project pursues its aims by engaging the approaches of feminist rhetorical critics and any potential allies also working in modern rhetoric. For example, both Wire's and Wuellner's rhetorical hermeneutical work explored the relevance of the "New Rhetoric," the theory of argumentation developed by Lucie Olbrechts-Tyteca and Chaïm Perelman.[34] Olbrechts-Tyteca and Perelman's conception of rhetoric plays a pivotal role in this study as it did in Wuellner's call for a "rhetoric revalued."[35] Though they produced a volume that offers four main categories for argumentative techniques, Olbrechts-Tyteca and Perelman persistently characterize these categories as flexible and interdependent. They note that it is only in this "interaction of arguments" that a rhetorical act becomes convincing.[36] Rhetoric is interactive, rather than static, because the argumentation must address itself to the audience. In their view argumentation requires that a rhetor find a way to appeal to the reasonableness

---

[34] Wire, *The Corinthian Women Prophets*, 1–11; Watson and Hauser, "Notes," 114–115; Hester Amador, *Academic Constraints*, 88, 97–101, 105–107, 112, 208–239; Watson, "Rhetorical Criticism," 401. Wuellner first proposed the usefulness of "New Rhetoric" to biblical interpretation in a seminar paper in 1976: "Methodological Considerations Concerning the Rhetorical Genre of First Corinthians," (paper presented at SBL Pacific Coast Regional Paul Seminar, March 26, 1976). On the "New Rhetoric," see the work of Lucie Olbrechts-Tyteca and Chaïm Perelman, as well as that of their contemporaries Stephen Toulmin and Kenneth Burke: Olbrechts-Tyteca and Perelman, *The New Rhetoric: A Treatise on Argumentation* (trans. John Wilkinson and Purcell Weaver; Notre Dame: University of Notre Dame Press, 1969), originally published as *La Nouvelle Rhétorique: Traité de l'Argumentation* (Paris: Universitaires de France, 1958); Toulmin, *The Uses of Argument* (Cambridge: Cambridge University Press, 1958); Burke, *A Rhetoric of Motives* (Berkeley: University of California Press, 1950). Typically, Perelman is credited with the work of the New Rhetoric to the exclusion of Olbrechts-Tyteca. Though all indications lead to their full partnership in the conception, research and writing of *The New Rhetoric*, Olbrechts-Tyteca's name and role are literally being written out of the history of rhetoric. It is for this reason that this project lists the two authors in reverse order to the title page, following the usual alphabetical order of last names. For more on Olbrechts-Tyteca and Perelman, see below, Chapter IV, and Chapter V.

[35] Wuellner, "Where," 453. The term comes from a collection edited by Brian Vickers, *Rhetoric Revalued: Papers from the International Society for the History of Rhetoric* (Medieval and Renaissance Texts and Studies 19; Binghampton, N.Y.: Center for Medieval and Renaissance Studies, 1982). See also Vickers, *In Defense of Rhetoric* (Oxford: Clarendon, 1988); and in similar veins with different emphases, *The Recovery of Rhetoric: Persuasive Discourse and Disciplinarity in the Human Sciences* (ed. Richard H. Roberts and James M. M. Good; Knowledge, Disciplinarity and Beyond; Charlottesville: University Press of Virginia, 1993); *Reclaiming Rhetorica: Women in the Rhetorical Tradition* (ed. Andrea A. Lunsford; Pittsburgh Series in Composition, Literacy, and Culture; Pittsburgh: University of Pittsburgh Press, 1995); and the titles in the series edited by Karlyn Kohrs Campbell and Celeste Michelle Condit, *Revisioning Rhetoric* (London: The Guilford Press).

[36] Olbrechts-Tyteca and Perelman, *The New Rhetoric*, 460–508.

of the audience.[37] This emphasis upon the audience and their adherence is one of the notable advances Olbrechts-Tyteca and Perelman make to rhetorical theory.

In this way the approach of New Rhetoric is focused pragmatically upon the function of arguments. Techniques of argumentation are discussed in terms of what they "do" or how they function in the convincing process. Arguments by dissociation are prominent both in this discussion of New Rhetoric and in my study of Philippians' rhetorics. As the classificatory innovation of Olbrechts-Tyteca and Perelman, dissociation explains arguments that separate elements of a concept already associated, resulting in a restructuring of the relationship between these elements.[38] This description is pivotal for the following examination of Philippians, as Paul is particularly adept at this technique. In the end this approach to rhetorical analysis facilitates the critical task of evaluating the power dynamics that inhere in the argumentation, while avoiding the rigid limits of approaches based primarily upon ancient models of rhetoric.[39]

C. FURTHER REFLECTIONS ON FEMINIST RHETORICAL APPROACHES

Feminist interpreters explicitly begin with different goals from most biblical scholars, including rhetorical critics. As part of a movement for liberation and justice, feminists interpret in order to critique and change structures of oppression.[40] As noted above, feminist approaches are also evident in rhetorical criticism. Parallel to the aforementioned developments in contemporary rhetoric and rhetorical interpretation of the Bible, feminist interpreters examined the

---

[37] "There is only one rule in this matter: adaptation of the speech to the audience, whatever its nature." See Olbrechts-Tyteca and Perelman, *The New Rhetoric*, 25. On "adaptation to the audience," see Olbrechts-Tyteca and Perelman, *The New Rhetoric*, 14–26.

[38] Olbrechts-Tyteca and Perelman, *The New Rhetoric*, 191–192, 411–459. For more on dissociative arguments, see also Chapter V.A below.

[39] For more on the background and effect of Olbrechts-Tyteca and Perelman, see Conley, *Rhetoric*, 285–310; Bizzell and Herzberg, *Rhetorical Tradition*, 900–901, 906–907, 914–915 1066–1103; Foss, Foss, and Trapp, *Contemporary Perspectives*, 81–115. On the oft-ignored work of Susanne K. Langer, who preceded Olbrechts-Tyteca, Perelman, Burke, and Toulmin, see Arabella Lyon, "Susanne K. Langer: Mother and Midwife at the Rebirth of Rhetoric," in *Reclaiming Rhetorica*, 265–284; and Langer, *Philosophy in a New Key: A Study in the Symbolism of Reason, Rite, and Art* (3rd ed.; Cambridge, Mass.: Harvard University Press, 1979), first published in 1942.

[40] On the variety of definitions for feminism, especially as it impacts feminist biblical interpretation, see Tolbert, "Defining the Problem," 113–126; and, more recently, Phyllis A. Bird, "What Makes a Feminist Reading Feminist? A Qualified Answer," in *Escaping Eden: New Feminist Perspectives on the Bible* (ed. Harold C. Washington, Susan Lochrie Graham, and Pamela Thimmes; New York: New York University Press, 1999), 124–131; Thimmes, "What Makes a Feminist Reading Feminist? Another Perspective," in *Escaping Eden*, 132–140; Schüssler Fiorenza, *Wisdom*, 54–64

history of scholarship in their respective fields and found it sorely lacking.[41] It is for this reason that Schüssler Fiorenza advocates implementing a rhetoric of inquiry for feminist rhetorical interpretation of the Bible.[42] This rhetoric of inquiry encourages an analysis of the location and function of the disciplinary practices of scholars, an important topic for biblical studies in general, and rhetorical interpretation of the Bible, in particular. For example, Schüssler Fiorenza points to the lack of recognition among biblical scholars and especially rhetorical critics of the important and relevant work of feminist interpreters.[43] Followers of Muilenburg have ignored Phyllis Trible's work, while rhetorical scholars working in Pauline letters have neglected the contributions from Schüssler Fiorenza, Wire, and Castelli.[44]

The circumstances of such "malestream" short-sightedness are unfortunate, especially since these different groups of rhetorical critics could potentially

---

[41] Similar to the previous section of the introduction, the main goal of this section cannot be an overview of the significant history of feminist rhetorical studies or feminist studies in biblical interpretation. For the former topic, see: Karen A. Foss and Sonja K. Foss, *Women Speak: The Eloquence of Women's Lives* (Prospect Heights, Ill.: Waveland, 1991); Susan C. Jarratt, *Rereading the Sophists: Classical Rhetoric Refigured* (Carbondale: Southern Illinois University Press, 1991); Lunsford, *Reclaiming Rhetorica*; Cheryl Glenn, *Rhetoric Retold: Regendering the Tradition from Antiquity through the Renaissance* (Carbondale: Southern Illinois University Press, 1997); *Listening to Their Voices: The Rhetorical Activities of Historical Women* (ed. Molly Meijer Wertheimer; Studies in Rhetoric/Communication; Columbia: University of South Carolina Press, 1997); Sonja K. Foss, Karen A. Foss, and Cindy L. Griffin, *Feminist Rhetorical Theories* (Thousand Oaks, Calif.: Sage, 1999); *The Changing Tradition: Women in the History of Rhetoric* (ed. Christine Mason Sutherland and Rebecca Sutcliffe; Calgary: University of Calgary Press, 1999). For the latter topic, see below and the notes in Chapter III.B.

[42] Schüssler Fiorenza, *Rhetoric*, 83–102. Her essay "Challenging the Rhetorical Half-Turn: Feminist and Rhetorical Biblical Criticism," found in this volume, was originally published in *Rhetoric, Scripture, and Theology* (1996), 28–53. On the rhetoric of inquiry, see *The Rhetoric of the Human Sciences: Language and Argument in Scholarship and Public Affairs* (ed. John S. Nelson, Allan Megill, and Donald N. McCloskey; Rhetoric of the Human Sciences; Madison: University of Wisconsin Press, 1987); *Rhetoric in the Human Sciences* (ed. Herbert W. Simons; Inquiries in Social Construction Series; Newbury Park, Calif.: Sage, 1989); and Carole Blair, Julie R. Brown, and Leslie A. Baxter, "Disciplining the Feminine," in *Contemporary Rhetorical Theory: A Reader* (ed. John Louis Lucaites, Celeste Michelle Condit, and Sally Caudill; Revisioning Rhetoric; New York: The Guilford Press, 1999), 563–590.

[43] Schüssler Fiorenza, *Rhetoric*, 90–92.

[44] Trible, *God and the Rhetoric of Sexuality*; *Texts of Terror: Literary-Feminist Readings of Biblical Narratives* (Overtures to Biblical Theology 13; Philadelphia: Fortress Press, 1984); *Rhetorical Criticism: Context, Method, and the Book of Jonah* (GBS Old Testament Series; Minneapolis: Fortress, 1994); Schüssler Fiorenza, "Ethics;" "Rhetorical Situation;" "Rhetoricity;" "Challenging the Rhetorical Half-Turn;" and *Rhetoric*; Wire, *The Corinthian Women Prophets*; Castelli, *Imitating Paul*.

INTRODUCTION   13

make suitable allies or collaborators.[45] Feminist scholars engaging in rhetorical interpretation note many of the same shortcomings in the initial rhetorical analyses offered for biblical studies. Concern with the rigidity of the application of rhetorical terminologies echoes through much feminist rhetorical work.[46] These feminist rhetorical interpreters have moved away from antiquarian approaches that subordinate the interpretive task to that of producing only historical observations.[47] Finally, and most importantly, feminist rhetorical interpretations have repeatedly called for a critical turn in biblical interpretation, so as to evaluate the functionality and relevance of various rhetorical acts, both in biblical materials and in scholarship on these materials.[48]

Yet, beyond making such observations in tandem, rhetorical interpreters with these reservations already in mind could benefit even further from the insights of feminist rhetorical work. In the case of Pauline letters, most interpreters begin with the assumption that Paul's view was normative to the communities he wrote. Such an assumption reinscribes Paul into a position of authority that is not necessarily evident in the process of his correspondence. Wire argues that conceptualizations like these at the foundations of biblical interpretation actually rob the field from a full appreciation of the letters as rhetoric: "Because an argument Paul makes cannot be rejected as unconvincing, it also cannot convince. In this way the authority we attribute to Paul prevents him from persuading us."[49] The letter as argumentation makes the most sense in a context where authority is still a contested issue and the issues discussed are not settled dogma but living concerns.[50] The approach of the letters demonstrates that Paul believes he needs to convince the communities of something, a purpose that varies from letter to letter.

Thus, insights from feminist rhetorical critics emphasize the importance of seeing Paul involved in a rhetorical exchange between the communities and

---

[45] Schüssler Fiorenza comments that she explicitly moved to rhetorical models for interpretation "in the belief that the 'natural' allies of feminist biblical studies would be scholars who blaze the trail of the New Rhetoric." See Schüssler Fiorenza, *Rhetoric*, 90.
[46] Schüssler Fiorenza, *Rhetoric*, 86, 88, 131; Wire, *The Corinthian Women Prophets*, 4, 197–198; Castelli, *Imitating Paul*, 30–32, 54.
[47] Schüssler Fiorenza, *Rhetoric*, 31–55, 83–102; Wire, *The Corinthian Women Prophets*, 2–11; Castelli, *Imitating Paul*, 21–58. Again, similar to observations from scholars using modern rhetoric, here Schüssler Fiorenza is also critical of the methods of socio-rhetorical criticism as extolled by Robbins. See Schüssler Fiorenza, *Rhetoric*, 86–88.
[48] Schüssler Fiorenza frequently refers to the feminist hermeneutical project as engaging in "critical rhetoric." See Schüssler Fiorenza, *Rhetoric*, 26–102. On critical rhetoric see also Raymie E. McKerrow, "Critical Rhetoric: Theory and Praxis," in *Contemporary Rhetorical Theory*, 441–463. On the need to be critically reflective on the function and analysis of biblical rhetorics, see also Wire, *The Corinthian Women Prophets*, 2–11, 197–199; Castelli, *Imitating Paul*, 21–33, 119–136.
[49] Wire, *The Corinthian Women Prophets*, 10.
[50] Wire, *The Corinthian Women Prophets*, 9–11; Castelli, *Imitating Paul*, 24–33.

himself. Beginning with this understanding of the rhetorical act is clearly compatible with Olbrechts-Tyteca and Perelman's focus upon "adaptation to the audience" in argumentation.[51] Wire perceptively notes this connection and, as a result, implements their perspective in her feminist rhetorical analysis of the Corinthian correspondence.[52] This study's analysis of Philippians' "evolving rhetoric" and "prevailing rhetoric" draws upon this instructive precedent.[53]

In a significant manner this study is also shaped by the feminist hermeneutical frameworks developed by Elisabeth Schüssler Fiorenza. Over the years, as she persistently tried to improve upon the expressions of her feminist biblical critical project(s), the terms moved increasingly toward the domain of rhetoric: from pastoral-theological, liberationist-cultural, feminist-postcolonial emancipatory, and ethical-political to public-rhetorical, rhetorical-ethical, rhetorical-political and rhetorical-emancipatory.[54] In addition, the turns in what Schüssler Fiorenza has dubbed the "dance of interpretation" have been revised, expanded and renamed, coming to one of their fullest descriptions in her more recent rhetorical-ethical work.[55] This dance of interpretation works on two levels: the level of the biblical text and the histories of its interpretations as well as the level of contemporary readers and reading practices and their locus in kyriarchal systems.[56] Since this study frequently draws upon these rhetorical turns in its analysis, it seems relevant to provide a brief overview of the seven moves or turns in Schüssler Fiorenza's "dance."

Though the following seven steps are not necessarily to be practiced sequentially, the first is at least an important starting point, while the seventh and final involves the goal and climax of the entire process.[57] Schüssler Fiorenza

---

[51] See n. 37 above.
[52] Wire, *The Corinthian Women Prophets*, 2–4, 6–8.
[53] The distinction made in this study between evolving (or developing) rhetoric and prevailing rhetoric is in keeping with the approach of Wire's study of 1 Corinthians. It differs from this study, however, in the order of presentation, and the descriptive terms used (evolving rather than "structural," prevailing in place of "textual"). See Wire, *The Corinthian Women Prophets*, 6–9, 12–180. For more on the procedure, see Chapter IV and Chapter V below. For more on the influence of Wire's approach here and in the rest of her work, see *Distant Voices Drawing Near: Essays in Honor of Antoinette Clark Wire* (ed. Holly E. Hearon; Collegeville, Minn.: Liturgical Press, 2004).
[54] Schüssler Fiorenza, *Rhetoric*, 32, 44. For previous listings, see such works as *Bread Not Stone: The Challenge of Feminist Biblical Interpretation* (rev. ed.; Boston: Beacon Press, 1995); *In Memory of Her: A Feminist Theological Reconstruction of Christian Origins* (10th anniversary ed.; New York: Crossroad, 1994); and *But She Said: Feminist Practices of Biblical Interpretation* (Boston: Beacon Press, 1992).
[55] Schüssler Fiorenza, *Rhetoric*, 48. For her initial and continuing expressions of this dance, "stew," or "struggle," see Schüssler Fiorenza, *Bread*, 15–22; and *But She Said*, 52–76; *Wisdom*, 165–190.
[56] Schüssler Fiorenza, *Rhetoric*, 48–49; *Wisdom*, 169.
[57] Schüssler Fiorenza, *Rhetoric*, 49, 53; *Wisdom*, 171, 186.

INTRODUCTION 15

labels this first move *the hermeneutics of experience and social location*.[58] The liberative interpretive process begins with the critical reflection upon one's own experience(s) of oppression and privilege. As with any rhetorical interaction, where one begins affects what one sees. This first move not only allows for critical conscientization but it also functions to put that experience at the center of this process, rather than the malestream traditions typically prized as canonical. This first turn leads into *the analytic of domination* necessary to the practice of a feminist rhetoric of liberation.[59] In particular, Schüssler Fiorenza has developed the concept of *kyriarchy* in order to comprehend the complex and interlocking systems of oppression that are embodied in sexism, racism, classism, heterosexism, colonialism, and nationalism (among others).[60] The next part of the dance detailed by Schüssler Fiorenza is *a hermeneutics of suspicion*.[61] Such a rhetorical-hermeneutical stance realizes that the picture one has is a distorted one, conditioned by androcentric language and malestream tendencies. This androcentric or, better yet, *kyriocentric* language does not cover over "the reality" of things, but constructs realities. Thus, a hermeneutics of suspicion does not seek to unveil some hidden truth, rather it is a way to learn how to read against the grain of texts and interpretations which have produced the marginalization of women and other oppressed groups.[62]

While the feminist rhetorical critic reads with a hermeneutics of suspicion, s/he can also assess a text with *a hermeneutics of ethical and theological evaluation*.[63] This practice allows for the evaluation of the rhetorics of a text or an interpretation with a feminist scale of values in mind. Ethical evaluation inquires in a non-dualistic fashion as to what extent a rhetorical act or work has contributed to emancipation and/or oppression. Schüssler Fiorenza's dance of interpretation also includes *a hermeneutics of remembrance and reconstruction*.[64] This move acknowledges that there are voices, besides the hegemonic ones, that have been marginalized in biblical texts, while emphasizing the importance of re-membering these voices. Such a move clearly does not give up on the prospects of historical reconstructions, yet it does not pretend that these reconstructions are not rhetorical themselves. Remembrance

---

[58] Schüssler Fiorenza, *Rhetoric*, 49; *Wisdom*, 169–172.
[59] Schüssler Fiorenza, *Rhetoric*, 50; *Wisdom*, 172–175.
[60] Schüssler Fiorenza coined the term *kyriarchy* many years ago in order to move beyond the gender dualism of the term patriarchy, and has been implementing an analysis of kyriarchal texts, practices and institutions ever since. For an introductory definition to this neologism, see Schüssler Fiorenza, *Rhetoric*, ix; *Wisdom*, 211. See also Schüssler Fiorenza, *Bread*, 211 n. 6; and *But She Said*, 8, 117.
[61] Schüssler Fiorenza, *Rhetoric*, 50–51; *Wisdom*, 175–177.
[62] Schüssler Fiorenza, *Rhetoric*, 51; *Wisdom*, 175–176.
[63] Schüssler Fiorenza, *Rhetoric*, 51; *Wisdom*, 177–179.
[64] Schüssler Fiorenza, *Rhetoric*, 51–52; *Wisdom*, 183–186.

does not presume to reveal "what really happened," but it does seek to enrich and deepen our perspectives on history by focusing on the neglected voices.

Such a step in interpretation entails also a complementary move of *a hermeneutics of imagination*.[65] Every act of interpretation involves the imagination, and it takes a great deal of it to begin envisioning both past interpretations and future hopes in new and non-dominating ways. Of course, these acts of imagination and remembrance do not go unchecked, since they are growing out of the same process which includes critically reflected upon experience, an analysis of dominating structures, and a suspicion about one's own predispositions. Finally, the dance of interpretation has as its goal *a hermeneutics of transformation*.[66] It is hoped that this process will lead to action for change: the changing of oppressive dynamics in people's lives and in people's interpretations. As a result, the entire process remains accountable to all those engaged in the struggle against kyriarchal systems.[67]

Thus, when this study approaches the letter to the Philippians and previous scholarship on this text, it is shaped by two feminist rhetorical perspectives: Elisabeth Schüssler Fiorenza's dance of interpretation and Antoinette Clark Wire's implementation of New Rhetoric perspectives. Upon turning to Philippians, then, it is not surprising to find that this study's examination of Paul's argumentation differs in significant ways from other scholarly assessments.

D. PRELIMINARY ISSUES IN THE STUDY OF PHILIPPIANS

My reading of Paul's letter to the Philippians differs in significant ways from most assessments of the letter. The acclaim accorded to Paul or the letter to the Philippians by biblical scholars is remarkably widespread. Paul is characterized as "very personal and warm"[68] and according to at least one interpreter, attempting to console the Philippians.[69] The letter is labeled "a jewel

---

[65] Schüssler Fiorenza, *Rhetoric*, 52–53; *Wisdom*, 179–183.
[66] Schüssler Fiorenza, *Rhetoric*, 53–54; *Wisdom*, 186–189.
[67] For further indications of the utility and influence of Schüssler Fiorenza's critical project(s), see *Walk in the Ways of Wisdom: Essays in Honor of Elisabeth Schüssler Fiorenza* (ed. Shelly Matthews, Cynthia Briggs Kittredge, and Melanie Johnson-DeBaufre; Harrisburg, Penn.: Trinity Press International, 2003); *On the Cutting Edge: The Study of Women in Biblical Worlds: Essays in Honor of Elisabeth Schüssler Fiorenza* (ed. Jane Schaberg, Alice Bach, and Esther Fuchs; New York: Continuum, 2003); and *Toward A New Heaven and A New Earth: Essays in Honor of Elisabeth Schüssler Fiorenza* (ed. Fernando F. Segovia; Maryknoll, N.Y.: Orbis Books, 2003).
[68] Gordon D. Fee, *Philippians* (IVP New Testament Commentary Series; Downers Grove, Ill.: Intervarsity Press, 1999), 11.
[69] Paul A. Holloway, *Consolation in Philippians: Philosophical Sources and Rhetorical Strategy* (SNTSMS 112; Cambridge: Cambridge University Press, 2001).

of the Pauline corpus,"[70] since it "sparkles with joy . . . life-giving, heart-refreshing joy."[71] In comparison to other Pauline letters, it is "one of Paul's most eloquent and cordial letters."[72] As Gordon D. Fee and others maintain, "many of us like Philippians because we like the Paul we meet here."[73] Frequently commentators refer to the "friendliness" of Paul's communication with the Philippians, a perspective that this study examines in some detail.[74]

Needless to say, most of these commentators are not proceeding with a hermeneutics of suspicion. Very few note any of the feminist frameworks for biblical interpretation already outlined in this introduction.[75] Because of these tendencies most biblical scholars have missed the other side of these apparently "friendly" rhetorics, particularly in their attempts to construct an authoritative position for Paul in the eyes of the Philippian community.[76] Thus, in order to examine and assess the argumentation of Philippians, this study proceeds differently, with the aid of feminist rhetorical analysis.

The aim of this study, then, is to initiate a reading of Philippians that analyzes how Paul implements multiple rhetorical strategies in the letter. These arguments are deployed to promote a particular version of unity with a specific set of model figures. This view of the letter's argumentation differs significantly from much previous work on the letter, since typically the perceived lack of sharp contention has led many scholars to overlook Philippians' complex argumentation. Yet, the rhetorical analysis cannot end with this detailed rendering of the interlocking argumentative techniques. Because these rhetorical strategies turn out to be Paul's attempts to establish a kyriarchal relationship between the Philippian community and himself, a feminist rhetorical analysis also requires reading these rhetorics in imaginative resistance. Such an approach can show the relevance of biblical interpretation, as it facilitates an assessment of the rhetorical impact of the letter and subsequent scholarship on the letter.

---

[70] Carolyn Osiek, *Philippians, Philemon* (ANTC; Nashville: Abingdon Press, 2000), 32.
[71] Markus Bockmuehl, *The Epistle to the Philippians* (BNTC; London: Hendrickson, 1998), 1.
[72] Ben Witherington III, *Friendship and Finances in Philippi: The Letter of Paul to the Philippians* (The New Testament in Context; Valley Forge, Penn.: Trinity Press International, 1994), 137.
[73] Fee, *Philippians*, 11. Similarly, Osiek comments about the letter: "It reveals Paul at his best." See Osiek, *Philippians*, 32.
[74] See Chapter II below.
[75] The exception being the commentary by Osiek, who had also contributed the chapter on "Philippians" to *Searching the Scriptures: A Feminist Commentary* Vol. 2 (ed. E. Schüssler Fiorenza; New York: Crossroad, 1993), 237–249.
[76] Here, and at several other key points, this study shares the same view of Philippians as explicated by Cynthia Briggs Kittredge in *Community and Authority: The Rhetoric of Obedience in the Pauline Tradition* (HTS 45; Harrisburg, Penn.: Trinity Press International, 1998). Kittredge's study demonstrates the relevance and explanatory power of a feminist rhetorical interpretation of this letter.

Over the years Philippians has received relatively less attention than those letters that are believed to contribute classically "Pauline" theological insights. Often the hymn of 2:6–11 has received more attention than the letter as a whole. This analysis of Philippians addresses these oversights by taking seriously that any part of the text can be better understood if one grasps its rhetorical function within the whole letter. As a result, the hymn receives attention only as it contributes to the identification and evaluation of the argumentative techniques of Philippians. Since it plays an important role in the argumentation of the letter, it merits examination. However, my focus on the letter's rhetorical function parts from the typical interests in historical relevance and theological meaning.[77]

In past analysis of the letter, the literary integrity of Philippians was a hotly contested issue, as redaction and source criticism was applied to the letter in order to argue that 4:10–20 and part(s) of Philippians 3 and 4 comprised fragments separate from the remainder of the letter.[78] Recently, however, the tide of scholarship on Philippians has turned, as the integrity is now more widely accepted than the variety of partition theories.[79] While the evidence for these

---

[77] For the differing ways traditional biblical scholarship engages the hymn in 2:6–11, see, for example, Ernst Lohmeyer, *Kyrios Jesus: Eine Untersuchung zu Phil. 2, 5–11* (SHAW Philosophisch-historische Klasse. Jahrgang 1927/28; 4. Abhandllung; Darmstadt: Wissenschaftliche Buchgesellschaft, 1961 [1928]); Ernst Käsemann, "A Critical Analysis of Philippians 2:5–11," *JTC* 5 (1968): 45–68. On Lohmeyer and Käsemann, and more recent discussion of the hymn, see *Where Christology Began: Essays on Philippians 2* (ed. Ralph P. Martin and Brian J. Dodd; Louisville, Ky.: Westminster John Knox Press, 1998). See also Chapter IV.D and Chapter V.D.2 below.

[78] For an impressive list of the proponents of the various partition hypotheses, see Jeffrey T. Reed, *A Discourse Analysis of Philippians: Method and Rhetoric in the Debate over Literary Integrity* (JSNTSup 136; Sheffield: Sheffield Academic Press, 1997), 127–129. Reed's lists are not quite comprehensive. Though he knows and cites the work of John Reumann and Philip Sellew in both the body and the bibliography of his monograph, he fails to list them amongst those who are convinced of and argue for the three-part division of the letter. See Sellew, "*Laodiceans* and the Philippians Fragment Hypothesis," *HTR* 87 (1994): 17–28; "*Laodiceans* and the Philippians Revisited: A Response to Paul Holloway," *HTR* 91 (1998): 327–329; Reumann, "Contributions of the Philippian Community to Paul and to Earliest Christianity," *NTS* 39 (1993): 438–57; "Justification and the Imitatio Motif in Philippians," in *Promoting Unity: Themes in Lutheran-Catholic Dialogue* (ed. H. G. Anderson and James R. Crumley, Jr.; Minneapolis: Fortress Press, 1989), 17–29, 92–99; and "Theologies of 1 Thessalonians and Philippians: Contents, Comparison, and Composite," *SBL Seminar Papers, 1987* (SBLSP 26; Chico, Calif.: Scholars Press, 1987), 521–36. See also Ulrich B. Müller, *Der Brief des Paulus an die Philipper* (THKNT 11:1; Leipzig: Evangelische Verlagsanstalt, 1993).

[79] For a list of scholars who maintain the integrity of the letter, again see Reed, *Discourse Analysis*, 127–129. To the list of recent scholars, the following should be added: Wayne Meeks, "Man from Heaven in Paul's Letter to the Philippians," in *The Future of Early Christianity: Essays in Honor of Helmut Koester* (ed. Birger A. Pearson; Minneapolis: Fortress, 1991), 331; L. Gregory Bloomquist, *The Function of Suffering in Philippians* (JSNTSup 78; Sheffield: JSOT Press, 1993); Wendy Cotter, "Our *Politeuma*

partition theories are too weak to make an issue of the letter's integrity, my study of the consistent arguments in Philippians can contribute to the current demonstrations of its coherence and unity.

Is In Heaven: The Meaning of Philippians 3.17–21," in *Origins and Method: Towards a New Understanding of Judaism and Christianity* (ed. Bradley H. McLean; JSNTSup 86; Sheffield: Sheffield Academic, 1993), 92–104; John W. Marshall, "Paul's Ethical Appeal in Philippians," in *Rhetoric and the New Testament: Essays from the 1992 Heidelberg Conference* (ed. Stanley E. Porter and Thomas H. Olbricht; JSNTSup 90; Sheffield: JSOT Press, 1993), 357–372; A. H. Snyman, "Persuasion in Philippians 4:1–20," in *Rhetoric and the New Testament*, 325–337; Witherington, *Friendship*; Nils A. Dahl, "Euodia and Syntyche and Paul's Letter to the Philippians," in *The Social World of the First Christians: Essays in Honor of Wayne A. Meeks* (ed. L. Michael White and O. Larry Yarbrough; Minneapolis: Fortress, 1995), 3–15; Davorin Peterlin, *Paul's Letter to the Philippians in the Light of Disunity in the Church* (NovTSup 79; Leiden: Brill, 1995); Craig S. Wansink, *Chained in Christ: The Experience and Rhetoric of Paul's Imprisonment* (JSNTSup 130; Sheffield: Sheffield Academic Press, 1996); Bockmuehl, *Epistle to the Philippians*; Kittredge, *Community*; Holloway, *Consolation*; Peter S. Oakes, *Philippians: From People to Letter* (SNTSMS 110; Cambridge: Cambridge University Press, 2001); and Demetrius K. Williams, *Enemies of the Cross of Christ: The Terminology of the Cross and Conflict in Philippians* (JSNTSup 223; London: Sheffield Academic Press, 2002). What is noteworthy about this shift is that even a few of the scholars who previously agreed with the partition theorists have altered their views in light of recent arguments for the integrity of the letter. See, for example, Meeks, "Man," 331; Williams, *Enemies*, 42–54 (Williams' position changed between the acceptance of his dissertation in 1997 and its published revision in 2002).

Part One

Setting the Stage

Chapter II

Critical Overview of Scholarship on Prominent Images in Philippians

I begin by presenting two contexts for my interpretation: contemporary scholarship on Philippians in this chapter and key aspects of the situation of first century Philippi in the next.

At first, this chapter will proceed in a rather standard way, providing a brief overview of two major proposals in current scholarship as to the letter's dominant imagery. As a feminist analysis, this study does not and cannot leave off with such an overview of these suggestions. Instead, it will proceed to analyze the power dynamics that inhere in both friendship and military images and in the arguments for their relevance to interpretation of the letter. Maintaining a feminist perspective should offer this study cues as to how to proceed with a feminist rhetorical interpretation of the letter to the Philippians.

In order for the conversation about the main imagery of the letter of Philippians to begin in earnest, several long-standing tendencies in scholarship needed to be overcome.[1] For many scholars the letter appears to be rather transparent and artless.[2] Pollard held that "it consists of a 'stream of consciousness' rather than follows a predetermined plan."[3] These impressions of artlessness and a rambling or unclear structure have been supported over the years by the belief that Philippians is such a deeply personal and, thus, informal,

---

[1] For an excellent overview of many of the purposes posited by scholars, normally connected to which image-sets are argued to be prominent, see Timothy C. Geoffrion, *The Rhetorical Purpose and the Political and Military Character of Philippians: A Call to Stand Firm* (Lewiston, N.Y.: Mellen, 1993), 2–22.
[2] For example, Jean-François Collange, *The Epistle of Saint Paul to the Philippians* (trans. A. W. Heathcote; London: Epworth Press, 1979), 9, 14; Gerald F. Hawthorne, *Philippians* (WBC; Waco, Tex.: Word Books, 1983), 14, 176; T. E. Pollard, "The Integrity of Philippians," *NTS* 13 (1966–1967): 65.
[3] Pollard, "Integrity," 59.

letter.⁴ Even recent formal arguments about the letter's structure argue it is a rather loose adaptation of family letters whose occasion for writing is no greater than the circumstance that a messenger was traveling to Philippi.⁵

The current state of scholarship, however, seems to be shifting toward arguing for the importance of a single group of images for the letter. Ernst Lohmeyer was the first scholar to attempt to identify one major image shaping the message for Philippians: the situation of martyrdom.⁶ While Lohmeyer's thesis has found virtually no acceptance, it marked an important shift as scholars began to focus on bringing out one major topic or image-set for the entire letter.⁷ Though there have since been a number of different proposals for the dominant set of images for Philippians, the two that have drawn the most attention and can contribute the most to this study are the arguments for friendship imagery and military imagery in the letter.

A. PROMINENT IMAGERY IN PHILIPPIANS

1. FRIENDSHIP IMAGERY

One of the most prominent recent developments in Philippians' scholarship has been the consideration of friendship language from the Greco-Roman context. Though Philippians was first classified as "a letter of friendship" in the 1950s, it has taken nearly a full generation for this identification to be reflected in biblical scholarship.⁸ Drawing upon Abraham Malherbe's initial work on the moral philosophical terminology of 1 Thessalonians,⁹ L. Michael White and John T. Fitzgerald were among the first in the field to suggest the relevance of

---

⁴ "Philippians is clearly the most 'personal' of Paul's letters." See Pollard, "Integrity," 59.
⁵ Loveday Alexander, "Hellenistic Letter-Forms and the Structure of Philippians," *JSNT* 37 (1989): 99. The exchange of news is really the only subject of the letter in Alexander's analysis. See Alexander, "Hellenistic Letter-Forms," 95.
⁶ Ernst Lohmeyer, *Die Briefe an die Philipper, an die Kolosser und an Philemon* (KEK 9; Göttingen: Vandenhoeck & Ruprecht, 1964 [1930]).
⁷ Though his thesis has been rejected by many scholars, it has functioned to call special attention to the topic of suffering in the letter. For an excellent study of both the history of thought about and the rhetorical function of suffering in Philippians, see L. Gregory Bloomquist, *The Function of Suffering in Philippians* (JSNTSup 78; Sheffield: JSOT Press, 1993).
⁸ Heikki Koskenniemi, *Studien zur Idee und Phraseologie des griechischen Briefes bis 400 n. Chr.* (Suomalaisen Tiedeakatemian toimituksia, Sarja B. 102, 2; Helsinki: Suomalainen Tiedeakatemia, 1956), 115–127. See also Klaus Thraede, *Grundzüge griechisch-römischer Brieftopic* (Zetemata 48; Munich: Beck, 1970).
⁹ Abraham J. Malherbe, *Paul and the Popular Philosophers* (Minneapolis: Fortress, 1989); *Paul and the Thessalonians* (Philadelphia: Fortress, 1987).

friendship language to the study of Philippians.[10] Since these initial developments friendship has become a major buzzword for Philippians' scholarship.[11] For many interpreters of this letter, it is easy to see why Alan C. Mitchell states: "Perhaps the richest Pauline treasure of friendship is his letter to the Philippians."[12] For example, the topic of Paul's absence and his attempts to communicate his desire to be in the Philippian community's presence (1:7–8, 19–26, 27; 2:12, 24; 4:1) reflect a stock motif of ancient friendship.[13]

---

[10] L. Michael White, "Morality Between Two Worlds: A Paradigm of Friendship in Philippians," in *Greeks, Romans and Christians: Essays in Honor of Abraham J. Malherbe* (ed. David L. Balch, Everett Ferguson and Wayne A. Meeks; Minneapolis: Fortress Press, 1990), 201–15; John T. Fitzgerald, "Philippians in the Light of Some Ancient Discussions of Friendship," in *Friendship, Flattery and Frankness of Speech: Studies on Friendship in the New Testament World* (ed. John T. Fitzgerald; NovTSup 82; Leiden: Brill, 1996), 141–160; "Philippians, Epistle to the," *ABD* V: 318–326. See also Stanley K. Stowers, *Letter Writing in Greco-Roman Antiquity* (LEC 5; Philadelphia: Westminster, 1986), 58–78; Malherbe, "Ancient Epistolary Theorists," *Ohio Journal of Religious Studies* 5 (1977): 31, 65, 71; and *Moral Exhortation: A Greco-Roman Sourcebook* (LEC 4; Philadelphia: Westminster, 1986), 144, 154.
[11] For recent examples, see Gordon D. Fee, *Philippians* (IVP New Testament Commentary Series; Downers Grove, Ill.: InterVarsity, 1999), 13–20; Fitzgerald, "Paul and Friendship," in *Paul in the Greco-Roman World: A Handbook* (ed. J. Paul Sampley; Harrisburg, Penn.: Trinity Press International, 2003), 319–343. For an inventory, accompanied by a critique, of the study of friendship in Philippians, see Reumann, "Philippians, Especially Chapter 4, as a 'Letter of Friendship': Observations on a Checkered History of Scholarship," in *Friendship, Flattery and Frankness of Speech*, 83–106. Reumann is particularly critical of what he maintains to be a lack of precision in defining the parameters of friendship language's influence on the letter. He does, in fact, point out the inconsistency in the use of the term, as in the case of Pheme Perkins' two articles. The first includes friendship in the title, yet by its 1991 revision, the title and subject are missing: "Christology, Friendship, and Status: The Rhetoric of Philippians," *SBL Seminar Papers 1987* (SBLSP 26; Atlanta: Scholars, 1987), 509–520; "Philippians: Theology for a Heavenly Politeuma," in *Pauline Theology*, Vol. 1: *Thessalonians, Philippians, Galatians, Philemon* (ed. Jouette M. Bassler; Minneapolis: Augsburg Fortress Press, 1991), 89–104. Similarly, Ben Witherington III uses friendship in his commentary's title, yet he fails to treat friendship as a topic beyond a few brief comments: *Friendship and Finances in Philippi: The Letter of Paul to the Philippians* (The New Testament in Context; Valley Forge, Penn.: Trinity Press International, 1994). Paul A. Holloway believes that friendship is a related, but "secondary description" of the consolation language in Philippians. See Holloway, *Consolation in Philippians: Philosophical Sources and Rhetorical Strategy* (SNTSMS 112; Cambridge: Cambridge University Press, 2001), 2.
[12] Alan C. Mitchell, "'Greet the Friends by Name': New Testament Evidence for the Greco-Roman *Topos* on Friendship," in *Greco-Roman Perspectives on Friendship* (ed. John T. Fitzgerald; Resources for Biblical Study 34; Atlanta: Scholars Press, 1997), 233.
[13] Fitzgerald, "Philippians," 147; Stanley K. Stowers, "Friends and Enemies in the Politics of Heaven: Reading Theology in Philippians," in *Pauline Theology*, Vol. 1

Explaining the striking or distinctive terminology in Philippians is the first step in identifying a predominant set of images for the letter. Scholars preferring to explain the letter in terms of "friendship" have frequently turned their attention to terms such as *koinēnia* and *to auto phronein*, arguing that they belong among the technical vocabulary of friendship.[14] "Thinking the same thing" (2:2; 4:2) is a typical part of Greco-Roman friendship, as reflected in the works of Plato, Cicero and Dio Chysostom (among others).[15] *Koinēnia* ("partnership/fellowship," 1:5, 7; 2:2; 3:10; 4:14, 15) serves as Aristotle's quick definition of friendship ("friendship is *koinēnia*"), while the phrase *koina ta philēn* ("the things of friends are (held) in common") is proverbial by the time of Plato.[16] As Fitzgerald has persuasively argued, this friendly "having things in common" explains not only the letter's *koinēnia* language, but is also reflected in the focus upon shared joy, the frequent use of *syn* compounds, and the concern with sameness (*autos*) in Philippians.[17] These observations are

---

(1991), 109; James L. Jaquette, "A Not-So-Noble Death: Figured Speech, Friendship and Suicide in Philippians 1:21–26," *Neotestamentica* 28 (1994): 187–188; Fitzgerald, "Paul," 338.

[14] White, "Morality," 210; Ken L. Berry, "The Function of Friendship Language in Philippians 4:10–20," in *Friendship, Flattery and Frankness of Speech*, 118; Fitzgerald, "Paul," 332–334. This reading is in contradistinction to the work of J. Paul Sampley's suggestion that these terms fit better in the Roman *societas* system. See Sampley, *Pauline Partnership in Christ* (Philadelphia: Fortress, 1980). For further support of this reading of *phroneē* and *koinēnia* contra Sampley, see Stowers, "Friends," 110–112.

[15] Fitzgerald, "Philippians, "145–146; Malherbe, "Paul's Self-Sufficiency (Philippians 4:11)," in *Friendship, Flattery and Frankness of Speech*, 127; Fitzgerald, "Paul," Plato, *Alc.*, 126–127; Cicero, *Amic.*, 15; *Planc.*, 2.5; Dio Chrysostom, *Or.*, 34.20.

[16] Aristotle, *Eth. Nic.*, 9.8.2; Plato, *Ly.*, 207C; *Resp.* 449C, 449D, 450C. See Fitzgerald, "Philippians," 146; Stowers, "Friends," 111; Berry, "Function of Friendship," 117; Malherbe, "Paul's Self-Sufficiency," 127; Fitzgerald, "Paul," 326; Cicero, *Off.*, 1.51

[17] Fitzgerald, "Philippians," 146; Luke Timothy Johnson, *The Writings of the New Testament: An Interpretation* (Philadelphia: Fortress, 1986), 341–342. *Chara* (joy) and related words appear 21 times in the letter (1:2, 3, 4, 7, 18 twice, 25; 2:2, 17 twice, 18 twice, 28, 29; 3:1; 4:1, 4 twice, 6, 10, 23), *syn* appears as a prefix or preposition 20 times (1:1, 7, 23 twice, 27; 2:2, 17, 18, 22, 25 twice; 3:10, 17, 21; 4:3 four times, 14, 21), and *pas, pasa, pan* ("all" or "every") appears 36 times (1:1, 3, 4 thrice, 7, 8, 9, 13, 18, 20 twice, 25; 2:9, 10, 11, 12, 14, 17, 21, 26, 29; 3:8 twice, 21; 4:4, 5, 6, 7, 12 twice, 13, 18, 19, 21, 22). For more on the frequency and distribution of vocabulary, especially as it impacts upon the question of the letter's integrity, see Pollard, "Integrity," 62–65; David E. Garland, "The Composition and Unity of Philippians: Some Neglected Literary Factors," *NovT* 27 (1985): 158–162; Robert Jewett, "The Epistolary Thanksgiving and the Integrity of Philippians," *NovT* 12 (1970): 51–53; R. Alan Culpepper, "Co-Workers in Suffering: Philippians 2:19–30," *Review & Expositor* 77 (1980): 350–351; Bloomquist, *Function*, 101–103; Duane F. Watson, "A Rhetorical Analysis of Philippians and Its Implications for the Unity Question," *NovT* 30:1 (1988): 64–67, 82–83; and Holloway, *Consolation in Philippians*, 27–31.

complemented by the importance of friends demonstrating their oneness, expressed as sharing "one soul" (*mia psychē*, 1:27).[18] This concept is implemented with variations in other parts of the letter, including the description of Timothy as *isopsychos* (2:20) and the synthesis of many of these terms in 2:2 (*autos* twice, *phroneē* twice, *syn* and *psychē* together as *sympsychoi*).[19]

A considerable test for these theories about the predominant imagery or theme of the letter is how well assertions about the terminology aid in explaining the organization of the whole. Among the researchers in friendship language, Stanley Stowers is quite persuasive in this regard. By expanding the topics of investigation to include both friends and enemies (a common topic in ancient friendship), Stowers demonstrates how most of the sections of Philippians reflect friendship motifs.[20] The letter introduces the topic of enemies early (1:15–18; 29–30) while the remainder of the letter presents a series of antithetical models.[21] The Christ hymn (2:6–11) is identified as a case of narrative modeling, showing the kind of friendship advocated for the Philippians: a selfless, sacrificial humbling in the vein of the ideal expressed in Lucian's *Toxaris*.[22] Indeed, Jaquette also suggests that Paul uses himself as an example of this sacrificial form of friendship in a previous section, where he is considering his own mortality (1:21–26).[23] The section following the hymn (2:14–18) is meant to connect the audience to this sacrificial pattern, as is the description of Timothy as the right kind of friend, selfless and concerned (2:19–24, see *isopsychos* in 2:20).[24] The whole of Phil. 3, then, is an opportunity to

---

[18] Aristotle, *Eth. Nic.*, 9.8.2; Plutarch, *De am. mult.*, 96F; *Diogenes Laertius*, 5:20. See Fitzgerald, "Philippians," 144–145; White, "Morality," 211; Stowers, "Friends," 112; Malherbe, "Paul's Self-Sufficiency," 127; Fitzgerald, "Paul," 327, 332.

[19] Fitzgerald, "Philippians," 144–145.

[20] For example, see Mary Whitlock Blundell, *Helping Friends and Harming Enemies: A Study in Sophocles and Greek Ethics* (Cambridge: Cambridge University Press, 1989).

[21] Stowers, "Friends," 114–115.

[22] Stowers, "Friends," 119; White, "Morality," 213; Jaquette, "A Not-So-Noble Death," 185. In chapters 29–34 of *Toxaris*, a young noble Demetrius cast aside his status to be placed into jail with his slave Antiphilus. Christ, like Demetrius, takes "the form of a slave" (2:7) as the supreme act of friendship.

[23] Jaquette, "A Not-So-Noble Death," 184–191. See also Jaquette, "Life and Death, Adiaphora, and Paul's Rhetorical Strategies," *NovT* 38 (1996): 33–38.

[24] Stowers, "Friends," 114; Jaquette, "A Not-So-Noble Death," 185. Certainly, Epaphroditus (2:25–30) is also functioning as an example here, as he served the community nearly to his death (2:27, 30), and he longed to be in their presence again (2:26), an observation which would only strengthen Stowers' argument. For the role of Epaphroditus as an example, see also Watson, "Rhetorical Analyis," 71–72; Bloomquist, *Function*, 128–129, 175–178.

contrast Paul's own model, following in this pattern set in the previous two chapters, with the counter-models of the "enemies" (*echthrous*, 3:18).[25]

The concluding chapter of Philippians is claimed by some to be the culmination of friendship language in the letter.[26] The specific exhortations to Euodia and Syntyche in 4:2–3 are expressed with four *syn* compounds as well as the key phrase "think the same thing" (*to auto phronein*, 4:2).[27] Furthering the argument that the letter is attempting to express the appropriate form of friendship for the community, 4:8 lists the virtues that show the truest form of friendship, while 4:9 presents Paul as the model for these virtues.[28] Berry argues that *phronein* (4:10) indicates the concern one has for a friend, a concern that is not false since the relationship continues despite *thlipsis* (4:14).[29] Even the high concentration of commercial language (such as *doma* and *karpos* in 4:17), which previously led scholars to see 4:10–20 as a thank you note or receipt for aid, was typical amongst friends who expected reciprocity in the exchange of gifts and favors.[30]

These observations about the letter's imagery and structure have led friendship scholars to identify Philippians as primarily a hortatory letter somehow involving friendship.[31] The imagery is presumed to demonstrate something about the nature or quality of Paul's relationship with the community at Philippi, as he is addressing a community of his friends.[32] Thus, Paul is writing for the community's benefit, so that they might make progress (*prokopē*: 1:25) in some way, specifically in the realm of morals.[33] Most of these scholars

---

[25] Stowers, "Friends," 116.
[26] Fitzgerald, "Philippians," 149; Malherbe, "Paul's Self-Sufficiency," 128. See also Fitzgerald, "Paul," 332–338.
[27] Fitzgerald, "Philippians," 149; Stowers, "Friends," 112.
[28] Fitzgerald, "Philippians," 151–152; White, "Morality," 207. Fitzgerald is the strongest proponent of the thesis that the purpose of the letter "is attempting to correct the Philippians' understanding of friendship." See Fitzgerald, "Philippians," 142.
[29] Berry, "Function of Friendship," 110–111, 116–117; Stowers, "Friends," 110. For more on *phronein* as a synonym for friendship in Philippians, see Wolfgang Schenk, *Die Philipperbriefe des Paulus* (Stuttgart: Kohlhammer, 1984), 65.
[30] Martin Ebner, *Leidenslisten und Apostelbrief: Untersuchungen zu Form, Motivik und Funktion der Peristasenkataloge bei Paulus* (FB 66; Würzburg: Echter, 1991), 331–364; Berry, "Function of Friendship," 118–119; Fitzgerald, "Paul," 332–333. For more on the commercial language in this section, see for example, Joachim Gnilka, *Der Philipperbrief* (HTKNT, 10.3; Freiburg: Herder, 1968), 178–180.
[31] White labels the letter as "primarily a friendly hortatory letter." See White, "Morality," 206. Stowers argues that it is "a hortatory or psychagogic letter of friendship." See Stowers, "Friends," 108, 121.
[32] Fitzgerald, "Philippians," 147, 156.
[33] White, "Morality," 207, 211 (see also the title of White's article, "Morality Between Two Worlds"); Stowers, "Friends," 108; Fitzgerald, "Philippians," 147.

argue, then, that Paul is functioning in a paradigmatic or model fashion in the letter,[34] with the aim of "correcting" the community's views of friendship.[35]

2. MILITARY IMAGERY

Though taken up by fewer scholars than the topic of friendship, an examination of military language has been equally provocative in the study of Philippians. It has proven to be particularly topical since it calls attention to Philippi's significant history as a colony and area of veteran settlement.[36] Edgar Krentz's initial study on military language in 1:27–30 surveyed the importance of this language as a *topos* in many areas of Greco-Roman society: politics, biographical writing, and philosophy (in particular, ethics).[37] Both Krentz and his student Timothy Geoffrion read the letter with this ethical backdrop, where

---

[34] White, "Morality," 201; Fitzgerald, "Philippians," 155, 158–160; Berry, "Function," 114–115, 122. Somewhat differently, but related to this argument, is that of Stowers, who maintains that Paul is playing the role of "community psychagogue," preparing them for God. See Stowers, "Friends," 118.
[35] Fitzgerald, "Philippians," 142; Berry, "Function," 114–115.
[36] For more on the Roman colonial background of Philippi, see Lukas Bormann, *Philippi: Stadt und Christengemeinde zur Zeit des Paulus* (NovTSup 78; Leiden: Brill, 1995); Craig S. De Vos, *Church and Community Conflicts: The Relationship of the Thessalonian, Corinthian, and Philippian Churches with Their Wider Civic Communities* (SBLDS 168; Atlanta: Scholars, 1999), 233–250, 275–287; Lilian Portefaix, *Sisters Rejoice: Paul's Letter to the Philippians and Luke-Acts As Received by First-Century Philippian Women* (ConBNT 20; Stockholm: Almqvist & Wiksell, 1988), 59–60; Paul Collart, *Philippes: Ville de Macédoine depuis ses origins jusqu'à la fin de l'époque romaine* (Paris: École Française d'Athènes, 1937); Peter Pilhofer, *Philippi I: Die erste christliche Gemeinde Europas* (WUNT 87; Tübingen: J. C. B. Mohr, 1995); Peter Oakes, *Philippians: From People to Letter* (SNTSMS 110; Cambridge: Cambridge University Press, 2001), 1–54. See also Chapter III.D. below. For an abbreviated analysis of these images with some reflections on the first two chapters of Philippians, see Joseph A. Marchal, "Military Images in Philippians 1-2: A Feminist Analysis of the Rhetorics of Scholarship, Philippians, and Current Contexts," in *Her Master's Tools? Feminist and Postcolonial Engagements of Historical-Critical Discourse* (ed. Caroline Vander Stichele and Todd Penner; Global Perspectives on Biblical Scholarship 9; Atlanta: Society of Biblical Literature, 2005), 265-286.
[37] Edgar M. Krentz, "Military Language and Metaphors in Philippians," in *Origins and Method: Towards a New Understanding of Judaism and Christianity* (ed. Bradley H. McLean; JSNTSup 86; Sheffield: Sheffield Academic, 1993), 105–109. Though primarily focused upon "celestial citizenship," Lilian Portefaix's study (which predates Krentz's offering here) on the reception of Philippians by first-century women offers several initial points about the potential military connotations in the letter. See especially Portefaix, *Sisters*, 140–141.

the faithful soldier is the example for the ethical life.[38] These initial forays into military imagery in the letter has provoked further consideration by Craig S. de Vos, Raymond H. Reimer, and John Paul Schuster.[39] Beyond pointing out the rather obvious uses of military terms in the letter, such as *praitēriē* (1:13) and *systratiētēs* (2:25),[40] these studies also argue that the military imagery plays a more direct role in the purpose of the letter: to exhort the Philippians to stand firm.[41]

Following Watson's division of the letter's rhetorical structure, Krentz, Geoffrion, and Reimer focus on 1:27–30 as the section that establishes the purpose of the argument.[42] By paying close attention to the wording and argument of this section, they find that a number of the terms are found in speeches of encouragement given by commanders to their troops when they seem discouraged or intimidated. For example, the verb *politeuesthe*, especially when paired with *euangeliou* in 1:27, recalls the proper way to live out one's obligations to the imperial cult.[43] The second allusion to this good news in the

---

[38] Krentz, "Military Language," 109; Geoffrion, *Rhetorical Purpose*, 38. Geoffrion calls this the *topos* of *militia spiritualis*, see Geoffrion, *Rhetorical Purpose*, 38–42. See also David McInnes Gracie, "Introduction," in Adolf von Harnack, *Militia Christi: The Christian Religion and the Military in the First Three Centuries* (trans. and intro. D. M. Gracie; Philadelphia: Fortress, 1981), 19–20.

[39] De Vos, *Church and Community Conflicts*, 277–287; Raymond Hubert Reimer, "'Our Citizenship Is in Heaven': Philippians 1:27–30 and 3:20–21 As Part of the Apostle Paul's Political Theology" (Ph.D. diss., Princeton Theological Seminary, 1997); John Paul Schuster, "Rhetorical Situation and Historical Reconstruction in Philippians" (Ph.D. diss., The Southern Baptist Theological Seminary, 1997).

[40] Von Harnack, *Militia*, 36; Portefaix, *Sisters*, 140; Krentz, "Military Language," 109–110; "Paul, Games, and the Military," in *Paul in the Greco-Roman World*, 360, 362. See also Schuster, "Rhetorical Situation," 45; Reimer, "'Our Citizenship,'" 191–192, 201–202. Reimer, in particular, emphasizes that the prosopographical studies show that many of the Macedonian soldiers in the Praetorian Guard can be identified as from Philippi. See Theodoros Ch. Sarikakēs, "Des Soldats Macedoniens dans l'armée romaine," *Ancient Macedonia II: anakoinēseis kata to Deutero Diethues Symposio, Thessalonikē, 19–24 Augoustou 1973* (Thessaloniki: Institute for Balkan Studies, 1977), 431–464; and also Davorin Peterlin, *Paul's Letter to the Philippians in the Light of Disunity in the Church* (NovTSup 79; Leiden: Brill, 1995), 164.

[41] Krentz, "Military Language," 113, 115; Geoffrion, *Rhetorical Purpose*, 23; De Vos, *Church and Community Conflicts*, 278–279; Krentz, "Paul," 362.

[42] Krentz, "Military Language," 113; Geoffrion, *Rhetorical Purpose*, 25, 35–82; Reimer, "'Our Citizenship,'"136. Here they follow Duane F. Watson, in identifying 1:27–30 as the letter's *narratio*, see Watson, "A Rhetorical Analysis," 60, 65–67.

[43] Krentz, "Military Language," 115–116; Geoffrion, *Rhetorical Purpose*, 45–47; Reimer, "'Our Citizenship,'" 144–146; Krentz, "Paul," 355, 359–360. See also R. R. Brewer, "The Meaning of *politeuesthe* in Phil. 1:27," *JBL* 73 (1954): 76–83. Schuster argues for the importance of the use of *politeuesthe* as an alliance term in a treaty between Rome and Maroneia; see Schuster, "Rhetorical Situation," 53, 64, 70–72, 177–

verse (*tē pistei tou euangeliou*) could then be referring to a soldier's pledge of allegiance to the general and the emperor.[44] Even the adverb *axiēs* (1:27) can be used to denote excellence in combat.[45] The purpose of such language is not to endorse emperor worship, but to exhort the community in an analogous fashion to live in accord with their new ruler Christ, rather than Claudius or Nero.

The military imagery extends beyond the initial clause of this verse, though. As with friendship imagery above, the theme of absence and presence is also important for military situations, since a commander's presence in battle is often depicted as a necessary positive example for the troops (1:27, see also 2:25, 28).[46] The third clause (*stēkete en heni pneumati, mia psychē synathlountes*) summons the image of soldiers standing side by side in proper formation.[47] Furthermore, *stēkete* is an antonym for fleeing (*pheugein*) as well as an important aspect of how to live worthily as citizens of the empire (*politeuesthe*), especially in times of war.[48] The unity and togetherness (*en heni pneumati, mia psychē synathlountes*) noted by friendship scholars is also the desired mental attitude for the army, since group action is the hallmark of a successful campaign.[49] The rest of this section only seems to reinforce the battlefield

---

178. While Krentz and Geoffrion attempt to establish that military terms were generally "in the air" for ethical topics, Schuster's comparative thesis is often premised upon the letter *directly* alluding to such sources as Appian's and Dio Cassius' accounts of the battle of Philippi (see Schuster, "Rhetorical Situation," 114). While such a thesis is problematic and difficult to demonstrate, Schuster's study does further demonstrate the wide semantic field for military language and is therefore useful for the purposes of this overview.

[44] Von Harnack, *Militia*, 28–29; Geoffrion, *Rhetorical Purpose*, 62–65; Reimer, "'Our Citizenship,'" 149–150. In the imperial context *euangelion* frequently referred to the good news of an important military victory or the rise of a new emperor (who often bears the title *sētēr*, see 1:28; 3:20). See Krentz, "Military Language," 117–118; Geoffrion, *Rhetorical Purpose*, 49–50; Reimer, "'Our Citizenship,'" 175–177; De Vos, *Church and Community Conflicts*, 274; Krentz, "De Caesare et Christo," *CurTM* 28 (2001): 343–344.

[45] Geoffrion, *Rhetorical Purpose*, 44–45; Reimer, "'Our Citizenship,'" 143–144; De Vos, *Church and Community Conflicts*, 278.

[46] Krentz, "Military Language," 119; "Paul," 355.

[47] Portefaix, *Sisters*, 140; Krentz, "Military Language," 120; Geoffrion, *Rhetorical Purpose*, 60–61; Reimer, "'Our Citizenship,'" 147–149; Schuster, "Rhetorical Situation," 79–81; De Vos, *Church and Community Conflicts*, 277–278.

[48] Krentz, "Military Langauge," 121; Geoffrion, *Rhetorical Purpose*, 24, 36, 55; Reimer, "'Our Citizenship,'" 146; De Vos, *Church and Community Conflicts*, 278; Krentz, "Paul," 362. Hawthorne notes that *stēkete*, as well as *synathloun, agēn* and *paschein*, could be either military or athletic terms. See Hawthorne, *Philippians*, 54.

[49] Krentz, "Military Language," 122–123; Geoffrion, *Rhetorical Purpose*, 59; Reimer, "'Our Citizenship,'" 148; De Vos, *Church and Community Conflicts*, 277–278. The image of "contending together" might be especially potent for veterans to recall as a group; see Geoffrion, *Rhetorical Purpose*, 53. Three of the key terms here (*stēkete,*

imagery, as the audience is exhorted not to be intimidated (*mē ptyromenoi*, 1:28) with a term typically reserved for frightened and disorderly horses in the midst of a battle.[50] The antithetical language of destruction (*apēleias*) and salvation (or safety, *sētērias*) in the next clause emphasizes the potential outcomes of any military conflict.[51] One of the soldier's expectations going into battle would certainly have been the possibility of suffering injury (*paschein*, 1:29) from another combatant.[52] Finally, the use of the term for opponents (*antikeimenēn*, 1:28) among this dense cluster of military terms seems to confirm that *agēna* (1:30) should be read primarily as a military, rather than an athletic, term.[53]

As before with friendship, those arguing for the importance of military images in Philippians need to show that such language plays a major role in the organization of the whole, not just one of its parts. It is essentially this endeavor that Geoffrion's monograph takes up, expanding upon Krentz's initial article.[54] Geoffrion attempts to show that the concerns of the other sections are all ultimately related to the dominant purpose of the letter as argued in military terms: steadfastness. Such steadfastness is demonstrated in military terms by both staying in line (three forms of *menē* in 1:24–25) and by advancing or making progress (*prokopē* in 1:12, 25).[55] The community's shared identity is required to remain steadfast together, as the *koinēnia* language (1:5, 7; 3:10; 4:14, 15) and the frequent appeals to joy are meant to reflect.[56] The exhortations

---

synathlountes, and *politeuesthe*) are also repeated in 3:17–4:3; see Schuster, "Rhetorical Situation," 25.

[50] Geoffrion, *Rhetorical Purpose*, 66; Reimer, "'Our Citizenship,'" 150–151; Schuster, "Rhetorical Situation," 83; De Vos, *Church and Community Conflicts*, 278.

[51] Reimer, "'Our Citizenship,'" 155–156.

[52] Krentz, "Military Language," 126; Geoffrion, *Rhetorical Purpose*, 71–77; Reimer, "'Our Citizenship,'" 156–158.

[53] Martin Dibelius, *An die Thessalonischer I–II; An die Philipper* (HNT 11; Tübingen: Mohr Siebeck, 1925), 71; Portefaix, *Sisters*, 140; Krentz, "Military Language," 126; Geoffrion, *Rhetorical Purpose*, 69–70; Reimer, "'Our Citizenship,'" 152, 159–160; Schuster, "Rhetorical Situation," 84. Appian used *agēn* to describe the battle at Philippi; see Schuster, "Rhetorical Situation," 88–89.

[54] More recently, Krentz provides an overview in Sampley's handbook on *Paul in the Greco-Roman World* of the relevance for this language to the whole of Philippians. See Krentz, "Paul," 355–363. In his summary, Krentz states, though there are other suggestions for relevant *topoi* in the letter: "But I am convinced that the greatest of these is military language." See Krentz, "Paul," 363.

[55] Geoffrion, *Rhetorical Purpose*, 59; Reimer, "'Our Citizenship,'" 190; Schuster, "Rhetorical Situation," 58, 62; Krentz, "Paul," 361.

[56] Geoffrion, *Rhetorical Purpose*, 82–84, 105–117; Krentz, "Paul," 356–357. Schuster sees *koinēnia* as an alliance term in Josephus and Appian; see Schuster, "Rhetorical Situation," 50–53, 177.

to joy reflect the expectation that a good soldier would do his duty joyfully, just as Paul does, even while suffering (1:18).[57] The role of examples is vital both in military situations and in the organization of the letter to the Philippians. Since the army requires submission and obedience, the Christ hymn could function as a model of such humble obedience (2:7–8).[58] Paul, like a military leader, seems to be playing the role of both a model (*typos*, 3:17, see also 4:9) and an authority figure, since he calls for obedience from the audience (2:12) without grumbling (2:14), even in his absence (1:27).[59] Clearly, Timothy and Epaphroditus (the *systratiētēn* in 2:25) are also presented as models of steadfast devotion.[60] The description of Timothy as *isopsychon* (in 2:20) to Paul might reflect the role of "a confidant" serving especially in military situations.[61] The presentation of their positive models only heightens the following chapter's contrast between the negative model of the *echthroi* (3:18) and the positive one of Paul. If one finds this polarization between enemies and allies to be reminiscent of the sides lined up in formation in 1:27–30, then the imagery seems to be even more forcefully pointing the audience in only one direction.[62] This sharp contrast is especially important to make so that the audience will assent to the calls for unity addressed to Euodia and Syntyche (4:2–3) and the continued modeling of Paul (4:8–9). The military associations of these calls for unity are stressed by the description of Euodia and Syntyche as at one time struggling alongside (*synēthlēsan*, 4:3) of Paul as his "co-combatants."[63] In the meantime the community members are encouraged to "guard" (*phrourēsei*, 4:7) their hearts and minds.[64]

As a result of the prominence of military imagery in 1:27–30 and its argumentative compatibility throughout the rest of the letter, scholars favoring this set of images maintain that the letter is meant as an encouragement for

---

[57] Geoffrion, *Rhetorical Purpose*, 41, 118–120; Krentz, "Paul," 357. According to Geoffrion both joy and steadfastness are part of the *topos* of *militia spiritualis*.
[58] Geoffrion, *Rhetorical Purpose*, 41, 134–140; Reimer, "'Our Citizenship,'" 197–199; De Vos, *Church and Community Conflicts*, 280–281; Krentz, "Paul," 356.
[59] Geoffrion, *Rhetorical Purpose*, 85, 100–104, 129–133; Krentz, "Paul," 356–357. In a similar vein the letter uses many imperatives and refers to Paul's *stephanos* (4:1); see Geoffrion, *Rhetorical Purpose*, 101, 206–207; Reimer, "'Our Citizenship,'" 206–207; Snyman, "Persuasion," 333–334; Krentz, "De Caesare," 344.
[60] Geoffrion, *Rhetorical Purpose*, 140–146; Reimer, "'Our Citizenship,'" 201–202; De Vos, *Church and Community Conflicts*, 278; Krentz, "Paul," 361–362.
[61] Reimer, "'Our Citizenship,'" 201; Krentz, "Paul," 362. See also Panayotis Christou, "*ISOPSYCHOS*, Phil 2:20," *JBL* 70 (1951): 293–296; Peterlin, *Paul's Letter*, 163.
[62] Geoffrion, *Rhetorical Purpose*, 152–158.
[63] Portefaix, *Sisters*, 141; Geoffrion, *Rhetorical Purpose*, 209–210; Reimer, "'Our Citizenship,'" 207–208; Krentz, "Paul," 362.
[64] Reimer, "'Our Citizenship,'" 209–210; Krentz, "De Caesare," 344; "Paul," 362–363.

steadfastness.[65] Most of the time, these scholars cite the heritage of military colonists in Philippi as one that would give added credence to the importance and persuasiveness of such images, since they would be familiar as well as favorably viewed.[66] In this regard Paul plays an important and "peculiar" role as one with authority. Though Paul apparently has limited authority here, he presumes his calls for steadfastness and obedience will be followed.[67] Thus, scholars interested in the military imagery in Philippians hold (like the friendship scholars above) that the audience was receptive to the means, the message and the sender of the letter.

B. FEMINIST ASSESSMENT

Before embarking upon this section, though, it might be appropriate to further elaborate how this chapter as "a critical overview" is different from the more common procedure of beginning a work with "a survey of previous scholarship." By attempting to engage in a critical overview, this project hopes that it does not simply summarize where scholarship has been before on these issues, as we proceed to go somewhere else. This chapter also is not meant to demonstrate how previous scholars have been "wrong" where this project will soon be "correct." Rather, as a critical overview, this chapter seeks to evaluate the usefulness of these proposals about dominant images in the letter in the pursuit of a feminist rhetorical interpretation of the letter. Since this is the aim of the project, the purpose of the following sections is to understand how these proposals do not supplant but contribute to a feminist interpretation, particularly where they have addressed or can be applied to various power relations within the letter's rhetorics.

Recalling the seven steps in the "dance of interpretation," developed by Elisabeth Schüssler Fiorenza and introduced in the previous chapter, this study proceeds with a feminist rhetorical analysis of these scholarly suggestions, in

---

[65] Krentz, "Military Language," 115, 127; Geoffrion, *Rhetorical Purpose*, 115; Krentz, "Paul," 362.

[66] Krentz, "Military Language," 127; Geoffrion, *Rhetorical Purpose*, 25; Krentz, "De Caesare," 344; "Paul," 355, 358–359. Geoffrion maintains that the audience would have consisted of "citizens or residents of a Roman colony," both of whom (he presumes) would receive a letter with such images quite amicably. See Geoffrion, *Rhetorical Purpose,* 23.

[67] Geoffrion repeatedly emphasizes this "limited authority figure" conception of Paul. See Geoffrion, *Rhetorical Purpose*, 85, 100–104. Here he is following the thought of Wayne A. Meeks (among others) who see Paul as being "suggestive rather than prescriptive." See Meeks, *The First Urban Christians: The Social World of the Apostle Paul* (New Haven: Yale University Press, 1983), 139 (whom Geoffrion cites approvingly in this section).

preparation for a feminist rhetorical analysis of Philippians itself.[68] This reconsideration will most obviously reflect Schüssler Fiorenza's calls for an *analytic of domination*, as it explains some of the roles friendship and military imagery play in scholarly constructions of Greek and Roman culture.[69] It will also reflect a *hermeneutics of suspicion* and a *hermeneutics of experience and social location*[70] and point the way to a *hermeneutics of ethical and theological evaluation*.[71]

1. RECONSIDERING FRIENDSHIP IMAGERY

Though these investigations of friendship images begin to explain what thematically the letter is attempting to achieve, they largely ignore the issues of class privilege implicit in the terminology of ancient friendship or fail to follow up on other factors, including gender, ethnicity, and colonial status. For example, Stowers straightforwardly admits: "My sketch of major features of friendship in Philippians lacks one essential element: Greek friendship was highly agonistic, that is, competitive."[72] His attention to the topic of enemies attempts to cover this gap, yet the study still fails to explicate who has the advantage in such a conceptualization of friendship. As Cicero wrote on the reasons to enter into a friendship:

> It is far from being true that friendship is cultivated because of need (*indigentiam*); rather it is cultivated by those who are most abundantly blessed with wealth and power and especially with virtue, which is man's best defence; by those least in need of another's help.[73]

Ancient discussions of friendship assume this hierarchical element to the friendship relationship; therefore, a full discussion of the use and effect of friendship language in Philippians should also comprehend and analyze this

---

[68] Elisabeth Schüssler Fiorenza, *Rhetoric and Ethic: The Politics of Biblical Studies* (Minneapolis: Fortress, 1999), 48–55; *Wisdom Ways: Introducing Feminist Biblical Interpretation* (Maryknoll, N.Y.: Orbis, 2001), 169–189. See also the overview of these seven steps in Chapter I above.
[69] Schüssler Fiorenza, *Rhetoric*, 50; *Wisdom Ways*, 172–175.
[70] Schüssler Fiorenza, *Rhetoric*, 49–51; *Wisdom Ways*, 169–177.
[71] Schüssler Fiorenza, *Rhetoric*, 51; *Wisdom Ways*, 177–179.
[72] Stowers, "Friends," 113. Here Stowers also refers to Peter Marshall, *Enmity in Corinth: Social Conventions in Paul's Relations with the Corinthians* (WUNT 2. Reihe; 23; Tübingen: Mohr, 1987), 35–67. For an acknowledgement of the agonistic nature of friendship, see also Jaquette, "A Not-So-Noble Death," 188.
[73] Cicero, *Amic.* 51; as quoted in Malherbe, "Paul's Self-Sufficiency," 136.

hierarchical element.[74] This seems to call for a shift in the scholarly discussion about friendship in Philippians: from *whether* the rhetorics of friendship are implemented in the letter to *how* the rhetorics of friendship are implemented. Stowers' article among others can be seen as an opportunity to provoke a fruitful exploration of what friendship entailed in the Greco-Roman world, and how this might impact interpretation of the letter to the Philippians.[75]

An attempt to further describe the theories, ideas and practices of ancient friendship is especially important, since it is to this cultural background which the friendship scholars refer when reading Philippians in this light. These scholars have gone to literary texts since the letter, in fact, never actually uses the direct terms for "friend" or "friendship" in Greek (*philos/philē* and *philia*), but associated terms and concepts. Yet, often times, by reference to *ancient* friendship ideas, the interpretations make the subtle (and often unnamed) jump that the letter itself or Paul are in some *de facto* fashion "friendly" in the *contemporary* sense for audiences today and in first century Philippi.[76] This involves an elision of what specifically ancient friendship involved, especially as it differs from modern, Western ideas of friendship, which seem more personal and egalitarian.

Before proceeding to an overview and analysis of ancient Greco-Roman ideas on friendship, then, we need to clarify the terms in this discussion. In particular, the term "friendship" in Greek (which, in turn, influences Roman notions) has a diversity of uses, an idea that is atypical for modern usage.[77] Even if we go as far back as the Homeric sources for friendship, the forms are diverse from the outset: some formal and practical, others more emotional and personal.[78] The important phrase in Philippians' study, "think the same thing" as a component of friendship is already evident in the *Iliad*, as when Agamemnon

---

[74] Comprehending this hierarchy both implicit and explicit in ancient friendship would call for further questions such as: who can be friends with whom, are these relationships equal and mutual or patronal and obligatory, and to whom would the imagery in Phil. most likely appeal?

[75] More recently, Fitzgerald's contribution to Sampley's handbook notes some of the political ramifications of ancient friendship in discussing the context; yet, upon turning to Pauline letters, he does not apply this knowledge to an analysis of the power relations that inhere in the letters' friendship rhetorics. See Fitzgerald, "Paul," 319–343.

[76] Fee notes that in Paul "we find a very personal and warm human being . . . many of us like Philippians because we like the Paul we meet here." See Fee, *Philippians*, 11.

[77] "We usually use 'friendship' to designate a rather narrow range of phenomena, but the Greeks use 'friendship' to designate a rather broad range of phenomena." See Paul Schollmeier, *Other Selves: Aristotle on Personal and Political Friendship* (SUNY Series in Ethical Theory; Albany: State University of New York Press, 1994), 4. See also Fitzgerald, "Paul," 325–326.

[78] Fitzgerald, "Friendship in the Greek World Prior to Aristotle," *Greco-Roman Perspectives on Friendship*, 21, 34.

and Odysseus are shown to think the same things.[79] Friends are described as "having one spirit" (*hena thuman echontes*).[80] This multiplication of roles friendship plays is reflective of friendship's great flexibility and wide applicability throughout the Greco-Roman period.[81]

a. THE ROOTS OF ANCIENT GREEK FRIENDSHIP IDEAS ARE ELITIST, ARISTOCRATIC AFFAIRS BASED ON INEQUALITIES IN WEALTH AND POWER.

Despite this diversity in the kinds of friendship, the roots of ancient Greek ideas on friendship are elitist and aristocratic. Again, this is reflected even in the work of Homer, with the ideal pair of friends, Achilles and Patroclus.[82] As Edward N. O'Neil comments, this pair like other "traditional pairs of friends which many writers list and hold up as models are usually not equal partners. In this respect, they may have originated in a type of patron-client or ruler-adviser relationship."[83] The idea of "guest-friendship" (*philoxenia*) is especially an aristocratic institution in its Homeric origins, as well as the basis for the conflict at the heart of the Trojan War.[84] Before Plato and Aristotle, it is Pythagoras who is credited with coining the phrase, "friends have everything in common" (*koina*

---

[79] Homer, *Iliad* 4.360–361. The opposite is also a reason for no truce between Achilles and Hector, since their state of mind is lacking *homophrona* ("concord"), but they are "evil minded" to each other (*kaka phroneousi*); see *Iliad* 22.262–265. Fitzgerald comments, "Homer regards *homophrosunē* as the greatest gift of the gods (*Ody.* 6.180–185)." See Fitzgerald, "Friendship in the Greek World Prior to Aristotle," 22.

[80] Homer, *Iliad* 15.710; 16.219; 17.267. See also Fitzgerald, "Friendship in the Greek World Prior to Aristotle," 22

[81] One of the primary sources for Greek theories of friendship, Aristotle, discusses the topic in such a variegated way that we can identify nine different kinds of Aristotelian friendship (personal and political divisions, further sub-divided according to altruistic or egoistic, and then useful and pleasant). See Schollmeier, *Other Selves*, 113. For extensive footnotes introducing the background(s) of friendship in the work of a wide distribution of both Greek and Roman thinkers (including Euripedes, Thucydides, Plato, Xenophon, Epicurus, Lucretius, Panaetius, Seneca, Epictetus, the Stoics, Catullus, Horace, Juvenal, and Roman poetry, among others), see Fitzgerald, "Introduction," *Greco-Roman Perspectives on Friendship*, 7–10.

[82] For their role as an exemplary pair, see Lucian *Tox.* 10; Plutarch, *De amic. mult.* 93E; 20, David Konstan, *Friendship in the Classical World* (Key Themes in Ancient History; Cambridge: Cambridge University Press, 1997), 20.

[83] Edward N. O'Neil, "Plutarch on Friendship," in *Greco-Roman Perspectives on Friendship*, 107. For more on the possibility of Greek friendship being involved with self-interest, see A. W. H. Adkins, "'Friendship' and 'Self-Sufficiency' in Homer and Aristotle," *Classical Quarterly* 13 (1963): 30–45. See also William F. R. Hardie, *Aristotle's Ethical Theory* (2nd ed.; Oxford: Clarendon Press, 1980), 327–329; Fitzgerald, "Paul," 329–330.

[84] Fitzgerald, "Friendship in the Greek World Prior to Aristotle," 24.

ta tēn philēn), a potentially more egalitarian perspective on communal sharing.[85] However, the Pythagoreans were not exactly inclusive in practice, as they were known for actively shunning friendships with non-Pythagoreans.[86]

Turning to Plato and Aristotle as major sources for Greek friendship does not alter this perception of the power relations presumed in friendships. The interest in friendship is mostly an upper-class one, as Aristotle states, "For both rich men and those possessed of office and dynasty seem to need friends the most."[87] Friendship is used to describe the bonds in many relationships in Greek thought, as Horst Hutter illustrates for Aristotle's descriptions that:

> The relations between parent and children, husband and wife, king and subject, ruler and citizen, host and guest, citizen and fellow citizen, and brother and brother are characterized by *philia*. In these relations, to be sure, *philia* assumes a form different from the one present in perfect friendship. In all such friendships, the partners are usually unequal.[88]

Most of the examples extolled in this way involve some kind of dominance over one party in the "friendship." For Aristotle, there are ideal or perfect friendships between equals at the top of the social pyramid, yet the realities reflect that "the majority of friendships involve some kind of superiority-inferiority relationship."[89]

Even after Aristotle, the participant in Greek friendship is also frequently presumed to be wealthy. Theophrastus of Eresus, for example, maintained that one could not have a true friendship if one of the friends was poor, since it was the sharing of wealth that characterized the relationship.[90] The chance to help one's friends through your monetary resources was seen as "one of the main

---

[85] Johan C. Thom, "'Harmonious Equality': The *Topos* of Friendship in Neopythagorean Writings," in *Greco-Roman Perspectives on Friendship*, 77, 92. Diogenes Laertius 8.10. See also Armand Delatte, *La vie de Pythagore de Diogène Laërce* (Brussels: Lamerton, 1922), 168.
[86] Porphyry, *Life of Pythagoras* 59–61. See also Thom, "Harmonious Equality," 94.
[87] Aristotle *Eth.* 8.1.1155a5–7, as translated in Schollmeier, *Other Selves*, 5.
[88] Horst Hutter, *Politics as Friendship: The Origins of Classical Notions of Politics in the Theory and Practice of Friendship* (Waterloo, Ont.: Wilfrid Laurier University Press, 1978), 109.
[89] Hutter, *Politics*, 111.
[90] See *Theophrastus of Eresus: Sources for His Life, Writings, Thought, and Influence* (ed. and trans. William W. Fortenbaugh, Andrew D. Barker, R. W. Sharples, and Pamela M. Huby; Philosophia antiqua; Leiden: Brill, 1992), 2.360, fr. 536; 2.360, fr. 537. See also Frederic M. Schroeder, "Friendship in Aristotle and Some Peripatetic Philosophers," in *Greco-Roman Perspectives on Friendship*, 46.

advantages of wealth."[91] Though there are occasionally other kinds of friendship in Chariton's novels, friendships between aristocratic men predominate in the narrative.[92] Though Stoics will also take up the principle of "friends having everything in common," this does not result in a questioning of the order of wealth and privilege amongst themselves, since they maintained inequalities in property and class.[93] The concept of unity and oneness in Greek friendship also managed to maintain these divisions, just as Stowers' article acknowledges regarding Plato and Aristotle:

> For these two philosophers, only the true and noble could be friends. These aristocratic friends would rule the lower classes in the ideal society. When the inferior classes submit to the rule of the upper class of "good men," who naturally have *homonoia* in their souls, there is also *homonoia* in the society as a whole.[94]

As Stowers' reflections indicate, this privileging of aristocrats as the exclusive candidates for friendship reinforced the connections between wealth, class, and the authority to rule evident throughout much of Greek thought about friendship.

b. ANCIENT FRIENDSHIPS WERE POLITICAL, INVOLVING ONLY A SMALL PORTION OF THE POPULATION.

The above observations from Stowers serve as an excellent transition to the next topic to be surveyed with regard to Greek friendship, that is, its political role. Amongst classical scholars, the dominant view of Greek friendship is that it was not very personal, but it was an institution with deep ties to the political and economic realms.[95] Again, unlike modern conceptions of a friend, "the appellation or categorization *philos* is used to mark not just affection but overridingly a series of complex obligations, duties and claims."[96] Indeed, the

---

[91] Hutter, *Politics*, 1, as well as 20. See also Jean Claude Fraisse, *Philia: La notion d'Amitié dans la philosophie antique* (Bibliothèque d'histoire de la philosophie; Paris: J. Vrin, 1974).
[92] Ronald F. Hock, "An Extraordinary Friend in Chariton's *Callirhoe*: The Importance of Friendship in the Greek Romances," in *Greco-Roman Perspectives on Friendship*, 158–159.
[93] Hutter, *Politics*, 125.
[94] Stowers, "Friends," 111. See also Andrew Erskine, *The Hellenistic Stoa: Political Thought and Action* (Ithaca, N.Y.: Cornell University Press, 1990), 30–33.
[95] Konstan, *Friendship*, 1–23, 60–67, 123–124; Hutter, *Politics As Friendship*, especially 25–55, 133–174.
[96] Simon D. Goldhill, *Reading Greek Tragedy* (Cambridge: Cambridge University Press, 1986), 82. See also Moses Finley, *The Ancient Economy* (2nd ed.; Sather Classical Lectures 43; Berkeley: University of California Press, 1973). Hutter also maintains that: "Whichever way friendship is defined in a given society, whether it is considered a

political use of *philos* for a "friend" to a ruler may be one of the oldest uses of the term.[97] Aristotle's ideas about friendship are also closely connected to his political theory. Aristotle indicates his favor for more hierarchical arrangements than the Athenian democratic model by placing kingship and aristocracy among the altruistic kinds of friendships and democracy among the egoistic.[98] The paternalistic bent of his ruling elite's "altruism" is accompanied by democracy being negatively described as a "masterless household."[99] Aristotle fails to explain why the kyriarch would be such an altruistic friend, but he "only asserts without explanation that a king rules for the common interest."[100] In this view of friendship, dominating forms of governance are not incompatible with virtuous aphorisms about friends having things in common.

Not only were kingship or aristocracy affirmed in these notions of friendship, but there are also many ways in which democracy was viewed as incompatible with ancient friendship. Friendship is seen as disruptive to a democratic order, since as a relationship it entails an exclusivity that, by nature, only includes a few people.[101] Despite this proclaimed incompatibility in the theory of Greek friendship, the elitist and aristocratic roots of friendship (as in the case of *hetaeries*, or "unions of friends"[102]) also had an effect on democratic forms, since:

> Athenian democracy was vitiated by the continuing practices of slavery and imperialism and the restriction of citizenship to a small minority of inhabitants. Hence, even the Aristotelian theory of the state as a friendship community suffers from the defects of aristocratic *hetaery* vis-à-vis those inhabitants who are outsiders and the large population of slaves.[103]

Just as friendship had been an exclusive rather than an inclusive concept, democracy was also embodied in a deeply exclusive way, especially with regard to gender (which the above quote ignores), class, status, and ethnicity (among others).

---

private concern or a public matter, it always is a political phenomenon." See Hutter, *Politics*, 9.
[97] O'Neil, "Plutarch," 110.
[98] Schollmeier, *Other Selves*, 75–96, 113–122, especially the helpful chart on 115.
[99] Aristotle *Eth.* 8.10.1161a6–9, as found in Schollmeier, *Other Selves*, 82.
[100] Schollmeier, *Other Selves*, 88.
[101] Hutter, *Politics*, 44–45. For more on how friendship and democracy are incompatible, see Herodotus *Histories* 3.80–82.
[102] Hetaeries were life-long friendship groupings maintained between elite, aristocratic males that solidified their bonds and their corporate dominance militarily, politically and legally. For more on *hetaeries*, see Hutter, *Politics*, 26–29, 35–36; Konstan, *Friendship*, 60–63
[103] Hutter, *Politics*, 47.

No matter which form of government was taken up, the need for a large number of friends in maintaining control and influence was evident to the Greeks.[104] By the time of the rise of the Macedonian kings, the term for "friend" also took on a meaning with a particularly political aspect, that of royal advisor. Since Macedonian rulers typically had a cabinet of friends as advisors, this tradition would then be extended to the Hellenistic courts of Alexander's time and beyond.[105] For example, these friends are noted next to the king on inscriptions in Hellenistic Syria, referring to "friends (*philoi*) and the military forces of land and sea (*dynameis*)."[106] Clearly, though, these relationships were not characterized by their equality, but were, in the words of Konstan, "a striking instance of the application of the language of friendship to distinctly hierarchical relations between people of different social station."[107] It is in this context that frankness of speech (*parrēsia*) becomes an especially important virtue of true friendships, as demonstrated by Plutarch's almost exclusive focus on the relations between kings and courtiers in his description of this virtue.[108]

As we turn to the Roman period, it becomes clear that, as with a great many other things, the Greek ideas and practices of friendship are continued and adapted by the Romans. Plutarch is a wonderful transition figure for these concepts, as he emphasizes that truly powerful friends, like the Romans, were indispensable.[109] It seems, then, that both Greek and Roman forms of friendship are often quite political. For example, classical scholar Peter Brunt maintains that, in the everyday language of Cicero's time, *amicus* simply meant a political follower.[110] Indeed, this seems to be the long-standing consensus amongst classical scholars of friendship, since *amicitiae* were seen as political

---

[104] Konstan, *Friendship*, 64–65. Oddly enough, one of Konstan's main goals in this study is an attempt to reemphasize the personal and affectional aspects of ancient friendship, in contradistinction to the majority of classical scholars' observations. However, by sheer bulk of reference to the political concerns, Konstan's work is an excellent resource for the political stress placed on friendships in the Greco-Roman world.
[105] Konstan, *Friendship*, 95–98; Hutter, *Politics*, 42–43; Fitzgerald, "Paul," 329. The advisers who aided the Roman emperor with administrative, legal, and military decisions would also be known as *amici*. See Susan P. Mattern, *Rome and the Enemy: Imperial Strategy in the Principate* (Berkeley: University of California Press, 1999), 1–8.
[106] D. Musti, "Syria and the East," in *The Cambridge Ancient History* (eds. F. W. Walbank, A. E. Astin, M. W. Frederiksen, and R. M. Ogilvie.; 2nd ed.; London: Cambridge University Press, 1984), 175–220, and esp. 179.
[107] Konstan, *Friendship*, 97.
[108] Konstan, *Friendship*, 104.
[109] Plutarch, *Political Precepts* 814c–d; 819b. See also Konstan, *Friendship*, 106.
[110] Peter A. Brunt, *The Fall of the Roman Republic and Related Essays* (Oxford: Clarendon Press, 1988), 353–353. See also Wilhelm Kroll, *Kultur der ciceronischen Zeit*, Vol. I (Leipzig: Dieterich, 1933), 55–57.

friendships, the connections needed for advancement, or just "the good old word for party relationships."[111]

c. ANCIENT FRIENDSHIP IS INTERTWINED WITH PATRONAGE AS A HIERARCHICAL SYSTEM.

The transition to the Roman provenance of this Greco-Roman concept, though, does entail some consideration of specifically Roman institutions, like the patron-client relationship. The terms for friendships and patron-client relations seem to overlap quite a bit in the literature, since *amicus* "is a nicely ambiguous word which applies equally well to political allies or personal intimates, to the patron or the client."[112] For example, in Cicero's recounting of his prosecution of Verres, he seems to be lumping *amici* together with *patroni*.[113] In a similar manner, M. Curius' letter to Cicero slips between referring to him as his *amicus* and *patronus*.[114] In fact, it seems that both patrons and clients are called "friends" in many places in Cicero's correspondence.[115] This ambiguity and possible compatibility is supported by epigraphy as well. In the case of the Therigny Marble (*CIL* 13.3162), Sollemnis uses both the terms *amicus* and *cliens* to describe his relationship with Paulinus. Richard Saller argues that this phenomenon "belies any thought that *amicitia* and *patronatus* were quite separate categories in the Roman mind."[116] Andrew Wallace-Hadrill also confirms that "if Roman manners distinguished *amici* (friends) from *clientes*, it was not an objective analytical distinction: they applied the same language of friendship, trust and obligation to both indifferently."[117] It seems, then, that patronage and friendship had some overlap in meaning; the images for friendship were descriptive for a number of different relations.

---

[111] Lily Ross Taylor, *Party Politics in the Age of Caesar* (Sather Classical Lectures 22; Berkeley: University of California Press, 1949), 8. See also Hutter, *Politics*, 141; Konstan, *Friendship*, 1–23, 123–135.

[112] Barbara K. Gold, *Literary Patronage in Greece and Rome* (Chapel Hill: University of North Carolina Press, 1987), 134.

[113] Cicero *Ad fam.* 2.1.28. See also Richard Saller, "Patronage and Friendship in Early Imperial Rome: Drawing the Distinction," in *Patronage in Ancient Society* (ed. Andrew Wallace-Hadrill; Leicester-Nottingham Studies in Ancient Society 1; London: Routledge, 1989), 53.

[114] Cicero *Ad fam.* 7.29. See also, Saller, "Patronage," 53–54; especially in reference to how Cicero mentions *amici, clientes* and *hospites* (guest-friends) in a series together twice in *Ad fam.* 1.20 and 5.8.5.

[115] David Braund, "Function and Dysfunction: Personal Patronage in Roman Imperialism," in *Patronage in Ancient Society*, 141–147. Cicero *Ad fam.* 8.9.4; 13.65; *In Verrem* 2.4.25.

[116] Saller, "Patronage," 56.

[117] Andrew Wallace-Hadrill, "Patronage in Roman Society: From Republic to Empire," in *Patronage in Ancient Society*, 77.

Though these patron-client styled "friendly" relations had obvious political connotations, the way friendships interacted with politics in Roman thought differed from the Greek theories of friendships in politics. Whereas Aristotle had seen friendship as foundational to the political order, Cicero perceived the relationship in reverse. For Cicero, if the political order was set and maintained well in a state of *concordia*, friendship would follow.[118] This helps to explain why friendships were always subordinated to patriotic duty, obligation to the state, and the love of Rome in Cicero's thought.[119] Loyalty to the state was always more important to Cicero than loyalty to friends.[120]

Given many of the main political trends in Cicero's time, this attitude is not surprising. During the period of the civil wars, Cicero focused on keeping the *status quo* in the Roman state in order to maintain his own relatively high standing in the republic. Loyalty to partisan friends over loyalty to the standing government fueled the changes, rather than resolving them peacefully. In this Roman's mind (and others'), one's attitudes toward friendship had a great deal to do with the machinations of political allegiance and influence. Friendships were so vital politically in the Roman world that they often became a matter of life and death, especially in terms of Cicero's own life. In the time of the civil wars, even Cicero's network of friends (and his matching awareness of their necessity) could not protect him from the frequent swings in allegiance, leading ultimately to his execution.[121] Cicero's execution was demanded because of his friendship with Brutus, a conspirator against Julius Caesar. As Octavian was rising in prominence, he turned on Cicero in order to shore up an, albeit tentative and brief, alliance with Antony.[122]

d. ANCIENT FRIENDSHIP REMAINS A MALE, UPPER-CLASS AFFAIR, EXPLOITATIVE TO WOMEN AND THE LOWER CLASSES.

Of course, these wranglings over power and the shape of the Roman government mostly involved only those at the very top of the social pyramid in Roman society. Since patronage and friendship had a great deal to do with politics, it is again not terribly surprising to find that, as in the Greek forms before, Roman friendships remained a mostly upper-class affair. Friendship was seen as "one of the decisive factors" as people contended in the arena of Roman politics and aristocratic society.[123] This is confirmed by the observation of Cicero (already cited above) that "it is far from being true that friendship is

---

[118] Hutter, *Politics*, 131.
[119] Cicero *Ad fam.* 2.5–6; *Philippics* 2.5–6. See also Konstan, *Friendship*, 125–127.
[120] Konstan, *Friendship*, 131.
[121] Benjamin Fiore, "The Theory and Practice of Friendship in Cicero," in *Greco-Roman Perspectives on Friendship*, 76.
[122] Hutter, *Politics*, 134–135.
[123] Fiore, "Theory," 68.

cultivated because of need (*indigentiam*); rather it is cultivated by those who are most abundantly blessed with wealth and power."[124] Since patronage relationships were based on providing support for the client from an excess of resources, rather than on the basis of need, classical scholars like Wallace-Hadrill hold that "patronage is seen as a characteristic activity of the upper class."[125] It seems, then, that these friendship and/or patronage relationships that were shaping the political order of Rome required wealth and power.

Not only were these relationships established by the wealthy and empowered class in Roman society, but these arrangements were also exploitative in nature to the majority of women and men in the lower classes. To the extent that we can link the friendship and patronage terms, images and systems together, these relations can both be defined in terms of their asymmetry.[126] Though the terms of patronage seem to indicate that joining in these friendly arrangements was voluntary, "there is nothing voluntary about a social system which succeeds in perpetuating inequalities."[127] *Amicitia*, then, is tied up in an exploitative system that kept the upper class nobles in control, while connecting the lower classes to the order that maintains their social and political inferiority.[128] It is important to keep clear the difference articulated here between modern Western and ancient Greco-Roman ideas, when using the terms of "friendship." As Saller insists, to speak in these instances of Roman arrangements

> in terms of 'friendship' seems to me misleading, because of the egalitarian overtones that word has in modern English. Though willing to extend the courtesy of the label *amicus* to some of their inferiors, the status-conscious Romans did not allow the courtesy to obscure the relative social standing of the two parties.[129]

Even in the mythic depictions of patronage, such as those that might be found in the work of Dionysius of Halicarnassus, the socio-political function of patronage as "an instrument of social control, that kept the population in subjection to the ruling class," is still evident.[130] Wallace-Hadrill posits that the

---

[124] Cicero, *Amic.* 51; as quoted in Malherbe, "Paul's Self-Sufficiency," 136.
[125] Wallace-Hadrill, "Patronage," 64.
[126] Richard P. Saller, *Personal Patronage Under the Early Empire* (Cambridge: Cambridge University Press, 1982), 1–6, 11–15.
[127] Wallace-Hadrill, "Introduction," *Patronage in Ancient Society*, 8.
[128] Fiore, "Theory," 70; Saller, "Patronage," 52; Wallace-Hadrill, "Patronage," 72. See also Neal Wood, *Cicero's Social and Political Thought* (Berkeley: University of California Press, 1988), 182–183.
[129] Saller, "Patronage," 57.
[130] Wallace-Hadrill, "Patronage," 73.

constant poverty, hunger and need of the clients in these arrangements and the exploitative maintenance of advantage by the patrons "need not be seen as arguments for the inadequacy of patronage, so much as the conditions of its flourishing."[131] To the extent, then, that friendship terms, images and institutions become intertwined and linked with this system that only worked when it was exploiting (rather than providing for) the majority in Roman society, "friendship" would carry some very un-friendly (in modern terms) associations for most people under Roman rule, including quite possibly Paul's audience at Philippi.[132]

Even when friendship's exploitative and hierarchical nature is detailed, most of the materials surveyed thus far in this overview and analysis of Greco-Roman friendship have neglected the issue of women's roles in Greco-Roman society. Perhaps this is because there is very little discussion about *amicitia* or *philia* between women and men in the classical sources. Konstan's study is an exception in this regard, though his treatment is quite brief. He suggests that the feminine term for friend in Latin, *amica,* had "pejorative connotations."[133] Cicero only discusses friendship with a woman in the case of befriending a widow, which would be regarded suspiciously when the man (the presumed initiator in friendships) had not previously been friends with either her father or husband.[134] Perhaps this was suspicious because, as Ovid suggests, faking a friendship might provide an opportunity for seduction.[135] Konstan also reports that the Greek term *philos* was used to describe "the clients or partners of a courtesan."[136] He surmises that this might explain why "respectable" women and men did not make use of the label *philē* or *philos* to describe their relationships. Friendship terminology provides yet another instance of dominant upper-class males attempting to circumscribe women's roles by associating them with sexuality, and, in particular, socially stigmatized sexual roles. Given the slant of much of the foundational thinking on Greek friendship by Aristotle, who had actively sought to maintain divisions in status between women and men,[137] it is not too far-fetched then to suggest that ancient Greco-Roman conceptions of friendship were not only exploitative toward the lower classes but also

---

[131] Wallace-Hadrill, "Patronage," 73.
[132] It seems that scholars who have interpreted Philippians with these friendship images in mind might not have fully considered this possibility when they have assumed a positive or receptive response to Paul, especially since this system was not "a particularly attractive system to live in." See Wallace-Hadrill, "Patronage," 85.
[133] Konstan, *Friendship*, 146.
[134] Cicero *Pro Caecina* 14. See also Plautus, *Bacchides* 193, *Curculio* 593; Epidicus 702. See Konstan, *Friendship*, 146.
[135] Ovid, *Art of Love* 1.720–722.
[136] Konstan, *Friendship*, 91; Xen. *Mem.* 3.11.
[137] Hutter, *Politics*, 59.

exploitative and exclusionary towards most (if not all) women. Friendship insulated the power and privilege of the upper class, while excluding women, the lower classes, and anyone outside of the center of power.

e. ANCIENT FRIENDSHIP TERMS WERE ALSO USED IN "INTERSTATE" RELATIONS.

Having already shown that "friendship" was connected to political convolutions in the Greco-Roman world as well as patron-client relations in Roman society, it also seems important to demonstrate additional ways "friendship" language and imagery functioned, not just in interpersonal relations but also in interstate relations. Though this seems most apparent in our sources for the Roman period, there are indications that even the Greek term *philia* was a "normal word for a treaty or alliance between states."[138] The exploitative patron-client arrangement described above by Wallace-Hadrill and others also applied to the expansion of Roman rule and the absorption of the colonized outsiders into the Roman system.[139] By socially integrating another state, city-state, colony or territory through these images (in the role of "client" and/or "friend"), the Romans came across an effective means for social control within their growing empire. We get glimpses of the Roman view of these interstate "friendships" through accounts like the ones found in Dionysius of Halicarnassus' *Roman Antiquities*. As David L. Balch summarizes one episode between the Romans and their "friends," the Alban people, typifying these political friendships: "acceptance of submission and friendship with the Romans may include being forced to give up ancestral homes and emigrating. The Romans are willing to forgive everything—if others submit."[140] Just as an asymmetrical relationship could be maintained between friends as personal patrons and clients, the Romans as a conquering people could consolidate their ties of friendship with another people, even as it demanded a relationship requiring submission. Just as Cicero had previously stressed, loyalty to Rome had priority in these relations as well. On these occasions, though, it was necessary on behalf of the subjected parties (whole populations, not just individuals) to demonstrate their loyalty and obedience above all other virtues.[141]

---

[138] Konstan, *Friendship*, 83.
[139] Wallace-Hadrill, "Patronage," 74. On the client states in the first century C.E., see Edward N. Luttwak, *The Grand Strategy of the Roman Empire: From the First Century A.D. to the Third* (Baltimore: Johns Hopkins University Press, 1976), 20–40.
[140] David L. Balch, "Political Friendship in the Historian Dionysius of Halicarnassus, *Roman Antiquities*," in *Greco-Roman Perspectives on Friendship*, 127. See Dionysius *Ant. Rom.* 3.
[141] Balch's later, chilling summary of the episode with the Alban peoples in Dionysius is also an aptly cautionary description here: "Deutschland über alles; love your country or leave it." See Balch, "Political Friendship," 143.

This system of patronal friendships transfers easily for the Romans as their influence around the Mediterranean grows. Since personal patronage had been so pervasive in Roman culture, it seems evident that this would then be reflected in Rome's imperial expansion and administration.[142] Foreign communities would be treated like an individual would have been, as more and more frequently these states, provinces or colonies would come under the patronage and authority of powerful Roman individuals, often bearing the name of their new "friendly" patron, as in the case of Philippi under Roman rule.[143] In fact, this became a primary method for the imperial administration of the provinces and other locales distant from Rome.[144]

Just as there had been an overlap between the terms for friendship and patronage relations in the personal instances above, the application of these terms to interstate relations functions rather analogously in combining these terms and images. While the Romans were increasingly making these peoples the subjects of their empire, their legal relationships were not always as clear. The main terms the Romans had for other states that they governed (or with whom they were otherwise linked) were *amicus* and *socius* ("ally").[145] Just as one was often still a social and political inferior in a friendship, the friend or ally state in these cases were still far from Rome's equal. John Rich makes this connection explicit, "Rome's 'friends' and 'allies' were in a position like that of a client vis-à-vis his patron . . . Both were unequal relationships, in which the weaker party looked to the stronger for protection and the stronger expected the weaker to show gratitude, loyalty and respect."[146] Rome's efforts at social control of the colonies and peripheries of its empire might have been effective precisely because of this flexibility and adaptability in the friendship-patronage terminology.[147] Rich speaks of the amalgamation of strategies used in the Greek East by the Romans, because "elements like 'friendship' were the common currency of diplomatic exchange throughout the Mediterranean world."[148] In administering and explaining its empire, the Romans capitalized on some of its own political traditions, which shared a common heritage with the Greeks, especially when it comes to images of friendship.

---

[142] Braund, "Function," 137.
[143] Hutter, *Politics*, 142; Wallace-Hadrill, "Patronage," 75–76.
[144] Braund, "Function," 139.
[145] John Rich, "Patronage and International Relations in the Roman Republic," in *Patronage in Ancient Society*, 128. Wallace-Hadrill adds "in law, the relationship of Rome to its subjects was complex and confused; they might be 'friends' and 'allies.'" See Wallace-Hadrill, "Patronage," 75.
[146] Rich, "Patronage," 119–120. See also Ernst Badian, *Foreign Clientelae (264–70 B.C.)* (Oxford: Oxford University Press, 1958), 1–153.
[147] Wallace-Hadrill, "Patronage," 78.
[148] Rich, "Patronage," 122–123.

f. THESE USES OF ANCIENT FRIENDSHIP TERMS MIGHT BE MORE DECEPTIVE THAN DESCRIPTIVE.

The use of these images to describe and administer its empire may not have been a case of circumstance, but a savvy technique to put "the best face" on the Roman Empire. Emphasizing the concept of patronage, as if the cities or states were individuals, helps to give the impression that the Roman form of governance had not changed from its humbler days as a simple city-state.[149] It appears only as a basic extension of the current state. This also seemed to be a way for the imperialists of Rome to stress the beneficence of their empire and its administration, just as personal patrons had previously done.[150] This has an obscuring effect, just as "when seeming amicability prevails between masters and slaves, the masters usually pose as the friends of their slaves. To be a servant is then thought to be a good thing for the servant and in his best interest."[151] The situation of Rome's rise to prominence in this period functions similarly, since Rome was clearly in a position of dominance in comparison to any other "friends" in interstate relations, but they still desired for the subjected "friends" to look amicably upon their asymmetrical arrangement.[152] It was for this reason that the Romans would

> use words like *amicus* ("friend") rather than *patronus* and *cliens* of what were in fact patronage relationships between individuals. For us to insist on using "friendship" where that is the term used in the sources would be to obscure both the function and inequality of these relationships. The point holds good for interstate relations as well. Client kings, for example, were usually called by the Romans "friendly and allied kings" (*reges socii et amici*), never *clientes*.[153]

The Roman choice to couch their "interstate relations" in terms of friendly relations between allies seems, then, an attempt to construct a particular vision of the Roman role in the administration and control of their empire. The use of friendship imagery could be seen as less a description of how the empire was

---

[149] Wallace-Hadrill, "Patronage," 75–76. Andrew Lintott maintains that patronage helps to give the *impression* of a unity in the empire, more likely to be a claim than a reality. See Lintott, *Imperium Romanum: Politics and Administration* (London: Routledge, 1993), 168–174, 186–194.
[150] Braund, "Function," 140–141.
[151] Hutter, *Politics*, 11.
[152] Rich, "Patronage," 128.
[153] Rich, "Patronage," 124.

run than how the Romans sought to be seen as offering a kind of "compassionate colonialism" to their annexed and conquered territories.[154]

g. SUMMARY AND INITIAL EVALUATIONS

The above considerations of ancient Greek and Roman terms for and forms of "friendship" demonstrated a wide variety of uses, which Philippians' scholarship would do well to consider more thoroughly. From its earliest articulations Greek "friendship" had its roots in elitist and aristocratic circles, maintaining an exclusive and limited application in Greek society. This becomes clearer when we see how "friendship" primarily functions in the political realm, which involved only a very small portion of the population, both in Greek and Roman forms of governance. Since "friendship" was intertwined with patronage as an institution and practice, it played a vital role in maintaining an inegalitarian status quo through a deeply hierarchical system. This system, in turn, functioned to exclude women in very specific ways, as well as the majority of the population in the lower classes. "Friendship" and patronage were also applied to interstate relations, especially evident in Rome's imperial agenda of expansion, submission, and colonization. This might have been a somewhat intentional strategic decision on the part of the Romans, as using these interlocking terms might have helped in their depiction of themselves as redeeming conquerors, beneficent rather than exploitative.

As mentioned in places throughout these reconsiderations, Philippians' scholars interested in friendship imagery have not totally ignored these considerations. The study of Stanley Stowers has proven exceptional in this regard, and was at least initially suggestive of these analyses. However, Stowers (and a great many of his colleagues) fail to develop their interpretations of friendship language in the letter along these lines. When these scholars have alluded to the classical sources for ancient "friendship," they have referred to many of the figures mentioned above, especially Plato and Aristotle. Yet, in their application of these Greek philosophers' conceptions, they do not explain how their ideas are at home in elitist and aristocratic (and, therefore, kyriarchal) thought. Frequently, they presume the "friendliness" of these images for

---

[154] For the use of Roman imperialism as a justification for modern colonialism and the beginnings of postcolonial approaches to classical archaeology, history, and art, see the contributions in *Roman Imperialism: Post-colonial perspectives* (ed. Jane Webster and Nicholas J. Cooper; Leicester Archaeology Monographs 3; Leicester: School of Archaeological Studies, 1996); *Dialogues in Roman Imperialism: Power, Discourse, and Discrepant Experience in the Roman Empire* (ed. David J. Mattingly; Journal of Roman Archaeology Supplementary Series; International Roman Archaeology Conference Series 23; Portsmouth, R.I.: Journal of Roman Archaeology, British Academy, 1997); and *Roman Imperialism and Provincial Art* (ed. Sarah Scott and Jane Webster; Cambridge: Cambridge University Press, 2003).

audiences both ancient and contemporary, without considering the valence of these terms, particularly if an audience (such as the community at Philippi) was diverse in terms of gender, class, status, or ethnicity (among other factors). Stowers and others do well when they demonstrate that Paul is making use of examples or models to discuss "friendship" in the letter, but their arguments could be strengthened by highlighting what kind of power dynamics are assumed in or constructed by these rhetorics, especially given the Greco-Roman conceptions of "friends." As the above reconsiderations have repeatedly shown, inequality and domination are not incompatible with "friendly" relations. Rather, these exploitative dynamics are prevalent and were more likely to be "heard" or expected by an ancient audience at Philippi. In the readings of the letter still to come, these connections will not seem strained, but will ring familiar, as Philippians similarly pairs submission and obedience to unity, friendship, and sameness.

2. RECONSIDERING MILITARY IMAGERY

a. MILITARY IMAGERY SHOULD ENCOURAGE A POSTCOLONIAL ANALYSIS OF THE LETTER.

Despite the relatively recent nature of these scholarly observations, the analysis of military language in Philippians has not been subjected to a postcolonial analysis. Since the military is one of the most obvious wings of a colonizing regime, postcolonial concerns seem to most certainly merit consideration once one identifies the prevalence of military imagery in the letter. Though the importance of the colonial status of the city of Philippi is often noted in these studies,[155] it has yet to lead to even a cursory suggestion of postcolonial interpretation by these scholars interested in military images.[156] By noting the

---

[155] See, for example, Krentz, "Military Language," 111–112, 127; Geoffrion, *Rhetorical Purpose*, 23. For more on the colonial background, see the Chapter III.D below and n. 36 above.

[156] Efrain Agosto has recently presented some initial "aspects of a postcolonial reading" for Philippians. See Agosto, "Paul vs. Empire: A Postcolonial and Latino Reading of Philippians," *Perspectivas: Occasional Papers* 6 (Fall 2002): 37–56. Agosto's comments focus upon Paul's imprisonment and the collection for the poor, with some very different results from my engagement with military imagery and the overall rhetorics of the letter. For brief introductions to postcolonial analysis in biblical interpretation (especially as it is partnered with feminist analyses), see Musa W. Dube, *Postcolonial Feminist Interpretation of the Bible* (St. Louis: Chalice Press, 2000); Kwok Pui-lan, *Discovering the Bible in the Non-Biblical World* (Bible & Liberation Series; Maryknoll, N.Y.: Orbis, 1995). See also Fernando F. Segovia, *Decolonizing Biblical Studies: A View from the Margins* (Maryknoll, N.Y.: Orbis, 2000); R. S. Sugirtharajah, *Postcolonial Criticism and Biblical Interpretation* (Oxford: Oxford University Press, 2002).

presence of veterans at Philippi and its status as a Roman colony, scholars focused upon military imagery have reminded interpreters of the neglected socio-political context of Philippians.[157] This is a helpful aspect of these scholars' work, preparing an opening for others willing and able to implement an analytic of domination.

Because of the limited reach of these studies examining military images, consideration of the letter's audience has been, in the end, partial and brief, especially in regards to its possible attitudes about or reactions to military images, since, as these scholars *have* acknowledged, these images could be connected to Philippi's multiple colonizations.[158] By turning to the work of some of the pioneers in postcolonial analysis of biblical texts, scholarship on the military imagery could have had models that would help to explain the variant, complex and sometimes compromised or ambivalent potential reactions of colonized subjects.[159] Perhaps this can begin to explain why most scholarship on the military images in the letter has not questioned the valence of such images for an audience among a subject people, a task I will briefly attempt below.

b. MILITARY IMAGERY PRESUMES AND INCLUDES VIOLENCE, BLOOD, AND DEATH.

Military images are also connected to violence. While this might be a rather obvious observation to be making, it is one rarely if ever made by scholars who propose the relevance of military imagery for the letter to the Philippians. The use of such images would not have been any less connected to violence in the Greco-Roman period. One of the virtues of the military scholars' explanations has, at times, been the vivid visualization of the images in the letter. Both Krentz and Geoffrion, for example, write of the battle lines being drawn, as they swing to face each other. The letter seems to point out to these "soldiers" the

---

[157] For recent efforts to correct this lack in Pauline studies, see, for example, *Paul and Empire: Religion and Power in Roman Imperial Society* (ed. Richard A. Horsley; Harrisburg, Penn.: Trinity Press International, 1997); *Paul and Politics: Ekklesia, Israel, Imperium, Interpretation* (ed. Horsley; Harrisburg, Penn.: Trinity Press International, 2000).

[158] For an overview of the Thasian, Macedonian and Roman colonizations of Philippi, see Chapter III.D below. By the mid-first century C.E., Philippi was under the authority of the Roman Empire and designated a *colonia iuris Italicum*. For more on this kind of colony, see De Vos, *Church and Community Conflicts*, 112–115, 246–247; Barbara Levick, ed., *The Government of the Roman Empire: A Sourcebook* (London: Croom Helm, 1988), 73–74, 316; Adrian N. Sherwin-White, *The Roman Citizenship* (2nd ed.; Oxford: Clarendon, 1973), 316–319.

[159] See, for example, the potential differences between various categories of reading communities in the dynamics between colonizer and colonized, articulated briefly in Musa W. Dube Shomanah, "Post-Colonial Biblical Interpretation," in *Dictionary of Biblical Interpretation* (2 vols.; ed. John H. Hayes; Nashville: Abingdon Press, 1999), 2: 299–303.

opposition, naming them the enemies (3:18). There is even some brief discussion of suffering. Yet, remarkably, there is very little acknowledgment that these machinations involve, or serve as preludes to, actual violence. The hearkening towards military images stops short, and the considerations are, as a result, quite bloodless.[160] Ironically enough, it has been precisely this issue of bloodshed that has been at the heart of previous debates among scholars of "early Christianity," as to whether faith in this movement could have been compatible with Roman military service. While some have explained the incompatibility of military participation for early believers by reason of the potential for idolatry, others maintain that it is specifically the violence and bloodshed that would have been especially prohibitive for them.[161]

In the case of the Roman army, this connection to violence can be stressed simply by looking at how the soldiers were trained. The process of recruitment and enlistment (required for entrance into military training) is primarily concerned with ascertaining whether the prospective soldier demonstrates the physical factors to be in proper "fighting shape," such as ruggedness, height, and age (among others).[162] The focus is on evaluating ahead of time one's physical potential to inflict damage in battle. Once accepted, the enlistee (*probates*) would not be advanced to the position of *miles* (soldier) until he endured and excelled in physical and weapons training.[163] It was success in these forms of training that was the basis for acceptance as a *miles*. This weapons training was quite extensive, as Vegetius attests "that the recruits and younger men were to have training in every type of weapon-exercise both morning and afternoon."[164] The range of this training was considered to be formidable for many recruits.[165]

---

[160] The analogy here to the terms of discussion for modern warfare (especially as it has been described of late by and for U.S. armed forces) is irresistible. Similarly, conversations stop short of speaking of blood and death, offering, rather, obfuscations and circumlocutionary terms, such as surgical strikes, precision targets, smart bombs and collateral damage.

[161] Jean-Michel Hornus, *It Is Not Lawful for Me to Fight* (trans. Alan Kreider and Oliver Coburn; A Christian Peace Shelf Selection; Scottsdale, Penn.: Herald Press, 1980); and C. John Cadoux, *The Early Christian Attitude to War* (Christian Revolution 3; London, Headley Brothers, 1918). See also Gracie, "Introduction," 14.

[162] Roy W. Davies, *Service in the Roman Army* (ed. David Breeze and Valerie A. Maxfield; New York: Columbia University Press, 1989), 3–9, 26. See also Antonio Santosuosso, *Storming the Heavens: Soldiers, Emperors, and Civilians in the Roman Empire* (History and Warfare; Boulder, Colo.: Westview Press, 2001), 89–116, in general, and, more specifically 91–93, for the physical qualifications of enlistment.

[163] Davies, *Service*, 14–15, 41–43.

[164] Davies, *Service*, 15. See Vegetius 1.11–14. See also Santosuosso, *Storming the Heavens*, 16–22.

[165] Vegetius 1.27; 3.4. See, Davies, *Service*, 41. Josephus comments on this unceasing regimen: "each soldier practices battle drill every day with great enthusiasm just as it

While soldiers were expected to accomplish other tasks, it is this kind of training that is stressed. As Davies, comments, "Although they were deployed in a considerable number of paramilitary and non-military duties, the men were first and foremost soldiers. Consequently, they must at all times be ready as *milites*."[166] It is their capacity as soldiers that makes them effective in their other roles, since they fulfill these roles backed by the threat of force, the skill they acquired in training and applied in operations. Thus, when one thinks of a soldier in the Roman army, the essential traits include being in a physical condition and having the facility with weapons so as to inflict harm and cause (mostly mortal) damage to other human beings.[167] If one cannot meet this qualification for committing acts of violence, one cannot effectively be a soldier in both his violent and threatening roles. As the training accounts bear out, this is what the soldier was equipped and expected to do. Thus, when language recalls the formations and encouragement of soldiers preparing for a battle as the letter of Philippians seems to do, it implies and anticipates an impending violent, bloody, and (for some) mortal resolution.

c. VETERAN LOYALTY IS A COMPLEX ISSUE AFTER THE YEARS OF CIVIL WARS.
Having made more explicit exactly what a Roman soldier was trained to do, we must now address how former soldiers might react to military images in a work like the letter of Philippians. Many scholars interested in military images in the letter have already stressed the fact that veterans had been settled in Philippi. This does not explain how these veterans (if they were in the audience of the letter) would find Paul's use of military rhetorics. In order to get some idea of veteran sentiment, though, we need to briefly consider the history of the civil wars that brought many of the veterans to Philippi and preceded the composition of the letter. If any members of the community at Philippi (in the mid-first century C.E.) would identify with these military images, it would most likely be the descendants of these veterans, settled in the latter half of the first

---

were in battle ... and their training maneuvers are *battle without bloodshed*, and their battle maneuvers *with bloodshed*." See Josephus, *Jewish War*, iii.72–76 (emphases mine). See also Santosuosso, *Storming the Heavens*, 92.

[166] Davies, *Service*, 41. On the make-up, training, and tasks in the Roman military, see Luttwak, *Grand Strategy*, 13–20, 40–49. For more on soldiers' "peaceful activities," see also Graham Webster, *The Roman Imperial Army of the First and Second Centuries A. D.* (London: Adam & Charles Black, 1969), 261–280.

[167] Indeed, the medical service in the field was mainly set up in anticipation of casualties in the Roman army. See Webster, *The Roman Imperial Army*, 250–253. On the role of threats in the empire, Mattern comments: "The Romans behaved on an international level like Homeric heroes, Mafia gangsters, or participants in any society where status and security depend on one's perceived ability to inflict violence." See Mattern, *Rome*, xii. On this "armed suasion," see also Luttwak, *Grand Strategy*, 46, 50.

century B.C.E.[168] Some classical scholars have argued that this history is also vital because these events were the foundation of the imperial army: "the army of the Roman Empire had substantial and evident roots in the civil wars of the Late Republic and that many, perhaps the great majority, of the legions found in service in Augustus' reign onwards were already in being before Actium, some indeed before the death of Caesar."[169]

The events of the civil wars and the years leading up to the middle of the first century C.E. were characterized by a number of sometimes rather swift and unexpected shifts in allegiance, especially in the case of the Roman military forces. For example, leading up to his conflict with Pompey, Julius took over some military units already in the process of forming on the side of Pompey.[170] After Julius' assassination, as Octavian and Antony prepared to face Brutus and Cassius, two of Antony's own legions switched to Octavian's control.[171] These machinations seemed to show that loyalty was never a certain thing in the Roman armed forces. This might have had a lingering effect on veterans' attitudes regarding their role in conflicts. For instance, after the battle at Philippi, the soldiers surviving from Brutus and Cassius' side (apparently 14,000 of them) were reincorporated into the ranks that had just defeated them.[172] As a result, their release from service and their expected settlement as veterans was delayed for further service, with a group to whom they were not necessarily loyal.

Indications that these divisions within Roman society, often causing changes in allegiance and alliance, had a mixed effect on the veterans of these wars are confirmed by the continuing troubles. By the early 30s B.C.E., relations between Antony and Octavian (once allies and two parts of a second Triumvirate of rulers) deteriorated, even as Antony continued working and fighting in the East. Despite support for Octavian (as Julius' adopted son) in the Senate, Antony "did not lack friends, who saw in him a more worthy successor to Caesar than the calculating Octavian, and risked all to follow him."[173] In this period any allusion to lingering loyalty to Julius would become a messy issue, as it seemed split between two parties at odds with each other.

In the case of Philippi, if there was any loyalty to a surviving member of the imperial government in this conflict between triumvirs, it would have been to

---

[168] For more on the chronology and history of colonization and veteran settlement at Philippi, see Chapter III. D below.
[169] Lawrence Keppie, *The Making of the Roman Army: From Republic to Empire* (London: BT Batsford, 1984), 132.
[170] Keppie, *Making*, 104.
[171] Keppie, *Making*, 115. On the frequency of such allegiance switching, predating even these wars, see Santosuosso, *Storming the Heavens*, 39–52.
[172] Keppie, *Making*, 121.
[173] Keppie, *Making*, 126.

Antony, who had ruled the provinces of Greece and Macedonia (among others) after the battle there.[174] These changes at the top would again end up affecting the soldiers under the authority of the contending parties, especially in the case of the defeated side. There are indications that Antony's troops, once beaten by Octavian's forces at Actium, were dissatisfied with being settled further away from Rome.[175] Not only the soldiers, but also the "communities which had sided with Antony were uprooted and transported to new homes in the provinces, to Philippi, Dyrrachium and other places."[176] For a veteran who expected rewards based on loyalty to his commander, it is easy to imagine bitterness in reaction to how political machinations at the top of the military and imperial ranks determined their settlement.

One might plead, though, that there is no way of knowing if soldiers cared about whom they served, or if they had any emotional reactions to the resolution of their years in the Roman army. However, there are indications that Roman veterans did previously have a cultural memory of the general or commander they followed. For example, Pompey was able to rely upon a legion of retired soldiers in the eastern provinces to come out on his side in his conflict with Julius.[177] Not only did they remember Pompey, but (once defeated) they also might not have cared for Julius and the resulting tussle to succeed him. It seems that Julius' assassination also struck a chord with those who had fought for him, as Keppie maintains: "The events of the Ides of March aroused the anger of the veterans, and both Antony and Octavian reconstituted several old Caesarian formations to bolster their forces and support their policies."[178] It was to the advantage of military leaders, then, to appeal to strong associations and memories, harnessing these veterans for their own ends. In the case of this conflict, Keppie presses this distinction between the respective commanders' reasons for war, and the veterans', since Octavian "was spoiling for a confrontation with Antony; but the veterans were more concerned with avenging Caesar's death."[179]

---

[174] Keppie, *Making*, 128.
[175] Keppie, *Colonisation and Veteran Settlement in Italy: 47–14 B.C.* (London: British School at Rome, 1983), 32.
[176] Keppie, *Colonisation*, 76. See Dio li.4.6.
[177] Keppie, *Making*, 106; Ernst Badian, *Roman Imperialism in the Late Republic* (Ithaca, N.Y.: Cornell University Press, 1968), 81.
[178] Keppie, *Making*, 133.
[179] Keppie, *Making*, 115. On Octavian exploiting the advantage of his adoption by Julius for his own advantage, see also Santosuosso, *Storming the Heavens*, 89–90, 105.

d. SETTLEMENT OF VETERANS WAS OFTEN PROBLEMATIC, ESPECIALLY IN THE EYES OF THE VETERANS.

Intensifying the mixed or potentially negative reactions to the frequent turmoil at the top of the Roman hierarchy in this period would also be the tricky matter of veteran settlement. For instance, after the battle at Philippi, most veterans wished to be and were settled in Italy.[180] Keppie states, in fact, that "all but a few were accommodated in Italy. The only known overseas colony of this time was at Philippi itself."[181] In the matter of veteran settlement, then, those most likely to be bitter were those settled in Philippi, since they seem to be the only ones not settled back home in Italy. This possibility can be confirmed by Antony's own complaints about Octavian not leaving enough settlement room in Italy.[182] In the Romans' eyes Philippi and Macedonia were not necessarily preferred as a power-base. During the rise of Octavian after the battle of Philippi, Antony had tried to trade Macedonia as a province for a Gallic one.[183] We know that the provinces, including Philippi, were where veterans were settled after defeats, as were Antony's veterans after Actium (31 B.C.E.).[184] Indeed, there seemed to be less than preferential treatment for most veterans, not just those on the losing side of these conflicts, since:

> The great majority of men placed in any colony can have had no previous links with, or knowledge of, the locality. There is little secure evidence that veterans had any choice in their place of settlement, either individually or collectively, or that they could opt (as many might have wished) for settlement close to their home towns, or indeed in the provinces where they may have developed interests or acquired property during service.[185]

Such practices in veteran settlement seem to have a high potential for dissatisfaction amongst the released soldiers.

Our sources for the Roman army indicate that soldiers and veterans would act on their dissatisfaction. Even before the decisive events of the battle of Philippi, the loyalty of soldiers was not always assured, as there are accounts of

---

[180] Keppie, *Colonisation*, 59; John C. Mann, *Legionary Recruitment and Veteran Settlement* (Occasional Publication 7; London: Institute of Archaeology, University of London, 1983), 1–11.
[181] Keppie, *Colonisation*, 60.
[182] Plutarch *Ant.* 55. See also Keppie, *Colonisation*, 73.
[183] Keppie, *Making*, 114.
[184] Keppie, *Making*, 128–129; *Colonisation*, 76; G. W. Bowerstock, *Augustus and the Greek World* (Oxford: Clarendon Press, 1965), 65.
[185] Keppie, *Colonisation*, 128.

insubordination and "near mutiny" in both 49 and 47 B.C.E.[186] It could take up to three years to acquire, survey, measure and divvy up land for veterans,[187] "a fact which the veterans themselves did not always appreciate. We hear repeated complaints at the slowness of the process."[188] Instances of dissent did not necessarily decrease over time; even after Actium, Octavian had to put down a mutiny of the Tenth Legion.[189] Rewards such as settlement were seen as rationales for serving, as Davies comments: "Life in the Roman army could be harsh and seem unrewarding, as the bitter complaints of the rebellious legionaries of Lower Germany in A.D. 14 show."[190] Even after the establishment of Augustus' "Pax Romana,"[191] the ranks of soldiers and veterans were not always at peace with the commanding hierarchy. These divisions between the upper echelon and the common soldier were maintained even in settlement, as land was allotted according to rank.[192] As a result, veteran settlement would continue as a lingering mark of one's place in social arrangements, yet another potential sore spot.

These complaints and potential revolts were often significant enough to be noticed by those at the top of the political-military hierarchy. As far back as Julius' own return from Egypt, we hear of veterans pressing for rewards and discharge.[193] On some occasions, though, the leaders could not manage to

---

[186] Keppie, *Colonisation*, 36. On the importance of settling these "near-mutinous soldiers," see Peter Garnsey and Richard Saller, *The Early Principate: Augustus to Trajan* (Greece & Rome: New Surveys in the Classics 15; Oxford: Clarendon Press, 1982), 8.
[187] Keppie, *Colonisation*, 70.
[188] Keppie, *Colonisation*, 87.
[189] Seutonius *Aug.* 24.2. See Keppie, *Making*, 135. Ironically enough, the notion of "veteran settlements were designed to convert professional soldiers into respectable citizens instead of their banding together and resorting to brigandage." See Webster, *The Roman Imperial Army*, 277.
[190] Davies, *Service*, 34. See Tacitus, *Annals* I.35. Further, Davies writes that: "Normal routine, plus army 'bull,' could be monotonous." See Davies, *Service*, 34. See also Mattern, *Rome*, 127–128.
[191] For two qualifying explanations of the ideology of "peace" in the Roman empire, see Greg Woolf, "Roman Peace," in *War and Society in the Roman World* (ed. John Rich and Graham Shipley; Leicester-Nottingham Studies in Ancient Society 5; London: Routledge, 1993), 171–194; and David Braund, "Piracy under the Principate and the Ideology of Imperial Eradication," in *War and Society in the Roman World*, 195–212.
[192] Keppie, *Colonisation*, 92. For land grants based on rank, see also John Patterson, "Military Organization and Social Change in the Later Roman Republic," in *War and Society in the Roman World*, 103. For more on the rare affluence of the veteran, and the divisions in reward, see Santosuosso, *Storming the Heavens*, 101–104.
[193] Keppie, *Making*, 110. The late republic, in general, shared this problem that "a large and increasing proportion of discharged veterans had little or no property to support them when they returned to their homes." See G. E. M. De Ste. Croix, *The Class Struggle in*

sufficiently assuage these concerns. After the battle at Philippi, Antony had so much difficulty collecting enough to pay his soldiers that Keppie claims: "there is no clear evidence that the bounty was ever paid."[194] Once Octavian tried to gain some advantage by succeeding where Antony was failing to pay, the plan backfired on Octavian as well, since "in October of the following year both he and Antony were faced by an angry deputation of colonised veterans seeking the promised money."[195] It seems that veteran settlement was a tricky enough enterprise that, even when the elite applied themselves to the issue, there were few assurances that the veterans were satisfied.

Later accounts of this period were often biased in their perspective, causing a lack of understanding about the cause of the veterans' unhappiness. Given the distance in time and the elite perspective from which later accounts were written, the legitimate complaints by the Roman soldiers were unsympathetically attributed to their "insatiable greed and a predilection for blackmail."[196] Reflecting further on the events coming on the heels of the battle at Philippi can remedy this elite slant. Keppie argues that it is instructive that only eight thousand of the thirty-six thousand soldiers eligible for discharge wished to stay enlisted. From this fact he maintains that "the citizen army of the Civil Wars contained two types of soldier: 1 the professional who was anxious for long protracted service, and liked the life (or knew no other), and 2 the short-stay recruit who was concerned to return to civilian life as soon as possible."[197] Many in the latter category were probably conscripted and, thus, desired release and their expected rewards, including settlement.[198] When thinking of the veterans settled at Philippi, then, it is those soldiers from the second category that probably predominated. However, by the time Roman writers sought to recount the history of these wars, they were more familiar with the first type of soldier.[199] As a result, they struggled to make sense of the negative and mixed reactions of soldiers and veterans who, at least in this instance, made up the

---

the Ancient Greek World: From the Archaic Age to the Arab Conquests (Ithaca, N.Y.: Cornell University Press, 1981), 357.

[194] Keppie, *Colonisation*, 41. There is some debate about whether only citizen soldiers received the cash bonus (*praemia*) upon retirement, or if the auxiliaries were included. See Mattern, *Rome*, 126–128.

[195] Keppie, *Colonisation*, 41. See Appian *BC* v. 13; Dio xlviii. 30.2.

[196] Keppie, *Colonisation*, 37. See also Appian *BC* ii. 47, Dio xli. 26 (for Placentia in 49 B.C.E.); Appian *BC* ii. 93, Dio xlii. 53, Seutonius *Caes.* 70 (for Rome in 47 B.C.E.); Appian *BC* v. 128, Dio xlix. 13 (for Messana in 36 B.C.E.).

[197] Keppie, *Making*, 145–146.

[198] The land grant in exchange for military service was used as an incentive for loyalty at the time of recruitment, especially during the civil wars. See Keppie, *Colonisation*, 40; Mattern, *Rome*, 126–128. The veterans, though in some way still invested in the imperial order, would have begun to *expect* the land grant, not necessarily be grateful for it.

[199] Keppie, *Making*, 146.

majority of the Roman army.[200] It seems, then, that most (if not all) of those settled did not look at their military service in the same happy or romantic light later expected of soldiers.

e. ROMAN MILITARY SERVICE WAS NOT ALWAYS VOLUNTARY AND WAS MET WITH SOME RESISTANCE.

From this distinction drawn by Keppie, we can surmise that soldiers were not always positive about continuing military service. This impression is reinforced by anecdotes about periods of conscription into the Roman army. That there was resistance to enlistment in these times is apparent from the order that "if when conscription had been introduced in time of war, a father mutilated his son, to make him physically unfit for service (*inhabilis militiae*), he was to be punished."[201] In one particular instance found in Seutonius, when a certain Roman knight cut off the thumbs of both of his sons, so that they would not be forced into the military, Augustus sold him and his property as punishment.[202] Apparently, this practice was not an uncommon way to avoid serving in the Roman army.[203]

Because of such incidents, it is difficult to ascertain how many of the soldiers were actually willing participants, especially within this time of frequent conscription during the civil wars.[204] For example, Keppie writes of Julius' campaign against Pompey, "Within a few months he had recruited, or pressed into service, about 80,000 men."[205] The relative frequency, abruptness and pace of these conflicts led to conscription as well as the use of non-Roman groups, as when Pompey raised legions from Asia and Macedonia.[206] This wave of pressing into service is also reflected in the epigraphic evidence for *legio* XXVIII, among others.[207] This legion is of special significance for Philippi since, after the city became the colony known as *Iulia Victrix Philippi* in 42 B.C.E., an inscription shows that a veteran of this legion settled there. Coins also show that former soldiers of the Praetorian cohorts were there as well.[208] Formed

---

[200] There is some uncertainty about how substantial the pay was for Roman soldiers. Deductions were apparently made for food, equipment and clothing. See Mattern, *Rome*, 127. In terms of social gains, Patterson holds: "Any social advancement would be largely accidental." See Patterson, "Military Organization," 99.
[201] Davies, *Service*, 7. See Arrius Menander, "On Military Matters" in *Digest* 49.16.4, 12.
[202] Seutonius *Augustus* 24.1. See also Davies, *Service*, 7.
[203] A. H. M. Jones, *Later Roman Empire* (Oxford: Oxford University Press, 1964), 618.
[204] Keppie, *Colonisation*, 37. See also Peter A. Brunt, *Italian Manpower, 225 B.C.–A.D. 14* (Oxford: Oxford Unversity Press, 1971), 391–394; Mattern, *Rome*, 83–88.
[205] Keppie, *Making*, 104.
[206] Keppie, *Making*, 141.
[207] Keppie, *Making*, 104–105.
[208] *L'Année Épigraphique* (Paris, 1924), 55. See also Keppie, *Making*, 121.

as part of the aforementioned rash of build-up before Julius' confrontation with Pompey, *legio* XXVIII fought with Julius in Africa against troops loyal to Pompey in 46 B.C.E.[209] The veteran that settled in Philippi from this legion, then, might have been one of those conscripted or forced into service against his will. Additionally, the Praetorian cohorts mentioned in coinage at Philippi could have fought for either Antony or Octavian, as they had been split on other occasions, such as the battle at Forum Gallorum.[210] These connections increase the likelihood, then, that veterans settled at Philippi might not have been inclined to look positively on their experience in the Roman army, either because of the way they joined (possibly against their will) or the way they were retired (after a defeat with non-preferential compensation).

f. VETERAN SETTLEMENT DID NOT NECESSARILY BENEFIT LOCAL POPULATIONS.

While it is vital to get a fuller picture of the range of reactions a veteran of the Roman army might have had to military images in Philippians, it is far from the whole picture as far as the potential audience of the letter. Studies in military imagery have tended to emphasize the privileges or advantages of being a Roman colony. Aside from the settled veterans, though, the local populations subject to colonization by Roman authorities certainly would have had cause for looking unfavorably on such actions. Regarding the previous inhabitants of colonized sites, Keppie argues that settlement was "undoubtedly a great shock for the inhabitants, bringing ruin to many."[211] Particularly after the battle at Philippi, there are accounts of residential unhappiness at veteran settlement in Italy (among other places). Like the protests of veterans mentioned above, these concerns would cause considerable problems for the imperial administration of Octavian.[212] By 41 B.C.E., Antony's wife Fulvia and his brother Lucius Antony had sided with the dispossessed residents, causing an "open conflict" with Octavian.[213]

Negative reactions by residents of colonized locales might have been exacerbated by their roles within the civil wars. In some instances it was apparent that non-Romans from these regions served in a military capacity, as when Pompey had raised legions in Asia and Macedonia, for example.[214] The

---

[209] Keppie, *Making*, 110–111.
[210] Keppie, *Making*, 115–117.
[211] Keppie, *Colonisation*, 101. Veteran settlement would only exacerbate any lingering enmity in general between civilians and soldiers. See Santosuosso, *Storming the Heavens*, 51.
[212] Keppie, *Making*, 122.
[213] Keppie, *Making*, 122. Luttwak adds: "resistance to the full impact of imperial taxation and conscription was often violent, sometimes more so than resistance to the initial conquest had been." See Luttwak, *Grand Strategy*, 18.
[214] Keppie, *Making*, 141.

"Liberators" (Brutus and Cassius) had also included non-Romans among their forces, which would later be reincorporated into Octavian's and Antony's armies.[215] This might have caused problems later, however, as Keppie claims, "local natives were doubtless attracted by the promise or prospect of full citizenship, and financial rewards in the event of victory, but few achieved them."[216] Though the native populations were expected to add to the infantry whenever Roman forces were outside of Italy, it seems that these "units were presumably paid for and kept supplied by their own communities."[217] This localized colonial taxation and recruitment into the Roman military forces even continued beyond Augustus' death in 14 C.E.[218]

The land taken away so that it might be granted to the veterans also disrupted the local power structures of the time, no doubt upsetting those already established in those structures. The sites for colonization were primarily selected on the basis of the city or town's already-established prosperity and fertility.[219] While scholars interested in military images in Philippians have stressed the boon of Philippi being selected as a colony, classical scholarship indicates that Philippi's selection meant it had already been prosperous before the Romans arrived, not necessarily in need of the added "advantage" of colonization.[220] One way the Roman administrators sought to appease the veterans in response to their increasing calls for speed in their system of veteran settlement was a change in method, mostly toward the form of "wholesale confiscation" of property.[221] This change demonstrates how the Roman policies could not appease both the veterans and the residents, for "the method of acquiring land was simple and callous: wholesale confiscation from owners mostly innocent of any disaffection or disloyalty."[222]

It was almost inevitable that these policies would eventually lead to resistance from the local populace in the form of violent confrontations. There are accounts of "street fighting" between arriving colonists and local residents in 41 B.C.E., and Keppie conjectures that "similar scenes on individual farmsteads

---

[215] Keppie, *Making*, 119–121.
[216] Keppie, *Making*, 144.
[217] Keppie, *Making*, 152. See also Keppie, *Making*, 150.
[218] Keppie, *Making*, 180–181.
[219] Keppie, *Colonisation*, 1, 128.
[220] As Badian comments: "No administration in history has ever devoted itself so wholeheartedly to fleecing its subjects for the private benefit of its ruling class as Rome of the last age of the Republic." See Badian, *Roman Imperialism*, 87.
[221] Keppie, *Colonisation*, 87.
[222] Keppie, *Colonisation*, 61. For more on this "balancing act" on the part of Octavian and his administration after the battle at Philippi, see Keppie, *Making*, 122. Settlement not only affected the wealthy propertied families, but also the poorer families, as Finley characterizes it as "an evasion, not a solution, of the needs of the poor." See Finley, *The Ancient Economy*, 172.

can be presumed."²²³ After Antony's defeat at Actium, these dispossessed local populations received more company, including veterans as well as other embittered, displaced civilians who had sided with Antony against Octavian.²²⁴ By the start of the first century C.E., these continuing problems again prompted a change in policy by the Roman imperial administration: Augustus began paying the soldiers through a series of taxes. The emperor judged this plan to be less problematic in comparison "to the dislocation, bad feeling and financial ruin, which had been the consequences of land settlement programmes of the preceding generation."²²⁵ Even Augustus had been forced to acknowledge the fundamental problems with the Roman policy of veteran settlement. The change hardly relieved all social ills. Alongside the policy of local sponsorship, this taxation plan still managed to place more of the financial burden on the non-elite populations of the empire.²²⁶

g. SUMMARY AND INITIAL EVALUATIONS

As with the Philippians' scholars interested in "friendship" imagery above, scholarly investigations into the range and impact of military language could benefit from some methodological expansions as well as some further consideration of the Roman military itself. These inquiries into military imagery have commendably noted the relevance of Philippi's status as a colony within the Roman Empire to the interpretation of the letter. However, they have yet to investigate the role of "empire" as the location for the rhetorical production and reception of these images, a task with which postcolonial critics of biblical literature could be of immediate and fruitful aid. While some of the interpretations have been evocative and visual, they have rarely made note of the clear implications of violence and mortal threat involved with these images. A soldier is trained to deliver effectively violent blows so as to defeat an enemy, primarily by causing serious to mortal damage to as many enemy combatants as possible. This fact most likely would not have been lost on an ancient audience living at the site of battles of historical significance for the Roman Empire such as Philippi. Thus, one who calls up the images of soldiers, enemies, and combat lines, while contrasting destruction with safety (or salvation), is interacting with an entire thought-world that also involves bloody suffering and death. Describing scenes like this is, rhetorically speaking, not too far a-field from actually threatening an audience.

---

²²³ Keppie, *Colonisation*, 101. See also Dio xlviii.9.
²²⁴ Keppie, *Colonisation*, 80.
²²⁵ Keppie, *Making*, 148. See also, Santosuosso, *Storming the Heavens*, 102–103; Garnsey and Saller, *The Early Principate*, 17.
²²⁶ As Keppie comments, "'a rich man's war and a poor man's fight' is an adage which can be applied to the Roman as well as to more modern worlds." See Keppie, *Making*, 181. See also Finley, *The Ancient Economy*, 96.

Given the vividness of these potential military images in the exhortations of Philippians, interpretations of the letter also might benefit from further examinations into the potential attitudes of veterans as a result of the swirl of events in the decades leading up to the letter's composition. Similar to Stowers above, Geoffrion effectively demonstrates how Philippians implements a series of examples or models in order to advocate for a particular course of action which is set in military terms such as steadfastness. The military imagery only accentuates our understanding of the letter's prevalent strategy of contrasting different sets of models with anti-models, since these images can be read as contending and opposing military formations. However, also like his colleague across this divide between friendship and military imagery, Geoffrion stops short of evaluating how these rhetorics construct and interact with certain power dynamics. The implications of these modeling rhetorics vis-à-vis relations between the audience, the rhetor, and the surrounding community could be further elucidated by rethinking the complex role of veterans in colonized locales.

Veteran loyalty to the emperor was less than assured in these time periods, because of the frequent shifts at the top of the socio-political and military hierarchies. Occasions for veteran and resident dissatisfaction at settlement were not rare, a phenomenon advanced perhaps by conscription or by failure to deliver upon promises of reward expected for service. Turning to the specific situation of Philippi, veterans were more likely to be unhappy if settled there, since its location far from Italy was not preferred. Furthermore, many could have been settled at Philippi as a result of being "on the wrong side at the wrong time," and, for this reason, would have had no lingering affection for the reigning administration that placed them there. These events present problems to scholars who wish to portray veterans and their descendents at Philippi as a monolithic entity, sharing the same positive outlook on their time in the Roman military and the resulting colonization and settlement.

Even if one were to assume that military imagery would have some inherent appeal to the veterans of Roman campaigns, it does not explain why scholars have presumed that the military language as a rhetorical practice would have had an appeal across the diversity of the Philippian community. Such scholarship has not adequately explained why people other than former veterans such as women and local Macedonians and Thracians would be inclined to react favorably to such terminology.[227] For the most part the people of the Greco-Roman world

---

[227] This is a particular weakness of Schuster's thesis, as his study presumes that the military families will recall specific speeches and accounts of the military history in the language of Philippians; see Schuster, "Rhetorical Situation," 141. Commentators often hold that the audience at Philippi would be proud or honored at the use of such language. See, for example, Witherington, *Friendship*, 51; Carolyn Osiek, *Philippians, Philemon* (ANTC; Nashville: Abingdon Press, 2000), 48. For an audience-oriented approach to the

64   HIERARCHY, UNITY, AND IMITATION

would have experienced the military as a wing of dominating rule, most recently in the form of Roman imperial government, with its accompanying requirements of subordination and obedience (outlined above in the Reconsidering Friendship Imagery section). The military is not a disconnected entity used only for battle. As a standing army, it functions as an extension of the Roman Empire's power and a tool for the maintenance of their domination through confiscation, taxation, and the continuing threat of force.[228] If these kinds of arrangement were associated with the military imagery presented in the letter, this could be a liability for the development of Paul's argument as a "limited authority figure."[229] One has to wonder how effective calls to obedience through military steadfastness would be, given the variegated context of Philippi. Yet, for the most part, Paul's rhetorical success has been presumed rather than argued for or explained by scholars interested in military imagery in Philippians.

3. RECONSIDERING THE CONNECTIONS BETWEEN FRIENDSHIP AND MILITARY IMAGERY

While the previous two sections have gone a long way towards reconsidering the Greco-Roman background to the use of friendship and military images in Philippians, it has yet to consider how, in fact, these two different sets of images are associated with each other. Such an observation has been made in at least a preliminary way by some of the commentators on the letter. Though his work remains predominantly focused on the topic of friendship, Fitzgerald is

---

letter that considers the way women would have received the letter, see Portefaix, *Sisters*. For the prominent role of women in Philippi's cultic activities (all but ignored in many of these studies), see Valerie Abrahamsen, "Women at Philippi: The Pagan and Christian Evidence," *JFSR* 3 (1987): 17–30; "Christianity and the Rock Reliefs at Philippi," *BA* 51 (1988) 46–56; *Women and Worship at Philippi: Diana/Artemis and Other Cults in the Early Christian Era* (Portland, Maine: Astarte Shell Press, 1995); and Chapter III.A below.
[228] On the importance of the imperial control of the military in order to increase the exploitation of the majority, especially as Rome's principate arose from the republic, see De Ste. Croix, *The Class Struggle*, 374–392.
[229] Geoffrion, *Rhetorical Purpose*, 85, 100–104. For a similarly defensive view of Paul's modeling, see Frederick W. Weidmann, "An (Un)Accomplished Model: Paul and the Rhetorical Strategy of Philippians 3:3–17," in *Putting Body and Soul Together: Essays in Honor of Robin Scroggs* (ed. Virginia Wiles, Alexandra Brown, and Graydon F. Snyder; Valley Forge, Penn.: Trinity Press International, 1997), 245–257; and Andrew D. Clarke, "'Be Imitators of Me': Paul's Model of Leadership," *Tyndale Bulletin* 49 (1998): 329–360. Weidmann's article is, in part, in response to Robert T. Fortna, "Philippians: Paul's Most Egocentric Letter," in *The Conversation Continues: Festschrift for J. Louis Martyn* (ed. Robert T. Fortna and Beverly R. Gaventa; Nashville: Abingdon, 1990), 220–234.

aware that arguing Philippians is *only* a letter of friendship could unnecessarily lead to the neglect of other major features in the letter.[230] Fitzgerald notes, for example, how friendship language combines with the other major theme discussed so far, military terminology, in the exhortation in 4:3 (*synēthlēsan*).[231] But the connections between military imagery and friendship are deeper than can be suggested in brief notes such as these.

From some of the earliest Greek expressions of these ideas, military and friendship conceptions were affiliated.[232] The original ideal pairs of friends were figures partnered in military activities. The most notable example of such a pair would be Achilles and Patroclus, but, in general, Homeric examples of friendships are linked by their military roles, since the conflict driving the *Iliad* is a military one.[233] This is, of course, intimately tied to friendship's political role in Greek thought, "friendship in ancient Greece, far from being a private matter, was a major cause of war."[234] Friendship was seen as an essential encouragement to bravery in battle, as one sought to imitate a brave friend and not be shamed in front of the same friend.[235] The later philosophical theories of friendship such as Aristotle's drew upon these archaic stories "associated with the cult of the fraternity-in-arms. This cult, in turn, arose in the context of the warrior aristocracies of the early Greek invaders."[236] Not only, then, are Greek theories of friendship based on an aristocratic and elitist perspective, but the beginnings of military and friendship imagery's interconnections are similarly from this perspective. This helps to explain why Aristotle's theory would be inclined to classify relations between soldiers as friendships.[237]

Over time, Achilles and Patroclus became traditional in their exemplary role as a pair of friends.[238] The influence of model figures like these had a broad range, as other pairs of friends (like Chaereas and Polycharmus in *Callirhoe*)

---

[230] Fitzgerald, "Philippians," 143.
[231] Fitzgerald, "Philippians," 151.
[232] The realms of friendship and the military are also reflected in civic imagery in Greco-Roman culture. For more on the relevance of civic imagery to the letter of Philippians, see Chapter III.C below.
[233] Fitzgerald, "Friendship in the Greek World Prior to Aristotle," 21–24; Konstan, *Friendship*, 27–42, especially 41–42.
[234] Hutter, *Politics*, 25.
[235] Hutter, *Politics*, 62–63. See also Plutarch, *Pelopidas* XVIII. Such a phenomenon has clear ramifications for interpreting Philippians' calls for imitation, presentation of models, and exhortations about fear.
[236] Hutter, *Politics*, 26.
[237] Schollmeier, *Other Selves*, 11. See, for example, Aristotle *Eth.* 8.9.1160a14–20, 28–30.
[238] See Lucian *Tox.* 10; Plutarch *De amic. mult.* 93E. See also Hock, "An Extraordinary Friend," 147, 156.

similarly bonded over military activities.[239] The conception of these roles of friend and co-combatant became so intertwined, that Lucian's *Toxaris* seems to be lampooning such an idea.[240] Pervo suggests that Lucian finds Greeks to be typically living in peace, yet "the traditional icons of Greek friendship are pairs of heroes whose exploits were essentially military."[241]

Ideas about the military and friendship were connected in corporate as well as individual aspects. As remarked above, friendship had been a term used for a treaty or an alliance, which clearly entailed the close or resolution of an armed conflict, as well as an attempt to avoid a later irruption into military conflict.[242] By the time of widespread Hellenistic rule, "friends" played such an important advisory role to the king that these "friends" are paired with the military forces (*philoi* and *dynameis*) as institutions in the ruling ideology.[243] It is also in the Hellenistic period that the term *xenos*, normally affiliated with guest-friendship and foreign peoples, shifts as Greeks "participated in wars between imperial powers as nationals and hired troops (the term *xenos* in this period had as its primary meaning 'mercenary soldier')."[244]

Even as the Romans become increasingly dominant around the Mediterranean, this link between friendship and military images remains. During the turbulent era of the late Roman republic, clients, friends, and armies were all linked, as is made apparent by the example of Scipio: "the 500 'clients [*pelatai*] and friends' that the young Scipio collected as part of his private militia in 134 B.C. (Appian, *Roman History* 6.14.84) were presumably distinct groups, though Scipio is said to have the label 'troop of friends' to the entire company of 4000."[245] In Roman politics, it became increasingly important to have a crowd of clients and friends who would follow you into military action, if necessary.[246] Military campaigns expanded people's client-friend networks, which in turn fueled factional politics at Rome.[247] Struggles over military and political dominance were often matters of controlling more friends, as well as staking claim to new friends. During Octavian's rise to power, "Caesar's legions

---

[239] Hock, "An Extraordinary Friend," 151, 154. As in the letter to the Philippians, we also find plenty of *syn-* compounds for these friendly co-fighters in Chariton, including the term *systratiētai* (Chariton, *Callirhoe* 8.2.10). See Hock, "An Extraordinary Friend," 156–158.
[240] Richard I. Pervo, "With Lucian: Who Needs Friends? Friendship in the *Toxaris*," in *Greco-Roman Perspectives on Friendship*, 163.
[241] Pervo, "With Lucian," 174.
[242] Konstan, *Friendship*, 83; Schroeder, "Friendship," 36. See, for example, Xenophon, *Mem.* 2.2.2; 3.7.9.
[243] Musti, "Syria," 179.
[244] Konstan, *Friendship*, 120.
[245] Konstan, *Friendship*, 136.
[246] Hutter, *Politics*, 142.
[247] Hutter, *Politics*, 149.

could be thought of as part of Octavian's inheritance—they were his father's friends (*patrikoi philoi*)."[248] As a conflict loomed between Octavian and Antony, Antony's own friends also played a role in the military wrangling.[249]

To the extent that patronage ideas became intertwined with friendship terms, the connections between military and friendship images continued as Augustus consolidated his role. In fact, it was this mixing of terms that facilitated these imperial arrangements, since "Augustus maintained, or wished to be seen as maintaining a close bond as *patronus* with individual veterans."[250] In writing the letter to the Philippians, Paul acts similarly to Augustus in mixing friendly emotions with his "soldiers":

> Throughout his reign Augustus was concerned to maintain a bond between the soldiers and himself, he was their patron, they his clients. Their loyalty, and the closeness of the bond, were continually emphasised, especially on the coinage, which the soldiers received from Augustus as their pay. Victories were his, and to be publicized.[251]

In Philippians Paul also sought to stress the bond between the community and himself, calling them "my crown" (*stephanos mou*, 4:1) while exhorting them to act properly for his own boasting (*eis kauchēma emoi*, 2:16).

The use of friendship language for the Romans' "interstate relations" was also intertwined with the order of military dominance they achieved. When the Romans depicted their imperial relations with the colonies in the ambiguous terms of friendly patronage, their ability to maintain these "friendly relations" become firmly associated with their advantageous military position.[252] This meant that, in order to have successful political relations with the Romans, other peoples needed to mix friendships with military ties. King Prusias of Bithynia seems to have done just that on his visit to Rome in 167 B.C.E., when he requested time to visit with friends: "The essential success of Prusias in the Senate was, according to Livy, due at least in part to the favour shown him by the generals who fought in Macedonia. No doubt these were among the friends whom he had taken care to visit before his audience in the Senate."[253]

Whereas Prusias' mixture of friendship with military ties saved him, the example of Cicero's life and death provides a counter-point, showing the

---

[248] Keppie, *Colonisation*, 31–32. See Nic. Dam. F130.115; Appian *BC* iii. 42; Cicero *Phil*. iv. 3
[249] Antony "did not lack friends who saw in him a more worthy successor to Caesar than the calculating Octavian, and risked all to follow him." See Keppie, *Making*, 126.
[250] Keppie, *Colonisation*, 113. See Seutonius *Aug*. 56
[251] Keppie, *Making*, 149.
[252] Wallace-Hadrill, "Patronage," 63–87; Rich, "Patronage," 117–135.
[253] Braund, "Function," 138. See Livy 45.44.

difficulty of handling this connection. In Cicero's time, having a consul friend (Quintus Metellus Celer) meant that the consul should respond to his friend's offense with all his powers, including military, "since Cicero had been attacked without provocation, Metellus should have come to his assistance, army and all."[254] Though Cicero survived this instance and quite a bit more turmoil in his time, ultimately he ended up on the wrong side of friendships with political and military ramifications, leading to his execution.[255] If ever there were an indication of how vital it was to manage the interconnections between friendships and military relations in the Greco-Roman world, the example of Cicero's life and death drives home the point.

It seems clear, then, that ancient friendship and military structures overlapped in the Greco-Roman world. Both functioned as institutions of exploitation that helped to maintain social control and, in the case of Rome, imperial domination for an elite few. Participation at the highest ranks of these institutions was almost entirely reserved for the elite, propertied males from the currently dominant ethnic group. These connections between military and friendship concepts and practices have been rarely recognized by scholarship on the letter of Philippians, yet it is precisely in this letter that we have some of the strongest arguments for the presence of *both* kinds of imagery. It is possible, then, that just as these institutions worked together in order to foster and maintain exploitative systems of rule, the confluence of these thought-worlds in Philippians was also meant to argue for a more dominating version of communal life, including calls for conformity, obedience, and loyalty to designated models.

4. SUMMARY

The aim of the preceding sections that reconsidered the relevance, impact and interconnections between ancient friendship and military images was not to demonstrate where previous scholarship has gone "wrong." Rather, the hope was, by proceeding differently, this project might be able to expand upon the observations and arguments of previous scholarship in order to more effectively develop a feminist rhetorical interpretation of the letter to the Philippians. The interpretation of Philippians can benefit from these reconsiderations in several ways. First of all, we are able to recognize the connections between ancient friendship and military imagery for the Greco-Roman world, especially as they function together in an order of domination and submission. Secondly, we can continue to emphasize that ancient friendship was a different institution from the modern, Western practice that carries with it more personal, egalitarian overtones. Ancient friendship was deeply entrenched within elite political

---

[254] Konstan, *Friendship*, 126. See Cicero *Ad fam.* 2.9.
[255] Hutter, *Politics*, 134–135; Fiore, "Theory," 76.

practices and was malleable enough to be entwined with patronage and colonizing relations in producing asymetrical power arrangements. As a result, ancient friendship was yet another means for excluding and exploiting the vast majority of people under its authority, most especially women and the non-elite classes.[256] Thirdly, we can recall the range of associations military images would have had for audiences. We should not overlook the violent implications of such images, or the potential for deeply mixed and ambivalent reactions from both veterans and residents in a colonized locale. That the military was, and in certain regards still is, an important wing in the acquisition and maintenance of dominating control of less-powerful populations should not be obscured or forgotten.

Both sets of imagery considered by interpreters of Philippians are overdue for an analysis in terms of their kyriarchal structures and effects. The term kyriarchy is here preferred over patriarchy since it emphasizes a more comprehensive view of how oppression functions.[257] Rather than a simplified, dualistic analysis of power in gendered terms, kyriarchy highlights how multiple and mutually influential structures of oppression function together and are evident not only in sexism, but also in racism, classism, ethnocentrism, heterosexism, colonialism, nationalism, and militarism (among others). The interlocking nature of various relations of domination emphasized in this definition helps to elucidate that friendship and military images work *together* as part of a complex system of domination and control. Thus, whether one is considering these images together or on their own, it is vital for any interpretation that is intended for the liberation of all people to recognize, name and analyze how friendship and military images function to oppress the vast majority of people. Interpreters of Philippians have rarely scrutinized these images for signs of an exploitation and domination that would be deeply

---

[256] Oakes estimates that about three percent of the population in Philippi could be designated as the Roman landowning elite rulers (all adult males). The remainder of the population was either disenfranchised since they were not citizens or, if they were, they lacked the wealth to truly exercise influence. See Oakes, *Philippians*, 47. De Vos approaches the problem from a different vantage point than Oakes, but mostly confirms the extent to which the Roman elite dominated the political, economic, and legal realms in the eastern colonies. See De Vos, *Church and Community Conflicts*, 111–115. Both emphasize the wide socioeconomic gap between the majority living marginally on a subsistence level and the small group of wealthy land-owners, De Vos, *Church and Community Conflicts*, 89–99, 115; Oakes, *Philippians*, 27–35.

[257] The term "kyriarchy," based on the Greek word for lord, has been coined by Elisabeth Schüssler Fiorenza to treat exactly this phenomenon. For an introductory definition to this neologism, see Schüssler Fiorenza, *Rhetoric*, ix. See also Schüssler Fiorenza, *Bread Not Stone: The Challenge of Feminist Biblical Interpretation* (rev. ed.; Boston: Beacon Press, 1995), 211 n. 6; and *But She Said: Feminist Practices of Biblical Interpretation* (Boston: Beacon Press, 1992), 8, 117.

troublesome to modern audiences of this letter.[258] It is hoped that this study, among others, might begin to remedy this gap in current scholarship.

C. CUES FROM THIS ASSESSMENT FOR THE STUDY

I began with these two proposals for prevalent imagery in the letter of Philippians not because of their inadequacy, but because of their productivity. Both sets of scholarship have already, to my mind, demonstrated the relevance of ancient friendship and military imagery to the interpretation of Philippians. Both have made strong arguments explaining both the uniqueness of some of the letter's terminology, while the exceptional studies have outlined how these images appear throughout and help to organize the whole of the letter. Scholars favoring ancient friendship as an important backdrop or reason for writing the letter at least initially demonstrated the difference between ancient Greco-Roman and modern, Western ideas of friendship. Scholars interested in military imagery recalled the importance of the community's location at Philippi, emphasizing that socio-political factors are relevant when interpreting Pauline letters. Both groups demonstrated the prevalence of the appeals to unity and to certain models and anti-models in Philippians. These points will hopefully not be lost as this project proceeds to its own reading of the rhetorics of the letter.

However, my project can benefit from comprehending not only where these interpretations have ventured, but also where they have yet to go. In particular, the sections reconsidering the ancient friendship and military images used in interpretations of Philippians have shown the relevance and importance of proceeding with feminist models and practices in mind, in order to produce a responsible and liberating reading of the letter. This difference in intent and procedure can be at least partially explained in terms of the steps in Elisabeth Schüssler Fiorenza's "dance of interpretation."

Because most biblical scholarship was not done with a concern for analyzing the potential dominating impact of the text, it seldom noted how friendship imagery and military imagery are connected to each other through their own interactions in kyriarchal systems in Greco-Roman antiquity. My study began with a hermeneutics of suspicion, holding that the language in Philippians does not simply re-present what was happening between Paul and the community at Philippi. Feminist interpretation follows an analysis of these images with questions of how these image-sets might be constructing our

---

[258] One notable exception among Philippians' scholarship would be the work of Cynthia Briggs Kittredge. See Kittredge, *Community and Authority: The Rhetoric of Obedience in the Pauline Tradition* (HTS 45; Harrisburg, Penn.: Trinity Press International, 1998). In a secondary fashion, since the work does not focus on Philippians as a whole, see also Elizabeth A. Castelli, *Imitating Paul: A Discourse of Power* (Literary Currents in Biblical Interpretation; Louisville, Ky.: Westminster/John Knox Press, 1991).

impression of the situation and producing the marginalization of women and other disempowered groups, just as it had done, in general, in Greek and Roman culture.

With few exceptions those who noted the relevance of friendship or military imagery did not consider issues of gender, race, class, orientation, colonial status or any other critical factors for systems of oppression, like the Roman Empire. The scholars rarely connected their observations about the imagery in the letter with critically conscious notes about their own social location or experiences, such as the role the figure of Paul plays within their own culture or denomination. Because these starting points or assumptions were rarely considered, many of their readings of the letter's images proceeded on "face value," rather than further exploring their role within potentially oppressive and/or liberating practices. This is perhaps why the uses of friendship imagery seemed "friendly" and why the implementation of military imagery seemed a neutral or positively unifying alternative.

Since I have consciously tried to demonstrate the relevance of these (and other) steps and integrate them into my readings, I have also highlighted the non-liberating aspects of Philippians and much of the current reflections on the letter. These images do not present some kind of paternalistic beneficence or "compassionate colonialism" practiced by the Roman elite for the good of their imperial subjects. Phrases like "troops of friends" evoke the interlocking network of hierarchical structures at work in cultures of oppression as varied as the ancient Greco-Roman and the contemporary, Western, neocolonial worlds. This letter is yet another rhetorical sign of the struggle between accommodation to and resistance of such kyriarchal arrangements.

The above reflections can provide cues for the rest of this study as to how best to produce an adequate feminist rhetorical interpretation of the letter to the Philippians. One point has been clearly demonstrated by the sections reconsidering the ancient friendship and military imagery: their inherent connection to kyriarchy. Both the military and friendship as institutions are at home in kyriarchal social relations in the Greco-Roman world. As such, both sets of imagery work together to contribute to this order of domination and oppression. Such an analysis highlights the utility of kyriarchy as a concept for interpreting these texts and interpretations. It should prove useful, then, as a companion for the readings of the rhetorics of Philippians. Therefore, the *first cue* developed from these reconsiderations is a call to pay attention to the potentially oppressive power relations reflected in the letter, with the analytical concept of kyriarchy as an important aid to such an endeavor.

The second item that was reflected not just in the content, but also in the arrangement of the "reconsidering" sections, was that two seemingly disparate sets of images or rhetorics are, in fact, connected. Ancient friendship and military images have an interrelated history in the thought of the Greeks and the

Romans. Not only historically, but also ideologically speaking, the military and friendship institutions together play a vital role in maintaining a status quo of domination that exploits and subjects the vast majority of the people under the authority of the Roman Empire. These images are overlapping, interconnected and mutually influential. A *second cue* for a feminist rhetorical interpretation, then, is to recognize that even if there are multiple rhetorical strategies, they could be interrelated and mutually supporting in the argumentation. In fact, it is often precisely the places where they work towards oppressive ends that they can be shown to intersect, overlap and interact with each other.

Thus, this critical overview of the scholarship on prominent images in Philippians has functioned not simply as a summary of where scholarship has already been. This chapter contributes two important cues for the remainder of the study to follow in order to produce its feminist rhetorical reading of Philippians. When the project turns in the following chapters to this task, it seeks to: 1.) pay attention to the potentially oppressive power relations reflected in the letter (with the help of feminist conceptualizations, such as kyriarchy), and 2.) understand the letter's rhetorics in their multiple specificity *and* in their mutually supporting interactivity, especially where they might function in potentially oppressive or even liberating ways.

Chapter III

Situating the Rhetorics of Philippians

The preceding chapter's critical overview of the scholarship on prominent images in Philippians (II above) functioned not simply as a summary of where scholarship has already been. Rather, through its critical attention to the way scholars articulated and developed their arguments for these images in the letter, it contributed two important cues for the remainder of the study to follow in order to produce its feminist rhetorical reading of Philippians. First, the study needs to track the potentially oppressive power relations reflected in the letter, with the help of feminist conceptualizations, such as kyriarchy. Second, the study needs to distinguish the letter's rhetorics in their multiple specificity *and* in their mutually supporting interactivity, especially where they might function in potentially oppressive or even liberating ways.

The four sections of this second contextual chapter each take up one or both of these cues in support of the aims of the overall project. The need for feminist analytic work (the first cue) is demonstrated through an examination of women's participation in both the cults at Philippi (III.A.) and in the early Jesus movement(s) at Philippi (III.B.). The assumed inactivity and/or insignificance of women in both classical and biblical examinations of ancient Philippi is resisted and de-centered by feminist approaches to these materials. The latter two sections of this chapter, then, primarily address themselves to the multiple and interlocking nature of power relations with rhetorical practices, in both the civic unity speeches of the Roman East (III.C.) and Philippi's military history and colonial status (III.D.), particularly as they help to elucidate potentially problematic elements to the rhetorics of Philippians.

A. WOMEN'S PARTICIPATION IN CULTS AT PHILIPPI

Turning first to the lives of women in ancient Philippi, recent studies of the archaeological and textual evidence have demonstrated the relevance of feminist analysis of the ancient world. Whereas previous work on Philippi has tended to treat references to women's realities, their cultic observances, and the role of goddesses in both as insignificant, scholars such as Lilian Portefaix and Valerie A. Abrahamsen have begun to place women at the center of their scholarly inquiry in an effort to achieve a fuller picture of Philippi.[1] Their efforts reflect the development of feminist modes of inquiry not only within biblical studies, but also within the fields of classical literature and history.[2]

Abrahamsen in particular examines the remarkable nature of the archaeological record for women in ancient Philippi, since the vast majority of the rock carvings on the hill of the city's acropolis depict female figures.[3] Of these rock reliefs, 138 of them appear to be female figures, while only 19 are male figures.[4] Initially at least, Portefaix held that it was difficult to ascertain exactly which cult was observed through these carvings, yet it seemed apparent that they were "recording some kind of fellowship of female worshippers."[5] This initial hesitancy seems appropriate considering both the number of goddess cults and the level of women's involvement in cultic life at Philippi. The interpretation of these rock reliefs can be further elucidated, then, by the following brief survey of the evidence for these two factors: women's cultic involvement and the variety of cults active in ancient Philippi.

Perhaps the most important figure for women's worship practices in Philippi was the goddess Diana.[6] While no sanctuary or temple of Diana can be found at Philippi, there is an altar at the acropolis, most likely an artifact of an open-air sanctuary for the goddess.[7] Abrahamsen has argued that the location of the acropolis carvings of female figures near depictions of Diana demonstrates

---

[1] Lilian Portefaix, *Sisters Rejoice: Paul's Letter to the Philippians and Luke-Acts as Received by First-Century Philippian Women* (ConBNT 20; Stockholm: Almqvist & Wiksell, 1988); and Valerie A. Abrahamsen, *Women and Worship at Philippi: Diana/Artemis and Other Cults in the Early Christian Era* (Portland, Maine: Astarte Shell Press, 1995). For a critique of previous archaeological studies of Philippi, see Abrahamsen, *Women*, 3.

[2] See, for example, Sarah B. Pomeroy, *Goddesses, Whores, Wives, and Slaves: Women in Classical Antiquity* (New York: Schocken Books, 1975); Mary R. Lefkowitz and Maureen B. Fant, *Women's Life in Greece & Rome: A Source Book in Translation* (2nd ed.; Baltimore: Johns Hopkins University Press, 1992); and Nancy Sorkin Rabinowitz and Amy Richlin, eds., *Feminist Theory and the Classics* (Thinking Gender; New York: Routledge, 1993).

[3] Abrahamsen, *Women*, 1, 26.

[4] Abrahamsen, *Women*, 26. Previous to Abrahamsen's study, Portefaix noted that 40 of the rock carvings on the acropolis portrayed female figures. See Portefaix, *Sisters*, 96; who also cited Paul Collart and Pierre Ducrey, *Philippes I: Les reliefs rupestres* (Athens and Paris: BCH Supplément 2, 1975), 28, nos. 98–137.

[5] Portefaix, *Sisters*, 98.

[6] On the role of Diana in ancient Philippi, in general, see Portefaix, *Sisters*, 75–98; and Abrahamsen, *Women*, 31–79.

[7] Portefaix, *Sisters*, 78.

the influence of priestesses in the Diana cult at Philippi.[8] In relation to these reliefs at Philippi, Portefaix more generally examined the importance of Diana to women at Philippi, as marked by the roles Diana was believed to play within women's lives in the Greco-Roman world.[9] Diana was reflected in the activities of her devotees in midwifery, puberty rites, healing processes, and funerary preparations.[10] This link between Diana and crucial moments in women's lives is in keeping with Diana's affiliation with both childbirth and the netherworld.[11] These typical activities and the prevalence of female figures at the acropolis stress how the Diana cult at Philippi was primarily made, paid for and organized by women.[12] Since the adherents were mostly women, the leadership and administrative roles were most likely also filled by women.[13]

In order to explain the relevance of these observations from second century C.E. rock reliefs to first century C.E. Philippi, though, we must examine the links between Diana and other goddesses in the Greco-Roman world. In the imperial era the Greek goddess Artemis was typically identified with the Roman goddess Diana.[14] Artemis had a temple cult in Philippi dating back to the second half of

---

[8] Abrahamsen, *Women*, 31.
[9] Portefaix, *Sisters*, 84. Portefaix is more uncertain about the role of these carvings than Abrahamsen: "the exact significance of these carvings for women is extremely difficult to determine since adequate inscriptions are lacking." See Portefaix, *Sisters*, 84. There are similar carvings of Diana linked with women in this period at Mesembria and Rome. See Portefaix, *Sisters*, 88–93; Gawril Kazarow, *Grabstele von Mesembria* (Jahreshefte des Österreichischen Archaeoloigschen Institutes, Bd. XXVI, 1930), 111, fig. 63.; and Henning Wrede, *Das Mausoleum der Claudia Semne und die bürgerliche Plastik der Kaiserzeit* (Mitteilungen des Deutschen Archaeologischen Instituts, Roemische Abteilung, Bd. 78, 1971), 138–141.
[10] Portefaix, *Sisters*, 81–84; Abrahamsen, *Women*, 75–78. For an inscription depicting a woman's invocation for her daughter's healing, see Collart and Ducrey, *Philippes*, 170, no. 149.
[11] Portefaix, *Sisters*, 77. Women also would have identified with Diana because she is often depicted as the "ideal woman" in literature of the time. See Portefaix, *Sisters*, 94–95. For example, see Homer, *Iliad*, 21, 489–496; Homer, *Odyssey*, 6, 102ff.; and Virgil, *Aeneid*, 1, 496–504; 7, 812–817.
[12] Abrahamsen, *Women*, 38. Abrahamsen argues that: "goddess cults such as Diana's required the almost exclusive participation of female devotees at Philippi." See Abrahamsen, *Women*, 74.
[13] Abrahamsen, *Women*, 79. Abrahamsen argues from the Philippian rock reliefs and inscriptions from the region that women were priestesses of the Diana cult in Philippi during the imperial era, the relevant time period for Paul's letter to the Philippians. See Abrahamsen, *Women*, 78.
[14] Abrahamsen, *Women*, 46. Portefaix affirms the connection between Diana, the Thracian goddess Bendis, and the Greek Artemis, while also stressing possible connections to the Greek goddess Hecate. See Portefaix, *Sisters*, 75–81. On the lingering importance of Artemis for first century CE Philippi, see Chaido Koukouli-Chrysantaki, "Colonia Iulia Augusta Philippensis," in *Philippi at the Time of Paul and After His Death*

the fourth century B.C.E.[15] The city of Thasos, which has close links to Philippi (as the history of colonizations will show in the fourth section of this chapter), was also a site of the Artemis cult since the sixth century B.C.E.[16] This Thasian site has an inscription, dating to the first century C.E. commemorating how "a woman dedicated the restoration and construction of the propylon to Artemis Eileithyia and to the people."[17] The prominent role of this woman in the Artemis cult of Thasos into the first century C.E. only reaffirms the possibilities of women's roles in the affiliated Diana cult at Philippi. Though the material remains of the Diana acropolis start around the end of the second century C.E., as Abrahamsen argues, "cults rarely come into being out of nothing just because a forum was built."[18] Given the long-standing presence of the Artemis cult and the syncretic process between Artemis and Diana, it seems likely that the Artemis/Diana cult was influential well before the creation of the surviving rock reliefs. This syncretic movement had most likely begun with the coming of the Romans to the region, that is, since at least 42 B.C.E. Since women played important roles in the Artemis/Diana cults, it seems reasonable to suggest that women were prominently involved in the Diana cult at Philippi in the first century C.E.

Though the Diana cult might be the most prominent center for women's involvement at Philippi, there are a number of other cults that reflect the activities of Philippian women. Seven of the rock reliefs at the acropolis hill depict the Thracian god Heros, or the Horseman.[19] The presence of this god is commensurate with the prominence of Diana on the hill since the Thracian Horseman is typically linked to the Thracian goddess Bendis, who over time becomes associated with Artemis/Diana.[20] This association is not surprising given the Horseman's role as another god of the afterlife, one whom the devotee can become united with after death. In fact, Heros is found depicted throughout the region on the grave stelai of women, men and children, indicating the likelihood of wide participation in the cult in the early empire.[21] Though the Horseman is also linked to rituals of healing, it is in this funerary function that

---

(ed. Charalambos Bakirtzis and Helmut Koester; Harrisburg, Penn.: Trinity Press International, 1998), 24; François Salviat, "Une nouvelle loi thasienne," *BCH* 82 (1958): 261–263.
[15] Abrahamsen, *Women*, 48; Demetrios Lazarides, "Philippi," in *Princeton Encyclopedia of Classical Sites* (ed. Richard Stillwell; Princeton, N. J.: Princeton University Press, 1976), 704.
[16] Abrahamsen, *Women*, 48; Ecole Française d'Athènes, *Guide de Thasos* (Paris: Editions E. de Boccard, 1968), 39.
[17] Abrahamsen, *Women*, 48.
[18] Abrahamsen, *Women*, 64.
[19] Abrahamsen, *Women*, 26, 70. See also Koukouli-Chrysantaki, "Colonia," 24–25.
[20] Abrahamsen, *Women*, 70.
[21] Abrahamsen, *Women*, 71; Ralph F. Hoddinott, *The Thracians* (Ancient Peoples and Places 98; New York: Thames and Hudson, 1981), 174.

the god was occasionally assimilated to Dionysus, another prominent deity in Philippi.[22] In terms of material remains, only two smaller Dionysiac shrines have been found in Philippi, one at the acropolis and another in the center of town.[23]

Concerning the epigraphy of the seventeen inscriptions linked with Dionysus, seven of them mention women, dedicated by women alone or along with a husband.[24] These inscriptions indicate a degree of economic independence and a desire to play leadership roles in the Dionysiac cult.[25] According to Herodotus, the oracle at Mount Pangaion (near Philippi) was attended by a priestess of Dionysus, while women are generally affiliated with ecstatic practices in the literature of the time.[26] There are strong indications, then, that Philippian women played a range of roles in the cults dedicated to male as well as female deities.

Though potentially most relevant for a period later than the one under consideration, the influence and popularity of the goddess Isis at Philippi cannot be overlooked. Among the three Egyptian gods that the Roman Empire initially resisted (Isis, Serapis, and Harpocrates), Isis would become the most popular at Philippi and throughout the empire.[27] Abrahamsen attributes Isis' prominence to "not only her overall strength in Thrace and Macedonia but also the propensity of the general populace toward a female deity (until recently, Diana) and the influence of her proselytizers to promote her qualities."[28] It seems that Isis worship was present at Philippi by the time of the Romans, possibly arriving by the third century B.C.E. via trade connections with Alexandria or Asia Minor.[29] While Portefaix asserts that the Isis temple on the acropolis dates to the Augustan era, Abrahamsen is less certain of such an early date.[30] She notes that

---

[22] Abrahamsen, *Women*, 70–72; Collart, *Philippes: Ville de Macédoine depuis ses origins jusqu'à le fin de l'époque romaine* (Paris: École Française d'Athènes, 1937), 413–423; Koukouli-Chrysantaki, "Colonia," 24. Portefaix's study is especially focused on the role of Dionysus in Philippian women's lives. See Portefaix, *Sisters*, 98–114.
[23] Portefaix, *Sisters*, 99. The shrine in town seems to have been a meeting-place for a thiasus of maenads. See Portefaix, *Sisters*, 99; Collart, *Philippes*, 414.
[24] Portefaix, *Sisters*, 99–101; Collart, *Philippes*, 414, no.1 and 415, no. 4; Holland L. Hendrix, "Philippi," *ABD* V. 315.
[25] Hendrix, "Philippi," 315.
[26] Herodotus, 7, 111. See Portefaix, *Sisters*, 99–104; Abrahamsen, *Women*, 71.
[27] Abrahamsen, *Women*, 34; Portefaix, *Sisters*, 114, 118–119; Rex Witt, "The Egyptian Cults in Ancient Macedonia," in *Ancient Macedonia* (ed. B. Laourdas; Thessaloniki: Institute for Balkan Studies, 1970), 329.
[28] Abrahamsen, *Women*, 66.
[29] Portefaix, *Sisters*, 70, 114; Collart, *Philippes*, 453–454.
[30] Portefaix, *Sisters*, 115, citing the evaluation of R. Salditt-Trappmann, *Tempel der ägyptischen Götter in Griechenland und an der Westküste Kleinasiens* (Leiden: 1970), 52–53.

the inscriptions there date probably to the early third century C.E.,[31] while holding out for the possibility that the temple could have been constructed during the second century.[32]

While Isis' popularity was not limited to women, the evidence for large numbers of female adherents are particularly clear in a time span stretching from the third century B.C.E. to the third century C.E.[33] Women and men were both participants in and officials of the Isis cult.[34] The base of a statue dedicated to a woman was unearthed at the acropolis temple site,[35] reflecting the appeal of Isis to women and their everyday realities.[36] The myths surrounding the Isis cult depict her as an ideal wife and mother and, as noted in the case of the deities above, involved in mourning rituals.[37] For Abrahamsen this latter association, alongside her healing properties,[38] could explain why Isis has an appeal similar to the goddess Diana, who preceded her in prominence at Philippi.[39] She argues that the growth of the Isis cult was a result of adherents leaving more gender-segregated cults, like the primarily female Diana cult and mostly male Sylvanus cult.[40] Abrahamsen accounts for Philippian women's shift away from Diana: "an Isis temple might have been attractive to those women who had been 'relegated' to carving open-air reliefs to their goddess, having had no elaborate temple like their male counterparts in the Sylvanus cult."[41] Through several centuries and several different cults (Diana/Artemis, Heros/Dionysus, and Isis), Philippian women sought active roles and practices compatible to their expectations.

Though less ubiquitous than the more traditional cults surrounding deities, the worship of the Roman emperor and his wife and daughters also reflects the experiences of Philippian women.[42] Julia, the daughter of Augustus, was revered

---

[31] Abrahamsen, *Women*, 34–35; citing Collart, "Le sanctuaire des dieux égyptiens à Philippes," *BCH* 53 (1929): 69–100.

[32] Abrahamsen, *Women*, 34.

[33] Portefaix, *Sisters*, 115; Sharon K. Heyob, *The Cult of Isis among Women in the Graeco-Roman World* (EPRO 51; Leiden: Brill, 1975), 86.

[34] Abrahamsen, *Women*, 34; Portefaix, *Sisters*, 115–116; Witt, "Egyptian Cults," 328; Heyob, *Cult*, 10.

[35] Portefaix, *Sisters*, 50, 115–116; Collart, *Philippes*, 446, no. 1.

[36] Portefaix, *Sisters*, 117.

[37] Portefaix, *Sisters*, 121–126.

[38] Portefaix, *Sisters*, 118; Abrahamsen, *Women*, 34; Collart, *Philippes*, 452. See also the inscription in Collart, "Le sanctuaire," 83, no. 7.

[39] Abrahamsen, *Women*, 59.

[40] Abrahamsen, *Women*, 38–39. In fact, some of the reliefs now identified as Diana were originally believed to depict Isis. See Abrahamsen, *Women*, 30; Collart, *Philippes*, 448. For more on the Sylvanus cult in Philippi, see Abrahamsen, *Women*, 35–38, 64–66

[41] Abrahamsen, *Women*, 39.

[42] For emperor and empress worship, in general, see Abrahamsen, *Women*, 79–82; Portefaix, *Sisters*, 48–51.

in Philippi in this time period.[43] More prominently in terms of material remains, though, is the figure of Livia, the wife of Augustus, who was part of a monument at a Philippian temple dating from the second half of the first century or the second century C.E.[44] While it is uncertain whether Livia ever visited Philippi before her death in 29 C.E., it seems that her subsequent proclamation as "diva" (in 42 C.E. by Claudius) so inspired worshippers in the Philippian colony that her cult lasted for over a century.[45] The monument base dedicated to Livia at Philippi depicts five priestesses of the deified empress, including Maecia C. F. Auruncina Calaviana, named twice on the monument, as priestess and as the donor of the monument.[46] Because of the extent of this honor to Livia and the sheer number of priestesses on this monument, Abrahamsen surmises that Philippi must have been especially "supportive of women, girls, goddesses and divinized females."[47] The role of Maecia and the others on the monument would not have been rare for the cult of the empress. Priestesses were common in this cult, as attested for Philippi in this monument and in other inscriptions.[48] Sarcophagi from Philippi's port (Neapolis) also attest to at least one other priestess of the city's Livia cult, named Cornelia Asprilla, active possibly in the first century C.E.[49]

Yet, Portefaix stresses that Philippian women's cultic experiences were not limited to these prominent, public worship opportunities. In a more private sphere of activity, the wife of the *paterfamilias* would effectively be the priestess of the family's domestic religion.[50] In this capacity, women would lead in the worship of the household deities, performing regular sacrifices and prayers as well as other duties on special occasions (certain meals or banquets).[51] Indeed, most family celebrations (like weddings and burials) would

---

[43] Abrahamsen, *Women*, 11; Collart, "Philippes," *Dictionnaire d'archéologie chrétienne*, Vol. 14 (1939), 722.
[44] Abrahamsen, *Women*, 80; Michel Sève and Patrick Weber, "Un monument honorifique au forum de Philippes," *BCH* 112 (1988): 474; Koukouli-Chrysantaki, "Colonia," 16.
[45] Abrahamsen, *Women*, 80–81; Sève and Weber, "Un monument," 470; Koukouli-Chrysantaki, "Colonia," 16; G. Grether, "Livia and the Roman Imperial Cult," *American Journal of Philology* 47 (1946): 222–252.
[46] Abrahamsen, *Women*, 80; Sève and Weber, "Un monument," 467–479.
[47] Abrahamsen, *Women*, 81.
[48] Portefaix, *Sisters*, 50, 65; Collart, *Philippes*, 265.
[49] Koukouli-Chrysantaki, "Colonia," 10; Leon A. Heuzey and H. Daumet, *Mission archéologique de Macédoine* (Paris: Librarie de Firmin-Didot et Cie, 1876), 15–21, nos. 1–4; Kavala Museum Inv. No. Λ275.
[50] Portefaix, *Sisters*, 43.
[51] Portefaix, *Sisters*, 43–46.

include a cultic element where women performed rituals.[52] As leaders in these practices, then, the older women were also responsible for instructing the younger women and girls in the proper ways to keep them.[53] Like these "sacra privata" observances, women's activities in mystery or "folk" religions might also be easy to overlook. As noted above with regard to the Dionysiac cult, mystery religions were often concerned with the transition from this life, a ritual occurrence of special significance for women.[54] For those women not associated with a temple or major deity, acting on one's own might be classified as participating in "folk" religion.[55] There would be little difference between a priestess in an accepted cult system and the folk practitioner, or sorceress, in terms of activity. The folk practitioner would offer her services to whoever was in need, functioning as a dream interpreter, consoler, or ritual purifier (especially at birth and death).[56] It seems possible, then, that women also took the lead and participated in a range of cultic activities beyond the more formal worship settings available in Philippi.

From this rather cursory sketch of women's participation in Philippi's cults, following primarily the studies of Abrahamsen and Portefaix, it becomes clear that women were engaged in a range of activities. Significantly, for the examination of the letter to the Philippians, it seems that women held leadership positions in these cults before, during and after the time of Paul.[57] While the leadership and participation of women might have been highest in the Diana cult, Philippian women also shared leadership in more mixed settings, including the Isis, Dionysus, and Thracian Horseman cults.[58] The popularity of empress worship within the imperial cult and the additional roles played within smaller, or more private settings fill out an already rich portrait of Philippian women's

---

[52] Portefaix, *Sisters*, 46–48. See, in general, Hugo Blümner, *Die römischen Privataltertümer* (Handbuch der klassischen Altertums-Wissenschaft, 4. Bd., 2. Abt., 2. T; München, Beck, 1911), 335–357.
[53] Portefaix, *Sisters*, 40–42, 45. See also the observations below regarding the mother's role in the education and organization of other females' imitation of these practices.
[54] Portefaix, *Sisters*, 51–55.
[55] Portefaix, *Sisters*, 55–58.
[56] Portefaix, *Sisters*, 56–57. See, also Blümner, *Die römischen Privataltertümer*, 304; Georg Luck, *Hexen und Zauberei in der römischen Dichtung* (Lebendige Antike; Zurich: Artemis, 1962).
[57] For a similar summary, see Abrahamsen, *Women*, 8. For more on the lingering significance of these cultic tendencies and women's leadership for Philippi heading into the early Byzantine period, see Abrahamsen, *Women*, 86–90, 164–172, and Chapter III.B below.
[58] See the overview above, and Abrahamsen, *Women*, 78. Furthermore, Abrahamsen comments: "The fact that two goddesses were the most common inhabitants of the acropolis hill—Diana, depicted ninety times on the reliefs, and Isis, with her own sanctuary close by—is a major reason to postulate the high involvement of women in this part of the city." See Abrahamsen, *Women*, 104.

participation in cultic life. The variety of these options and the importance of women within these cultic realms suggest that any other movement introduced to Philippi would have to contend with *expectations* about women's roles. As Abrahamsen has maintained: "The combined influence of Isis, Diana, the Horseman and Dionysos vis-à-vis female cult officials—the *assumption* that women were to be among the leaders of any religious organization—was felt by the Christian community."[59] These potential assumptions and expectations about women's participation and leadership would have affected the reception of the letter to the Philippians, and should affect any interpretation of the early community receiving the letter, especially a feminist interpretation.[60]

EXCURSUS: IMITATION OF WOMEN IN CULTIC LIFE

Since it was expected that women would have participated and led within the cultic life of Philippi, it seems that these activities would also encourage Philippian women to play yet another role, that of model. Whenever they depicted a priestess of Diana, those remarkable rock reliefs at Philippi's acropolis served as a visual exhortation for other Diana devotees to imitate the deceased priestess.[61] Portefaix even suggests that the goddess Diana herself "was the model for all members of her sex."[62] Within the Diana cult, the almost exclusively female environment would have had an impact on the next generation:

> girls had access to important female role models in a structured context at a young age that greatly influenced their development. Such role models were women who worshipped a same-sex deity and were active participants and leaders in the community. This positive bonding between older and younger women would be a significant factor in a city's socio-political situation: in many spheres of life, women would not be dependent on men nor subservient to them. Rather, they would be able to fashion their own destiny to a large

---

[59] Abrahamsen, *Women*, 91. Emphasis original.
[60] It is essentially this point (that women's activities at Philippi would effect the reception of New Testament documents such as the letter to the Philippians and Luke-Acts) that Portefaix's study first made in a detailed yet understated manner. See, for example, the summary of her extensive study of women's social and religious backgrounds, and the following interpretation, respectively, in Portefaix, *Sisters*, 127–128, 131–154. Abrahamsen deduces that these documents must have been received in a particular fashion given the continuing prominence of women at Philippi later in antiquity and into the Byzantine era.
[61] Abrahamsen, *Women*, 53–56.
[62] Portefaix, *Sisters*, 94. This identification with Diana might have inspired women to aspire to relative positions of freedom or equality. See Portefaix, *Sisters*, 94–95.

degree, a destiny which would combine domestic life with public and religious service.[63]

Beyond the Diana cult, the role of statues and figurines cannot be underestimated in their roles as models. The priestesses on the Livia monument were no doubt meant to be public models of devotion to the empress, while smaller plaster or wax figurines of deceased female ancestors would have aided in educating children in the private sphere.[64]

During childhood both female and male children would be instructed in cultic matters by women of the family, whether they were mothers, older sisters, grandmothers, or nurses (in wealthier families).[65] Since learning frequently occurred through imitation in antiquity, the children would learn through the model of women, receiving the myths and worship procedures passed on to them through women. Children would learn through observation as well, watching how these women participated in rituals in both the formal cults and in familial gatherings around the home shrine.[66] This activity was necessary for the child's formation, since later they themselves would be expected to perform such duties.[67] Thus, in the education and upbringing of Philippian women (and often also young males), they would have encountered a range of female models: goddesses, priestesses, ancestors, fellow devotees, and family members. It seems, then, that women in Philippi would have been accustomed to the idea of imitating other women in everyday as well as cultic settings.

---

[63] Abrahamsen, *Women*, 81. Here, Abrahamsen demonstrates the potential for a more positive take on modeling than is typically in evidence for discussions of the social, pedagogical, and ethical roles of imitation (or *mimōsis*) in antiquity. As Elizabeth A. Castelli capably highlights in her examination of imitation, there is an ambiguous or paradoxical quality to imitation. Imitation requires the higher evaluation of a model, in a relationship that is both asymmetrical and hierarchical. Yet, the call to imitate implies that one should attempt to be *like* the model, to become equivalent to or the same as the model. Though this could be seen as involving a more egalitarian view of the relationship between model and copy (it is possible to become like the model), ultimately the imitation will be incomplete, reinscribing the elevated status of the model. This creates a tension since "mimesis consists of both the emulative and the authoritative." See Castelli, *Imitating Paul: A Discourse of Power* (Literary Currents in Biblical Interpretation; Louisville, Ky.: Westminster/John Knox Press, 1991), 140–141. For more on this tension, see Castelli, *Imitating Paul*, 16, 21–22, 30–31, 68–71. For the possibility that *mimōsis* as a term originated in a cultic setting, see Castelli, *Imitating Paul*, 60–62.

[64] Abrahamsen, *Women*, 81; Portefaix, *Sisters*, 38. These figurines were typically part of mourning rituals in imperial times. See Heinrich Drerup, "Totenmaske und Ahnenbild bei den Römern," *Mitteilungen des Deutschen archaeologischen Instituts, Roemische Abteilung*, 87 (1980): 122–123.

[65] Portefaix, *Sisters*, 34–35.
[66] Portefaix, *Sisters*, 36–42
[67] Portefaix, *Sisters*, 45.

B. WOMEN'S PARTICIPATION IN THE EARLY JESUS MOVEMENT AT PHILIPPI

Perhaps the shortest way to set this study and the issue of Philippian women's participation in these communities within the current context of biblical studies is to present in full this comparative insight from one of the pioneers of feminist biblical interpretation:

> I can remember that in the late 1960s, when the so-called "second wave" of the wo/men's movement first emerged on the scene, I devoured everything that appeared on any wo/men's or feminist topic. In the 1970s, I could still read anything that appeared in the area of feminist theology or feminist studies in religion. In the 1980s, I was no longer able to keep informed and to read everything that appeared in feminist critical studies but could still keep abreast of most of the publications in my own area of expertise, biblical studies. In the 1990s, I have had a tough time reading the literature appearing even in my field of specialization, Christian Testament Studies.[68]

Elisabeth Schüssler Fiorenza's comments here demonstrate the near impossibility of surveying and/or summarizing all of the relevant findings in biblical interpretation to explain the many roles women played in the developing communities of the early Jesus movement(s). Over the past decades, feminist scholars have convincingly argued that women played important roles within these movements, often in the face of malestream scholarly inattention (both historically and ongoing).[69] Without these predecessors and companions in struggle, the aims of this project simply would not be possible.

---

[68] Schüssler Fiorenza, *Wisdom Ways: Introducing Feminist Biblical Interpretation* (Maryknoll, N.Y.: Orbis, 2001), 9.

[69] While it is not possible to present a completely comprehensive bibliography of feminist work in biblical studies (and related fields), there are many resources for beginning the process of navigating this significant body of work. Some of the earliest feminist resources include: Schüssler Fiorenza, *In Memory of Her: A Feminist Theological Reconstruction of Christian Origins* (New York: Crossroad, 1983) (also available in a Tenth Anniversary edition, 1994); Mary Ann Tolbert, ed., *The Bible and Feminist Hermeneutics*; *Semeia* 28 (1983); Letty Russell, ed,, *Feminist Interpretation of the Bible* (Philadelphia: Westminster, 1985); and Adela Yarbro Collins, ed., *Feminist Perspectives on Biblical Scholarship* (Chico, Calif.: Scholars Press, 1985). The first feminist commentary collections include: Carol A. Newsom and Sharon H. Ringe, eds., *Women's Bible Commentary* (Louisville, Ky.: Westminster/John Knox, 1992) (An Expanded Edition with Apocrypha was available in 1998) and Schüssler Fiorenza, ed., *Searching the Scriptures*, 2 vols. (New York: Crossroad, 1993–1994). More recently, introductory textbooks and dictionaries have provided excellent starting points for feminist study: Ross Shepard Kraemer and Mary Rose D'Angelo, *Women & Christian Origins* (New York: Oxford University Press, 1999); Carol Meyers, Toni Craven, and

A feminist approach to biblical literature, though, is not simply a matter of supplementing previous scholarship by including women; it is not an "add women and stir" approach. To begin, there is the issue of taking the information about women from these textual traditions at "face value" when these texts are kyriocentric.[70] Kyriocentric texts do not mirror women's realities, but construct them in order to produce women as silenced or marginalized.[71] Because of the nature of these sources (as well as the historical fields of interpretation), feminist biblical interpreters cannot simply plug "women" as an object of study into previous scholarly paradigms without reinscribing women's marginalization.[72] As Schüssler Fiorenza has articulated it, one of the main tasks of feminist biblical interpretation is not just to *understand* biblical texts, but also to *change* the way we analyze them.[73]

Given the strides made in feminist biblical interpretation, then, this study seeks such a change by beginning with different assumptions, expectations, and goals.[74] As has been discussed previously, as part of a hermeneutics of re-membering and reconstruction, feminist interpretation begins first with the *assumption* that women were present and able to play a number of roles within the developing communities of the early Jesus movement(s).[75] Second, wherever we find an argument for or presentation against certain practices for women, we can *expect* that women were likely to have been engaged in just such practices.[76] This expectation recognizes that these arguments are more often prescriptive than descriptive about women. Third, one of the *goals* of a feminist interpretation is an analysis of the various contexts for the rhetorics of a text, recognizing how these rhetorics might interact within structures of domination and/or movements for change.[77]

Ross S. Kraemer, eds., *Women in Scripture: A Dictionary of Named and Unnamed Women in the Hebrew Bible, the Apocryphal/Deuterocanonical Books, and the New Testament* (Grand Rapids, Mich.: Eerdmans, 2000); and Schüssler Fiorenza, *Wisdom Ways: Introducing Feminist Biblical Interpretation* (Maryknoll, N.Y.: Orbis, 2001).

[70] Schüssler Fiorenza, *But She Said*, 31, 53–54.
[71] Schüssler Fiorenza, *But She Said*, 83. See also, in general, the introduction to feminist rhetorical analysis in biblical interpretation in Chapter I above.
[72] See the previous notes, as well as Schüssler Fiorenza, *Bread Not Stone*, 109.
[73] Schüssler Fiorenza, *Rhetoric and Ethic*, 46, 60; *Wisdom Ways*, 89–91.
[74] While such critical work can be done because of the struggles of feminist and other liberation-oriented approaches to interpretation, it is important to stress that the field of biblical studies as a whole has not embraced this transformative shift. On the dangers of positing feminist scholarship as a completed project and consumerist "success story," (especially as it is related to males in feminism), see Esther Fuchs, "Men in Biblical Feminist Scholarship," *JFSR* 19:2 (2003): 93–114.
[75] For this step in Schüssler Fiorenza's "dance of interpretation," see Chapter I above as well as Schüssler Fiorenza, *Wisdom Ways*, 183–186.
[76] Schüssler Fiorenza, *Wisdom Ways*, 185. See also Wire, *The Corinthian Women Prophets*, 9.
[77] Schüssler Fiorenza, *Wisdom Ways*, 185.

Of these three differences in approach, this section is most concerned with considering the first of these, the assumption that women were active. Yet this study does not plan to leave behind the remaining two. The second of these differences will aid in this study's "reading against the grain" in both the initial contextual sections and the latter interpretive sections. The third of these differences in approach has already been highlighted in the previous chapter's attention to the interlocking and mutually supporting nature of argumentation in this letter.[78] It will be further pursued as one of the crucial cues for the final two sections of this chapter and for the overall task of producing a feminist rhetorical interpretation of Philippians.

Turning to this study's particular analysis of the letter to the Philippians, then, we will assume that women were present in the community to which Paul wrote at Philippi and that some women played prominent roles within the community. By beginning with such an assumption, instead of the traditional scholarly expectation of women's absence or insignificance, much work that precedes this study has shown the relevance of feminist approaches to not only Pauline letters, in general, but also to the specific case of Philippians.[79] Two women, Euodia and Syntyche, are specifically addressed in the letter (4:2–3) and are described in ways that indicate that they were prominent members of the community. Here, Paul notes that Euodia and Syntyche are "co-workers" and "those who struggled with me in the gospel" (4:3), terms typically reserved in Pauline letters for those engaged in leadership activities in these early communities.[80] This first assumption (of women's presence and activity) has been affirmed by the albeit-brief allusion to two women leaders in the community at Philippi. This should not surprise us, nor should it be the final stop in a feminist examination of the letter to the Philippians.

For a feminist analysis of the letter to the Philippians, it is not enough to simply point out that women are mentioned in this text. While an examination of the role of Euodia and Syntyche in the argumentation of this letter is included (in IV and V below), I also argue that the context of first century Philippi shows

---

[78] See especially Chapter II.D above.
[79] Abrahamsen, "The Women at Philippi: The Pagan and Christian Evidence," *JFSR* 3 (1987): 17–30; Portefaix, *Sisters*; Mary Rose D'Angelo, "Women Partners in the New Testament," *JFSR* 6 (1990): 65–86; Castelli, *Imitating*; Carolyn Osiek, "Philippians" in *Searching the Scriptures: A Feminist Commentary*, Vol. 2 (ed. Schüssler Fiorenza; New York: Crossroad, 1994), 237–249; Kittredge, *Community*. For more on feminist approaches to Pauline literature, in general, see the entries in Newsom and Ringe, eds., *Women's Bible Commentary*; Schüssler Fiorenza, ed., *Searching the Scriptures: A Feminist Commentary*, Vol. 2; and Kraemer and D'Angelo, eds., *Women & Christian Origins*.
[80] D'Angelo, "Women Partners," 75–77; Kittredge, *Community*, 91–95, 105–108. See also Rom 16:1–16.

that it is, in fact, not exceptional to find women in leading roles here. As the preceding section has shown (III.A. above), women played a variety of leading and otherwise active roles in several cults at Philippi. Even beyond women's participation in these cults, women at Philippi continue to play significant roles in the developing communities of the early Jesus movement(s) well past the first century C.E.

For example, in treating the identity and leadership of Euodia and Syntyche, biblical scholars have often noted the prominent role Lydia plays in Luke-Acts' account of Paul's arrival in Philippi (Acts 16).[81] Occasionally, scholars have tried to identify either Euodia or Syntyche with the figure of Lydia in Acts, with no great degree of success.[82] However, linking the possible leadership of a woman (Lydia) with such a story of the beginnings of the community at Philippi is intriguing considering the roles we assume Euodia and Syntyche most likely played in Philippi. Further consideration of the narrative in Acts 16:11–40 and the rhetorical function of female figures in this passage could prove useful.

The four main characters of this narrative set at Philippi are Paul, Lydia, a slave girl with mantic capabilities, and the jailer. Though it is notable that two female characters play a role here, the passage is primarily focused upon the heroic actions and stature of Paul. In terms of Paul's encounters with the other characters, the episode with the jailer is extended and dramatic (16:23–36) in comparison to the brief passages involving Lydia (16:13–15, 40) and the slave girl (16:16–18).

Upon receiving a vision where a *man* of Macedonia (*anēr Makedōn*, 16:9) exhorts him to travel to the region, Paul arrives in Philippi and encounters a group of women at a *proseuchō* (16:13) on the Sabbath.[83] Lydia, described as "a dealer in purple from the city of Thyatira" and "a worshipper of God" (16:14), is among these women. Upon hearing Paul speak, Lydia is baptized with her

---

[81] For more on Lydia and Acts 16, see Portefaix, *Sisters*, 169–173; Luise Schottroff, *Let the Oppressed Go Free: Feminist Perspectives on the New Testament* (trans. Annemarie S. Kidder; Gender and the Biblical Tradition; Louisville, Ky.: Westminster/John Knox, 1991), 131–137; Turid Karlsen Seim, *The Double Message: Patterns of Gender in Luke & Acts* (Nashville: Abingdon, 1994); Clarice J. Martin, "Acts of the Apostles," in *Searching the Scriptures: A Feminist Commentary.* Volume 2 (ed. Elisabeth Schüssler Fiorenza; New York: Crossroad, 1994), 763–799; Ivoni Richter Reimer, *Women in the Acts of the Apostles: A Feminist Liberation Perspective* (trans. Linda M. Maloney; Minneapolis: Fortress, 1995), 71–149; Shelly Matthews, *First Converts: Rich Pagan Women and the Rhetoric of Mission in Early Judaism and Christianity* (Contraversions; Stanford: Stanford University Press, 2001), 51–100.

[82] See, for example, Davorin Peterlin, *Paul's Letter to the Philippians in the Light of Disunity in the Church* (NovTSup 79; Leiden: Brill, 1995), 128–130.

[83] Though the Lukan author chooses not to call it a *synagōgō*, this location can be identified as a synagogue with some confidence. See Reimer, *Women*, 78-92; Bernadette J. Brooten, *Women Leaders in the Ancient Synagogue* (BJS 36; Atlanta: Scholars, 1982), 139–140.

household and then persuades Paul to stay at her home (16:15). At the end of his stay in Philippi, Paul again visits Lydia before departing to Thessalonica (16:40). From these scant verses, a few things are initially worthy of note. Lydia is presented as the first resident of Philippi to join the early Jesus movement. She is described in terms used for "God-fearers," Gentiles who show some degree of interest in Jewish cultic practices and are often linked with synagogues.[84] Lydia also seems to have some status, given the notes about her household and her trade.[85]

Over the course of a few days, Paul repeatedly encounters a slave girl on the way to the *proseuchō* (16:16, 18). She is gifted with a Pythian spirit (*pneuma puthōna*, 16:16) and prophesies for the gain of her masters. Her incessant, but accurate, exclamations that Paul and Silas are "servants of the most high god" (16:17) cause Paul such great annoyance that he casts the spirit out of her (16:18). Because this authoritative act deprives the slave's owners of future profits, they bring Paul and Silas before the imperial magistrates, who throw them into prison (16:19–23). After a miraculous earthquake (16:26) and a near-suicide (16:27), the jailer accepts Paul's message. The jailer and his household are baptized (16:33) and share a meal with Paul and Silas (16:34). The episode with the slave-girl provides only the context for this dramatic episode.

In order to assess the relevance of these events in Acts 16 for women in the Philippian community, we must first understand the events in terms of the Lukan author's rhetorical strategy. Given Luke-Acts' repeated pairing of women and men,[86] Lydia could be a parallel to either Cornelius (another "God-fearer" in Acts 10:1–43)[87] or the jailer (another "householder" who joins Paul).[88] As a follower of Paul with some degree of status, Lydia is also presented in contrast to the other female character in Acts 16, the slave-girl who prophesies through the power of Apollo.[89] These details fit the overall narrative's interest in

---

[84] For more on "God-fearers" as a group distinct from Jews and proselytes, see Reimer, *Women*, 93–98; Matthews, *First Converts*, 66–71.
[85] Matthews' accounting for Lydia's elevated status convincingly reestablishes the standard scholarly evaluation over against the assertions of Reimer and Luise Schottroff. See Matthews, *First Converts*, 85–89; in response to Reimer, *Women*, 98–114; Schottroff, *Let the Oppressed*, 131–137. In particular, Matthews demonstrates how such a description of Lydia fits with the rhetorical strategy of Luke-Acts.
[86] Seim, *Double Message*; Martin, "Acts," 768–769, 777–778, 784–785.
[87] Martin, "Acts," 784; Matthews, *First Converts*, 59, 88–89.
[88] Martin, "Acts," 770, 778; contra Seim, *Double Message*, 14.
[89] Matthews, *First Converts*, 87, 89–92, 94–95. This could be an understated instance of what Barbara R. Rossing calls the "two-women *topos*" in moralistic literature and Revelation. See Rossing, *The Choice Between Two Cities: Whore, Bride, and Empire in the Apocalypse* (HTS 48; Harrisburg, Penn.: Trinity Press International, 1999), especially 17–59.

displaying Paul's greater "respectability" and power in comparison to other cults in the Roman Empire.[90]

In order to show that the early Jesus movement can fit into the world of the empire, Acts 16 emphasizes the harmony of Paul's communities.[91] Lydia and the jailer accept Paul without a hint of dissension, while the major source of conflict for the passage comes out of Paul's encounter with someone from another cult. This picture of the community at Philippi differs significantly from the indicators of conflict in Philippians, 1 Thessalonians (especially 2:1–2), and later sources.

Indeed, the female figures' roles in Acts 16 are best understood in terms of this Lukan "rhetoric of apologetics."[92] Though Lydia is the first person to join Paul's community at Philippi, her role is significantly circumscribed in comparison to some of the prominent women mentioned in Paul's letters.[93] Acts seems to distance Paul from more active women like his *synergoi* Euodia and Syntyche (Phil 4:2–3), the *apostolos* Junia (Rom 16:7), or the *diakonos* and *prostatis* Phoebe (Rom 16:1–2). In fact, the only female character shown speaking prophetically in Acts is this slave-girl, who does not join up with Paul. Matthews explicates how Acts appropriates the *topos* of a high-standing Gentile woman supporter in order to present a more palatable form of this movement to audiences in the Roman Empire.[94] Acts 16 shifts the blame for conflicts outside of the early Jesus movement and onto lower-status figures, effectively distancing Paul's leadership from lower-status women. Yet, Acts' employment of this *topos* is more likely the Lukan author's *reaction to* certain situations in the early communities, than a direct *reflection of* them. In fact, if other sources for the Philippian community are any indication, Acts 16 might be substituting this version with Lydia as the author styles her for an account involving more

---

[90] Reimer, *Women*, 172; Matthews, *First Converts*, 89–92. On the possibility that this entire narrative echoes a pattern found in Euripides' *Bacchae*, see Portefaix, *Sisters*, 169–173; Matthews, *First Converts*, 72–78. This might be especially significant for women at Philippi because of the influence of the Dionysus cult there and at Mount Pangaion nearby. See Portefaix, *Sisters*, 98–114; Chapter III.A. above.

[91] There are several textual indications of interaction with the Roman imperial mindset. The Lukan author notes Philippi as a *kolōnia* (16:12), stresses the shift in the identification of Paul as a *Ioudaios* (16:20) to a *Rōmaios* (16:37, 38), and connects the order for Paul's release with *eirōnō* (16:36). Paul's prison experience and ability to convince the jailer to join him here provides an interesting echo to notes in Phil 1:12–14 and 4:22.

[92] Matthews, *First Converts*, 62–71, 85–95.

[93] Schüssler Fiorenza, *But She Said*, 52–76; Seim, *Double Message* 249–260; Martin, "Acts," 777; Matthews, *First Converts*, 53. Portefaix characterizes Lydia's model character not in terms of her action, but her accommodation. Lydia is "unselfish," because of her "readiness to place her home at the disposal of the apostles." See Portefaix, *Sisters*, 172–173.

[94] Matthews, *First Converts*, 61–66, 85–95.

active women (possibly of lower-status) and a measure of conflict or disagreement.[95]

Acts 16 yields little information about specific women in the community at Philippi. However, as one author's reaction to the roles of conflict and lower-class women in the early Jesus movements, it does resonate with the general evidence for women in these early communities. Beyond these initial references in Philippians 4 and Acts 16, there seems to be a persistent focus on women's activities at Philippi, even after the mid-to-late first century C.E. In Polycarp of Smyrna's letter to the Philippians (ca. 110 C.E.), he singles out only two groups in seeking obedience and conformity to his authority: Docetists (6.3–7.2) and women (4.2; 5.1–3).[96] In particular, Polycarp seems concerned with female ascetic practices (5.3) and their potential to disrupt the communal order he prefers for the Philippian assembly. Reading against the grain of Polycarp's injunctions towards women, a feminist interpretation of the situation at Philippi *expects* that Polycarp's attempts to control these women are not descriptive of women's obedience to established authorities. Rather, it more likely indicates that women were engaging in ascetic practices running counter to the dominant culture of the time.[97] Furthermore, these expectations about women's asceticism at Philippi might be supported by the apocryphal Acts of Paul (late 2nd century C.E.), which enthusiastically depict female converts to an ascetic message delivered by Paul.[98] A fragmentary section of these apocryphal stories is set at Philippi. There, Paul raises a woman named Frontina to life after her execution, apparently having previously converted her to this ascetic message.[99]

Though we might be uncertain as to how much these 2nd century C.E. traditions and stories reflect women's experiences at Philippi, it is notable how persistently women's activity and possible leadership are found affiliated with Philippi in these traditions. This remains a notable trend even further forward in time, into the early Byzantine period, since women continue to appear as leaders

---

[95] See discussions in Chapter IV and Chapter V below and the conclusion of Matthews in *First Converts*, 93.

[96] Abrahamsen, *Women*, 84–85. Polycarp's letter can be found in *Early Christian Fathers* (ed. Cyril C. Richardson; LCC 1; New York: MacMillan, 1978), 121–137.

[97] Abrahamsen, *Women*, 85. See, in a related vein, Dennis R. MacDonald, *The Legend and the Apostle: The Battle for Paul in Story and Canon* (Philadelphia: Westminster, 1983), 50–53, 74.

[98] *New Testament Apocyrpha; Volume II: Writing Related to the Apostles, Apocalypses and Related Subjects* (ed. Edgar Hennecke and Wilhelm Schneemelcher; trans. R. McL. Wilson; Cambridge: James Clarke & Co.: 1992), 213–270. For more on women in the apocryphal acts, see Virginia Burrus, *Chastity as Autonomy: Women in the Stories of the Apocryphal Acts* (Studies in Women and Religion 23; Lewiston, N.Y.: Edwin Mellen Press, 1987); Stevan Davies, *The Revolt of the Widows: The Social World of the Apocryphal Acts* (Carbondale: Southern Illinois University Press, 1980).

[99] *New Testament Apocrypha*, 256–257.

at Philippi. Abrahamsen's archaeological studies point to the evidence for two female deacons in inscriptions on grave monuments dating to the fourth or fifth centuries C.E.[100] Additionally, a grave inscription in this find describes a woman named Posidonia as a *kanonikō*, possibly a member of a consecrated order of virgins or widows.[101] The material record indicates that women held specific positions in the community at Philippi even into the early Byzantine period. Not only did women's roles in the early church continue, but we also find goddess and other feminine imagery at the Christian basilicas dating from this period.[102] Some of this may be due to the survival of both the Diana and the Isis cults (detailed in III.A. above) into this time period as well.[103]

The persistence of women's activities and leadership in several cults (Diana, Isis, and what will eventually become "Christianity") at Philippi from the time both preceding and following the mid first century C.E. seems significant to this study's feminist analysis of Paul's letter to the Philippians. This persistence indicates that women's leadership and participation in cultic life would *not* have been viewed as *anomalous* at Philippi. Instead, there is a distinct possibility that it would have been *expected* in Philippi. This expectation might have been even greater for a relatively new cultic group attempting to explain itself to an audience that possibly worked from "the *assumption* that women were to be among the leaders of any religious organization."[104]

In this way, feminist approaches to biblical interpretation have continued to demonstrate their utility and explanatory power for setting the context of the letter of the Philippians. When combined with the observations from the preceding section, we see the importance of paying attention to the potentially oppressive tendencies of malestream classical and biblical scholarship. By focusing as much on *how* we pursue an examination of these contexts, as *what* we can find from these contexts, these two sections have demonstrated the kyriarchal bias of scholarship that assumes that women would be absent or insignificant in the cults of Philippi. Beyond this demonstration, though, we have also generated a useful picture of women's leadership and activity at Philippi. Thus, when we examine the argumentation of Paul's letter to the Philippians, we can operate with the assumption that Paul's naming and ascribing of leadership roles to Euodia and Syntyche were not a "glitch," but part of a persistent phenomenon for Philippi.

---

[100] Abrahamsen, *Women*, 86–87. See also Paul Lemerle, *Philippes et la Macédoine Orientale à l'époque chrétienne et byzantine: Recherches d'histoire et d'archéologie* (Bibliothèque des Ecoles françaises d'Athènes et de Rome 158; Paris: Boccard, 1945), 92–94.
[101] Abrahamsen, *Women*, 86–89.
[102] Abrahamsen, *Women*, 164–167.
[103] Abrahamsen, *Women*, 194.
[104] Abrahamsen, "Women," 29.

C. UNITY RHETORICS IN ANCIENT CIVIC SPEECHES

The concept of unity is crucial for any study of the letter of Philippians. This observation is made evident by the assessment of the friendship and military imagery for Philippians (II above) and can be further emphasized by the examination of the rhetorics of the letter (IV and V below). Fortunately, the ancient stress on political unity has already been examined by other scholars of Pauline letters, especially with regard to the letters to the Corinthians.[105] It seems appropriate, then, for this study to attempt to comprehend the role of unity rhetorics more broadly within the realm of civic thinking in the Greco-Roman world.

For example, some of the same language utilized in the letter to the Philippians is prominent in conceptions of the *polis* in the Greek-speaking world. Among the unity concepts, *homonoia* (concord or oneness in mind) is one of the most prominent in speeches on the city,[106] notable from the time of Isocrates to that of Dio Chrysostom and Aelius Aristides.[107] This kind of unity is concerned with avoiding or ending *stasis* (strife, discord, or factionalism), the

---

[105] Margaret M. Mitchell, *Paul and the Rhetoric of Reconciliation: An Exegetical Investigation of the Language and Composition of 1 Corinthians* (HUT 28; Louisville, Ky.: Westminster/John Knox, 1991); Dale B. Martin, *Slavery as Salvation: The Metaphor of Slavery in Pauline Christianity* (New Haven: Yale University Press, 1990), 142–148; *The Corinthian Body* (New Haven: Yale University Press, 1995), 38–47, 57–59, 92–95, 160, 196; L. L. Welborn, *Politics and Rhetoric in the Corinthian Epistles* (Macon, Ga.: Mercer University Press, 1997). In a related vein, but focusing on Romans (and Philippians, briefly), see Bruno Blumenfeld, *The Political Paul: Justice, Democracy and Kingship in a Hellenistic Framework* (JSNTSup 210; London: Sheffield Academic Press, 2001).

[106] See here especially, A. R. R. Sheppard, "*Homonoia* in the Greek Cities of the Roman Empire," *Ancient Society* 15–17 (1984–1986): 229–252. See also Mitchell, *Paul*, 1–2, 15, 24, 31, 60–64; Martin, *Corinthian Body*, 38–47, 57–59, 92–95, 160, 196; Welborn, *Politics*, 7, 72. Ben Witherington III argues that Paul's primary goal in Philippians is the establishment of *concordia*. See Witherington, *Friendship and Finances in Philippi: The Letter of Paul to the Philippians* (The New Testament in Context; Valley Forge, Penn.: Trinity Press International, 1994), 13–15.

[107] For example, Isocrates, *Or.* 4 (*Panegyricus*), 5 (*To Philip*), 8 (*On The Peace*); Dio Chrysostom, *Or.* 38 (*To the Nicomedians, on Concord with the Nicaeans*), 39 (*On Concord in Nicaea*), 40 (*On Concord with Apameia*), 41 (*To the Apameians, On Concord*); Aristides, *Or.* 23 (*Concerning Concord*); 24 (*To the Rhodians: Concerning Concord*). See also Harry Mortimer Hubbell, *The Influence of Isocrates on Cicero, Dionysius and Aristides* (New Haven: Yale University Press, 1913); Pieter W. Van Der Horst, *Aelius Aristides and the New Testament* (SCHNT 6; Leiden: Brill, 1980).

opposite of *homonoia*.[108] It is not uncommon for this situation of strife to be characterized in terms of *eris* (rivalry, or contentiousness),[109] with all parties looking out only for themselves.[110] L. L. Welborn emphasizes that, in the attempt to restore the situation to one of unity or amicability, the speaker often does not explicitly mention the source of strife.[111] Where relevant for the Pauline letters, this technique might help to explain scholars' difficulty in reconstructing other parties or "opponents" from the letters.

One way to exhort an audience to move increasingly toward a state of *homonoia* is to emphasize what they hold (or should hold) in common (*koinos, koinōnia*).[112] Margaret M. Mitchell and Dale B. Martin stress the frequency of appeals to "common advantage" (*to koinō sympheron*) in deliberative speeches of concord.[113] These unity exhortations may also implement the verb *phronein* in order to express the proper way of (or commonality in) thinking.[114] Indeed, it is used in one of Aristides' favorite phrases to describe unity, *tauta phronein* ("to think these things/the same things").[115] In setting out such arguments, it is customary also to point out *typoi* or *paradeigmata* (models, types, or examples) for the audience to imitate in a more unified course of action. When writing to Philip, Isocrates urges him to follow the general *paradeigmata* of his ancestors (5.113) and to imitate (*mimōsasthai*, 5.114) Heracles, in particular.[116] It is even possible to make use of oneself as an example in these arguments, as Paul does in both the Corinthian correspondence and Philippians.[117]

Since the unity of the community seems to be fundamental to the civic rhetorics of the ancient Greek city, it is not surprising that the obligation of living as a citizen of the *polis* (*politeuesthe*) is a common topic in these

---

[108] Sheppard, "*Homonoia*," 229, 239, 242–243; Mitchell, *Paul*, 1–2, 60–61; Martin, *Corinthian Body*, 39; Welborn, *Politics*, 8–9. Mitchell, in fact, argues that a situation of factionalism, or *stasis*, is addressed by the thesis of Paul's first letter to the Corinthians, which she identifies in 1:10. See Mitchell, *Paul*, 1, 24.

[109] Sheppard, "*Homonoia*," 241–243; Mitchell, *Paul*, 79–83; Welborn, *Politics*, 3–4.

[110] Welborn, *Politics*, 9–11.

[111] Welborn, *Politics*, 88–94.

[112] Sheppard, "*Homonoia*," 245; Mitchell, *Paul*, 31–32, 77, 89, 134–136; Martin, *Slavery*, 144; *Corinthian Body*, 45; Welborn, *Politics*, 69; Blumenfeld, *Political Paul*, 109–112. See, for example, Aristides, *Or.* 24.37.

[113] Mitchell, *Paul*, 31–32; Martin, *Slavery*, 143–144. See, for example, Dio Chrysostom, *Or.* 34. 19, 22; Aristides, *Or.* 24.5.

[114] Welborn, *Politics*, 59–61, 69, 74; Mitchell, *Paul*, 79, 84; Blumenfeld, *Political Paul*, 299–300. See, for example, Aristides, *Or.* 24.37.

[115] Aristides, *Or.* 23.31, 42, 43; 24.29. See Mitchell, *Paul*, 69–70, 100.

[116] Isocrates, *Or.* 5.113–114. See also Isocrates, *Or.* 8.36–37; Aristides, *Or.* 23.78; 24.32–33; Mitchell, *Paul*, 42–49, 138; Welborn, *Politics*, 62–63.

[117] Mitchell, *Paul*, 2, 23, 37, 45, 49–50, 53–56; Martin, *Corinthian Body*, 58–59, 61–63, 68; Welborn, *Politics*, 36, 62–63; Blumenfeld, *Political Paul*, 20, 299.

speeches.[118] Such considerations may cause the speaker to reflect upon their own or the audience's experiences of stress (*thlipsis*) or suffering, but they also involve the potential for progress or advancement (*prokopō*).[119] The stakes are high in achieving a state of concord, as failure to do so could end in destruction (*apōleia*), rather than safety (*sōtōria*).[120] To avoid this, the members of the audience need to work together (*synergein*), which is, perhaps, another antonym for *stasis*. Dio Chysostom asks the assembly at Prusa: "is it not disgraceful that bees are of one mind (*homonoousi*) and no one has ever seen a swarm that is fractious (*stasiazonta*) and fights against itself, but, on the contrary, they both work (*synergazontai*) and live together?"[121] Those who truly work together to achieve *homonoia*, or concord, in their city can also share in the rejoicing (*synchairein*) at their unity.[122]

While the precise terms *stasis* and *homonoia* do not appear in the letter to the Philippians, concerns about unity and difference are recurrent and a number of the terms surveyed above factor into the argumentation. Somewhat distinctively in this letter, Paul employs the civic term *politeuesthe* (1:27; 3:20) in urging the community to follow his arguments. The concept of oneness appears several times (1:27; 2:2, 2:20) and *koinōnia* even more frequently (1:5, 7; 2:2; 3:10; 4:14, 15), while calls for shared joy and joint action also appear quite frequently.[123] Just as Aristides employed the phrase *tauta phronein* to describe how unity is to be achieved, Paul implements the similar phrases *to auto phronein* and *touto phroneite* on more than one occasion in this letter (2:2, 5; 3:15; 4:2).[124] Paul faults his rivals for displaying *eris* and *eritheia* (1:15, 17; 2:3), while noting how he helps to bring about *prokopō* for the community (1:12, 25). The letter portrays the task of following its exhortations as a matter of

---

[118] Welborn, *Politics*, 72–73; Martin, *Corinthian Body*, 39–41; Blumenfeld, *Political Paul*, 182, 293–295. See also Jakob A. O. Larsen, *Greek Federal States* (Oxford: Oxford University Press, 1968).
[119] Welborn, *Politics*, 11, 77, 90.
[120] Mitchell, *Paul*, 103–104; Blumenfeld, *Political Paul*, 266–272, 295–297. See, for example, Aristides, *Or.* 24.51.
[121] Dio Chysostom, *Or.* 48.15. See also Aristides *Or.* 27.39; Mitchell, *Paul*, 98–99; Abraham J. Malherbe, *Moral Exhortation: A Greco-Roman Sourcebook* (LEC 4; Philadelphia: Westminster, 1986), 147.
[122] Mitchell, *Paul*, 162–163. See, for example, Isocrates, *Or.* 4.168; Dio Chrysostom, *Or.* 38.33, 43; 41.13; Aristides, *Or.* 23.29, 35.
[123] *Chara* (joy) and related words appear 21 times in the letter (1:2, 3, 4, 7, 18 twice, 25; 2:2, 17 twice, 18 twice, 28, 29; 3:1; 4:1, 4 twice, 6, 10, 23), *syn* appears as a prefix or preposition 20 times (1:1, 7, 23 twice, 27; 2:2, 17, 18, 22, 25 twice; 3:10, 17, 21; 4:3 four times, 14, 21), and *pas, pasa, pan* ("all" or "every") appears 36 times (1:1, 3, 4 thrice, 7, 8, 9, 13, 18, 20 twice, 25; 2:9, 10, 11, 12, 14, 17, 21, 26, 29; 3:8 twice, 21; 4:4, 5, 6, 7, 12 twice, 13, 18, 19, 21, 22). See Chapter II.A above.
[124] Aristides, *Or.* 23.31, 42, 43; 24.29.

attaining safety (*sōtōria*) from potential destruction (*apōleia*) (1:28; 2:12; 3:1, 19–20). Pointing out others as enemies (1:28; 3:18) and anti-models (1:15–17; 2:15; 3:2–3; 3:18–19), Paul offers himself and other *typoi* (3:17) as models to be imitated throughout the letter. In this vein, Paul discusses his own and the other models' stress and suffering (1:7, 12, 17; 2:7–8, 16–17, 21, 26–30; 3:8–10) and contrasts such people with those who look after only their own interests (1:15–17; 2:3, 21; 3:19).

All of these terms central to ancient Greco-Roman discourse on civic unity were also examined in the preceding treatment on friendship and military imagery (see II. A and B above). The correspondence of these concepts should not be surprising, given the considerable connections between civic thinking and the role of the military and friendships within the ancient *polis*. First, in the case of the military, the cause of *homonoia* could be and was implemented in an argument for war.[125] The best way for Isocrates, for example, to foster a Pan-Hellenic concord, a favorite dream of his, was to pose an outside "Barbarian" enemy as a common threat and advocate a united Greek military effort.[126] War was not only a cause of internal unity, but also a cause for discord. Welborn finds that *eris* "invariably appears in accounts of ancient political life the moment the pressure of circumstances, that is, the approach of an enemy army or the election of mutually hostile consuls, draws the citizens into confused knots."[127] Political factions are also often depicted as massed and organized armies, a common metaphor in civic speeches.[128] Drawing connections between assembled citizens and the military is common in Greco-Roman civic thought because one of the main topics for discussion in the *polis* is a decision to make war or peace.[129]

Second, in the case of ancient friendship, the virtue of friendship becomes intertwined with the concept of *homonoia*. Sheppard finds that the pairing of "friendship and concord" is in both the literature and the inscriptions of the Greek-speaking world.[130] To Aristotle, *philia* is an antidote for *stasis*, while Dio Chrysostom queries: "what is friendship (*philia*) save concord (*homonoia*)

---

[125] Sheppard, "*Homonoia*," 229, 238.
[126] For such a strategy, with the Persians as the enemy, see the whole of Isocrates, *Or.* 4 (*Panegyricus*). See also Werner Jaeger, *Paideia: The Ideals of Greek Culture, Volume 3: The Conflict of Cultural Ideals in the Age of Plato* (trans. Gilbert Highet; Oxford: Basil Blackwell, 1961), 71–83.
[127] Welborn, *Politics*, 3.
[128] Welborn, *Politics*, 15; Mitchell, *Paul*, 41, 99; Blumenfeld, *Political Paul*, 92. See, for example, Aristides, *Or.* 23.34, 78. The link between military and political imagery is evident even to some of the greatest proponents of military imagery in an analysis of the letter to the Philippians. See, for example, the title of Geoffrion's study, *The Rhetorical Purpose and the Political and Military Character of Philippians: A Call to Stand Firm*.
[129] Mitchell, *Paul*, 60. See, for example, Isocrates, *Or.* 8.2; Dio Chrysostom, *Or.* 25.2.
[130] Sheppard, "*Homonoia*," 249–250.

between friends?" (38.15).[131] As was made clear in the preceding overview of this topic, ancient friendship played a vital role in the political life, where one's power is measured by the number of one's clients and friends.[132] Friendships are political alliances, whether for individuals, parties or entire cities.[133] These alliances are the substance and concern of unity rhetorics. As Blumenfeld highlights, friendship is "the motive of social life and the *polis*'s means of existence."[134] Also, as previously noted, these realms (civic unity, the military, and friendship) are even further intertwined than these separate links to unity concerns indicate. For example, in the case of civic speeches determining whether to make war or peace (where unity rhetorics are particularly relevant), this topic is often connected to either the dissolution or the creation of "friendships" (e.g. treaties between city-states or alliances between factions). It seems, then, that these topics interact broadly within the same thought-world.

As a feminist study attempting to engage these materials with an analytic of domination, then, it seems vital to inquire to what end these ancient speeches focused on civic unity. Proceeding with a hermeneutics of suspicion, this study pursues whose concerns are addressed and which power relations are constructed or reinforced by reference to unity. In these speeches *homonoia* is linked with exhortations to obedience to the leaders of the time.[135] These leaders are not of the democratic variety, but represent the elite in the Greek cities. Unity under such leadership, then, mostly takes the form of monarchical or absolute rule, an ideal proclaimed from Isocrates and Plato through to Dio Chysostom and Aristides.[136] Even within his arguments for Pan-Hellenic

---

[131] Aristotle, *Nicomacean Ethics*, 8.1.4; Dio Chrysostom, *Or.* 38.15. See also the pairing of *philia* and *homonoia* in Dio Chrysostom, *Or.* 41.13 and the arguments and observations of Mitchell, *Paul*, 165–171. In the intervening years, for the Hellenistic Pythagoreans, political friendship is also linked to the order and concord of the universe. See Blumenfeld, *Political Paul*, 272; Holger Thesleff, *The Pythagorean Texts of the Hellenistic Period* (Acta Academiae Aboensis; Ser. 1, Humaniora 30:1; Åbo: Åbo Akademi, 1965), 81.21–22.

[132] Aside from Chapter II above, see also, Welborn, *Politics*, 10–11.

[133] For more on the treaty as "friendship," see also Mitchell, *Paul*, 167; Welborn, *Politics*, 72. In more "personalized" relationships (which still have clear political implications), the history of a friendship is important to review before discussing the matter of division. Welborn, *Politics*, 88. See, for example, Cicero, *Ad Fam.* 5.8.1–2.

[134] Blumenfeld, *Political Paul*, 109. Here Blumenfeld is examining the foundational role of Aristotle's work for the political thought of Hellenistic cities. See, Aristotle, *Politics*, 3.1280b39–40.

[135] Sheppard, "*Homonoia*," 249–251; Martin, *Corinthian Body*, 40–47. Popular philosophers also tended to emphasize obedience to established authorities. See Blumenfeld, *Political Paul*, 19.

[136] Sheppard, "*Homonoia*," 230, 249. See Isocrates, *Or.* 5.16; Dio Chrysostom, *Or.* 36.21; 41.12; Aristides, *Or.* 27.40–41. See also Blumenfeld, *Political Paul*, 265–266.

concord, Isocrates privileged parties within this "unity:" first Athens over the other Greek city-states, then the figure of Alexander as an absolute ruler over all of Greece.[137]

In the eyes of the Roman empire, though, this Greek tradition of aspiring towards dominance might encourage resistance, if not accommodated. The role of Greek apologists for the Romans becomes especially important, then, for equating concord with loyalty and submission to the empire.[138] *Homonoia*'s connection to absolute rule makes just such a transition possible, as does the continuing benefits for Greek aristocrats if they promoted this vision of concord in the empire.[139] Dio Chrysostom and Aelius Aristides extolled a narrative where the Romans brought unity and solved the problem of *stasis* for the Greeks.[140] Subjects of the empire should act with appropriate respect to the rulers that brought this state of affairs to them. Dio Chrysostom endorses the form of a "world emperor," while Aristides maintains that tyrannical rule is preferable to disorder.[141] In fact, as Sheppard has shown, Aristides provides the strongest statements justifying the status quo of Roman imperial rule through appeals to concord.[142] This version of unity is reinforced by the argument that the king or emperor rules in the interests of the subjects.[143]

Such an argument for hierarchical rule is co-extensive with the hierarchy of the household in the Greco-Roman world.[144] As Aristides calls for *homonoia*, he exhorts his audience: "Imitate the form and fashion of a household. What is this?

---

[137] For this consistent tendency toward hierarchy even within unity, and the shift toward Alexander, contrast Isocrates, *Or.* 4 (emphasis upon Athens) and 5 (emphasis upon Alexander).
[138] Sheppard, "*Homonoia*," 230, 238. See also, Blumenfeld, *Political Paul*, 279–281; Mitchell, *Paul*, 78; W. W. Tarn, *Alexander the Great*, Vol. II: *Sources and Studies* (Cambridge: Cambridge University Press, 1948), 416; John Ferguson, *Moral Values in the Ancient World* (London: Methuen, 1958), 127–132.
[139] Sheppard, "*Homonoia*," 246, 252.
[140] Dio Chrysostom, *Or.* 38.34; Aristides, *Or.* 23.8–12; 24.31. See Sheppard, "*Homonoia*," 239.
[141] Dio Chrysostom, *Or.* 49.3; Aristides, *Or.* 24.20. See Sheppard, "*Homonoia*," 237, 249. The concept of *pambasileus* (king/ruler over all) succinctly encapsulates the ties of unity rhetorics to dominating forms of rule. For the further justification of kingship by way of the king's association with the divine, see Blumenfeld, *Political Paul*, 183–184, 265–266, 270–272.
[142] Sheppard, "*Homonoia*," 239–240.
[143] Sheppard, "*Homonoia*," 240; Martin, *Corinthian Body*, 41–47; Welborn, *Politics*, 10–11; Blumenfeld, *Political Paul*, 92–93, 281. See, for example, Aristides, *Or.* 26.60. As it applies to both Hellenistic kingship and Roman imperial rule in Greece, Blumenfeld comments: "The modus operandi of any apologist for imperial autocracy was, as we have seen above, first to establish that the emperor was morally better than his subjects and/or opponents and, second, to prove that he ruled in his subjects' interest." See Blumenfeld, *Political Paul*, 281.
[144] Martin, *Corinthian Body*, 41–42.

SITUATING THE RHETORICS 97

There are rulers in the household, the fathers of the sons and the masters of the slaves."[145] In these unity speeches, submitting to the order of the empire is akin to accepting the rule of the slave-master and the *paterfamilias*, emphasizing the interlocking nature of systems of domination that comprise the form of kyriarchy. All of these hierarchical structures implement the argument, used in unity rhetorics, of paternalistic "care" through rule, even as they subordinate and exploit those whom they "unite" and "protect."[146] In the case of concord speeches, even Aristides could not pretend there was not an increasing gulf between the poor and the elite in the Roman empire.[147]

Yet, this state of affairs was acceptable to those who composed unity speeches in the ancient world, because they expected that conformity and hierarchy would accompany such "unity." Conformity to an order established from above was essential to achieving or maintaining concord.[148] As the similarities between Aristides' exhortation above and the *Haustafeln* sayings make clear, the political impact of these concord arguments is most commonly a socially conservative one.[149] To the extent that Paul's letters make use of this concept of unity, then, they also have a distinctly conservative and status quo sensibility.[150] Though it may appear that Paul and unity speeches, in general, offer a form of equality, most often it is a kind of "equality-within-hierarchy."[151] As Mitchell has already noted for 1 Corinthians, Paul seeks a "unity despite the differentiation of roles," so that the members of the community would be "unified in their submission."[152]

---

[145] Aristides, *Or.* 24.32, as translated in Mitchell, *Paul*, 130. See also Dio Chrysostom, *Or.* 38.15.
[146] Martin's work, in particular, addresses itself to this issue of "benevolent patriarchalism." See Martin, *Slavery*, 87–108; *Corinthian Body*, 42–47, 135, 160, 196. Martin highlights how this term is "oxymoronic," even as it represents the views of the elite Greco-Roman sources. In this way, Martin alters and critiques Gerd Theissen's proposal of a Pauline "love-patriarchalism." See Martin, *Corinthian Body*, 259; Theissen, *Social Setting of Pauline Christianity* (ed., trans, intro. John H. Schütz; Philadelphia: Fortress, 1982). For a thorough feminist examination and assessment of Theissen's proposal, see Schüssler Fiorenza, *In Memory*, 72–84.
[147] Aristides, *Or.* 26.65. See Sheppard, *"Homonoia,"* 240.
[148] Sheppard, *"Homonoia,"* 251.
[149] Sheppard, *"Homonoia,"* 249–252; Mitchell, *Paul*, 123, 281–283; Martin, *Corinthian Body*, 42–47.
[150] Mitchell, *Paul*, 123, 281–283; Blumenfeld, *Political Paul*, 290.
[151] Blumenfeld, *Political Paul*, 284. Blumenfeld also describes this type of ancient political thinking as endorsing "a republic of cheerful slaves." See Blumenfeld, *Political Paul*, 92.
[152] Mitchell, *Paul*, 164, 179. See 1 Cor. 12:28–30; 16:15–16. While Martin, with Mitchell, identifies the ideology of concord speeches as conservative ("to solidify the social hierarchy by averting lower-class challenges to the so-called natural status structures that prevail in society"), he maintains that Paul's arguments in 1 Corinthians

As this brief overview and analysis of unity rhetorics in ancient speeches has demonstrated, arguments for *homonoia* (concord, oneness, unity) are concerned with much more than unity for the sake of unity. The claims of these unity speeches to be reciprocal, or work for the common good, do not rule out the possibility that their arguments work to differentiate a power structure for the audience. In fact, it seems that most of the examples of unity rhetorics cited above do endorse and help to either found or reinscribe hierarchical arrangements. Underlying these unity rhetorics are claims to superiority, empire, and elite status, seeking an accompanying obedience, conformity, and subjugation. The use of unity as a topic in civic thinking, rather than running counter to these impulses, is so intertwined with such a kyriarchal orientation, that it easily transfers and re-applies from one hierarchical argument to the next. Isocrates adapts the priority of Athens to fit a newly idealized ruler (Alexander); Aristides shifts *homonoia* from a distinctly Greek tradition to an apology and legitimization of Roman imperial rule.

Tracing the use of unity rhetorics emphasizes, yet again, that these ancient sources do not as much *describe* a situation as they attempt to *construct* a certain view of the situation.[153] It demonstrates that, where unity rhetorics are implemented or echoed as they seem to be in Philippians, anyone reading for liberation should tread carefully.[154] Rather than presuming that it represents a view of the common good, a feminist study of such argumentation should inquire where there might be uneven differentiation within this unity, hierarchy in claims to equality or reciprocity, or calls for obedience and conformity in apparent commonality. This brief overview and analysis of unity rhetorics affirms the two cues garnered from the previous chapter. First, it remains crucial to pay attention to potentially oppressive power relations as they are constructed in the letter. Feminist conceptualizations, such as the analytic concept kyriarchy, have already proven useful in this regard. Second, it is necessary to understand the constellation of rhetorics in any body of literature, speech, or letter in their multiple and interlocking nature. It is not merely enough to describe unity

---

disrupt the dominant use of *homonoia* speeches by proposing an alternate system for status. See Martin, *Corinthian Body*, 47, 67–68.

[153] Again, we do not have to take Paul's letters at face value. He selects unity rhetorics in his argumentation in order to frame the situation from his perspective. It indicates not necessarily what was "the problem" in the Corinthian or Philippian community, but what Paul thinks is his problem. For factionalism as Paul's assessment of the problem (though with a slightly different emphasis than the above observation), see Mitchell, *Paul*, 1–2, 15, 23–24.

[154] While the relevance of unity rhetorics for the letter of Philippians can best be demonstrated by the argumentation of the letter (as addressed above and later, in Chapters IV and V), it is also important to note that these concerns with *homonoia* were echoed in sources involving both Macedonia (the location of the Philippian community) and Tarsus (Paul's hometown, according to tradition). See Sheppard, "*Homonoia*," 234–236, 238, 245.

rhetorics, for example, but we must also grapple with how such arguments support other rhetorics, especially where they might function in oppressive ways.

D. COLONIAL STATUS AND MILITARY SITUATION OF PHILIPPI

In order to continue reconsidering the relevance of the presence of military imagery in the letter to the Philippians, this study must proceed to a brief overview of the history of the settlement and colonization(s) of Philippi.[155] The site was originally known as "Krenides" ("springs") because of the relatively high number of streams and springs in the area.[156] In the earliest stages of its settlement, people were drawn to Krenides because of its valuable silver mines.[157] Mentioned as early as 490 B.C.E., the area was apparently first inhabited by Thracians, but by 360–356 B.C.E. Thasians founded a small mining colony on the site of Krenides.[158] Yet, before these settlers from the island of Thasos arrived, Oakes would even further specify the Thracian residents in more descriptive tribal terms as the Pieri and Edoni.[159] By 356 B.C.E., the Thasian

---

[155] See Chapter II above for the initial examination of and critical reflection upon military imagery for this letter, Philippi, and most generally, the Greco-Roman world. The following rather rudimentary review of the history of Philippi echoes many elements in previous work on Philippi and the letter to the Philippians. See Lukas Bormann, *Philippi: Stadt und Christengemeinde zur Zeit des Paulus* (NovTSup 78; Leiden: Brill, 1995); Craig S. De Vos, *Church and Community Conflicts: The Relationship of the Thessalonian, Corinthian, and Philippian Churches with Their Wider Civic Communities* (SBLDS 168; Atlanta: Scholars, 1999), 233–250, 275–287; Portefaix, *Sisters*, 59–60; Holland L. Hendrix, "Philippi," *ABD* V.313–317; Paul Collart, *Philippes*; Peter Pilhofer, *Philippi I: Die erste christliche Gemeinde Europas* (WUNT 87; Tübingen: J. C. B. Mohr, 1995); Raymond Hubert Reimer, "'Our Citizenship Is in Heaven': Philippians 1:27–30 and 3:20–21 As Part of the Apostle Paul's Political Theology" (Ph.D diss., Princeton University: 1997), 56–80; Koukouli-Chrysantaki, "Colonia," 5–35; Peter S. Oakes, *Philippians: From People to Letter* (SNTSMS 110; Cambridge: Cambridge University Press, 2001), 1–54.
[156] Strabo 7, frag. 34, 41; Appian, *BC* 4.105; Hendrix, "Philippi," 313; Koukouli-Chrysantaki, "Colonia," 5; Reimer, "'Our Citizenship,'" 56; De Vos, *Church and Community Conflicts*, 234; Oakes, *Philippians*, 22.
[157] Herodotus, 7.112; Collart, *Philippes*, 135; Portefaix, *Sisters*, 59–60; Reimer, "'Our Citizenship,'" 57; Oakes, *Philippians*, 12.
[158] Herodotus, 7.112; Appian, *BC* 4.105; Collart, *Philippes*, 54, 133–160; Portefaix, *Sisters*, 59–60; De Vos, *Church and Community Conflicts*, 234; Reimer, "'Our Citizenship,'" 58; Koukouli-Chrysantaki, "Colonia," 5; Oakes, *Philippians*, 12.
[159] Oakes, *Philippians*, 10. See also Fanoula Papazoglou, *Les Villes de Macédoine à l'époque Romaine* (*BCH* Supplement 16; Paris: École Française d'Athènes, 1988), 385. In the remainder of his examination, though, Oakes will embrace the term "Thracian" to describe these two separate tribal groups, following the lead of Collart. See Collart, *Philippes*, 55.

settlers and these local Thracian tribes were fighting for control of the area. Ironically, when the Thasians called for assistance in this conflict from Philip II of Macedonia, Philip settled the dispute by taking over the region himself.[160]

It is at this point in 356 B.C.E. that the settlement gains its more familiar name of Philippi, as the conquering Philip II renamed the city after himself.[161] Philip would also eventually fortify the city, building a wall and placing soldiers there.[162] It is here that many of the surveys begin to part ways or make judgments about activity at Philippi. Evaluations differ based on the relative productivity of the silver mines and its importance to maintaining a vital population there. Several historical surveys argue that Philip so exploited the mines that he exhausted their resources and Philippi soon fell in utility and prominence.[163] Reimer maintains that Philippi became "not much more than an inconsequential provincial town for most of the next two centuries,"[164] a point with which many others (Portefaix, Bormann, De Vos) would concur. The problem is the relative silence of our sources for the period in between Philip II and the rise of the Romans. More recently, Oakes has cautioned against arguing too strenuously for Philippi's "obscurity" from this silence, while Koukouli-Chrysantaki states simply: "little is known about its history in the Hellenistic period."[165] This issue of uncertainty and differing ways of interpreting this silence about Philippi will continue to be relevant even as the city enters into its "Roman" period.

Philippi would remain under the authority of Macedonian kings until 168 B.C.E., when Perseus, the son of Philip V, was defeated by Roman forces in what Romans called the Third Macedonian War.[166] Shortly thereafter, Macedonia would be officially annexed by the Romans and incorporated as a province in the empire in 146 B.C.E.[167] Once again, we know relatively little about Philippi in the years between Macedonia's annexation and the events of 42 B.C.E., a

---

[160] Diodorus Siculus 11.70.5; 12.68.1–3; 16.3.7; 16.8.6–7; Collart, *Philippes*, 68–85, 138, 152–160, 258; Hendrix, "Philippi," 314; Portefaix, *Sisters*, 60; De Vos, *Church and Community Conflicts*, 234–235; Koukouli-Chrysantaki, "Colonia," 7; Oakes, *Philippians*, 12.
[161] Diodorus Siculus 9.6; 16.3.7; 16.8.6–7; Appian *BC* 4.105; Collart, *Philippes*, 134–155; Hendrix, "Philippi," 314; Pilhofer, *Philippi I*, 86–87, 90; Reimer, "'Our Citizenship,'" 58.
[162] Collart, *Philippes*, 177.
[163] Here, scholars cite Diodorus Siculus 16.8.6–7 in discussions of how rapidly Philip II extracted the precious metals from the local mines.
[164] Reimer, "'Our Citizenship,'" 59. On the relative unimportance of "pre-colonial" Philippi, see Portefaix, *Sisters*, 60; Bormann, *Philippi*, 19–20; De Vos, *Church and Community Conflicts*, 235.
[165] Oakes, *Philippians*, 19–24; Koukouli-Chrysantaki, "Colonia," 7–8.
[166] Polybius 31.29; Livy 45.29.5–9; Hendrix, "Philippi," 314; Reimer, "'Our Citizenship,'" 60.
[167] Koukouli-Chrysantaki, "Colonia," 8; Reimer, "'Our Citizenship,'" 61.

period lasting over a century. As the previous chapter made clear, scholars have especially focused on the battle of Philippi because of its historical significance for both the Roman Empire and the city of Philippi. To re-state briefly, Philippi was the location of the deciding battle between the forces of Brutus and Cassius and the victorious armies of Antony and Octavian.[168] After the battle Octavian and Antony settled some of their veterans at Philippi, designating the city as a colony named after the event, Colonia Victrix Philippensium.[169]

More veterans were settled at Philippi in 31 B.C.E., after Octavian defeated his former ally Antony at Actium. Those veterans of Antony's forces which had already been settled closer to home in Italy were then displaced to the Philippian colony.[170] It is on this occasion that Octavian renamed the city Colonia Iulia Philippensis after his predecessor Julius (rather than after his daughter Julia, as was once thought).[171] In 27 B.C.E. the colony is yet again renamed as Colonia Iulia Augusta Philippensis, in honor of both Julius and Octavian (now known as Augustus).[172] These events inevitably altered the political landscape of Philippi, as Roman rule and veteran settlement would have brought a host of changes. It seems that at least some of the Roman veterans benefited from these arrangements and became local officials at Philippi.[173]

Since this would remain the current form of governance into the mid first century C.E., it seems important to further sketch the ramifications of Roman colonization of Philippi, especially as it might have an impact on the interpretation of the mid first century letter to the Philippians. Scholars who see this colonization as a positive moment in the history of Philippi highlight the

---

[168] Appian *BC* 4.105–138.
[169] Strabo 7.331 (frag. 41); Pliny 4.42; Collart, *Philippes*, 227; Portefaix, *Sisters*, 60; Koukouli-Chrysantaki, "Colonia," 8; De Vos, *Church and Community Conflicts*, 234; Oakes, *Philippians*, 13.
[170] See Chapter II above, and Collart, *Philippes*, 236; Hendrix, "Philippi," 314; Reimer, "'Our Citizenship,'" 63–64; Koukouli-Chrysantaki, "Colonia," 8.
[171] On this correction, see especially Pilhofer, *Philippi I*, 47. Colonies would take the honorific name Iulia or Augusta after the Caesars Julius and Augustus, respectively, as a sign of their benefaction. See Peter A. Brunt, *Italian Manpower: 225 B.C.–A.D. 14* (Oxford: Oxford University Press, 1971), 234; Oakes, *Philippians*, 13. Pilhofer corrects this tendency evident in some biblical scholarship. See, for example, Hendrix, "Philippi," 314; Reimer, "'Our Citizenship,'" 64.
[172] Collart, *Philippes*, 224–237; Bormann, *Philippi*, 35; Reimer, "'Our Citizenship,'" 64; Pilhofer, *Philippi I*, 47; Oakes, *Philippians*, 13. It is here that De Vos seems to be compressing history a bit, affiliating this final Roman name change to the events of 31 BCE. See De Vos, *Church and Community Conflicts*, 235–236.
[173] See especially the inscriptions in Collart, *Philippes*, 262, 288, 293, 499. See also Hendrix, "Philippi," 315; Bormann, *Philippi*, 52; Reimer, "'Our Citizenship,'" 63, 68.

privileges of a city attaining the status of *colonia iuris Italici*.[174] Under this kind of colony, Roman citizens had access to most of the same processes that were available to them in Italy: trade, marriage, inheritance, and other legal structures.[175] Citizens voted for magistrates, who would make up the decision-making body that nominated *aediles*, *quaestores*, and *duoviri*, who in turn ran the markets, treasuries, and courts, respectively.[176]

The key to understanding these advantages for Philippi as a colony, though, is to focus on the issue of Roman citizenship. In most cases, it was quite rare to grant citizenship to the natives of a colonized locale, with the possible exception of the local elite.[177] For the vast majority of the residents of Philippi, then, the designation as a Roman *colonia* would not have brought any direct benefits. The ability to affect those decision-making bodies was limited to a very small group of residents: Roman citizens. Bormann's arguments, then, for the extreme "Roman-ness" of the city, while reflecting the influence and power of the few Romans in charge of Philippi, do not reflect the likely attitude of the majority of the populace in the colony.[178]

The assumption that Roman colonization brought benefits to the city of Philippi also rests on the assumption that Philippi was in a state of decline previous to 42 B.C.E.[179] As highlighted above, this assumption is based upon an

---

[174] Reimer, "'Our Citizenship,'" 63; Krentz, "Military Language," 111–112, 115; Geoffrion, *Rhetorical Purpose*, 36–38; Krentz, "De Caesare," 344; R. R. Brewer, "The Meaning of *politeuesthe* in Phil. 1.27," *JBL* 73 (1954): 80.

[175] Reimer, "'Our Citizenship,'" 66–69; De Vos, *Church and Community Conflicts*, 111. For more on this kind of colony, see Barbara Levick, ed., *The Government of the Roman Empire: A Sourcebook* (London: Croom Helm, 1988), 73–74, 316; Adrian N. Sherwin-White, *The Roman Citizenship* (2nd ed.; Oxford: Clarendon, 1973), 316–319.

[176] A. H. M. Jones, *The Roman Economy* (Oxford: Blackwell, 1974), 13; Peter D. A. Garnsey and Richard P. Saller, *The Early Principate: Augustus to Trajan* (Greece & Rome: New Surveys in the Classics 15; Oxford: Clarendon, 1982), 2; De Vos, *Church and Community Conflicts*, 111–112.

[177] Appian *BC* 2.140; Brunt, *Italian Manpower*, 247, 254; Sherwin-White, *Roman Citizenship*, 248–249; Jones, *Roman Economy*, 3; De Vos, *Church and Community Conflicts*, 111–113; Oakes, *Philippians*, 27. Oakes has most recently commented: "However, in Philippi there is no evidence of the persistence of any town-based Greek élite." See Oakes, *Philippians*, 27.

[178] Bormann, *Philippi*, 52. The dominance of Roman figures and Latin language in inscriptions at Philippi *do* demonstrate Roman influence and power. See, for example, Collart, *Philippes*, 315; Pilhofer, *Philippi I*, 92. However, this does not demonstrate that Romans were in the majority in Philippi, or that the majority somehow benefited from Roman colonization. See De Vos, *Church and Community Conflicts*, 242–247; Oakes, *Philippians*, 35.

[179] The records on Philippi and Macedonia in general for this time period are relatively few. While the Macedonian Wars would have involved costly indemnities and Roman spoiling for precious metals, Jakob A. O. Larsen cautions: "It is necessary, nevertheless, to avoid exaggerating the effects of the Roman confiscations." See Larsen, "Roman

SITUATING THE RHETORICS 103

argument from silence. Since we hear little of Philippi in our sources for the Hellenistic period, we assume Philippi declined. However, Roman tendencies in colonization seem to negate such an assumption about the relative state of Philippi. Sites for colonization were primarily selected on the basis of the city or town's already-established prosperity and fertility.[180] While some scholars stress the boon of Philippi being selected as a colony, classical scholarship indicates that Philippi's selection meant it had already been prosperous before the Romans arrived, not necessarily in need of the added "advantage" of colonization.[181]

Since the city was more likely to be prosperous or at least healthy prior to Roman colonization, the wresting of control by Roman citizens would have meant a loss (rather than a gain) on the part of the local populations. Because the key to participation in the avenues of power is dependent upon citizenship, almost all of the residents prior to the Romans would be at a loss, since "few of the native Macedonians and Thracians, if any, would have been enfranchised."[182] Not only were these Philippians displaced from the governing structure, but the accompanying veteran settlement also required confiscation of the Philippians' land. In order to speed the sometimes-lengthy process of colonial settlement, the Roman administration adopted a policy of "wholesale confiscation" of property.[183] This change demonstrates how the Roman colonial policies could not benefit both the veterans and the residents at the same time, for "the method of acquiring land was simple and callous: wholesale confiscation from owners mostly innocent of any disaffection or disloyalty. With good reason could the dispossessed complain of the injustice of their plight."[184] The conditions of Roman colonization would only exacerbate whatever resentment existed between the retiring military forces and the local populations.

Some of these arguments about Philippi's "pride" in its status in the Roman empire focus less on the continuing residents and more upon the more recent

---

Greece," in *An Economic Survey of Ancient Rome*, Volume IV (ed. Tenney Frank; Baltimore: Johns Hopkins Press, 1938), 324.
[180] Keppie, *Colonisation*, 1, 128.
[181] As Badian comments: "No administration in history has ever devoted itself so wholeheartedly to fleecing its subjects for the private benefit of its ruling class as Rome of the last age of the Republic." See Badian, *Roman Imperialism*, 87.
[182] De Vos, *Church and Community Conflicts*, 246.
[183] Keppie, *Colonisation*, 87.
[184] Keppie, *Colonisation*, 61. For more on this "balancing act" on the part of Octavian and his administration after the battle at Philippi, see Keppie, *Making*, 122. Settlement not only affected the wealthy propertied families, but also the poorer families, as Finley characterizes it as "an evasion, not a solution, of the needs of the poor." See Moses I. Finley, *The Ancient Economy* (2nd ed.; Sather Classical Lectures 43; Berkeley: University of California Press, 1985), 172.

occupants, the Roman veterans and their families. Bormann, in particular, emphasizes the high proportion of veterans among Philippi's authorities in order to explain the colony's acceptance of imperial policy.[185] This argument holds initial sway because of the extensive efforts at settling these veterans in Philippi. Surely, since they received the land that was confiscated from the residents of Philippi, these veterans would have had close bonds to the empire that established them there. However, such an argument fails to take into account a range of factors for the veterans of Roman military campaigns. After the years of civil wars that brought these veterans to Philippi in the first place, veteran loyalty was a complex issue, involving sudden defeats and shifts in command structure. The process of and locations for their settlement were regular sources of contention, made especially problematic for those left to colonize Philippi, since it was far removed from the preferred Italian territories.[186] In fact, Philippi was used as an area of settlement for those soldiers on the defeated side in these civil wars, as Antony's troops were after Actium in 31 B.C.E.[187] Once we factor in the role of conscription and involuntary service in these Roman armies, the picture of a uniform group of satisfied and loyal colonizing veterans and their descendants becomes even further strained.[188]

Far from a series of speculations, a number of these factors for veteran experience can be shown to be especially relevant for the settlement at Philippi. After defeating Antony, Octavian sought to consolidate control and loyalty close to home. As a result, not only Antony's soldiers but also the "communities which had sided with Antony were uprooted and transported to new homes in the provinces, to Philippi, Dyrrachium and other places."[189] Earlier, after the initial Roman colonization of Philippi in 42 B.C.E., an inscription shows that a veteran of *legio* XXVIII settled there. Such epigraphical evidence raises the possibility that conscripted soldiers were left at Philippi, since this legion was among those that fought with Julius in 46 B.C.E. after he pressed large numbers into service.[190] Even the coinage that mentions retired members of the Praetorian cohorts at Philippi[191] does not assure us of satisfaction among their ranks, as

---

[185] Bormann, *Philippi*, 28, 52.
[186] For Antony's complaints about Octavian not leaving enough settlement space in Italy, see Plutarch *Ant*. 55; Keppie, *Colonisation*, 73. For more on this factor, see Chapter II above.
[187] Keppie, *Making*, 128–129; *Colonisation*, 76; G. W. Bowerstock, *Augustus and the Greek World* (Oxford: Clarendon Press, 1965), 65.
[188] Keppie, *Colonisation*, 37. See also Brunt, *Italian Manpower*, 391. For example, Keppie writes of Julius' campaign against Pompey, "Within a few months he had recruited, or pressed into service, about 80,000 men." See Keppie, *Making*, 104. For more on this factor, see Chapter II above.
[189] Keppie, *Colonisation*, 76. See Dio li.4.6; Bormann, *Philippi*, 22.
[190] Keppie, *Making*, 104–105, 110–111.
[191] *L'Année Épigraphique* (Paris, 1924), 55. See also Keppie, *Making*, 121.

these soldiers could have fought for either Antony or Octavian.[192] The varied picture sketched above and in the previous chapter, then, seems also to be relevant for the situation at Philippi.

Those biblical scholars who have attempted to describe the social relations evident at Philippi can lend some additional help in articulating a picture different from the previously assumed one that included a group of uniformly positive veterans in this colony. Whether veterans and their families were pleased with the outcome or not, they received confiscated Philippian land on which to settle. However, Oakes' model of the colony's social development stresses the likelihood of consolidation of this land into the hands of a small group of the wealthiest Romans.[193] The concentration of land-ownership meant that some of the colonist farmers were going into debt to these elites, eventually losing their land to them. In Oakes' terms, there was a "double land-loss," "first by Greek and then by many of the poorer Roman colonists."[194] This indicates that, even when some veterans benefited from the allocation of land at Philippi, not all of these settlers and their descendants enjoyed stability, let alone prosperity, in the years between initial colonization and the mid first century C.E.[195]

It seems important, then, to not overlook the hierarchical arrangements that dictated living both within and without the Roman military. For example, even when groups of veterans were settled in an area, their land was not allocated in an even-handed manner. The division between the members of the commanding hierarchy and the common soldiers was reinforced by the preference the former

---

[192] The Praetorian cohorts were split between these two leaders on other occasions, such as the battle at Forum Gallorum. See Keppie, *Making*, 115–117.

[193] Oakes, *Philippians*, 33–35. Here Oakes is making use of a model including debt, foreclosure, and concentration provided by Douglas E. Oakman, "The Countryside in Luke-Acts," in *The Social World of Luke-Acts* (ed. Jerome H. Neyrey; Peabody, Mass.: Hendrickson, 1991), 157. See also the more visual representation of Oakes' model in the figures reproduced for Oakes, *Philippians*, 16–17.

[194] Oakes, *Philippians*, 49.

[195] The late republic, in general, shared this problem that "a large and increasing proportion of discharged veterans had little or no property to support them when they returned to their homes." See G. E. M. De Ste. Croix, *The Class Struggle in the Ancient Greek World: From the Archaic Age to the Arab Conquests* (Ithaca, N.Y.: Cornell University Press, 1981), 357. In terms of relevance for the community receiving the letter to the Philippians in the mid first century CE, one of the relative strengths of Oakes' modeling is its attention to the effects of colonization for the succeeding generations. On the *development* of the colony, see Oakes, *Philippians*, 24–40. Similarly, De Vos notes: "With successive generations a standard Roman stratification would have evolved." See De Vos, *Church and Community Conflicts*, 245.

were given in settlement programs. Land was allocated according to rank.[196] Similar divisions were reflected in the social arrangements of Philippi, as power would remain concentrated in the hands of the wealthiest Romans. As De Vos points out for Philippi, "Like other Roman *coloniae*, the average citizen would have had limited political power given the strongly hierarchical and oligarchic system."[197] Even if one were a Roman citizen, then, one only had power in the rare cases where one managed to have wealth, property and a significant patronage network as well.

These descriptions of social relations have mostly focused upon the differences amongst veterans and citizens, that is, Romans. While this brief examination of social relations demonstrates how variant these relations were for Romans, depending upon a range of factors, the picture of this colony becomes even more complex once one considers the longstanding, non-Roman residents of Philippi. As the above cursory survey of the multiple colonizations of this territory has shown, several ethnic groups resided at Philippi. After the Thracians the territory was colonized by Thasians and Macedonians, over time drawing a number of migrant-workers and slaves from the Greek East.[198] Yet, the persistence of the Thracian tribes in maintaining their identity through these multiple colonizations is remarkable and has been noted often in the literature.[199] Their continuing influence has already been noted in the previous examination of women's roles in Philippi's cultic life.

The aforementioned dispossession of land experienced by a number of the veterans and their descendants would have occurred with greater frequency for these various "Greek" populations.[200] First, it was these residents' land that was

---

[196] Keppie, *Colonisation*, 92. For more on the rare affluence of the veteran, and the divisions in reward, see Antonio Santosuosso, *Storming the Heavens: Soldiers, Emperors, and Civilians in the Roman Empire* (History and Warfare; Boulder, Colo.: Westview Press, 2001), 101–104.

[197] De Vos, *Church and Community Conflicts*, 247. For the social-political relations in Roman colonies and Philippi specifically, see De Vos, *Church and Community Conflicts*, 110–115, 245–247.

[198] Oakes, *Philippians*, 73–74. While De Vos takes issue with many of Oakes' precisely enumerated figures for the make-up of Philippi (and the community to which the letter was written), most of his observations about the population of the colony do not significantly contradict the general trajectory of Oakes' evaluations. For example, in the case of these multiple "Greek" ethnic groups, De Vos disputes the high number Oakes assigns to the population of the city overall, yet broadly agrees that there was significant ethnic diversity, including Thracians and Macedonians among the Greek-speaking populace. See De Vos, *Church and Community Conflicts*, 240–244.

[199] Hendrix, "Philippi," 314; De Vos, *Church and Community Conflicts*, 240, 243; Oakes, *Philippians*, 30, 73.

[200] Oakes argues that, as the years pass, the Thasian and Macedonian colonizers became indistinguishable from each other, which is why he uses the more general term "Greeks" for them. Eventually in his study, Oakes adopts "Greeks" as a term for all residents in the

confiscated in large quantities by the Romans when they initially settled the veterans and others.[201] Second, already at a disadvantage after the first colonizing wave, those Greeks who still held some land would have been even more vulnerable than the colonist farmers to the structures of debt and foreclosure that allowed for wealthier Romans to consolidate smaller plots into larger estates.[202] Without access to the mechanisms of power through status, land, or citizenship, these non-Roman populations would remain subjugated to the Roman dominance politically, economically, and socially in Philippi.[203]

Those who were at the apex of these interlocking hierarchical (kyriarchal) arrangements made up a very small portion of the population in Roman Philippi. Oakes estimates that about three percent of the population in Philippi could be designated as the Roman landowning elite rulers (all adult males).[204] The remainder of the population was either disenfranchised since they were not citizens or, if they were citizens, they lacked the wealth and property to truly exercise influence.[205] Though De Vos approaches the problem of percentiles from a different vantage point than Oakes, he mostly confirms the extent to which the Roman elite dominated the political, economic and legal realms in all of the eastern colonies.[206] Both emphasize the wide socioeconomic gap between the vast majority living marginally on a subsistence level and the small group of wealthy landowners.[207] Both studies also further classify the socioeconomic stratification of the colony into groups beyond this elite/non-elite differentiation. De Vos notes that the non-elite population could be further divided between other Romans, freed slaves, and native inhabitants,[208] while Oakes specifies

---

colony that are clearly not Roman, including Thracians and later Greek-speaking arrivals. See Oakes, *Philippians*, 12, 18, 73–74.
[201] Oakes, *Philippians*, 24–29.
[202] Oakes, *Philippians*, 34–35, 74–75.
[203] De Vos, *Church and Community Conflicts*, 245–250; Oakes, *Philippians*, 74–76.
[204] Oakes, *Philippians*, 16–17, 47. For the virtual monopoly the Romans held on positions within the imperial government of Philippi, see Pilhofer, *Philippi I*, 91.
[205] Larsen's survey of wages, living costs, slavery and poverty for ancient Greece and Macedonia are often too general to be helpful in any precise way. Yet, based on information from Delos, he does surmise a degree of discontent among agricultural workers and the persistence of slave labor in the region. See Larsen, "Roman Greece," 408–417.
[206] De Vos, *Church and Community Conflicts*, 111–115.
[207] De Vos, *Church and Community Conflicts*, 89–99, 115; Oakes, *Philippians*, 27–35. De Vos emphasizes how those elite maintained their power by developing strong boundaries to other groups joining their group socially. See De Vos, *Church and Community Conflicts*, 245.
[208] De Vos, *Church and Community Conflicts*, 245. This description emphasizes the particular role of *liberti* (freed slaves) in maintaining the "Roman-ness" of Philippi and increasing the patronage networks of the leading Romans in the colony. See De Vos, *Church and Community Conflicts*, 245–247. One such *libertus* appears to have been

landowners, farmers, service providers, slaves and the poor as the major social roles for the colonial population.[209]

By briefly examining the history of military campaigns, colonial forces, and their socio-political impact upon Philippi, we have a more complicated picture of the Roman colony in the mid first century C.E. Rather than assuming that all in the colony benefited from and remained pliant to the order established by the Roman Empire, we have a picture of a colony marked by distinct socioeconomic stratification. An oligarchic political structure was maintained by an elite in the severe minority, while the population was distinguished by significant diversity in ethnicity, economic and legal status, and potential loyalty. The history of the city has included up to three different colonizing forces (Thasian, Macedonian, and Roman). In the last of these colonizations, the settlement processes managed to marginalize both previous inhabitants and eventually some of those "rewarded" for making this colonization possible. Though a Roman style of governance predominates, its success in maintaining a monopoly on power does not necessarily reflect a warm acceptance of Roman ideas, military images, or colonial organization by the subjects at Philippi. Rather, it seems, it could be providing the conditions under which most Philippians would recognize and resent this Roman dominance.

While several of the studies drawn on above present a multi-factored analysis of the social, economic and political relations in the colony of Philippi, they rarely explicitly consider the role of women in these relations. Admittedly, the resources for seeking women's realities in first century Philippi are scant. However, the resources for non-elites are perhaps just as difficult to find and interpret, yet they are frequently represented in the models of social relations at Philippi. As previous sections of this chapter have indicated, women played vital roles within their communities at Philippi. Beginning with Philippi's various cultic systems, some women were sponsors and/or priestesses in these cults, indicating that they might have had some status relative to other members of the cultic community.[210] Thus, within these layered socioeconomic and legal descriptions, it is possible to place some women as among either the elite or those Romans and "Greeks" who had some land, property, status, and/or wealth.

---

elected *aedile* at Philippi. See De Vos, *Church and Community Conflicts*, 245; *CIL* 3.633.1–2.

[209] Oakes, *Philippians*, 76. Oakes' "standard scenario" of the population's composition includes 37% service, 20% slaves, 20% colonist farmers, 20% poor, and 3% elite; 60% of which are "Greek" and 40% Roman. See Oakes, *Philippians*, 17, 50. In Oakes' classification of the "poor," while nearly all of the population could be defined as poor (at or near subsistence level), he chooses to specify further in order to get a sense of the contours of this massive, subsistence group. Thus, the "poor" are those who are regularly and unhealthily below subsistence level. See Oakes, *Philippians*, 48. Oakes places most *liberti* within the service provider groups. See Oakes, *Philippians*, 49–50.

[210] See Chapter III.A above and Abrahamsen, *Women*; Portefaix, *Sisters*.

Yet, wherever an adult, free female had access to such avenues of power, it was most likely because of a connection to an adult, propertied, free male who had greater access or control over these advantages. For example, this overview of Philippi's colonial structures has stressed the importance of Roman citizenship as one factor in maintaining access to a range of political, social and economic benefits.[211] While it has been noted that very few if any "Greeks" were granted citizenship rights, these studies have failed to mention that all women, even those in elite circles, would have been excluded from Roman citizenship.[212] As Pomeroy has succinctly expressed: "Roman women were given no true political offices and were forced to exert their influence through their men."[213] To the extent that citizenship afforded access to these benefits, then, elite women would have to try to work vicariously through elite, propertied, citizen men. Though we can, and should, differentiate between elite and non-elite females, as well as between elite and non-elite males, these distinctions are not equivalent, but mitigated by a kyriarchal bias toward adult, elite, free, propertied, Roman citizen male heads of household (*paterfamilias*).[214]

Once we depart from an analysis of the elite ranks of Roman legal and socioeconomic arrangements, we see women in a range of roles alongside of men. Across those socioeconomic differentiations made by Oakes and De Vos, we find women as well as men working in farming, crafts and other services.[215] A brief glance at the sources for women's lives in Greco-Roman antiquity shows women engaged in a variety of tasks: laboring in skilled trades, working in markets, beginning apprenticeships, practicing medicine, and serving as slaves

---

[211] Indeed, the sole instance where a woman might have had access to power beyond the control of the *paterfamilias* would be as the daughter of a Roman citizen. In some cases the dowry accompanying propertied daughters into marriage would give them the potential for power and independence within their new families. Granted, this benefit emanates from her father's *potestas*, but it does keep her from being completely subsumed under the husband's *dominium*. For more on dowries and the Roman family, in general, see Richard P. Saller, "Dowries and Daughters in Rome," in *Patriarchy, Property and Death in the Roman Family* (Cambridge Studies in Population, Economy, and Society in Past Time 25; Cambridge: Cambridge University Press, 1994), 204–224; Beryl Rawson, ed., *The Family in Ancient Rome: New Perspectives* (Ithaca, N.Y.: Cornell University Press, 1986); *Marriage, Divorce and Children in Ancient Rome* (Oxford: Oxford University Press, 1991); Susan Treggiari, *Roman Marriage: 'Iusti Coniuges' from the Time of Cicero to the Time of Ulpian* (Oxford: Oxford University Press, 1991).
[212] Pomeroy, *Goddesses*, 149–189. For more on the legal status of women in the Roman world, as well as their limited roles in political life, see Lefkowitz and Fant, *Women's Life*, 94–119, 142–155.
[213] Pomeroy, *Goddesses*, 189.
[214] For more on the near-absolute authority (the *patria potestas*) in Roman law for the *paterfamilias*, see Pomeroy, *Goddesses*, 150–152, 213; Leftkowitz and Fant, *Women's Life*, 98–100; Portefaix, *Sisters*, 15–17.
[215] Portefaix, *Sisters*, 23–28.

and freedwomen.[216] We would expect, then, that at Philippi women were involved in most of the same occupations as men, especially in those all-too-common cases where their survival depended on these activities. Though we might expect to find women among the colonist and non-colonist farmers, the service providers, slaves, and the poor, their legal and social capacities would typically be limited in comparison to their male counterparts in class, status and property.

This preceding sketch of the history of the colonization(s) of Philippi and its political, social, and economic impact gives us a basic notion of the conditions under which a community in this colony received a letter in the mid first century C.E. Though there are limitations for a continuation of this examination, it might still be relevant to attempt to explain where the community to which Paul wrote fell in this complex web of relations at Philippi. For example, it seems unlikely that veterans (or their descendants) were members in any significant way of the relatively small audience Paul was addressing in the Philippian community.[217] In general, the appeal of this movement was not to elite members of society, but to an ethnically and socially diverse mix of subsistence-level (or lower) populations. More recent scholarship that has attempted to model the "church" community at Philippi confirms that this tendency would have been operative at Philippi as well. De Vos writes that it was "unlikely that there were any in the church who were descendants of the original colonists. Certainly nothing remotely hints at his [Clement, 4:3] being a member of the ruling elite."[218] Oakes stresses how Paul's likely inability to access the upper echelons of Philippian society would be reflected in the makeup of the community.[219]

Oakes further estimates that if there were any descendants of veterans in the community, they would have been farmers who had fallen on bad times economically, having lost their land.[220] Indeed, by stressing that the community most likely did not include many Romans, elites, or land-owning veterans, Oakes manages to address the role of women at Philippi: "It is characteristic of much of scholarship that Karl Bornhäuser can look at a letter, two out of three of whose named addressees are Greek women, and take as his exegetical

---

[216] Lefkowitz and Fant, *Women's Life*, 208–224, 264–272.
[217] Oakes, *Philippians*, 53. For the importance of veteran presence at Philippi as applied to an interpretation of the letter to the Philippians, see Bormann, *Philippi*, 52.
[218] De Vos, *Church and Community Conflicts*, 255. Here De Vos disputes Peterlin's assumption that Clement's name indicates he is of "military stock." See Peterlin, *Paul's Letter*, 168–169. See also Oakes, *Philippians*, 57–61.
[219] Oakes, *Philippians*, 57–61.
[220] Oakes, *Philippians*, 60–61. Oakes also notes: "there was probably a negligible proportion of veterans among the hearers of the letter." See Oakes, *Philippians*, 53. For the city of Philippi, "the proportion of veterans in the population was extremely small." See Oakes, *Philippians*, 53.

foundation the idea that the recipients are Roman, male, ex-soldiers."[221] Oakes' comment lays bare the scholarly tendency to take one factor, Philippi as a Roman colony, and read it in a rather limited fashion into all situations for the letter, ignoring especially the role of women. This tendency (that Oakes explicitly names) also shows how traditional biblical and classical scholarship has identified first with elite men, who produced and preserved most of our sources for the ancient world. My study demonstrates the necessity of the feminist analytic of domination to accompany any accounting of the colonial status of Philippi and its impact on the community that received Paul's letter to the Philippians.

Both De Vos and Oakes stress the likelihood of the community being composed of people with lower status. On the basis of those named in the letter (Epaphroditus, Euodia, Syntyche, and Clement) and Paul's own status, De Vos maintains that the community would have likely been comprised mostly of subsistence-level artisans, merchants, and *liberti*.[222] Working from his model for the whole population of Philippi, Oakes also makes use of the accessibility factor, in terms of geography, society and religion.[223] Applying this limiting factor, then, Oakes argues that the community was mostly composed of service providers, slaves, and the poor, with some farmers.[224] While his model does not exclude outright the possibility of elite in the community, Oakes agrees that "there are no indicators of élite members."[225] Thus, though these two approaches ultimately differ some in their assessment of how "Roman" the community could have been, their approximations for the social make-up of the community converge in significant ways.[226]

---

[221] Oakes, *Philippians*, 63–64. Here he is referring to D. Karl Bornhäuser, *Jesus imperator mundi (Phil 3, 17–21 u. 2, 5–12)* (Gütersloh: Bertelsmann, 1938).
[222] De Vos, *Church and Community Conflicts*, 250–261.
[223] Oakes, *Philippians*, 57–59.
[224] Oakes, *Philippians*, 59–63. Oakes' model gives precise numbers as well as reasonable ranges for each of these groups. For example, he maintains that the community would be: 35–55% service groups, 20–40% poor, 12–25% slaves, 15–23% commuting peasant colonists, and 0.5–1.5% elite. See Oakes, *Philippians*, 60–61.
[225] Oakes, *Philippians*, 61. Here, Oakes refers to Justin J. Meggitt, *Paul, Poverty and Survival* (Studies of the New Testament and Its World; Edinburgh: T & T Clark, 1998), 97.
[226] De Vos argues that the majority of the community would be Roman, mostly because of the number of *liberti*. Oakes estimates that the community could be 25–40% Roman, drawing from the colonist farmer ranks, and about a third of the service groups and a quarter of the poor. See De Vos, *Church and Community Conflicts*, 251–252, 258–261; Oakes, *Philippians*, 61–63. Though it seems difficult to arbitrate between the two positions, this study will lean more towards Oakes' evaluations specifically because of his model's attention to changes in the development of the colony from its mid first century B.C.E. founding to the situation in the mid first century C.E.

By briefly examining the history of military campaigns and colonial forces and considering their impact upon Philippi and the possible audience of the letter to the Philippians, we have drawn a more complicated picture of the Roman colony in the mid first century C.E. Rather than assuming monolithic representations of these populations, their colonial "benefits," and the community to which Paul wrote, we have reflected upon the significant ethnic and socioeconomic differences within the city, a dominant political power structure which ensured privileges only for the very few, and a community that most likely rested in the lower ranks of these stratifications. Such an albeit truncated overview has demonstrated the continued importance of applying a multi-factored analysis and an analytic of domination to the colonial situation at Philippi.

Part Two

How Philippians Implements These Rhetorics

Chapter IV

Evolving Rhetoric:
The Interaction of Arguments As They Appear

Having set the stage by examining the contexts of both the letter and the interpretation of the letter, the second half of this study now turns to an analysis of the rhetorics of Philippians. In this and the following chapter, the argumentation is examined from two different vantage points. First, we approach Philippians by considering its evolving rhetoric, assessing the arguments in the order that they appear in the letter, as they build upon and interact with each other. Second, the letter's prevailing rhetoric is discussed, evaluating the arguments once they are grouped together according to type, so that we can examine what is characteristic about the letter's rhetoric.[1] Thus, this chapter is a section-by-section analysis of Philippians' rhetorics, while the next chapter functions as an overview of the argumentation noted in this analysis.

By considering some of the strongest suggestions about dominant images in the letter, military images and ancient friendship images, we have established two cues from an assessment of previous scholarship about how to proceed with a feminist rhetorical interpretation of the letter. The first cue demonstrates the necessity of paying attention to the potentially oppressive power relations reflected in and constructed by Philippians with the aid of the analytical concept of kyriarchy. The relevance of this concept for a feminist interpretation has already been demonstrated (see Chapters II and III). The second cue involves comprehending how multiple rhetorical strategies overlap and, thus, mutually reinforce each other, even as they seem to come from separate thought-worlds.

---

[1] The distinction made in this study between evolving (or developing) rhetoric and prevailing rhetoric is in keeping with the approach of Antoinette Clark Wire's study of 1 Corinthians implementing Olbrechts-Tyteca and Perelman's argumentative techniques. It differs from this study, however, in the order of presentation, and the descriptive terms used (evolving rather than structural, prevailing in place of textual). See Wire, *The Corinthian Women Prophets: A Reconstruction through Paul's Rhetoric* (Minneapolis: Fortress Press, 1990), 6–9, 12–180.

It is on this matter of the second cue that the work of rhetorical scholars becomes especially relevant.[2] For example, the work of Lucie Olbrechts-Tyteca and Chaïm Perelman played a pivotal role in founding the most recent revival of rhetorical studies, often dubbed the New Rhetoric.[3] Working in Europe after the Second World War, Olbrechts-Tyteca and Perelman reflect upon the crisis of modernity and the concomitant problems of misunderstanding and injustice. They claim that understanding between humans does not grow out of formal logic and the self-evidence of statements, but from people's value judgments and the measuring of opinions.[4] In their view argumentation requires that a rhetor find a way to appeal to the reasonableness of the audience.[5] This

---

[2] For more on the background of rhetorical approaches in general, as well as the more recent developments in rhetorical interpretation (especially as they involve Olbrechts-Tyteca and Perelman), see Chapter I above.

[3] Typically, Perelman is credited with the work of the New Rhetoric to the exclusion of Olbrechts-Tyteca. Though all indications lead to their full partnership in the conception, research and writing of *The New Rhetoric: A Treatise on Argumentation* (trans. John Wilkinson and Purcell Weaver; Notre Dame, Ind.: University of Notre Dame Press, 1969), Olbrechts-Tyteca's name and role are literally being written out of the history of rhetoric. It is for this reason that this project lists the two authors in reverse order to the title page, following the usual alphabetical order of last names. On Olbrechts-Tyteca's background, contribution to this study, and later work, see Barbara Warnick, "Lucie Olbrechts-Tyteca's Contribution to *The New Rhetoric*," in *Listening to Their Voices: The Rhetorical Activities of Historical Women* (ed. Molly Meijer Wertheimer; Studies in Rhetoric/Communication; Columbia: University of South Carolina Press, 1997), 69–85. On the prominent role assigned to Perelman in North American and European scholarship, see James L. Golden and Joseph L. Pilotta, eds., *Practical Reasoning in Human Affairs: Studies in Honor of Chaïm Perelman* (Synthese Library 183; Dordrecht, Netherlands; D. Reidel, 1986); and Ray D. Dearin, ed., *The New Rhetoric of Chaïm Perelman: Statement & Response* (Lanham, Md.: University Press of America, 1989).

[4] "Values enter, at some stage or other, into every argument." See Olbrechts-Tyteca and Perelman, *The New Rhetoric*, 75. For the role of values in rhetoric, see Olbrechts-Tyteca and Perelman, *The New Rhetoric*, 1–4, 74–79. For more on the probability of reasoning in communication and argument, see Stephen Toulmin, *The Uses of Argument* (Cambridge: Cambridge University Press, 1958). For more on the relation between Toulmin and Perelman (again, to the exclusion of Olbrechts-Tyteca), see Conley, *Rhetoric*, 285–304; Bizzell and Herzberg, *The Rhetorical Tradition*, 912–95. See also the work of their contemporary, Kenneth Burke, *A Rhetoric of Motives* (Berkeley: University of California Press, 1950).

[5] "There is only one rule in this matter: adaptation of the speech to the audience, whatever its nature." See Olbrechts-Tyteca and Perelman, *The New Rhetoric*, 25. On "adaptation to the audience," see Olbrechts-Tyteca and Perelman, *The New Rhetoric*, 14–26. This view of rhetoric is a departure from the dominance of the rhetor (in line with the "great man" theories of history and ideas) and from the view of rhetoric as manipulation by stylistics. This latter view was one of the main reasons for rhetoric's degradation at the hands of philosophy over the centuries. See Wilhelm Wuellner, *Hermeneutics and Rhetorics: From "Truth and Method" to Truth and Power* (Scriptura Special Issue S3; Stellenbosch, RSA: Centre for Hermeneutical Studies, 1989).

emphasis upon the audience and seeking its adherence is one of the notable advances Olbrechts-Tyteca and Perelman make to rhetorical theory. This orientation toward the audience requires that the rhetor actually care about and in some way esteem or value the other person's (or people's) opinions and reactions. Since audiences are normally composite, the rhetor will have to use a multiplicity of arguments to convince.[6] It is here that we can begin to see how Olbrechts-Tyteca and Perelman's vision of rhetoric coincides with the second cue (multiple, interlocking nature of rhetoric) developed earlier in this project.

Olbrechts-Tyteca and Perelman's work also includes a rather detailed elucidation of the various techniques of argumentation one could use in assembling this multiplicity of arguments.[7] They group these argumentative techniques into four broad, descriptive categories based upon what the techniques "do" or how they function in the convincing process. The first set of argumentative techniques they label *quasi-logical arguments*, since they draw rhetorical strength from their similarity to already well-established modes of reasoning like formal proofs.[8] The second category of techniques is what Olbrechts-Tyteca and Perelman call *arguments based on the structure of reality*.[9] These arguments attempt to link the accepted judgments or general perceptions of reality of an audience with the position one is trying to promote.[10] Close to this second category, the third group of rhetorical techniques is described as *arguments establishing the structure of reality*.[11] This kind of argument seeks to add specific perceptions and evaluations to the beliefs already accepted as accurately portraying the reality of the audience's experiences.[12] The distinctive category in Olbrechts-Tyteca and Perelman's work is the fourth and final set detailed, *arguments of dissociation*.[13] Whereas the previous three sets sought to bring together concepts or propositions not normally associated with

---

[6] Olbrechts-Tyteca and Perelman, *The New Rhetoric*, 21–26.
[7] In fact, the investigation, explication and exemplification of these argumentative techniques make up the bulk of *The New Rhetoric* volume. See Olbrechts-Tyteca and Perelman, *The New Rhetoric*, 185–459. It has been surmised that these techniques (especially dissociation) were Olbrechts-Tyteca's major contribution to their collaborative effort. See Warnick, "Lucie Olbrechts-Tyteca's Contribution," 70.
[8] Olbrechts-Tyteca and Perelman, *The New Rhetoric*, 193–260.
[9] Olbrechts-Tyteca and Perelman, *The New Rhetoric*, 261–349.
[10] Olbrechts-Tyteca and Perelman, *The New Rhetoric*, 191, 261–263.
[11] Olbrechts-Tyteca and Perelman, *The New Rhetoric*, 350–410.
[12] Olbrechts-Tyteca and Perelman, *The New Rhetoric*, 191.
[13] Olbrechts-Tyteca and Perelman, *The New Rhetoric*, 411–459. Dissociation remained a topic of primary focus for the remainder of Olbrechts-Tyteca's career and, therefore, was most likely one of her innovative contributions to *The New Rhetoric*. See Olbrechts-Tyteca, *Le Comique du discours* (Bruxelles: Editions de l'Université de Bruxelles, 1974); and "Les Couples philosophiques: Une nouvelle approche," *Revue internationale de philosophie* 33 (1979): 81–98.

118   HIERARCHY, UNITY, AND IMITATION

each other and specified their relationship, dissociation is focused upon separating elements or a concept already associated, typically to make new associations.[14] Stated in brief, dissociation breaks the connecting links upon which previous arguments or perceptions were based.

The strength of Olbrechts-Tyteca and Perelman's categorization lies not just in the manner they have divided and organized rhetorical practices, but also in their flexible and interdependent conceptualization of argumentation itself. While their four main categories are fluid and overlapping, the value of dividing arguments is in seeing how a rhetorical act works best when it integrates different kinds of argumentative techniques from more than one category so that they build upon or complement each other. It is in this "interaction of arguments" that the rhetoric becomes convincing and can produce different effects.[15] Rhetoric does not function statically, but interactively, thus one's approaches to and analysis of a rhetorical act must enter into the process with an eye towards this interaction of arguments, just as this study's second cue has indicated.

As it has been made clear in this brief re-introduction to the "New Rhetoric," the model for rhetoric presented by Olbrechts-Tyteca and Perelman can serve as an excellent partner in the following analysis of Philippians' evolving rhetoric. Fortunately, in the case of biblical studies, this study has a number of antecedents in scholars who have already pursued rhetorical readings with the help of Olbrechts-Tyteca and Perelman's techniques of argumentation.[16] Even more specifically for this project, Antoinette Clark Wire's work stands as an insightful precedent-setter in her implementation of Olbrechts-Tyteca and Perelman's categories in a feminist rhetorical analysis of another Pauline letter, First Corinthians.[17]

This study now turns to an overview of the argumentative techniques within the letter of Philippians in order to better understand the rhetorics of the whole as well as the power relations at work in these rhetorics. Since the aim is also to

---

[14] Olbrechts-Tyteca and Perelman, *The New Rhetoric*, 191–192, 411–415.
[15] Olbrechts-Tyteca and Perelman, *The New Rhetoric*, 460–508.
[16] See, for example, J. David Hester Amador, *Academic Constraints in Rhetorical Criticism of the New Testament: An Introduction to a Rhetoric of Power* (JSNT Sup 174; Sheffield: Sheffield Academic Press, 1999), especially 60–87; Yehoshua Gitay, *Prophecy and Persuasion: A Study of Isaiah 40–48* (Forum theologiae linguisticae 14; Bonn: Linguistica Biblica Bonn, 1981); and *Isaiah and His Audience: The Structure and Meaning of Isaiah 1–12* (SSN 30; Assen, The Netherlands: Van Gorcum, 1991); Steven J. Kraftchick, "Why Do the Rhetoricians Rage?" in *Text and Logos: The Humanistic Interpretation of the New Testament* (ed. Theodore W. Jennings, Jr.; Homage Series 16; Atlanta: Scholars Press, 1990), 55–79; Gary Salyer, *Vain Rhetoric: Private Insight and Public Debate in the Book of Ecclesiastes* (JSOTSup 327; Sheffield: Sheffield Academic Press, 2001); and Folker Siegert, *Argumentation bei Paulus, gezeigt an Römer 9–11* (WUNT 34; Tübingen: J. C. B. Mohr/Paul Siebeck, 1985).
[17] Wire, *The Corinthian Women Prophets*.

produce a feminist rhetorical interpretation of the letter, this analysis also reflects upon the ethical import of these rhetorics in the mode of Schüssler Fiorenza's and Wire's approaches. Specifically, attention is given to claims to authority, developments of structures of subordination, and specific figures within these relations (including Paul, Christ, Timothy, Epaphroditus, Euodia and Syntyche). This focus on the letter's techniques[18] follows the arguments as they interact with each other and thus takes them in the order that they appear.[19] This study holds that the letter's rhetoric can be more broadly separated into two overarching, yet still interconnected, strategies: the rhetorics of commonality and the rhetorics of differentiation. A closer examination of the argumentative techniques should confirm this suggestion and provide a more thorough analysis of the argumentative techniques.[20]

A. 1:1–11

Even before the thanksgiving section (1:3–11) begins, a few observations can be made that could be of relevance as we continue through the letter.[21] Paul's choice of the term *douloi* ("slaves/servants," 1:1) to describe Timothy and

---

[18] While it would be desirable to read this text with many turns or interpretations, the constraints of this current project provide the opportunity for only an initial reading. This rhetorical choice is not meant to indicate that this is the only legitimate or correct interpretation, but it is one amongst several potential readings. For more on the utility of multiple readings, see Daniel Patte, *Ethics of Biblical Interpretation: A Reevaluation* (Louisville, Ky.: Westminster John Knox Press, 1995), 27–30; and Chapter VI below.
[19] This approach differs from Wire's use of Olbrechts-Tyteca and Perelman, since she first grouped the argumentative techniques together according to category before proceeding section by section through the letter. See Wire, *The Corinthian Women Prophets*, 12–38. It is hoped that this difference in approach suits the considerably more compact Philippians while demonstrating the way the arguments build upon each other as the letter continues.
[20] At several key points this study shares the view of Philippians explicated in Cynthia Briggs Kittredge's book, *Community and Authority: The Rhetoric of Obedience in the Pauline Tradition* (HTS 45; Harrisburg, Penn.: Trinity Press International, 1998). Kittredge demonstrates the relevance and explanatory power of a feminist rhetorical interpretation of this letter. Yet, given these similarities in orientation, this study's differences in emphasis and approach will merit the effort and enrich our understanding of the letter.
[21] Though this study occasionally draws upon the terminology and divisions of the more form-oriented rhetorical studies, it does not articulate its own set of divisions. The focus here is upon the interaction and additive effects of the rhetorics throughout the letter, rather than any artificially stressed boundaries between the argumentative sections. For a consideration of the ample supply of rhetorical structures offered by biblical critics, see L. Gregory Bloomquist, *The Function of Suffering in Philippians* (JSNTSup 78; Sheffield: Sheffield Academic Press, 1993), 72–138.

himself as the senders of the letter should not be overlooked. Such a description has possible associations with the model provided by the Christ hymn in 2:5–11, where Christ takes the form of a slave (2:7).[22] It is also within these initial verses (of both the salutation and the thanksgiving) that Paul modifies the rule of justice (quasi-logical argument). In rhetorical terms the rule of justice refers to an argument that strives to show the application of the same principle or standard to similar situations.[23] The first reference in greeting "all the holy ones" (1:1) introduces Paul's care for *all* of the Philippian community, stressed also in very next sentence: *epi **pasō** tō mneia hymōn **pan**tote en **pasō** deōsei mou hyper **pantōn** hymōn* (1:3–4). Even as the letter begins with these strong demonstrations toward universal concern, there are also indications that there are some differentiations at work. The letter addresses not only "all the holy ones" in Philippi, but also the "overseers and servers" (1:1),[24] and even the formulaic greeting of 1:2 portrays some of the senders as the ones conveying the grace and peace from God and Jesus, most likely the ultimate figures of authority for the community at Philippi.[25]

The associations with the rule of justice in these opening verses are strengthened as the letter further describes the relationship between the community and Paul as a *koinōnia* ("partnership," 1:5), for which Paul is thankful. In the following sentence the community members are also called *synkoinōnous mou* ("partners with me," 1:7). The note on the duration of this partnership hints at a point of concern for Paul, since the community has had this relationship "from the first day up to/until now" (1:5). The temporal emphasis suggests that this could be the beginning of an argument of waste (based on the structure of reality).[26] Up to this point the letter considers them

---

[22] The only other occurrence of the *doul-* word-group in the letter, aside from 1:1 and 2:7, is another clear case of positive modeling, again regarding Timothy (*edouleusen*, 2:22).

[23] Olbrechts-Tyteca and Perelman note that "the rule of justice requires giving identical treatment to beings or situations of the same kind." See Olbrechts-Tyteca and Perelman, *The New Rhetoric*, 218. For more on the rule of justice in argumentation, see Olbrechts-Tyteca and Perelman, *The New Rhetoric*, 218–220; and Chapter V.B.1 below.

[24] This matter of differentiation can be overread, however, as Peterlin does by seeing the signs of division in these scant references. See Davorin Peterlin, *Paul's Letter to the Philippians in the Light of Disunity in the Church* (NovTSup 79; Leiden: Brill, 1995), 20–24. The point seems to be that, even when Paul writes the community in terms of unity and oneness, he does not see all people the same way.

[25] The brief notes about God and Jesus could be construed as arguments from authority/divine authority (based on the structure of reality) or even arguments by transitivity (quasi-logical). For more on these argumentative techniques, see below, especially Chapter V.B.4 and V.C.4.

[26] Building on a current state of affairs, the argument of waste maintains that not acting or thinking a particular way would wastefully negate previous efforts to establish the current state. For more on the argument of waste, see Olbrechts-Tyteca and Perelman, *The New Rhetoric*, 279–281; and Chapter V.C.1 below.

partners, suggesting that what they do in the present and near future determines whether they will remain in this kind of relationship, or whether their efforts at maintaining *koinōnia* will have gone to waste. This orientation toward the near-future seems especially important, since the lengthy sentence concludes with the anticipation of their completion at the day of Christ (1:6). By expressing a universal concern for the community and defining their relationship as a partnership, the letter's rhetorics of commonality attempt to bridge the distance between Paul and his audience with a particular vision of communal identity. In fact, this opening section might be contrasting the assurance of Paul's constant concern (*pantote*, 1:4) with the unresolved question of the Philippian community's response (an argument by comparison, a quasi-logical argument) to intensify this call for a particular communal response.[27]

When the letter turns to a definition (quasi-logical argument)[28] of what is just or right (*dikaion*) for Paul to think or feel (*phronein*) about the audience (1:7), it reinforces the impression that Paul is being presented as a model (argument establishing the structure of reality)[29] for the Philippians. The strength of this modeling is based upon the expression of (at least) two rhetorical techniques. First, Paul's prayers, concerns and actions (1:3–7) act as an argument drawn from the relationship between a person and her/his acts (argument based on the structure of reality), since it is often presumed that a person's actions can tell one something about that person's character.[30] It seems that all forms of modeling are in some way dependent upon this interaction

---

[27] On the argument by comparison, see Olbrechts-Tyteca and Perelman, *The New Rhetoric*, 242–247; and Chapter V.B.2 below. While these parties (Paul and the Philippian community) are being contrasted here, the contrast could be based upon a traditional dissociation between duration and eternity. See Table III in Olbrechts-Tyteca and Perelman, *The New Rhetoric*, 421.

[28] For an explanation of and examples for the argument by definition, see Olbrechts-Tyteca and Perelman, *The New Rhetoric*, 210–214; and Chapter V.B.3 below.

[29] On the use of models in argumentation, see Olbrechts-Tyteca and Perelman, *The New Rhetoric*, 362–368; and Chapter V.D.1–5 below. On imitation in Paul's letters in general, see Elizabeth A. Castelli, *Imitating Paul: A Discourse of Power* (Literary Currents in Biblical Interpretation; Louisville, Ky.: Westminster John Knox Press, 1991); Benjamin Fiore, "Paul, Exemplification, and Imitation," in *Paul in the Greco-Roman World: A Handbook* (ed. J. Paul Sampley; Harrisburg, Penn.: Trinity Press International, 2003), 228–257. Brian J. Dodd argues that "Paul in fact explicitly places himself as a model for his readers through his letters and he implies he did so when he was present with his newly founded churches." See Dodd, *Paul's Paradigmatic "I": Personal Example as Literary Strategy* (JSNTSup 177; Sheffield: Sheffield Academic Press, 1999), 13. Markus Bockmuehl maintains that "the theme of imitation recurs as an integrating focus in every major section of Philippians." See Bockmuehl, *The Epistle to the Philippians* (BNTC; London: Hendrickson, 1998), 254.

[30] On the relation between "the person and his [sic] acts," see Olbrechts-Tyteca and Perelman, *The New Rhetoric*, 293–305; and Chapter V.C.2 below.

between act and person. Even as the section argues for Paul's model character, the "rule of justice" continues to influence the rhetoric, as it is repeatedly mentioned how Paul feels this way about "all of you" (1:7 twice, 1:8, see also *synkoinōnous mou* in 1:7, mentioned above).[31]

The character of Paul in his model desire for the community is attested in a second way by the witness of God (1:8) in the ultimate version of the argument from authority (based upon the structure of reality).[32] Any allusion to authority also implicitly entails some sort of hierarchical difference in order to explain the figure's claim to authority. Thus, alongside the continuing rhetorics of commonality, these references to divine authority and the model of Paul evoke a separate rhetorics of differentiation. Paul's elevated status is one potential premise for the presumed effects detailed in the final sentence of the thanksgiving section (1:9–11). The letter asserts that Paul's prayer will have an efficacy that benefits the community by a series of causal links (argument based on the structure of reality).[33] By way of two *hina* clauses (1:9, 10) and an infinitive of result (*eis to dokimazein*, 1:10), the argument articulates a series of

---

[31] Scholars interested in friendship imagery have highlighted *phroneō* and *koinōnia* as key terms. See L. Michael White, "Morality Between Two Worlds: A Paradigm of Friendship in Philippians," in *Greeks, Romans and Christians: Essays in Honor of Abraham J. Malherbe* (ed. David L. Balch, Everett Ferguson and Wayne A. Meeks; Minneapolis: Fortress Press, 1990), 210; Ken L. Berry, "The Function of Friendship Language in Philippians 4:10–20," in *Friendship, Flattery and Frankness of Speech: Studies on Friendship in the New Testament World* (ed. John T. Fitzgerald; NovTSup 82; Leiden: Brill, 1996), 118; Stanley K. Stowers, "Friends and Enemies in the Politics of Heaven: Reading Theology in Philippians," in *Pauline Theology*, Vol. 1: *Thessalonians, Philippians, Galatians, Philemon* (ed. Jouette M. Bassler; Minneapolis: Augsburg Fortress Press, 1991), 110–112; Fitzgerald, "Paul and Friendship," in *Paul in the Greco-Roman World*, 332–334. Sampley suggests that these terms fit better in the Roman *societas* system. See Sampley, *Pauline Partnership in Christ* (Philadelphia: Fortress, 1980). For more on *phroneō* as a synonym for friendship in Philippians, see Wolfgang Schenk, *Die Philipperbriefe des Paulus* (Stuttgart: Kohlhammer, 1984), 65.

[32] On the argument from authority, see Olbrechts-Tyteca and Perelman, *The New Rhetoric*, 305–310; and Chapter V.C.4 below. The use here is particularly strong, since for an authoritative proof, "The extreme case is the divine authority which overcomes all the obstacles that reason might raise." See Olbrechts-Tyteca and Perelman, *The New Rhetoric*, 308. The causal link also plays a role within this definition and model argument, in both 1:7 and 1:8. The close ties between the arguments by the model of Paul and the arguments from divine authority throughout this letter demonstrate how hierarchically-oriented Philippians' modeling rhetorics tend to be. On the tension between sameness and hierarchy in imitation, see Castelli, *Imitating Paul*, 16, 21–22, 30–31, 68–71, 140–141.

[33] On the use of the causal link in argumentation, see Olbrechts-Tyteca and Perelman, *The New Rhetoric*, 263–292; and Chapter V.C.5 below. For the difference between the outcome focused means-end arguments and the fact focused fact-consequence argument, see Olbrechts-Tyteca and Perelman, *The New Rhetoric*, 270–278.

benefits that will come to the community as a result of Paul's prayer.[34] The effects again emphasize Paul's connection to the divine realm, since these effects will prepare them for "the day of Christ" (1:10), and give them blessings that come "through Jesus Christ for the glory and praise of God" (1:11). While the emphasis here seems to be more on the range of positive effects than Paul's prayerful action (more a means-end argument than a fact-consequence argument), it nevertheless reinforces Paul's model status by way of an association with authority. This final connection between Paul, Christ, and God comes close to an argument by transitivity (quasi-logical).[35] Since Paul's prayer has certain results and at least one of these results (the "fruit of righteousness," 1:11) comes through Christ and for God, Paul's role in the community is explicated here as very close to the roles of Christ and God.

B. 1:12–26

This initial thanksgiving introduced both the topics of commonality and Paul's model status, but the next section marks the first instance of the dissociative rhetoric that will remain prominent throughout the remainder of the letter. Dissociative arguments restructure the relationship between two previously-associated elements of an argument in order to associate them in a different way.[36] For example, the first use of dissociation in Philippians is based upon Olbrechts-Tyteca and Perelman's classic dissociation of appearance from reality,[37] as Paul insists that his imprisonment *has* in fact "advanced the gospel"

---

[34] Paul A. Holloway argues that 1:9–10a is the thesis of Paul's rhetorical goal of consolation, as he seeks for the audience to discern the things that do and do not matter. See Holloway, *Consolation in Philippians: Philosophical Sources and Rhetorical Strategy* (SNTSMS 112; Cambridge: Cambridge University Press, 2001), 45–78, 94–100.

[35] Transitivity expands upon the associative principle in argumentation, maintaining that "because a relation holds between *a* and *b* and between *b* and *c*, it therefore holds between *a* and *c*." See Olbrechts-Tyteca and Perelman, *The New Rhetoric*, 227. If operational in this passage, this argument shows that because Paul (*a*) is connected to Christ and God (*b*), and Christ and God (*b*) are connected to the potential audience (*c*) as authorities, Paul's status (*a*) in the eyes of the audience (*c*) might then share in this authority. For more on the argument by transitivity, see Olbrechts-Tyteca and Perelman, *The New Rhetoric*, 227–231; and Chapter V.B.4 below.

[36] For Olbrechts-Tyteca and Perelman's extensive treatment of arguments by dissociation, see Olbrechts-Tyteca and Perelman, *The New Rhetoric*, 411–459. Unlike most argumentative techniques based on making new connections, dissociations break connecting links; not simply to dissolve the relation between the elements of the argument, but to modify the previous formulation of their relation. See also Chapter V.A below.

[37] On the appearance-reality pair, see the above discussion, Olbrechts-Tyteca and Perelman, *The New Rhetoric*, 415–420; and Chapter V.A.1 below.

(1:12), as opposed to some other (possibly expected) negative outcome (*mallon*, "rather," 1:12). This dissociation between appearance and reality is articulated in terms of the results of the imprisonment (an argument from causal link). While it might appear that Paul's imprisonment would block or limit his mission, the letter conveys that in reality progress (*prokopōn*, 1:12) has been made.[38] While the mission might seem to have been limited, the letter argues to the contrary, by means of a dissociative definition,[39] that "my chains are for Christ" (1:13). Following the series of events in the subsequent *hōste* clause (1:13–14), the imprisonment has been re-cast as an opportunity to reach the praetorian guard (1:13), as well as most of the community there (1:14). These community members are now fearlessly speaking about their beliefs because of Paul's chains (1:14). This argument from causal link shows how the fact of Paul's imprisonment has led to many positive consequences. When combined with the following statement that most "have been made confident by my chains" (1:14), it confirms the initial impression that the letter is continuing to argue from and for the model of Paul.[40]

Before leaving this sentence, though, it might be important to consider the brief note about the praetorian guard (in 1:13).[41] The descriptions of whom Paul

---

[38] On the importance of the term "progress"' for the military language proposals for the letter, see Timothy C. Geoffrion, *The Rhetorical Purpose and the Political and Military Character of Philippians: A Call to Stand Firm* (Lewiston, N.Y.: Mellen, 1993), 59; Raymond Hubert Reimer, "'Our Citizenship Is in Heaven': Philippians 1:27–30 and 3:20–21 As Part of the Apostle Paul's Political Theology" (Ph.D. diss., Princeton Theological Seminary, 1997), 190; John Paul Schuster, "Rhetorical Situation and Historical Reconstruction in Philippians" (Ph.D. diss., The Southern Baptist Theological Seminary, 1997), 58, 62; Edgar M. Krentz, "Paul, Games, and the Military," in *Paul in the Greco-Roman World*, 361.

[39] On the use of definition after or as part of the dissociative process, see Olbrechts-Tyteca and Perelman, *The New Rhetoric*, 444–450; and Chapter V.B.3 below. The use of definition as either a dissociative argument or a quasi-logical argument is an excellent example of the inventional flexibility of both rhetoric itself and Olbrechts-Tyteca and Perelman's description of rhetoric.

[40] On the difference between an example and model, see Olbrechts-Tyteca and Perelman, *The New Rhetoric*, 350–357, 363–371. In particular, "as an example, it makes generalization possible . . . as a model, it encourages imitation." See Olbrechts-Tyteca and Perelman, *The New Rhetoric*, 350. These instances referring to Paul above are labeled modeling because of an implicit drive for imitation that will later become increasingly explicit (see 1:30–2:5 and especially 3:17).

[41] Scholars interested in military images were among the first to point out the relevance of this language for understanding Philippians. See Adolf Von Harnack, *Militia Christi: The Christian Religion and the Military in the First Three Centuries* (trans. and intro. D. M. Gracie; Philadelphia: Fortress, 1981), 36; Lillian Portefaix, *Sisters Rejoice: Paul's Letter to the Philippians and Luke-Acts as Received by First-Century Philippian Women* (ConBNT 20; Stockholm: Almqvist & Wiksell, 1988), 140; Krentz, "Military Language and Metaphors in Philippians," in *Origins and Method: Towards a New Understanding of Judaism and Christianity* (ed. Bradley H. McLean; JSNTSup 86; Sheffield: Sheffield

is reaching in this section follow the pattern already established in the preceding section's use of the rule of justice. The success was not partial, but it reached "the *whole* praetorian guard and *all* of the rest" (1:13). Since the letter is advocating a certain kind of communal identity, the emphasis on reaching the whole praetorian guard stands out in the argumentation. It is possible that Paul is making an argument here in terms of the group and its members (argument based on the structure of reality).[42] If the community at Paul's imprisonment site now includes those functioning within the Roman imperial system, what does this say about "all the rest" now? How does the act of including the praetorian guard there impact the definition of community boundaries in Philippi?

The letter continues to make use of dissociation as it opposes those who proceed with envy and rivalry from those with good will and love (1:15–16). Since the issue is contextualized by Paul as a matter of contentious divisiveness (*eritheias*, 1:17), this dissociation embodies the letter's rhetorics of commonality by differentiating division and difference (the devalued, term I) from unity and sameness (the preferred, term II).[43] As an affiliated move, then, this dissociation of division/unity also clarifies a distinction between these "others" and Paul (1:17–18). The continuing strategy of depicting Paul as a model is aided by the addition of another argumentative technique, the use of anti-models.[44] Like the arguments from a model before them, the anti-models are shown to be so by

---

Academic Press, 1993), 109–110; "Paul," 360. See also Schuster, "Rhetorical Situation," 45; Reimer, "'Our Citizenship,'" 191–192, 201–202. For military imagery in Philippians, in general, see Chapter II above.

[42] On the use of an argument based on the group and its members, see Olbrechts-Tyteca and Perelman, *The New Rhetoric*, 321–327; and Chapter V.C.3 below. This argument is similar in principle to the argument based on a person and her/his acts, since it is assumed a member can be representative of the group.

[43] While the argument proceeds by way of comparison, and in fairness can also be labeled thus in terms of Olbrechts-Tyteca and Perelman's techniques, the technique of dissociation seems to fit better in this case than comparison. In the case of those who preach divisively, they seem to have been considered part of the community, and most might have made no differentiation between them (as Paul does, as well, in the end regarding the results of their preaching in 1:18). The letter is attempting to argue that, though they might appear to be part of an original unity, they are evaluated as quite different from those who preach "from good will" (1:15). For more in this vein on the definition of dissociation as different from the breaking of connecting links between independent elements, see Olbrechts-Tyteca and Perelman, *The New Rhetoric*, 411–412. For the dissociation of multiplicity from unity or plurality from unity as traditional philosophically, see Tables I and II in Olbrechts-Tyteca and Perelman, *The New Rhetoric*, 420–421.

[44] For the use of anti-models with or without the contrasting models in argumentation, see Olbrechts-Tyteca and Perelman, *The New Rhetoric*, 366–368; and Chapter V.D.4 below. The topic of enemies is common in discussions of ancient friendship. See Stowers, "Friends," 114–115; Fitzgerald, "Paul," 334–337.

virtue of their actions, conveying something about the character of the person (interaction of act and person). The techniques start to pile up and build upon each other. The word or place where the rhetorics of differentiation part from the rhetorics of commonality blurs, to what seems to be even greater argumentative effect. While it seems important in the letter to differentiate the way the anti-models worked from the way others do (1:15–17), the letter also ultimately defines a common end for both patterns of behavior: Paul's rejoicing (1:18).[45]

This oft-repeated topic of joy serves as a transition to the next sentence in the letter. Paul's rejoicing is not only in the present, but will also continue, but for a different reason. The reason for joy is presented as a three-part causal link assertion. First, Paul will rejoice because he knows he will be safe (*eis sōtōrian*, 1:19). Second, his safety or deliverance will be brought about "through your prayers and the resources of the spirit of Jesus Christ" (1:19). Third, this course of events will ensure that "Christ will be made great/glorified in my body" (1:20). These three causal links in the argumentation make clear Paul's conceptions of the interpersonal links between the community, Christ, and himself. The second link anticipates both the community's and Christ's desire to bring about his safety, or salvation. He assumes they care, and the matter of his safety is prominent enough to merit the community's prayers and the intervention of Jesus' spirit. The third link maintains that Paul will not be the only beneficiary of these actions, but that Christ will also gain esteem in some way. In fact, Paul is so certain of this result that it is communicated in now-familiar universal terms, "in all frankness now as always" (*en pasō parrōsia hōs pantote kai nun*, 1:20). Paul presumes his relationship with Christ is so close as to almost be reciprocal in form in these last couple of expressions: as Christ will help Paul, Paul will be a cause of exaltation for Christ. The exaltation of the admired authority figure for this community (Christ) would only enhance Paul's model status, while drawing him closer to this accepted authority.

This preceding round of causal links ends with an unusual qualifying clause ("either by life or by death") that helps to transition to the subject of the following assertions. Here, the letter again combines definition and dissociation in order to re-define how the community should see things more from Paul's perspective. As this unusual appendage hints, the potential of death in prison is not seen as a liability in this letter, as Paul re-defines: "For to me to live is

---

[45] Joy is an important repetitive theme for both friendship and military scholars. Shared joy is just one characteristic of an ancient friendship. See John T. Fitzgerald, "Philippians in the Light of Some Ancient Discussions of Friendship," in *Friendship, Flattery and Frankness of Speech*, 146. Geoffrion maintains that joy and steadfastness are part of the *topos* of *militia spiritualis*. See Geoffrion, *Rhetorical Purpose*, 41, 118–120. Both groups of scholarly inquiry tend not to ask to what end this joy is extolled. This tendency predominates in the commentaries, where the letter is often characterized primarily in terms of this joyfulness. Bockmuehl enthuses: "St. Paul's letter to Philippi sparkles with joy . . . life-giving, heart-refreshing joy." See Bockmuehl, *Epistle*, 1.

Christ, and to die is gain" (1:21). The statement creates the dissociation between this life and the life with Christ that values death over this life, reversing the usual relation between life and death. Appearance is not reality; the life that appears preferable is not really so for Paul.[46] These dissociative re-definitions are based upon new causal links (1:21–23): death will be better because he will be with Christ (the focus is on the end, rather than the means in this causal link argument). Since it is a choice between the two, this life is not preferred since it is not yet considered being with Christ.

This reversal of sorts also functions as a premise for the next argument by dissociation.[47] Paul explains how living, though not preferable for him, is "more necessary because of you" (*anankaioteron di' hymas*, 1:24) and is "for your progress and joy" (*eis tōn hymōn prokopōn kai charan*, 1:25) establishing a dissociation of Paul's self-benefit from the community benefit.[48] Though Paul would benefit from being with Christ in death, he maintains that he must remain because of the community (another causal link argument).[49] Such a dissociation attempts to draw the community closer to Paul (the rhetorics of commonality) while still showing his model behavior on their behalf (rhetorics of

---

[46] It is possible that these dissociations reflect a reversal of expectations not only regarding life and death, but also regarding how to be "with Christ." That dying is linked in these dissociations with "gaining" Christ suggests that Paul may be trying to argue dissociatively here in order to convince people that they have not gained Christ already. Members of the community may have already experienced life in Christ as a benefit in some way in this life.

[47] Olbrechts-Tyteca and Perelman maintain that various dissociations of concepts influence each other and become interrelated in a networked fashion. See Olbrechts-Tyteca and Perelman, *The New Rhetoric*, 422.

[48] For the use of arguments dissociating self-benefit from community benefit in 1 Corinthians, see Wire, *The Corinthian Women Prophets*, 17–19. See also Chapter V.A.3 below. The appeal to "common advantage" over personal gain is evident in ancient speeches on civic concord (for example, in Dio Chrysostom, *Or*. 34.19, 22; Aristides, *Or*. 24.5). See Margaret M. Mitchell, *Paul and the Rhetoric of Reconciliation: An Exegetical Investigation of the Language and Composition of 1 Corinthians* (HUT 28; Louisville, Ky.: Westminster/John Knox, 1991), 31–32; Dale B. Martin, *Slavery as Salvation: The Metaphor of Slavery in Pauline Christianity* (New Haven: Yale University Press, 1990), 143–144. It should be noted that this argument is also used in support of the rhetorics of unity in 1 Corinthians, as in the case of 1 Cor. 1:10 and 3:3. For more on the rhetorics of unity in 1 Corinthians and ancient civic-political discourse, see Chapter III.C above.

[49] This causal link technique could be seen as both a means-end and a fact-consequence relationship. The emphasis articulated here is on remaining for the community's benefit, which is a strong causal argument on the basis of the end. The end is too important for Paul to pursue another avenue. At the same time, the rhetorics are resolutely interested in what Paul would choose or hope to do considering these two alternatives. That he chooses to stay places a firm stress on the fact of his model action, an action positive because of the positive consequences. Bockmuehl argues that this section functions as a *synkrisis*, or comparison. See Bockmuehl, *Epistle*, 87.

differentiation). That the rhetorics of commonality are still being forwarded is highlighted not only by this community benefit argument but also by the allusion to "all of you" (*pasin hymin*, 1:25) in this section. In this case Paul's status as a model is forwarded by the interaction between person and acts, as always. However, his role as model is also marked through an appeal to argumentation by sacrifice (quasi-logical argument).[50] According to the rhetorics of these dissociative reversals, Paul sacrifices the chance to be with Christ in order to remain for the Philippian community's benefit, demonstrating the worth of Paul's actions and the community benefits (for which he acted).[51] Since this sacrifice is articulated in terms of causality (the *hina* clause and *dia* prepositional phrase in 1:26, as well as the *eis* prepositional phrase in 1:25), Paul implies that his *not* remaining might have endangered this "progress and joy" (possibly an implicit argument of waste).[52]

C. 1:27–2:4

The letter moves from these reflections upon Paul's situation to some rather direct exhortations to the community. Having already established the dissociation of division from unity (1:15ff.), the letter proposes a course of

---

[50] For more on argumentation by sacrifice, see Olbrechts-Tyteca and Perelman, *The New Rhetoric*, 248–255; and Chapter V.B.5 below. Sacrifice argumentation might also be functioning (in a less obvious way) in 1:12–14: Paul clarifies that his imprisonment (which would have involved suffering on his part) has had positive effects. In other words, his chains are worth the progress made. On the issue of Paul's mortality and the argument from his sacrifice, especially in 1:21–26, see James L. Jaquette, "A Not-So-Noble Death: Figured Speech, Friendship and Suicide in Philippians 1:21–26," *Neot* 28:1 (1994): 184–191; "Life and Death, *Adiaphora*, and Paul's Rhetorical Strategies," *NovT* 38 (1996): 33–38; and Craig S. Wansink, *Chained in Christ: The Experience and Rhetoric of Paul's Imprisonments* (JSNTSup 130; Sheffield: Sheffield Academic Press, 1996), 96–125.

[51] An argument by sacrifice can elevate the prestige of the person undergoing the sacrifice, since "the meaning of this sacrifice in the eyes of others depends on the esteem enjoyed by the person." See Olbrechts-Tyteca and Perelman, *The New Rhetoric*, 249. Sacrifice argumentation also demonstrates the relative worth of the result, since someone is willing to sacrifice for it. See Olbrechts-Tyteca and Perelman, *The New Rhetoric*, 248. On the theme of suffering as it relates to this passage, see Bloomquist, *Function*, 152–157. On suffering as a central theme in the letter, see Nikolaus Walter, "Die Philipper und das Leiden: Aus den Anfängen einer heidenchristlichen Gemeinde," in *Die Kirche des Anfangs: Für Heinz Schümann zum 65. Geburtstag* (ed. Rudolf Schnackenburg, Joseph Ernst, and Joachim Wanke; ETS 38; Freiburg: Herder, 1978), 417–433; Bloomquist, *Function*; Peter S. Oakes, *Philippians: From People to Letter* (SNTSMS 110; Cambridge: Cambridge University Press, 2001), 77–102.

[52] Scholars interested in military imagery have identified the theme of steadfastness here. See Geoffrion, *Rhetorical Purpose*, 59; Reimer, "'Our Citizenship,'" 190; Schuster, "Rhetorical Situation," 58, 62.

action that will best achieve this unity: participating as citizens worthy of the gospel (1:27).[53] Paul proposes a causal link (*hina* clause, in 1:27, but extending through 1:30) that defines *politeuesthe* in terms of being unified "in one spirit, contending together with one mind" (*en heni pneumati, mia psychō synathlountes*, 1:27).[54] While the argument links these actions based on an appeal to commonality, these appeals are made from and for the benefit of Paul's own perspective. The purpose of the community "living as citizens" in this way is so that Paul might hear (*akouō ta peri hymōn*, 1:27) they are acting in terms of this "oneness" he is advocating. The rhetorics stress that it is Paul who seeks this result ("whether coming and seeing you or being away," 1:27), and defines Paul's hearing as sufficient motivation for the community at Philippi to take up the exhortations.[55] That their common attitude or action is primarily connected to Paul's own conception of an appropriate attitude is confirmed by the later expectation that they would have "the same fight" (*ton auton agōna*, 1:30) as Paul's ("in me" twice in 1:30). The argument by causal link posits that following Paul's agenda (rhetorics of differentiation) will lead to a beneficent unity and oneness in the community (rhetorics of commonality).

---

[53] How to live as a citizen of a *polis* (*politeuesthe*) is a common topic in concord speeches. See L. L. Welborn, *Politics and Rhetoric in the Corinthian Epistles* (Macon, GA: Mercer University Press, 1997), 72–73; Dale B. Martin, *The Corinthian Body* (New Haven: Yale University Press, 1995), 39–41; Bruno Blumenfeld, *The Political Paul: Justice, Democracy and Kingship in a Hellenistic Framework* (JSNTSup 210; London: Sheffield Academic Press, 2001), 182, 293–295. 1:27–30 in particular is important for scholars interested in military images. See Krentz, "Military Language," 113; Geoffrion, *Rhetorical Purpose*, 25, 35–82; Reimer, "'Our Citizenship,'"136; Krentz, "Paul," 355, 359–360. Here they follow Duane F. Watson, in identifying 1:27–30 as the letter's *narratio*, see Watson, "A Rhetorical Analysis of Philippians and Its Implications for the Unity Question," *NovT* 30:1 (1988): 60, 65–67.

[54] On the use of such unity language in military situations, see Portefaix, *Sisters*, 140; Krentz, "Military Language," 120; Geoffrion, *Rhetorical Purpose*, 60–61; Reimer, "'Our Citizenship,'" 147–149; Schuster, "Rhetorical Situation," 79–81; Craig S. De Vos, *Church and Community Conflicts: The Relationship of the Thessalonian, Corinthian, and Philippian Churches with Their Wider Civic Communities* (SBLDS 168; Atlanta: Scholars, 1999), 277–278. For the place of *mia psychō* in friendship language, see Fitzgerald, "Philippians," 144–145; White, "Morality," 211; Stowers, "Friends," 112; Abraham J. Malherbe, "Paul's Self-Sufficiency (Philippians 4:11)," in *Friendship, Flattery and Frankness of Speech*, 127; Fitzgerald, "Paul," 327, 332.

[55] Such an argument makes clear that the analysis of the argumentation in the letter must do more than simply identify the imagery (whether military, ancient friendship, or civic-political), it should also recognize the implications of the argument, especially as it contributes to a developing picture of the power relations of these rhetorics. Here preceding scholarship has stopped short, failing to recognize how the rhetorics construct a preeminent role for Paul through such argumentation.

This initial look at the exhortations to unity in attitude and purpose is far from completing an understanding of the argumentative techniques functioning in this dense and lengthy sentence (1:27–30). Introducing the subject of opponents and their potential fate (1:28) at this point in the argument emphasizes the advisability (in an almost threatening manner) of following the course the letter is attempting to propose.[56] The letter evokes a series of dissociations in differentiating between the opponents (*antikeimenōn*, 1:28) and the community members at Philippi.[57] While the former will receive destruction (*apōleias*), the latter will have safety or salvation (*sōtōrias*, 1:28). Thus, there is an additional causal link tying the contrast (opponents/Philippians) to this first dissociation (destruction/salvation): if the Philippians follow the proper course of unity, they will be safe, while those who are opposed, will not (an end-oriented causal link argument). While it is from God (*apo theou*, 1:28) that the Philippians will receive protection, the opponents will, by implication, only have the fruitless protection of their human devices (human/divine dissociation).[58] Perhaps, this statement is itself meant to propose an appearance/reality dissociation in regard to these opponents, who probably did not anticipate divine condemnation. The divine aspect gives the dissociation added force, as mentioned above, since the best way to enhance an argument from authority is to make it from the ultimate authority.[59] Thus, the letter presents another anti-model (rhetorics of differentiation) for the Philippians not to follow, while continuing its rhetorics of commonality.

The imperative that begins this sentence (*politeuesthe*, 1:27), then, is linked causally as both a positive course of action to be followed and a sign (*endeixis*, 1:28) of the negative result for those opposed. While the specter of opponents and destruction might be functioning as a not-so-veiled threat, it might also be

---

[56] Olbrechts-Tyteca and Perelman write that "[r]ecourse to argumentation assumes the establishment of a community of minds, which, while it lasts, excludes the use of violence." See Olbrechts-Tyteca and Perelman, *The New Rhetoric*, 55. There is an extent to which, then, that rhetoric implies either an unwillingness to use or an alternative to force. For more on violence and argumentation, see Olbrechts-Tyteca and Perelman, *The New Rhetoric*, 54–59.

[57] This description of "those who stand against/opposite" (*antikeimenōn*, 1:28) does not explicitly name against whom they are standing. Since they are being used in a contrast with the community at Philippi, it is typically assumed that they are seen as the opponents of the Philippian community. However, the lingering focus on Paul and his exhortations to a certain kind of unity within this section leaves open the possibility that this participle can be read as "those who stand opposite/against me (Paul)." This description of opposition is also a great aid to the arguments and vibrant descriptions of the military scholars.

[58] For an example of the tradition behind the human/divine dissociation, see Table II in Olbrechts-Tyteca and Perelman, *The New Rhetoric*, 421.

[59] On the "extreme case" of divine authority in an argument, see Olbrechts-Tyteca and Perelman, *The New Rhetoric*, 308–309; and Chapter V.C.4 below.

viewed as an argument from waste. The letter is attempting to demonstrate what would be lost if one were to become like "those opposed," reinforcing the strong encouragement to not be a waste, to not be afraid, by following the course set out by Paul. The argumentation is nuanced in this sentence, though, finessing the important difference between the threat of destruction (1:27–28) and the expectation of suffering (*paschein*, 1:29–30). The same God who insures safety (1:28) is (presumably) also the one granting that the community members should suffer (1:29). That they do so "on behalf of Christ" (1:29) could be seen as an argument from sacrifice. Their suffering may be seen as a worthy sacrifice for what they gain by acting for Christ (and potentially for what they avoid, the aforementioned destruction). The presence of this argumentative technique seems even more likely, since they are said to share the same struggle with Paul (1:30), to whom this kind of argument has already been applied in the letter (1:24–26). Though indirectly, Paul has again been presented as a model for the audience (rhetorics of differentiation), even as they are exhorted to act as one and join him (rhetorics of commonality).

With these dissociations, results, and models still fresh, the letter proceeds to another lengthy and convoluted imperatival sentence. In this section the importance of sameness is particularly emphasized with regard to the state of mind of the community. First, the characteristics of a unified community, such as encouragement and communal sharing (*koinōnia*), are specifically linked with figures such as Christ and the spirit (2:1), perhaps again to emphasize the divine privileging of these relations in contrast to human ones (the above-mentioned human/divine dissociation).[60] These characteristics are conditional preludes (four *ei* clauses in 2:1) to the task Paul seeks from the audience: completing his joy (*plērōsate mou tōn charan*, 2:2). Just as the preceding sentence was concerned with Paul hearing of certain results in the Philippian community, this sentence implores the community to act in order to bring about Paul's joy. Indeed, all of the clauses within 2:1–4 are dependent upon this imperative: the conditionals preceding it as well as the compound *hina* clause governing the remainder of 2:2–4. The imperatival clause is at the center of two causal links. The letter argues that if the community members have any of the listed virtues (2:1), they will be able to fulfill Paul's joy. To do so, though, they should act in accordance with densely packed expressions of unity in the following verse: "in order that you might think the same thing, having the same love, sharing (or

---

[60] Because of the reference to the "spirit," some commentators make an unlikely connection between this exhortation and trinitarian theological concepts. See, for example, Ben Witherington III, *Friendship and Finances in Philippi: The Letter of Paul to the Philippians* (The New Testament in Context; Valley Forge, Penn.: Trinity Press International, 1994), 61–62; Gordon D. Fee, *Philippians* (IVP New Testament Commentary Series; Downers Grove, Ill.: Intervarsity Press, 1999), 83.

together) in spirit, thinking the one thing" (*hina to auto phronōte, tōn autōn agapōn echontes, sympsychoi, to hen phronountes*, 2:2).[61]

The doubled use of the verb *phroneo* here in 2:2 and in the direct exhortation in 2:5 ("Think (*phroneite*) the same thing amongst yourselves, which [is] also in Christ Jesus") is striking, especially when considering the role the same term played earlier in 1:7's initial modeling of Paul. This particular emphasis on frame of mind suggests that it is one potential source of consternation and contrast for Paul and/or the audience. The letter seems to suggest that, sharing the same fight (1:30), Paul wishes the community would also share his way of thinking (1:7; 2:2ff.), evoking as an implicit foundation another potential contrast between (at least some) members of the community and Paul (1:15–18, 28–30). This connection enriches the resonance of these appeals to commonality in the background of previous dissociations of division from unity.

The completion of Paul's joy in this section is not only linked to these expressions of commonality and sameness. By exhorting the audience to not act according to contentiousness (*mōden kat' eritheian*, 2:3), the letter recalls the previous issue of difference and divisiveness as described by Paul (*erin*, 1:15; *eritheias*, 1:17). In addition, the letter weaves in another element from previous argumentation, the dissociation of self- from community-benefit (1:24–26), by encouraging the Philippians to put the interests of others (*allōlous*, 2:3; *ta heterōn*, 2:4) ahead of their own (*mō ta heautōn*, 2:4).[62] Since both of these arguments play upon elements already articulated in the letter, they also reinforce the actions and authority of the person who first responded to them: Paul. Paul offered himself as a model of how to respond to divisions (1:15–18) and how to act in terms of community benefit (1:24–26). That these actions take after the model of Paul in the letter only strengthens the possibility, then, that exhortations for a common frame of mind (2:1–2) should also be following Paul. Because the letter started early in its argument that Paul can define the right way to think (or feel, *phronein*, 1:7) about them, the call to "think the same thing" (2:2), accompanied by actions already modeled by Paul, could also be read as an instruction for the community to think the same thing *as Paul*.[63]

---

[61] This phrase has been highlighted by scholars interested in friendship imagery within Philippians. See Fitzgerald, "Philippians, "144–146; Malherbe, "Paul's Self-Sufficiency," 127. What is missing from these observations, however, is a recognition of this argument's relevance for structuring the relationship between Paul and the audience. Namely, the unity of this bond (whether it is "friendship" or not) is for the fulfillment of Paul's own joy.

[62] The self-benefit/community-benefit dissociation (as in 2:3–4) could also be linked to an argument by sacrifice, since Paul is attempting to argue that putting other's interests first will result in a certain kind of unity and closeness to Christ. Paul is trying to argue that their sacrifice will be worth this result.

[63] Following the possibility of an argument by sacrifice (as in the note above) also reinforces the possibility that the instructions are concerned with conformity with Paul's

D. 2:5-18

Though the argumentation shifts here to incorporate the hymn (2:6–11), it builds upon and continues many of the argumentative techniques in the immediately preceding section(s). The continuing concern with frame of mind in the transition to the hymn (2:5; cf. 2:2; 1:7) demonstrates this clearly enough. Since it is held that Paul is drawing upon a hymnic source in this instance, one can argue that the hymn functions rhetorically as an argument from a tradition (argument based on the structure of reality)[64] which would have presumably carried some type of authority or relevance to the audience. The introductory words immediately preceding the hymn (2:5) help to determine the manner with which the hymn should be taken: as an instance of how to imitate Christ (argument from a model, establishing the structure of reality).[65] That this introduction alludes to imitation can be shown by its utilization of the principle of transitivity (a quasi-logical argument). The Philippians are told to have a certain mindset (*touto phronein en hymin*), which is also in Christ (*ho kai en Christou*, 2:5). Given the relations between *a* (the Philippians) and *b* (this way of thinking) and between *b* (this way of thinking) and *c* (Christ), the Philippians

---

point of view, since the only other figure involved in an argument by sacrifice thus far was Paul (1:21–26, possibly also 1:12–14).

[64] While argument from a tradition is not a verbatim term from Olbrechts-Tyteca and Perelman, it still makes for an excellent fit with the goals of arguments based on the structure of reality, since they "make use of this structure to establish a solidarity between accepted judgments and others which one wishes to promote." See Olbrechts-Tyteca and Perelman, *The New Rhetoric*, 261. The section on the argument from authority is in Olbrechts-Tyteca and Perelman, *The New Rhetoric*, 305–310. For more examples of adaptation or expansion of arguments based on the structure of reality, see Wire, *The Corinthian Women Prophets*, 28–35. See also Chapter V.C.6 below.

[65] In contradistinction to many readings of Philippians (such as Watson, "A Rhetorical Analysis," 64, 67–72; Bloomquist, *Function*, 173–178; Geoffrion, *Rhetorical Purpose*, 125–146), this study envisions the following figures (Christ, Timothy and Epaphroditus) as not merely examples but as models, because of the imitative element of their rhetorical implementation in the letter. The long-standing debate about how to interpret the hymn involves whether or not to view the hymn as possible of imitation. Those readings that reject the hymn as a model for the audience to imitate do so primarily on theological, rather than rhetorical grounds. See Ernst Lohmeyer, *Kyrios Jesus: Eine Untersuchung zu Phil. 2, 5–11* (SHAW Philosophisch-historische Klasse. Jahrgang 1927/28; 4. Abhandllung; Darmstadt: Wissenschaftliche Buchgesellschaft, 1961 [1928]); Ernst Käsemann, "A Critical Analysis of Philippians 2:5–11," *JTC* 5 (1968): 45–68. On Lohmeyer and Käsemann, and more recent discussion of the hymn, see *Where Christology Began: Essays on Philippians 2* (ed. Ralph P. Martin and Brian J. Dodd; Louisville, Ky.: Westminster John Knox Press, 1998).

(*a*) are in relationship to Christ (*c*) via a certain way of thinking (*b*).[66] The subject of this mind-set has already been shown to be a central one for this letter's argumentation and will continue to be so, as its content is further explicated in the hymn (2:6–11) and the application following it (2:12–18).

The arc of the hymn, whereby Christ became human and humbled himself (2:6–8) only to later be exalted by God (2:9–11), plays upon the human/divine dissociation in order to show the remarkable extent of his obedience (*hypōkoos*, 2:8).[67] This dissociation is also linked to an appearance/reality dissociation. Since Christ shares in the divine realm by "being in the form of God" (2:6), the "taking the form of a slave" as a human (2:7) is not the final reality about Christ. The latter half of the hymn (2:9–11) only reinforces this dissociation by way of arguments by causal link. Because Christ humbled himself and became obedient (2:8), God exalts Christ (2:9; see *dio*, "therefore," linking 2:8 and 2:9). The further effects of this action are important to clarify, so as to note to what end this hymn portrays God as exalting Christ. As part of this exaltation, Christ is given (by God) "a name above every name" (2:9), effectively combining both commonality rhetorics (all or every) with differentiation rhetorics (above or over).[68] This rhetorical combination continues in the following result clause (*hina*, 2:10), since this name of Jesus will culminate in *every* knee bowing on all three cosmic plains (2:10) in acknowledgment of his lordship (*kyrios*, 2:11).[69] Since the argument includes the entire cosmos, this inclusive-styled rhetoric works simply to subordinate all under a figure described in terms of exclusive rule.

Even as the hymn attempts to argue for these results, it also points to the imitation (see 2:5) of the figure at the heart of these dissociations and argument links (Christ, as mentioned above). Recall that the actions of Christ that spurred

---

[66] For more on the argument by transitivity, and its relation to syllogistic reasoning (familiar to classical Greco-Roman rhetoricians as the enthymeme and the epicheirema), see Olbrechts-Tyteca and Perelman, *The New Rhetoric*, 227–231.

[67] The topic and rhetorical use of obedience is the major focus of Kittredge's interpretation of Philippians. For the rhetorical function of the hymn, see Kittredge, *Community*, 77–86.

[68] This and the following argument makes it clear that the rhetorics of obedience and friendship overlap and interact with each other, reinforcing the hierarchical ends toward which both work.

[69] That *kyrios* is the word at the root of the feminist analytical neologism "kyriarchy," used to describe the multiple oppressions functioning together in antiquity (as well as today), calls attention to a continuing need to address any confession or acknowledgement of a *kyrios* (now traditional for Jesus as well as, more generally, God) as something hostile (rather than liberating) to those disempowered by kyriarchal structures.

these effects were his humility and obedience (2:8).[70] As before with Paul (1:21–26), this model figure's obedience is also linked to mortal risk, highlighted by the clarifying repetition of *thanatou* in 2:8.[71] This emphasis on death also indicates an argument by sacrifice: demonstrating what Christ gave up to become human.[72] To the extent that Christ is depicted as sharing in the divine (*morphō theou*, 2:6; the regal imagery of 2:9–11),[73] the model status and quality intensifies: "The attribution of good qualities to superior beings makes it possible, if it is accepted, to argue from the model, and, if it is challenged, to enhance the value of the quality as being at least worthy of attribution to the model."[74] By arguing from a divine model, the letter combines the strength of arguments from a model with the argument from authority. As presented in the hymn, the model of Christ in obedience, deathly risk, and sacrificial willingness echoes similar qualities previously extolled through the model of Paul (1:21–26).

Just as the section introducing the hymn helps to determine its utility in the argumentation, the exhortations immediately following also reveal the direction of the rhetoric of modeling. The matter of how to apply the model of Christ to

---

[70] Humility and obedience would be virtues in a military situation. See Geoffrion, *Rhetorical Purpose*, 41, 134–140; Reimer, "'Our Citizenship,'" 197–199; De Vos, *Church and Community Conflicts*, 280–281; Krentz, "Paul," 356.

[71] On the possibility that Paul might have inserted the *thanatou de staurou* clause into the hymn, first suggested by Ernst Lohmeyer, see Ralph P. Martin, *Carmen Christi: Philippians 2:5–11 in Recent Interpretation and in the Setting of Early Christian Worship* (repr.; SNTSMS 4; Grand Rapids, Mich.: Eerdmans, 1983), 36–37, 220; and Charles J. Robbins, "Rhetorical Structure of Philippians 2:6–11" *CBQ* 42 (1980): 73–82.

[72] For the role of sacrifice in ancient friendship, see Stowers, "Friends," 119; White, "Morality," 213; Jaquette, "A Not-So-Noble Death," 185.

[73] It is here that this study parts ways with the analysis of the hymn offered by Kittredge and other feminist scholars. See Kittredge, *Community*, 99–100, 110; Luise Schottroff, *Lydia's Impatient Sisters: A Feminist Social History of Early Christianity* (trans. Barbara and Martin Rumscheidt; Louisville, Ky.: Westminster John Knox, 1995), 43–46. Though the hymn might have offered a pattern of reversal as a hope to those oppressed in various ways by the kyriarchal culture, its imagery and vocabulary are still embedded in this kyriarchal matrix of slave-master (2:7) and subject-ruler (2:9–11). For a similar assertion about the kyriocentric nature of this text, see Sheila Briggs, "Can an Enslaved God Liberate? Hermeneutical Reflections on Philippians 2:6–11," *Semeia* 47 (1989): 137–153. This analysis of the rhetoric also leads to the difference seen in the relationship between the respective rhetorical tendencies. While Kittredge sees a "discontinuity between the language of friendship and the language of obedience" (*Community*, 110), this study attempts to demonstrate how the rhetorics of commonality often cross paths and work with the rhetorics of differentiation in the letter.

[74] Olbrechts-Tyteca and Perelman, *The New Rhetoric*, 365. For more on the divine as a model, see Olbrechts-Tyteca and Perelman, *The New Rhetoric*, 368–371; and Chapter V.D.2 below.

the Philippian community is settled by the immediate connection ("therefore," *hōste*) to acting obediently (*hypōkousate*, 2:12).[75] It is this quality of obedience that is to be imitated, whether Paul is present or not. The issue of Paul's presence in relation to their obedience suggests that Paul could be the figure they are expected to obey.[76] The continuing expressions of Paul's model status, as well as the importance of holding in common certain views, confirm this suggestion as a suitable working presumption, but the study of the letter's rhetoric should still look for means to confirm or refute this working hypothesis.

The combination of inclusion and submission noted in the hymn continues in this exhortation, since the audience should act "just as you have always obeyed" (2:12). By alluding to what is assumed to be previous practice and highlighting their safety (*tōn heautōn sōtōrian*, 2:12) as their stake in this obedience, an argument from waste is developed. If the audience has already been obedient, they should continue to live accordingly, if only to preserve what their obedience was to insure. Obedience may not be entirely pleasant, no matter to whom it is due, since the audience is encouraged to act "with fear and trembling" (2:12). Calling for obedience in terms of acting with fear while keeping safe, then, might be re-invoking previous dissociations between destruction (*apōleia*) and safety (*sōtōria*, see 1:28). Thus, if obedience in this case should lead to safety, it remains implicit (especially when considering "fear and trembling") that disobedience would lead to danger or destruction.[77] That

---

[75] Kittredge, *Community*, 83–86. Kittredge clearly and convincingly demonstrates this point, one of the inventive strengths of her study.

[76] The analysis of the letter with military and friendship imagery would be demonstrably affected by such observations about the letter's argumentation. If scholars interested in military images would more fully acknowledge the authoritarian role of Paul in Philippians, their analysis would become more comprehensive. If scholars interested in friendship imagery grappled with this argument, they would be required to assess how submission and obedience are a part of ancient friendship.

[77] Instances of rhetorical interactivity such as these demonstrate the need for a reevaluation of Paul's role in the argumentation as authority. Where admitted in scholarship on the letter, the authority of Paul is often mitigated or qualified, particularly as a "limited authority figure." Geoffrion repeatedly emphasizes this conception of Paul. See Geoffrion, *Rhetorical Purpose*, 85, 100–104. Here he is following the thought of Wayne A. Meeks (among others) who see Paul as being "suggestive rather than prescriptive." See Meeks, *The First Urban Christians: The Social World of the Apostle Paul* (New Haven: Yale University Press, 1983), 139 (whom Geoffrion cites approvingly in this section). Stowers maintains that Paul is playing the role of "community psychagogue," preparing them for God, while Fitzgerald labels Paul "a paradigm of virtuous friendship." See Stowers, "Friends," 118; Fitzgerald, "Philippians," 155. For a similarly defensive view of Paul's modeling, see Frederick W. Weidmann, "An (Un)Accomplished Model: Paul and the Rhetorical Strategy of Philippians 3:3–17," in *Putting Body and Soul Together: Essays in Honor of Robin Scroggs* (ed. Virginia Wiles, Alexandra Brown, and Graydon F. Snyder; Valley Forge, Penn.: Trinity Press International, 1997), 245–257; Andrew D. Clarke, "'Be Imitators of Me': Paul's Model

the relationship to be imitated here between the authority and the obedient ones is a hierarchical relationship is only further underlined by the description of Christ's model obedience in becoming human as "taking the form of a slave" (*morphōn doulou*, 2:7). Thus, the human obedience expected in these circumstances (2:8, 12) could be seen as compulsory, as in the slave/master relationship.[78] Since God is described as present in these efforts at obedience (2:13), the differentiated relationship receives support by argument from divine authority. The establishment and maintenance of this hierarchical relationship is for God's pleasure or goodwill (*hyper tēs eudokias*, 2:13), just as preceding arguments were linked with God's glory (Paul's prayer, 1:11; Jesus' kyriarchal status, 2:11).

The likelihood that this obedience is due to Paul is bolstered by the immediately following direct address (or order) for the community to "do everything without grumbling or questioning" (2:14). The address assumes a relationship of authority and obedience between Paul and the audience (differentiation), seeking for them to universally (*panta*) apply their obedience, united in their lack of dissent (commonality). The purpose of this address is made clear by the results to come (causal link arguments, *hina* clause, beginning in 2:15; *hoti* clause in 2:16). The differentiation between "the crooked and twisted generation" and the Philippians' potential to be "children of God" (2:15) highlight the possible benefits of (and reason for) their obedience.[79] While their obedience could lead to this benefit, it is also primarily oriented towards another result: Paul's own ability to boast (*eis kauchēma moi*, 2:16). Since the content of this boast would be whether Paul's work was in vain (2:16), it also functions as an argument from waste, showing how hard the letter is working in trying to

---

of Leadership," *Tyndale Bulletin* 49 (1998): 329–360. Weidmann's article is, in part, in response to Robert T. Fortna, "Philippians: Paul's Most Egocentric Letter," in *The Conversation Continues: Festschrift for J. Louis Martyn* (ed. Robert T. Fortna and Beverly R. Gaventa; Nashville: Abingdon, 1990), 220–234.

[78] The dynamic between slave and master (often, *kyrios*) is governed in terms of the slavery/freedom dissociation, a traditional philosophical dissociation, as shown for example in Table III in Olbrechts-Tyteca and Perelman, *The New Rhetoric*, 421. On the connection between "fear and trembling" and the obedience of slaves in the Pauline corpus, see Carolyn Osiek, *Philippians, Philemon* (ANTC; Nashville: Abingdon Press, 2000), 70.

[79] Though being designated as "children of God" would be seen as a positive association with the divine, it should also not obscure the unmistakable hierarchical element entailed in the parent-child relationship in the ancient world. As such, the kyriarchal relational description is not a denial of the oppressive dynamic of patriarchal ("fatherly") relations, but an inclusion of this oppressive dynamic as interacting with and reinforcing other oppressive relationships or structures. On the non-affectionate, mostly hierarchical nature of ancient parent-child (especially father-child) relations, see Wire, *The Corinthian Women Prophets*, 45–47; Castelli, *Imitating Paul*, 99–102.

elicit responses of obedience from the audience.[80] Acting disobediently would waste not only the community's previous efforts (as argued above, for 2:12) but also Paul's own work (*ekopiasa*, 2:16).

By characterizing this effort on Paul's part as a "sacrifice and service" (*tō thusia kai leitourgia*, 2:17) for them, the letter's argumentation repeats previous strategies regarding Paul. Paul's repeated willingness to face death (here, as in 1:21–26) demonstrates a continuing argument from a model, only intensified by its similarity to Christ in the preceding hymn (2:8). That this death would be "for their loyalty/faith" recalls the dissociation of self- from community-benefit (1:25–26; 2:3–4) and rather explicitly an argument by sacrifice. The dissociations start to coalesce: division/unity are linked to obedience (the Philippians as slaves to Paul the master) through a destruction/safety dissociation. The self-benefit/community benefit dissociation supports Paul as a model in the argumentation, accompanied by an allusion to a vague group of anti-models ("crooked and perverse generation," 2:15). Even as the argument seeks obedient adherence to Paul's model, it also encourages the Philippians to rejoice with him (*synchairete*) in the same thing (*to auto*, 2:18). The doubled exhortation to co-rejoicing (2:17 and 2:18) delineates how the community should act in terms of Paul's actions, creating an argument based on the relationship between a group and its members. Paul is attempting to argue that behavior of one member (himself) should define how the group behaves. Even when alluding to a joyfully united attitude (commonality rhetorics), this letter appeals to the authority of the Pauline model (differentiation rhetorics).

E. 2:19–30

The remainder of the second chapter affords Paul the opportunity to present additional models for the Philippians to follow. Multiple models can forward the goals of argumentation, for: "Close adherence to a recognized model guarantees the value of the behavior. The person following the model enjoys an enhanced value, and can thus, in turn, serve as a model."[81] Before describing Timothy as a model, the letter offers the particular reason why he is being sent to Philippi through a causal link statement. Paul wants to send Timothy so that (*hina* clause) Paul might be happy (or pleased in mind/soul, *eupsychō*, 2:19), knowing about the community. Just as the community members were previously exhorted to respond in obedience for a result in terms of Paul's own boasting (2:14–16)

---

[80] Osiek highlights how Paul seems "manipulative" here: "if the Philippians do what he wants, he will be honored by Christ. If not, his honor is at risk—and it will be their fault." See Osiek, *Philippians*, 72.

[81] Olbrechts-Tyteca and Perelman, *The New Rhetoric*, 364. The recognition of more than one model as an argumentative technique also reflects the principle at work behind an argument by transitivity.

and joy (2:17–18), the dispatching of Timothy is also articulated as producing a result relative to Paul's positive reaction.

Paul's desire to send Timothy gives him a chance to extol Timothy's qualities in a two-fold manner. First of all, the letter maintains that Paul has no one "of similar mind/soul" (*isopsychon*, 2:20),[82] showing that Timothy aligns with the model of Paul in this important sense (see 1:7, 27; 2:1–5). Secondly, Timothy feels appropriately about the community (2:20), very much in keeping with the previous dissociation of self-benefit/community benefit (1:21–26; 2:3–4, 17). As has been the letter's practice thus far (1:15–17, 28; 2:14–16), Timothy's status is also contrasted with another party (an unspecified anti-model): those who "seek their own things" (2:21). Though he serves as a model of community benefit, the letter is careful to clearly state Timothy's relationship to Paul as an analogy in hierarchical terms, "as a child to a father" (2:22).[83] As in the opening words of the letter (where he is named as a co-sender, 1:1), Timothy is here again described as "serving" (*edouleusen*, 2:22). While recalling this initial designation, the verb also links him with the only other figure described as a slave or servant, Christ (2:7), strengthening the authority of his model in the letter. That Paul chose to describe yet another model with such terms (in just a brief span) increases the impression that the letter is seeking just such a subordinate obedience from its audience. In fact, it is these qualities (serving, being Paul's "child") that are most immediately connected (*oun*, "therefore," 2:23) to Paul's expression of hope for sending Timothy. While the dispatch of Timothy is important, it is still primarily linked to Paul's own welfare. As a note here (*aphidō ta peri eme*, 2:23), it is a brief reminder of Paul's status as a model because of his own efforts (1:12–14) and sacrifice (1:24–26; 2:17) on the community's behalf.

Epaphroditus is also doubly qualified in his role as model for the Philippians. Epaphroditus not only cared deeply for the community (2:26), but he had also shown a courageous dedication in the face of a potentially fatal illness (2:26–27, 30). Indeed, it is these two factors that are raised in establishing two causal links for why Paul is sending Epaphroditus. First, Paul finds it necessary to send him because (*epeidō*, 2:26) he had been longing for "all of you" (*pantas hymas*, 2:26), demonstrating a concern (that echoes Paul's own) with *all* of the community. Second, Epaphroditus yearns because of this common concern and "because you heard that he was sick" (*dioti* clause, 2:26). The seriousness with which his illness is described only heightens Epaphroditus'

---

[82] Here Timothy is tied to Paul in language reminiscent of ancient friendship imagery. See Fitzgerald, "Philippians," 144–145.
[83] On the non-affectionate, mostly hierarchical nature of ancient parent-child relations, see n. 79 above. For more on the argument by analogy (an argument establishing the structure of reality), see Olbrechts-Tyteca and Perelman, *The New Rhetoric*, 371–398.

status as a model, given what he endured to be their messenger (*hymōn apostolon*, 2:25) (an argument by sacrifice). Twice in this brief description Paul notes how close Epaphroditus came to dying (2:27, 30), the second occasion using the same phrase that described Christ's obedience, *mechri thanatou* ("up to/as far as death," 2:8, 30).

Epaphroditus' recovery from this grave illness is seen as a relief not only for Epaphroditus, but also for Paul (2:27). Paul's relief is not a throw-away note, though, as it again focuses the arguments around Paul's point of view. God's mercy prevents Paul's sorrow from being further compounded (in a negative result clause, *hina mō*, 2:27).[84] Just as Epaphroditus' recovery relieved Epaphroditus *and Paul* (2:27), Epaphroditus' return is doubly linked (*hina* clause) to positive reactions for the Philippian community members (joy) *and Paul* (less anxiety) (2:28). The occasion of Epaphroditus' illness and travels are used for the additional purpose of giving a generalized exhortation to treat "such people as honored" (*tous toioutous entimous*, 2:29) who risk their lives; an exhortation which could easily apply to Paul's own case as well as Epaphroditus'. Thus, the description of Epaphroditus brings him close to the models of Christ and Paul in his mortal risk (1:20–26; 2:8, 17) as well as shows a quality, like the one shared by Timothy and Paul (1:21–26; 2:3–4, 16–18, 20), based on the repeated dissociation of self-benefit from community benefit. Though he is a brother, co-worker and "co-soldier" (2:25) with Paul, Epaphroditus (like Timothy in 2:19, 23) can still be sent (2:25, 28) by Paul.

In the cases of both Timothy and Epaphroditus, the letter is establishing them as models and, in turn, arguing from their model status. Yet, it appears that Paul cannot leave off with simply arguing from a model, but in each case he reintroduces himself as a model.[85] The argumentation demonstrates that their model status is dependent upon and is, in a way, less significant than the model of Paul. At this point in the letter's evolving rhetorics, in order to accept Timothy and Epaphroditus as models, the audience must first accept the model qualities already defined by the character of Paul as a model: risking one's life and valuing community-benefit over self-benefit. Having established Paul as the

---

[84] As the closing notes about Timothy did above, these notes about Paul's relief and anxiety are possibly meant to remind the audience of Paul's imprisonment conditions, and his own model sacrificial actions. Attributing the prevention of Paul's sorrow to God gives further weight to the repeated calls for joy: since God does not want Paul to be unhappy, the community is implicitly enjoined to prevent Paul's sorrow or unhappiness. The added force from the divine authority presents the options in a greater argumentative contrast: if the Philippians fail (or refuse?) to bring about Paul's joy, they risk being on the opposite side of God.

[85] These connections between Paul, Timothy and Epaphroditus as models further demonstrate how much the principle of transitivity interacts with argumentation through modeling when there is more than one model at work rhetorically. Dodd notes that Paul uses the first singular adjective or pronoun more than 50 times in this letter. See Dodd, *Paul's Paradigmatic "I"*, 171.

prototype for these qualities, Christ's model reinforces the value of mortal risk, while introducing the additional quality of obedience, immediately applied in the letter's argumentation (2:8, 12). Though this call for obedience has yet to be applied to Paul, it potentially lies behind the descriptions of Timothy and Epaphroditus, especially as they are subject to Paul's instructions for travel (2:19, 23, 25, 28).

F. 3:1–11

Having presented a number of models hierarchically differentiated from Paul's model, the letter focuses with greater attention upon the character of its author. Though the reference made to writing them "the same things" (3:1) has been inferred to mean some previous form of correspondence, it can also be read as a brief apologia for continuing in the same rhetorical vein as the arguments thus far.[86] The topic of these "same things" is not a departure, but a continuation of some of the already-noted argumentative techniques. In describing writing these things as "not troubling for me, but safe for you" (3:1), Paul is hearkening again to the dissociation between self- and community-benefit. By defining the task at hand in terms of the community, the rhetorics display Paul's model care for them. In mentioning their safety (*asphales*, 3:1), the letter might also be alluding to the destruction/safety dissociation (1:28; cf. 2:12) as a way to highlight the stakes of their acceptance of these "same things" written by Paul. Following this note the letter gives a three-fold admonition to look out for "dogs . . . evil workers . . . the mutilation" (3:2); however, the passage does not seem so much to be "about" these potential dangers or opponents.[87] Paul quickly provides an emphatic contrast, in particular to "the mutilation" (*katatomō*): "For we ourselves are the circumcision" (*ōmeis gar esmen hō peritomō*, 3:3). Not only does Paul differentiate on this basis, but he also draws upon a classic dissociation between the flesh and the spirit in order to specify to and in whom

---

[86] For those scholars who hold to one of several partition theories for this letter, this verse was most frequently seen as a "hinge" or indicator of the composite nature of the letter. See also the notes on the letter's integrity in Chapter I above.

[87] The convoluted and much-debated topic of the identity of the "opponents" of Phil 3 is far too large and nuanced to do justice to in this discussion. The lack of consensus and multiple suggestions simply do not allow for an easy summary. For a thorough treatment of the issues surrounding opponents in Paul's letters, including at least eighteen different scholarly suggestions as to their identity in Philippians, see John J. Gunther, *St. Paul's Opponents and Their Background: A Study of Apocalyptic and Jewish Sectarian Teachings* (NovTSup 35; Leiden: Brill, 1973).

"we" worship and have confidence (3:3).[88] In order to think through what would constitute the views of a unified (and safe) community, Paul again gives voice to an anti-model in order to proceed by means of contrast.[89]

Yet, because Paul is an opportunistic rhetor, the matter of flesh is used as a departure for another demonstration of his model character. Drawing upon the appearance/reality dissociation, Paul gives a full listing (3:5–6) of how he *really* has more reason to boast in the flesh than any other, especially in terms of his ethnic, cultic and political identities (3:4–6). Yet, it is with this same dissociation that Paul also turns these sources of confidence on their ear (3:7ff.), privileging faith over the law in a new dissociation (3:9). The cause for this reversal is repeatedly stated in terms of Paul's relationship to Christ: "because of Christ" (3:7), "because of the surpassing value of the knowledge of Christ Jesus" (3:8), "in order that I might gain Christ" (3:8). With Christ as the cause, Paul is willing to lose all the things that gave him this status (3:7–8), demonstrating (through an argument by sacrifice) the value he places on his relationship to Christ.

It is in giving up this status that Paul attempts to parallel his own life with the arc of the hymn he presented a chapter earlier.[90] Christ is not only the cause but also a figure capable to be joined or imitated. Paul maintains that he suffered because of Christ, but also because he aimed to have a "share in his suffering, becoming like him in his death" (*koinōnian [tōn] pathōmatōn, symmorphizomenos tō thanatō autou,* 3:10) (causal link as a part of the consecutive infinitive clause, rendered as a result clause). Here the rhetorics of commonality are implemented in an attempt to move Paul closer to the authority of Christ. This depiction of Paul demonstrates his desire to be seen in parallel to the pattern of the hymn. By highlighting how he sacrificed his status, Paul directs attention to his suffering and away from his overall gain. Just as Christ moved through humility to death and, in turn, exaltation, Paul argues that he

---

[88] For the traditional philosophical dissociation between body and soul (analogous or at least related to flesh and spirit here), see Table II in Olbrechts-Tyteca and Perelman, *The New Rhetoric*, 421.

[89] Here Paul is arguing in order to draw lines around what he believes the community should and should not be by characterizing both "them" and "us." This rhetorical strategy draws upon the relationship between a group and its members (an argument based on the structure of reality).

[90] On the parallels between Paul's self-description in 3:4–11 and the Christ hymn in 2:6–11, see T. E. Pollard, "The Integrity of Philippians," *NTS* 13 (1966–1967): 62–65. On the use of terms from the hymn throughout Phil. 3, see R. Alan Culpepper, "Co-Workers in Suffering: Philippians 2:19–30," *Review and Expositor* 77 (1980): 350–351; David E. Garland, "The Composition and Unity of Philippians: Some Neglected Literary Factors," *NovT* 27 (1985): 157, 159. On the similarity in sacrifice, and the focus on Paul throughout the letter, see Fortna, "Philippians," 226–228. Dodd denies that Christ's example is reflected here in the description of Paul. See Dodd, *Paul's Paradigmatic "I"*, 193.

wanted to join Christ in suffering (3:8, 10) in death (3:10, recalling his earlier willingness to face death, 1:20–26; 2:8, 17), and in resurrection (*anastaseōs*, 3:10; *exanastasin*, 3:11).[91] Paul's reversal and conformity to Christ are reinforced by an argument from divine authority, since this process involves gaining a righteousness "from God" (*ek theou*, 3:9), as opposed to the law.[92] By virtue of this close association with Christ, then, the argumentation has the secondary effect of continuing to draw Paul upward in a hierarchy of models presented throughout the letter.

G. 3:12–21

Yet, Paul is careful not to press his association with divine authorities too far, qualifying the above rhetoric only as an assertion of a continuing goal and hope (3:12–14). The letter has attempted to frame much of the communal identity in terms of unity with Paul, but in this section the pursuit of this prize is phrased in Paul's first person singular (e.g. *diōkō* in both 3:12, 14). Here Paul is seeking to clarify that he is still in pursuit of this bond with Christ. Proceeding by means of a causal link, he maintains that the reason for his pursuit is the possibility of grasping ("but I pursue if I might also grasp," 3:12). The rationale for this pursuit is immediately explained by Christ's own "grasping" of Paul (*eph hō*, "because," or more literally "upon which," 3:12). Paul is still attempting to become like Christ since (in a semi-reciprocal arrangement) Paul seeks to attain what Christ has already attained with Paul. Though not yet achieved or completed (differentiation), this casts Paul in close relationship to Christ (commonality). As with other argumentative uses of Christ in this letter (2:6–11; 3:7–11), the link with Christ functions as an explication of Paul's own model status. That this pursuit results in a hierarchical differentiation benefiting Paul is further stressed by the end-centered argument that he pursues "for the prize of the upward call" (*eis to brabeion tōs anō klōseōs*, 3:14) in both God and Christ. The point of this pursuit for Paul is to ascend (*anō*) into a hierarchy closer to the divine realm.

---

[91] Both allusions to "resurrection" in 3:10–11 reflect causal link argumentation: the first included in the infinitive clause (*tou gnōnai*, 3:10), the second in his attempt to reach "to/for resurrection" (*eis tōn exanastasin*, 3:11). For a thorough, though traditional, syntactic examination of 3:7–11, see Veronica Koperski, *The Knowledge of Christ Jesus My Lord: The High Christology of Philippians 3:7–11* (CBET 16; Kampen, The Netherlands: Kok Pharos, 1996).

[92] The frequent appeals to God and Christ in this section as the source of faith and righteousness could also be playing upon the earlier human/divine dissociation, possibly characterizing the law as a human concern. Blamelessness under the law has certainly already been associated with status as a human for Paul (3:4–6).

This pursuit is applied ("therefore," *oun*) to the next argumentative differentiation: between "us" who "think this" (*touto phronōmen*, literally "let us think this/have this mind," 3:15) and "you" who "think anything other" (*ti heterōs phroneite*, 3:15). Drawing upon the frequent dissociation of division/unity (1:15–17, 27–30; 2:1–5), the difference-maker is couched again in terms of the content of thoughts or feelings (1:7; 2:2, 5). But what are the Philippians meant to think: what is the "this" (*touto*, 3:15a) which they should think? A great deal of rhetorical energy has been expended in the letter in order to offer Paul as a model of what they should think (and a number of supporting figures as models). Indeed, the immediately preceding sentences (3:12–14) focused on Paul's own first-person assertions of how he has pursued association with Christ. These dissociative arguments favoring unity are apparently calling for the community to have the same view as Paul.

The force of this argument, like several before it, is backed up by a divine authority. If the audience chooses to "think the other" instead of the "this" (*touto*, twice in 3:15), "God will also reveal *this* to you" (3:15). There is more than a faint sense of foreboding here for those who oppose Paul's exhortation.[93] By expressing this dissociation in divinely approved apocalyptic terms (literally, *apokalypsei*, in 3:15), the argumentation might also be recalling the previous dissociation between destruction and safety (1:28; cf. 2:12; 3:1). Aside from this potentially threatening reason, the audience is also exhorted to "think this" through an argument of waste. Though difficult to translate, it roughly states, "for where we have reached, stay in line in the same way" (3:16).[94] Paul is arguing that sharing the proper frame of mind preserves the position that they have already attained. Not only is this improper ("other") way of thinking not in line with what God would show, it would also mean that the community's previous efforts will be wasted. Departing from the perspective Paul has would involve loss for the community at Philippi.

Such a suggestion about how the Philippians are meant to think can also be confirmed by looking to see whom they are exhorted to imitate. While there have been a number of occasions where it appears the letter is arguing for the model of Paul (1:7, 12–14, 24–26; 2:17–18; 3:4ff.), there is no more explicit instance of this rhetorical technique than the exhortation to "become co-imitators of me" (*symmimōtai mou ginesthe*, 3:17). In this brief phrase Paul combines both commonality rhetorics and differentiation rhetorics, as the

---

[93] Osiek summarizes the verse in this fashion: "Those who think differently from the path Paul just laid out are promised/threatened that God will set them straight . . . The moderately coercive tone that comes through is no doubt intended." See Osiek, *Philippians*, 99.

[94] The use of the verb *stoichein* ("stay in line") in this verse, along with the drawing up of sides, and the potential threat in choosing to be on the wrong side all add to the impression here that the letter's rhetorics are drawing upon military imagery. See, for example, Geoffrion, *Rhetorical Purpose*, 60, 130, 197–201.

audience is encouraged to join together in order to imitate Paul.[95] As support for this exhortation, the letter also commends them to notice others whom "you have as a type/form in us" (*echete typon ōmas*, 3:17). Though it does not directly allude to them here, the letter has already taken pains to present as models first Paul and then Christ, Timothy, and Epaphroditus, who share certain qualities with Paul, such as concern with communal benefit or a willingness to sacrifice. Since the "type" referred to here is one the Philippians have in "us," and the rhetoric has worked to associate these other models with Paul, it seems safe to suggest that this second clause refers to this already-expounded group.[96]

In support of this argument, then, the letter also contrasts Paul and these "types" with "the enemies" (3:18) about whom Paul has apparently previously informed them.[97] This section's contrast between these two groups is based upon at least two dissociations. First is a dissociation of earthly from heavenly matters (3:19–21).[98] Specifically, these anti-models can be discerned since they have their minds (*phronountes*) upon "the earthly things" (*ta epigeia*, 3:19); whereas the "we" of the letter have a *politeuma* in the heavens (*en ouranois*, 3:20). This concern with the wrong frame of mind has been a regular bone of contention in the letter (1:7; 2:1–5; 3:15) and here leads these enemies to a terrible fate (*apōleia*, 3:19, also recall 1:28), returning the rhetoric to the safety/destruction

---

[95] On this combination of unity rhetorics with the call to imitation, see Castelli, *Imitating Paul*, 95–96.

[96] The direct exhortation to imitate Paul and other "types" could also be functioning to define what kind of group to which the community would belong as members. By pointing to Paul and a range of supporting models, the letter argues that they are, in some way, typical or definitive of what it means to belong in the community. Thus, in order to be identifiable as belonging to this group, one should be like Paul and/or the other models presented in the letter.

[97] For more on the use of models and anti-models, see Olbrechts-Tyteca and Perelman, *The New Rhetoric*, 362–368. Paul specifically labels them "enemies of the cross of Christ" (3:18). Demetrius K. Williams has argued that the cross terminology tell us less about the conflict than about Paul's strategy of advocating unity and contrasting his opponents with himself. For reasons like these, Williams calls the cross terminology Paul's "rhetorical find." See Williams, *Enemies of the Cross of Christ: The Terminology of the Cross and Conflict in Philippians* (JSNTSup 223; London: Sheffield Academic Press, 2002).

[98] The earth/heaven dissociation is closely connected to the dissociation between human and divine, a traditional dissociation, as alluded to in Table II, Olbrechts-Tyteca and Perelman, *The New Rhetoric*, 421.

dissociation.[99] While these enemies will be destroyed, those on the "right" side of this contrast will have Christ as a *sōtōr* and *kyrios* (3:20).[100]

This contrast does not present a choice, but places these two paths in bold opposition, arguing further that not being an enemy involves becoming like (*symmorphon*) Christ's body (3:21). This desire to take a form like Christ has already been modeled by Paul (*symmorphizomenos*, 3:10), making clear again that being on the "right" side of this contrast involves following Paul's model.[101] Yet, even as the audience is exhorted to move in a course in common with Paul's model, the terms demonstrate an ongoing differentiation. In describing the "bodies" to be changed, "our body" is one of humility or debasement (*to sōma tōs tapeinōseōs hōmōn*, 3:21), while Christ's is one of glory (*tōs doxōs*, 3:21). This transformation in becoming more like Christ's body is also effected by Christ's power "to subject all things to himself" (*hypotaxai autō ta panta*, 3:21). While the terms are reminiscent of the hymn (Christ's humbling, *etapeinōsen*, 2:8; a name above every name, *to hyper pan onoma*, 2:9; all knees bending, 2:10; all tongues confessing for glory, 2:11), they maintain a hierarchical differentiation between Christ as subjecter-ruler and the community ("we") as subjected-ruled. Though the community can benefit by virtue of their association with Christ rather than the "enemies" (commonality rhetorics), their safety and transformation is brought about only in terms of their humility before

---

[99] The contrast in fates through the safety/destruction dissociation is connected here with the political terminology of a group (*politeuma*), just as it was in the previous use of the related term (*politeuesthe*, 1:27–28).

[100] The political use of these terms in the Roman world is unmistakable, as both of them are typical descriptions for the Roman emperor. On the political valence of a great deal of Pauline vocabulary, see Richard A. Horsley, "Paul's Counter-Imperial Gospel: An Introduction," in *Paul and Empire: Religion and Power in Roman Imperial Society* (ed. R. Horsley; Harrisburg, Penn.: Trinity Press International, 1997), 140–147; Dieter Georgi, "God Turned Upside Down," in *Paul and Empire*, 148–157. An argument can be made that Christ's rule is here being favorably compared to the unjust Roman one and, thus, is a positive distinction for modern readers (and possibly also for Paul's audience at Philippi). However, the terms of this contrast remain in the domain of rule (*politeuma, sōtōra, kyrion, hypotaxai*). The argumentation does not pose Christ and this community (as defined by Paul in unity with his version of Christ) as separate from, or as an alternative to, this kind of domination or rule. Since Paul's argument here does not challenge this notion of rule, it is problematic for any modern interpreter concerned with an analysis of kyriarchal images and social arrangements. For a similar assessment in terms of another Pauline letter, see Kittredge, "Corinthian Women Prophets and Paul's Argumentation in 1 Corinthians," in *Paul and Politics: Ekklesia, Israel, Imperium, Interpretation* (ed. R. Horsley; Harrisburg, Penn.: Trinity Press International, 2000), 103–109; Wire, "Response: The Politics of the Assembly in Corinth," in *Paul and Politics*, 124–129.

[101] On the striking vocabulary parallels between 2:6–11 and 3:20–21, see Culpepper, "Co-Workers," 350–351; Garland, "Composition," 158.

authorities and imitation of certain empowered models, most especially Paul (differentiation rhetorics).[102]

H. 4:1-9

This next section begins with a causal link (*hoste*, 4:1), underlining the importance of comprehending Paul's argument as a whole. While setting up the following arguments, the call to "stand thus in the lord" is also hearkening back to the immediately preceding argumentation. In light of these previous dissociations, the brief exhortation asks the audience to position themselves on the "right side" (Paul's side), unless they want to be destroyed like the enemies and miss out on their chance at transformation (3:18-21). These exclusionary and contrasting arguments are now balanced by more inclusive expressions ("beloved" twice in 4:1), indicating that the audience still has the chance to be included in this group, if they take up Paul's model, laid out for them throughout the preceding chapters. Even within the "love"-fest, elements of the letter's hierarchical arrangements are evident in this section. Paul calls the audience not only his "beloved," but also his "crown" (*stephanos*, 4:1), the reward for victory in some kind of agonistic contest (whether in battle or athletic games). The hierarchical aspect of rule is difficult to shake here, as it comes on the heels of Paul's description of Christ's own subordinating rule (3:19-21).[103] In this letter Paul's authority is not entirely separate from or different than Christ's.

These reflections lead this study finally to one of its central interests: the role of Euodia and Syntyche in the rhetoric of Philippians. The first and only mention of these women is here, in a doubled exhortation for them "to think the same thing in the lord" (*to auto phronein en kyriō*, 4:2). Most traditional interpretations of the letter hold that Paul is encouraging Euodia and Syntyche to

---

[102] For more on the pairing of imitation with obedience, especially as it relates to Paul's view of Christ, see Stephen D. Moore, *God's Gym: Divine Male Bodies of the Bible* (New York: Routledge, 1996), 25-30.

[103] Images of hierarchical rule paired with "loving" language are not necessarily as incompatible or contradictory as contemporary eyes might assume. The topic of "loving" one's subjects is not uncommon in the expressions of emperors and kings seeking to depict themselves in a paternalistic and beneficent light. Dale Martin's work, in particular, addresses itself to this issue of "benevolent patriarchalism." See Martin, *Slavery*, 87-108; *Corinthian Body*, 42-47, 135, 160, 196. Martin highlights how this term is "oxymoronic," even as it represents the views of the elite Greco-Roman sources. In this way, Martin alters and critiques Gerd Theissen's proposal of a Pauline "love-patriarchalism." See Martin, *Corinthian Body*, 259; Theissen, *Social Setting of Pauline Christianity* (ed., trans, intro. John H. Schütz; Philadelphia: Fortress, 1982). For a thorough feminist examination and assessment of Theissen's proposal, see Schüssler Fiorenza, *In Memory*, 72-84. For more on the link between these types of images, see Chapters II and III above.

think the same thing *as each other*, presuming that the two women are in some kind of conflict.[104] However, the examination of the argumentative techniques in Philippians seems to indicate at least one other reasonable way of reading this passage.

As detailed above Paul combines the rhetorics of commonality and the rhetorics of differentiation throughout the letter. The letter's rhetoric regularly dissociates Paul and his view of the community from others (1:15–17, 27–28; 2:14–16, 20–22; 3:2–4, 15, 18–19), while stressing the importance of closeness or sameness (1:3–7, 24–26, 27–30; 2:1–5, 18, 20, 25; 3:1, 3, 10–11, 17). Paul has been frequently presented as a model (1:7, 12–14, 24–26; 2:17–18; 3:4–8, 13–15, 17), with supporting model figures (2:5–11, 19–24, 25–30; 3:17). Finally, the way to think properly (*phroneō*) has been emphasized on several occasions, in instances of both commonality rhetorics (2:1–5; 3:15) and differentiation rhetorics (1:7; 2:5; 3:15, 19, including anti-modeling). It is vital to the rhetorical design of the letter that the audience's way of thinking is changed to conform more to Paul's own model.[105]

This study argues that the exhortation to Euodia and Syntyche fits into this design exactly, in both its concern with frame of mind (*phronein*) and stress on sameness (*to auto*, 4:2). Paul's model status and closeness to Christ (*in kyriō*, 4:2, see also 1:8, 13, 21–23; 2:16–17; 3:7–11) have been extolled throughout Philippians, so that the members of the community will see things the same way as Paul. As possible prominent members of this community, Euodia and Syntyche's agreement would be quite important to the success of these rhetorics.[106] Therefore, it seems more likely that the exhortation to "think the same thing" here is meant, as in the rest of the letter, to encourage Euodia and Syntyche to think the same thing *as Paul*.

---

[104] See, among the most recent examples, Bockmuehl, *Epistles*, 238–242; Fee, *Philippians*, 167–171; Holloway, *Consolation*, 146–148; Oakes, *Philippians*, 114, 123–124; Carolyn Osiek, *Philippians*, 110–113; and Peterlin, *Paul's Letter*, 101–132. In the severe minority are those who hold that Euodia and Syntyche are not in a conflict with each other, but with Paul. See the argument below and Kittredge, *Community*, 105–108.

[105] Among those scholars interested in Philippians' friendship imagery, Fitzgerald has been the strongest proponent of the thesis that the purpose of the letter "is attempting to correct the Philippians' understanding of friendship." See Fitzgerald, "Philippians," 142.

[106] On the basis of the description of Euodia and Syntyche as "co-workers" and "those who struggled with me in the gospel" in 4:3, many scholars argue for their prominence and possible leadership roles in the community. For further considerations of their roles, see Portefaix, *Sisters*, 135–154; Mary Rose D'Angelo, "Women Partners in the New Testament," *JFSR* 6 (1990): 65–86; Wendy Cotter, "Women's Authority Roles in Paul's Churches: Countercultural or Conventional?" *NovT* 36 (1994): 350–72; Nils A. Dahl, "Euodia and Syntyche and Paul's Letter to the Philippians," in *The Social World of the First Christians: Essays in Honor of Wayne A. Meeks* (ed. L. Michael White and O. Larry Yarbrough; Minneapolis: Fortress, 1995), 3–15.

The difference between these positions (thinking the same thing as Paul and thinking the same thing as each other) can be explained by a difference in how an interpreter hears an argument by transitivity functioning here. If one sees this exhortation as an isolated one (as was previously traditional in Philippians' scholarship), it is easier to argue that the exhortation is self-contained. Since Euodia (*a*) is urged to think the same thing (*b*) (*a* R *b*), and Syntyche (*c*) is separately urged likewise (also *b*) (*b* R *c*), it is argued Paul is trying to get them to think the same thing as each other (*a* R *c*). However, by placing the sentence within the larger argumentative tendencies of the letter (as we have done above), the message is not as obvious and self-contained as once believed. Given the repeated concern with state of mind, the attempts to contrast groups and dissociate concepts, and the modeling of Paul (with supporting figures), "the same thing" is firmly related to the aim of these arguments. Since Paul (*a*) has modeled a particular way of thinking (*b*) (*a* R *b*) throughout the letter, in contrast to those who do not (with serious consequences), and Paul argues for Euodia and Syntyche (*c*) to think a particular way (*b*) (*b* R *c*), Paul is urging Euodia and Syntyche to think the same thing as him (*a* R *c*).

This passage is another instance of Paul's modeling rhetoric in Philippians. Euodia and Syntyche are entreated to take Paul as their model, so that they might change their minds in imitation of Paul and the wider set of models presented in the letter. The directed exhortation to Euodia and Syntyche in 4:2 may be echoing in a specific manner the more general exhortation to "become co-imitators" of Paul (3:17). That the preceding instances of *phroneō* (3:15, 19) stand on both sides of this most explicit call to imitate Paul only enhances the impression that 4:2 is in line with the letter's ongoing arguments from a model. Both of these instances are part of arguments that seek to contrast two paths (3:15, 19–21), with Paul closely tied to the "us" who have their minds on the right path. The arguments stress the urgency of choosing Paul's group, since choosing wrong will involve destruction (3:19) and/or some divine revelation (3:15). These arguments emphasize how this specific entreaty to Euodia and Syntyche is another occasion for Paul to argue in terms of group boundaries. In urging them to have the same state of mind as he, Paul attempts to continue drawing the lines around what is and is not acceptable in order to remain part of the community ("think the same thing as me, think the same thing as us").

That this exhortation to Euodia and Syntyche is part of an argument about belonging to the community can be confirmed by the terms invoked in the following appeals. Paul appeals to some third party, a "true yokeperson" (*gnōsie syzyge*), "to take hold with these (women)" (*syllambanou autais*, 4:3). The point of the second person singular is to get this person to work with Euodia and Syntyche in some way, as further emphasized by the four-fold repetition of togetherness terms (*syn-*) in the verse. The occasions where this terminology was last evident involved imitating Paul, both directly (*symmimōtai*, 3:17) and by becoming like Christ (*symmorphon*, 3:21, as Paul had sought in 3:10, *symmorphizomenos*). The exceedingly positive address for this person ("true yokeperson/comrade") is also in terms of belonging. The addressee is very well yoked to Paul. In terms of the contrasts functioning throughout the letter, this person would be among Paul's group, rather than that of the anti-models ("enemies"). By emphasizing this element of the person's identity, the appeal accentuates even further the contrast between the mind-set of Euodia and Syntyche and the mind-set of Paul and his yoke-friend.[107] Though they "have struggled alongside" him (*synōthlōsan*, 4:3),[108] Euodia and Syntyche are not as "truly" united with Paul as the "true comrade" is.

In the sense that they do not share with Paul this proper frame of mind (which presumably this comrade does), Euodia and Syntyche function as anti-models. However, the aim of the entreaty is to bring them into conformity with Paul's ideas (as they are presented in the letter). If these women in the Philippian community were to respond with favor to this exhortation, they would be added to the range of models offered as support to Paul's own model status. Euodia and Syntyche would be models for how members of the community at Philippi could properly "think this thing" (3:15). Their past inclusion in the work of the gospel (4:3) would only strengthen the efficacy of their model status, which might help to explain why they have been singled out in this instance. Yet, if they continue to "think something other" (3:15) than "the same thing" as Paul (4:2), they will be anti-models, and can be effectively incorporated in the series of contrasts and dissociations in the letter's argumentation. Paul's rhetoric has so closely connected group identity to his own model (and a range of anti-models) that, as he has defined it, inclusion within the community requires conformity and compliance to Paul's perspective. The argumentation of the letter insures that, no matter which way members of the Philippian community (including Euodia and Syntyche) respond, Paul's previous depiction of the situation can only label them as insiders or outsiders.

The final clause in 4:3 reflects in a similar way lines drawn between insiders and outsiders throughout the letter. The note about inclusion in "the book of life" (4:3) stands out as another apocalyptic image.[109] The idea that only some names will be written in the book of life is compatible with the typically

---

[107] From the wording of this passage, Paul seems to think that the community will know who this "true yokeperson" is. If someone was so clearly tied to Paul that s/he need not be named, it only accentuates the likelihood that there are members of the community who are just as clearly less linked to Paul.

[108] This expression about Euodia and Syntyche has a clear military resonance. See Portefaix, *Sisters*, 141; Geoffrion, *Rhetorical Purpose*, 209–210; Reimer, "'Our Citizenship,'" 207–208; Krentz, "Paul," 362.

[109] The term "book of life" appears in apocalyptic literature (Dan. 12:1; 1 Enoch 47.3; Rev. 3:5; 13:8; 17:8; 20:12, 15; 21:27). See also Exod. 32:32; Isa. 4:3; Ezek. 13:9; Ps. 69:28; Luke 10:20; Heb. 12:23.

dualistic pattern evident in the apocalyptic mind-set as well as in apocalyptic literature. Since only a few will have God's favor, while others will be left out in the end, the opposition between Paul's people and the "dogs" or "enemies" is reinforced by this allusion to the book of life. The question remains: whose names are meant in 4:3 (*hōn ta onomata*)? Does it include Euodia and Syntyche, who are clearly the referent in the first relative pronoun (*haitines*, 4:3) in the sentence? Or does it only refer to "the rest of my co-workers" (*tōn loipōn synergōn mou*, 4:3)? On the one hand, the sentence does not refrain from praising Euodia and Syntyche, so it seems likely that they could be included in this positive judgment. Yet, throughout the letter Paul has worked hard to associate himself, often hierarchically, with God, so that his arguments could be reinforced by a divine authority. He has also not shied away from describing threats when giving the options for the audience (1:28; 2:12; 3:15, 19). Since disagreement with Paul has frequently been associated with being on the wrong side of issues, it is certainly possible that the reference here to the book of life is another embodiment of this rhetorical strategy: any disagreement with Paul means exclusion of one's name from the book of life. This final clause articulates what Paul feels is at stake in his urging Euodia and Syntyche to conform with his position.[110]

This reading of Paul's exhortation to Euodia and Syntyche as a call to obediently imitate his model is confirmed by showing that these modeling rhetorics extend their interactions into other portions of this fourth chapter. As at the beginning of the letter, Paul calls twice for joy in terms of the rule of justice, at all times (4:4) and in every prayer (4:6).[111] The urgency of this call to joy is heightened by the claim that "the lord is near" (*kyrios engys*, 4:5). This expectation of the divine could be functioning both as an argument from divine authority and as an argument from waste. Paul is concerned that members of the community do what he has told them to do, especially now when the moment of truth is so near.[112] This impression is only furthered by the implicit causal link made between these calls to rejoice (4:4–6) and the peace of God that will guard

---

[110] Dahl, "Euodia," 7.
[111] This appeal to universal joy is echoed by a statement in the negative: "do not be concerned with anything" (*mēden merimnate*, 4:6). Is part of Paul's problem (or disagreement) with the audience at Philippi involving this concern, possibly about concrete realities (as in 3:19, where "enemies" think about "earthly things")?
[112] As with the reference to "the book of life" above, there may be an element of threat to this note about the nearness of the lord. Given the previous designations of what could happen (destruction or safety, 1:28; 2:12; 3:15, 19–21), depending on one's choices, divine involvement in this call to rejoice accentuates the danger in not following the exhortation.

(*phrourōsei*, 4:7) them, implying that the community members are in need of this divine protection.[113]

After this lobbying to rejoice, the letter utilizes a virtue list (4:8) to make an argument from tradition. At the same time Paul affiliates himself with these virtues by writing: "the things you have learned and received and heard and seen in me, do these things" (*ha kai emathete kai parelabete kai ōkousate kai eidete en emoi, tauta prassete*, 4:9).[114] Paul persists in using himself as the main model for this letter's argumentation, as this additional call to imitate makes clear. The causal link provided between the act of imitating Paul and the second reference to God's peace[115] for Paul's imitators (4:9) does additional duty as an argument from divine authority.[116] As a result, this argument enacts a hierarchy of authority that links Paul closely to God in a similar fashion to the links forged previously with Christ, Timothy and Epaphroditus. That these arguments based on Paul's own authority and status as model extend beyond the explicit reference to imitation in 3:17 confirms that his address to Euodia and Syntyche in 4:2–3, like his address to the community here at 4:8–9, also involves the imitation of Paul.

I. 4:10–23

The final major section of the letter repeats many of the argumentative techniques already noted. The section begins with Paul's statement that he is rejoicing as a result of the community's revival of concern for him (literally, "that you have blossomed regarding the thinking on my behalf," 4:10). This concern with Paul may be linked to his previous dissociating of self-benefit from community benefit, since Paul has certainly argued that supporting him was a good way to aid the community. This "thinking" about (or for) Paul is the same

---

[113] Scholars have commented upon the military resonance of this verb, even as they have not noted the potential danger or threat implicit in its usage here. See Reimer, "'Our Citizenship,'" 209–210; Krentz, "De Caesare et Christo," *CurTM* 28 (2001): 344; "Paul," 363.

[114] Some friendship scholars believe that Paul is alluding to the virtues of friendship in this list. See Fitzgerald, "Philippians," 151–152; White, "Morality," 207.

[115] The second reference to divine peace as a result of following Paul in these exhortations (peace of God, 4:7, God of peace, 4:9) stands out in this stage of the argumentation. The frequency of the military terminology in the letter and location of Philippi within the Roman empire suggests that this "peace" could be some kind of commentary upon, allusion to, or alternative to the "Pax Romana" established under Augustus' reign.

[116] The time element of the statement is 4:9 is also worthy of comment. Since Paul wrote that the peace *will* be with them (*estai*, 4:9), it is possible that Paul is intentionally stressing the "not-yet-ness" of this peace, in contradistinction to those who might believe God's peace is already present (see "day of Christ," 1:6, 10 and 2:16; "not yet perfect," 3:12–14, "earthly things," "awaiting a savior," 3:19–20; "lord is near" 4:5).

term (*phronein*, twice in 4:10) implemented in previous calls to unity in the face of other paths (2:2, 5; 3:15, 19; 4:2). With this recitation of joy, Paul is trying to reinforce the proper way to "think" as a member of the community, especially as it involves appropriate connections to Paul.[117] Though he is grateful, Paul also maintains that in every situation he is "self-sufficient" (*autarkōs*, 4:11).[118] Dissociating need from contentment, Paul shows a lack of concern with his own condition (4:11–12) and demonstrates the continuing devaluation of self-benefit in the letter. Paul also maintains that this self-sufficient contentment comes from another source: "the one who strengthens me" (4:13). Since Paul has worked so strenuously to link himself with divine forces throughout the letter, this most likely refers to either God or Christ, which, by way of association, further emphasizes Paul's model status as one close to the divine.

Even as he draws himself closer to divine authority, Paul also attempts to strengthen his bonds with the community. By emphasizing their help in sharing his problems (*synkoinōnōsantes*, 4:14) and stressing the history of this aid (4:15–16), Paul is hoping to maintain this support. This recitation of their previous and continuing relationship is an implicit argument from waste: having invested time and money in Paul, it would be a waste for the Philippian community to not keep their relationship with him. Recalling his past relationship with them reinforces the suitability of listening to his arguments now. Paul insists that he did not need their help, but that he allowed the relationship for the benefit of the community's own "fruit" (4:17), demonstrating his continuing model status as one more concerned with the community than himself (cf. 4:11–13). When Paul does discuss accepting their gift, he does so in liturgical terms of God's own pleasure (4:18). This shifting of the grounds of conversation to the divine realm

---

[117] This instance of *phronein* language shows how the certain mind-set advocated in the letter is primarily linked to support of Paul. Such a link is made more complex by the power dynamics involved in ancient patronage relationships, as they may be intertwined here and throughout 4:10–20. For more on *phronein* in this section, see Berry, "Function of Friendship," 110–111, 116–117; Stowers, "Friends," 110; Fitzgerald, "Paul," 332. On the commercial valence of this language (with *doma* and *karpos* in 4:17), see Joachim Gnilka, *Der Philipperbrief* (HTKNT, 10.3; Freiburg: Herder, 1968), 178–180; Martin Ebner, *Leidenslisten und Apostelbrief: Untersuchungen zu Form, Motivik und Funktion der Peristasenkataloge bei Paulus* (FB 66; Würzburg: Echter, 1991), 331–364; Berry, "Function of Friendship," 118–119; G. W. Peterman, *Paul's Gift from Philippi: Conventions of Gift-Exchange and Christian Giving* (SNTSMS 92; Cambridge: Cambridge University Press, 1997); Fitzgerald, "Paul," 332–334.

[118] Alongside of the observations about friendship and military imagery, the use of this term highlights the relevance of Greek philosophical concepts for understanding the thought-world of Paul. On the Stoic background of *autarkōs*, and the influence of Stoic concepts upon military and friendship concepts, see Troels Engberg-Pedersen, "Stoicism in Philippians," in *Paul in His Hellenistic Context* (ed. T. Engberg-Pedersen; Minneapolis: Fortress Press, 1995), 256–290.

recalls the previous causal links in the chapter (4:7, 9), resulting in God's favor. The gift they provided to Paul, pleasing to God (4:18), will result in God providing for the community (4:19). The reciprocal exchange occurs through God as proxy for Paul, demonstrating how closely linked Paul considers himself to be to the divine authority. Even when Paul is in someone's debt, he manages to communicate this relationship in terms of his own model status, heightened in a hierarchical relationship aligned with the divine.

Even the closing greetings reflect some of the argumentative tendencies of the whole letter. The greetings Paul exchanges are phrased in terms of the rule of justice. Paul greets "every holy one" in the community receiving the letter (4:21), and states that they are from "all the holy ones" (4:22) in the place of his imprisonment. While Paul has the authority to speak on behalf of everyone in his own current community, he also is at pains to mention "especially those out of Caesar's household" (4:22). Stressing "all" as the receivers and givers of greetings stresses the rhetorics of commonality present throughout the letter, while invoking a particular group with authority (in this case imperial authority) points out the persistent rhetorics of differentiation.[119]

J. SUMMARY OF THE ARGUMENTATIVE TECHNIQUES

At this point, some general observations can be made, before the study proceeds to a consideration of the letter's prevailing rhetoric. This examination has shown the argumentative techniques reach across all of Olbrechts-Tyteca and Perelman's four categories. Perhaps more importantly, an argument often operates in close proximity to and collaboration with many other arguments, typically to greater effect. The rhetorics overlap, not only in terms of these argumentative techniques, but also with respect to the two identifiable overarching strategies, differentiaton and commonality rhetorics. True to form for the "New Rhetoric," the arguments function interactively, working separately yet together, toward Paul's rhetorical ends.

The sequence of the argumentative techniques in Philippians emphasizes this interactive quality. Frequently, we saw an argument by dissociation followed shortly by an argument by causal link. Often, the use of a model or anti-model was implemented to reinforce these rhetorical combinations. On a wider view these arguments by model demonstrate a greater pattern evolving throughout the letter. The model quality of Paul is established first (1:3–11, 12–14, 24–26), before turning to other, more truncated arguments by model: Christ

---

[119] Scholars interested in military language in the letter would do well to explain how the mentioning of Caesar's household (4:22) and the praetorian guard (1:13) would fit into the appeal of the letter. Does it show that Paul's message is compatible with even the highest levels of the imperial administration? Or is it meant to show how far an alternative to this imperial order has come? Does Paul hope the audience will be impressed by his speaking about (or on behalf of) these groups of people?

(2:5-11), Timothy (2:19-24), and Epaphroditus (2:25-30). But the argumentation returns to the model of Paul throughout the remainder of the letter (3:7-11, 17; 4:2, 9, 11-13), often in their most explicit forms (3:17; 4:9). The other models are nestled into the middle of a series of arguments for Paul's model.

This detailing of the argumentative techniques in the letter of the Philippians has garnered some useful readings of Paul's rhetoric. The letter pursued both the rhetorics of commonality and the rhetorics of differentiation in an attempt to construct a particular, unified view of the way the community should think.[120] The path constructed by these rhetorics is modeled throughout the letter by Paul and his own perceptions of his relationship to a number of other models (Christ, Timothy, Epaphroditus, and some less explicit antimodels). Seen in the context of the whole letter, then, the exhortation to Euodia and Syntyche is a targeted and even climactic example of Paul's continuing calls for imitation.

The frequent use of dissociative arguments and the high level of rhetorical exertion required in this arguing for imitation suggest that the audience may not have naturally taken to Paul's construction of his own preeminently authoritative status. In support of the arguments for his own model status, Paul makes frequent appeals to the authority of the divine. As compatible with one of the main functions of dissociation,[121] the rhetorics of the letter also work hard to break the current patterns of thinking and draw the community to conform its thoughts to Paul's. Dissociation is not performed in a vacuum; it acts as an argument when one wants to change the audience's conceptions of an idea or structure. Rather than proposing a disagreement between Euodia and Syntyche as the background to 4:2-3, the above reading of the rhetorical techniques suggest some sort of difference in perspective between Paul and some of the Philippians including Euodia and Syntyche. Instead of locating "the problem" between these two prominent women, the rhetorics indicate it is Paul who has a problem with the Philippians.

One of the virtues of using Olbrechts-Tyteca and Perelman's argumentative techniques to analyze the letter of Philippians has been to hear these arguments

---

[120] In contradistinction to this study, Kittredge maintains that the two different kinds of language she finds in Philippians (friendship/partnership and obedience) come from two different sources (the community and Paul, respectively) and, thus, have different values. See Kittredge, *Community*, 56, 64-65. This study has shown how the different rhetorics have been intertwined in Paul's argument.

[121] Olbrechts-Tyteca and Perelman wrote that dissociation "involves a more profound change that is always prompted by the desire to remove an incompatibility arising out of the confrontation of one proposition with others." See Olbrechts-Tyteca and Perelman, *The New Rhetoric*, 413. Dissociation presumes a difference between the rhetor's assessment of the audience's views and the rhetor's own view.

chiefly in terms of their adaptation to an audience. Focusing on the interaction of these arguments gives us an opportunity to place Paul not at the center of "the meaning" of the letter. Reading with a hermeneutics of suspicion, the above rendering of the rhetorical techniques does not begin with the premise that Paul's status was authoritative. Rather, we have seen how Paul's rhetoric utilizes certain techniques as the letter constructs his authority in a call for imitation.[122] Such a rhetorical analysis does not simply list these arguments and conclude that they must be persuasive. On the contrary, the interaction between the commonality rhetorics and the differentiation rhetorics presumes the rhetor Paul is contending with different perspectives in the community. The letter is *an attempt* to convince the community to accept Paul's perspective on issues of communal identity and authority.

---

[122] The above reading of the letter's focus on imitation again stands in contradistinction to Kittredge's reading, namely, by holding that leadership is more than an "indirect concern" in the letter. See Kittredge, *Community*, 109.

Chapter V

Prevailing Rhetoric:
The Major Arguments

After the tasks and scope of this study were introduced, the next two chapters contextualized the analysis of Philippians in contemporary biblical interpretation and within the community at ancient Philippi. These examinations established two important cues for conducting a feminist rhetorical interpretation of Philippians: a) the relevance of a critical feminist analytic of power relations and b) the recognition of the interactivity of argumentation. With these two cues in mind, the analysis turned to an investigation of the rhetorics of Philippians, facilitated by Olbrechts-Tyteca and Perelman's techniques of argumentation. The preceding chapter approached the letter's rhetorics in the order that they evolved, as they were building upon and interacting with each other. This chapter describes the prevailing rhetoric, the kinds of arguments that are most characteristic of the letter.[1]

The previous chapter's examination of the letter's rhetoric as the arguments evolved was well suited to showing how these arguments interacted with each other, the second cue. This chapter's examination of the letter's prevailing rhetoric, taking similar arguments together, more closely attends to what kind of power relations Paul attempted to establish through the argumentation, the first cue. Rather than simply identify and group the argumentation in terms of a) dissociation, b) quasi-logical arguments, c) arguments based on the structure of reality, and d) arguments establishing the structure of reality, this chapter notes how these arguments function hierarchically, seeking to specify what kind of

---

[1] The distinction made in this study between evolving (or developing) rhetoric and prevailing rhetoric is in keeping with the approach of Antoinette Clark Wire's study of 1 Corinthians implementing Olbrechts-Tyteca and Perelman's argumentative techniques. It differs from this study, however, in the order of presentation, and the descriptive terms used (evolving rather than structural, prevailing in place of textual). See Wire, *The Corinthian Women Prophets: A Reconstruction through Paul's Rhetoric* (Minneapolis: Fortress Press, 1990) 6–9, 12–180.

power relations and authority claims are enacted through the letter's argumentation.[2] Here we will see a clearer explanation of the letter's rhetorical tendencies and press for the implications of the analysis for the role of the community at Philippi.

A. ARGUMENTS BY DISSOCIATION

This overview of Paul's argumentation in the letter to the Philippians begins with the arguments by dissociation. Of the four categories of argumentative techniques, this group is a classificatory innovation on the part of Olbrechts-Tyteca and Perelman.[3] Whereas the other three sets of techniques seek to bring together concepts or propositions not normally associated with each other, dissociative techniques are focused upon separating elements of a concept already associated, typically to make new associations.[4] Stated in brief, dissociation breaks the connecting links upon which previous perceptions were based, resulting in a restructuring of the relationship between elements previously associated in another way.[5] Dissociations are argumentative techniques of modification, "since they aim less at using the accepted language than at moving toward a new formulation."[6]

In terms of the two broad sets of rhetorics already identified in the previous chapter, dissocation seems to be an argumentative technique that more frequently contributes to the letter's rhetorics of differentiation. Even on those occasions where dissociative arguments refer to concepts of unity and communal benefit (topics at home in the rhetorics of commonality), the

---

[2] A compelling rhetorical analysis of this letter requires not only identifying the types of argumentation, but also explicating why these identifications matter, how they affect an understanding of the letter. This exercise is not identification for identification's sake, but identification of arguments with the hope of contributing something useful for a feminist analysis of Philippians. For similar observations on the utility of rhetorical interpretations and interpretations, in general, of biblical literature, see Mary Ann Tolbert, *Sowing the Gospel: Mark's World in Literary-Historical Perspective* (Minneapolis: Fortress Press, 1989), 13, 106–107; and Chapter I.B above.

[3] Lucie Olbrechts-Tyteca and Chaïm Perelman, *The New Rhetoric: A Treatise on Argumentation* (trans. John Wilkinson and Purcell Weaver; Notre Dame, Ind.: University of Notre Dame Press, 1969), 411–459. For more on Olbrechts-Tyteca and Perelman, see Chapter I and the beginning of Chapter IV above. Dissociation remained a topic of primary focus for the remainder of Olbrechts-Tyteca's career and, therefore, was most likely one of her innovative contributions to *The New Rhetoric*. See Olbrechts-Tyteca, *Le Comique du discours* (Bruxelles: Editions de l'Université de Bruxelles, 1974); and "Les Couples philosophiques: Une nouvelle approche," *Revue internationale de philosophie* 33 (1979): 81–98.

[4] Olbrechts-Tyteca and Perelman, *The New Rhetoric*, 191–192, 411–415.

[5] Olbrechts-Tyteca and Perelman, *The New Rhetoric*, 411–412.

[6] Olbrechts-Tyteca and Perelman, *The New Rhetoric*, 192.

technique seems to entail at least some level of differentiation. This might suggest that there is something distinctly hierarchical about the argument by dissociation. The devaluation of one term in the dissociation necessarily entails a process of privileging the other hierarchically.[7] In this portion of the overview of Philippians' argumentation, we examine key instances of the techniques of dissociation for any hierarchical tendencies.

1. DISSOCIATION OF APPEARANCE FROM REALITY

> But I want you to know, brothers, that the things concerning me have really happened for the progress of the gospel (1:12)

> Christ Jesus . . . being in the form of God . . . emptied himself, taking the form of a slave, becoming in the likeness of humans . . . Therefore God exceedingly exalted him and gave him a name over all names . . . (2:5–11)

> I myself have (reason for) confidence in the flesh. If any other supposes s/he has reason to be confident in the flesh, I have more: circumcised on the eighth day, out of the people Israel, of the tribe of Benjamin, a Hebrew out of Hebrews, according to the law a Pharisee, according to zeal a pursuer of the assemblies, according to righteousness in the law blameless. (3:4–6)

See also 1:28

The dissociation of appearance from reality is so common a distinction in argumentation that Olbrechts-Tyteca and Perelman make use of this dissociation as the explanatory example in their initial definition.[8] Of appearance/reality, they write: "We consider this dissociation to be the prototype of all conceptual dissociation because of its widespread use and its basic importance in philosophy."[9] The appearance/reality dissociation is such a common or classic argumentative technique that this study will have reason to refer back to it in sections to come in order to explain exactly how some of the other dissociations operate.

As it is defined by Olbrechts-Tyteca and Perelman and is also apparent in this letter's arguments, the second of the two terms in the argument (reality) is

---

[7] Though their study does not directly address itself to this consequence of dissociative argumentation, Olbrechts-Tyteca and Perelman do briefly allude to the role of hierarchical thinking patterns in the argument by dissociation. "The dissociation expresses a vision of the world and establishes hierarchies for which it endeavors to provide the criteria." See Olbrechts-Tyteca and Perelman, *The New Rhetoric*, 420.
[8] Olbrechts-Tyteca and Perelman, *The New Rhetoric*, 415–444.
[9] Olbrechts-Tyteca and Perelman, *The New Rhetoric*, 415.

the preferred term. By implementing this dissociative argument, Paul is attempting to convince the audience that what appears to be the case is not, in fact, the case. The first of these arguments asserts that Paul's imprisonment elsewhere (1:12–1:14) has not hindered the spread of the message, rather (or "really," *mallon*, 1:12) it has actually worked to advance it. The third argument from dissociation of appearance from reality (3:4–6) also involves impressions about Paul, clarifying exactly how much more confidence he should have.[10] Comparatively speaking, then, this dissociative argument forwards an argument that raises Paul's profile over others known by the community. While it may be coming from a source outside of Paul's own invention (see the argument from a tradition, below), the second instance of this dissociative argument establishes the kyriarchal supremacy ("Jesus Christ is lord," 2:11) of the model figure in the hymn, though it appeared he was in servitude as a human (2:7–8).

In general, dissociating appearance from reality is staking a claim on how to describe reality for the audience. The dissociative argument highlights how the audience is in need of correction in the eyes of the rhetor (Paul). According to Paul's vision in the letter, the members of the Philippian community are not seeing the whole picture, or are in need of corrective lenses prescribed by Paul. That two of the dissociative arguments are forwarded to instill a particular impression of Paul suggests that Paul is unhappy with how he is being perceived in the community (or at least how he perceives they are perceiving him). Thus, these arguments seem to be attempting to re-define who Paul is for the community (1:12; 3:4–6), and, by extension, what the community should seek to be (1:28; 3:4–6).

2. Dissociation of Division from Unity and Difference from Sameness

> Some preach Christ out of envy and rivalry, but others from good will. These (the second) do so out of love, knowing that I am placed for the defense of the gospel, but those (the first) proclaim Christ out of divisiveness . . . (1:15–17)

> Therefore if there is any appeal in Christ, any call to love, any partnership of the spirit, any affection and compassion, complete my joy in order that you might think the same thing, having the same love, sharing in spirit, thinking the one thing, not according to divisiveness nor conceit but in humility counting others over yourselves . . . (2:1–3)

> Therefore those who are mature, let us think this; and if you think anything other, God will also reveal this to you . . . (3:15)

---

[10] Wire notes that Phil 3:4 is one of only two instances (along with Gal 6:3) of this kind of "confident boast" outside of 1 Corinthians. See Wire, *The Corinthian Women Prophets*, 14.

These dissociative arguments seek to clarify the difference between those in the community who act in accordance with Paul's particular version of unity, and those who are, in the letter's terms, acting divisively. It initially appears that all who preach this message belong in the community, no matter how they preach (1:18). These dissociations of division from unity, however, seek to shift the argumentative ground to a description of *how* these people conduct themselves. Though once thought to be unified, these parties can be differentiated on the basis of how they think/feel (2:1–3; 3:15) and how they act (1:15–17; 2:1–3). Dissociation seeks to modify the way one looks at an entity once held to have a given unity and structure.[11]

Here, Paul is making an argument that the community should differentiate based on whether certain people act a particular way. How a party acts shows where they belong in the restructuring brought about by the dissociation. If a party is acting divisively (1:15–17; 2:1–3), they do not have the same mindset as "us." The unity of the community is forwarded by "having the same mind" (2:1–3; 3:15). Any departure from this particular kind of unity is classified as promoting strife (1:15) and will be met by an apocalyptic consequence from the divine realm ("God will also reveal," 3:15). Anyone keeping in line with the same idea of unity will be affiliated with the most positive attributes: good will, love, partnership, affection, joy and fulfillment. By implication, then, those who do not hold to the same vision look after only their own interests (see the next section) and fail to embody these virtues.

This kind of dissociation lies at the heart of Paul's argumentation in Philippians. While emphasizing unity, these arguments work to differentiate between different courses of action. This should not be surprising to us coming on the heels of the previous chapter's analysis, showing how even when the letter seems focused on commonality rhetorics, they are intertwined with the letter's differentiation rhetorics. Such careful reconsideration of these techniques demonstrates how Paul is arguing for a particular view of communal unity. It is not unity solely for unity's sake, but a kind of unity that promotes certain differentiations in keeping with Paul's view of his relationship with the community.

3. DISSOCIATION OF SELF-BENEFIT FROM COMMUNITY-BENEFIT

> But remaining in the flesh is more necessary because of you (pl.). And being convinced of this, I know that I will remain and stay beside all of you (pl.) for your (pl.) progress and joy of trust. (1:24–25)

---

[11] Olbrechts-Tyteca and Perelman, *The New Rhetoric*, 411–412.

not according to divisiveness nor conceit but in humility counting others over yourselves, each looking not to their own interests but to the interests of others. (2:3–4)

But even if I am poured upon the sacrifice and service of your (pl.) trust, I rejoice and I rejoice with all of you. (2:17)

For I have no one of similar mind/soul, who will truly care about the things concerning you (pl.). (2:20–21)

Since he was longing for all of you and was troubled, because you heard that he had fallen ill. (2:26)

To write the same things to you (pl.) is not troubling for me, but safe for you (pl.). (3:1)

Not that I seek the payment, but I seek the fruit which abounds to your (pl.) account. (4:17)

See also 4:10

Closely related to the previous argumentative technique dissociating difference from unity, the dissociation of self-benefit from community-benefit[12] recurs at a high rate for such a brief letter. It plays a vital role in Paul's description of himself (1:24–25; 2:17; 3:1; 4:17), some of his co-workers (Timothy 2:20–21; Epaphroditus 2:26), and what he seeks from the audience (2:3–4; 4:10). It is reminiscent of the argument for the common good, in unity rhetorics within Greek civic thought.[13] Yet most of the instances of Paul's dissociation differ from this argument for the common good in that the focus seems to remain squarely upon certain figures in the community who demonstrate the attitude of community benefit. The dissociation functions to display the value placed on the community by these model figures (see the arguments by model below), but these arguments are not extended meditations on what might be the common good for the audience. For example, Paul shows

---

[12] Wire's conceptualization of this dissociation for the first letter to the Corinthians has been particularly useful here. See Wire, *The Corinthian Women Prophets*, 17–19.

[13] The appeal to "common advantage" over personal gain is evident in ancient speeches on civic concord (for example, in Dio Chrysostom, *Or.* 34. 19, 22; Aristides, *Or.* 24.5). See Margaret M. Mitchell, *Paul and the Rhetoric of Reconciliation: An Exegetical Investigation of the Language and Composition of 1 Corinthians* (HUT 28; Louisville, Ky.: Westminster/John Knox, 1991), 31–32; Dale B. Martin, *Slavery as Salvation: The Metaphor of Slavery in Pauline Christianity* (New Haven: Yale University Press, 1990), 143–144. For more on unity rhetorics in ancient civic-political discourse, see Chapter III.C above.

all that he is willing to give up for the benefit of the community (such as a life with Christ in 1:24–25 or his own life in 2:17), thus continuing to raise his status for the audience. Timothy and Epaphroditus seem to display similar concern in these dissociative arguments (2:20–21, 26), elevating them in the argumentation to a role supporting Paul's model.

Along with the previous unity/difference dissociation, this recurring dissociation stresses the rhetorics of commonality at work in the letter. By placing community-benefit in the latter half of the dissociative pair, it is clearly the valued term, reinforcing the letter's interest in communal matters. Recall, however, that dissociations function to reorganize the perception of the relation between elements. By positing self-benefit as dissociated from community-benefit, the argumentation wants to demonstrate how these two may not be as compatible as previously thought. Those who seek "their own interests" now stand out as different from those who are "counting others over yourselves" (2:3–4). Thus, even as these dissociative arguments focus attention on the centrality of communal benefit, they do so in order to demonstrate who does and who does not embody this concern in an appropriate way. Yet again, the rhetorics of commonality are intertwined with the rhetorics of differentation to highlight the difference between how Paul and his associates act—with the "right" idea about community benefit—and how others might act.

4. DISSOCIATION OF DESTRUCTION FROM SAFETY OR SALVATION

> and not frightened by anything from those who stand against you, this is a sign to them of their destruction, and of your (pl.) safety . . . (1:28)

> Therefore, my beloved, just as you (pl.) have always obeyed, not only as in my presence but also now much more in my absence, bring about your (pl.) own safety with fear and trembling (2:12)

> Their end is destruction, their god is the belly and glory in their shame, having their minds on the earthly things. For our *politeuma* is in heaven, out of which we also wait for a savior, lord Jesus Christ. (3:19–20)

> See also 3:1 and 3:15

Perhaps the starkest of these dissociations is this destruction/safety pair. In the argumentation of Philippians, it is not simply a contrast or comparison. This kind of rhetoric seems better explained as a dissociative argument since it seeks to disrupt the assumption of safety for all in the audience. Since Paul works to build an appeal in these terms, it could indicate that he believes that the audience assumes they are all safe. According to Paul's arguments the opponents of his perspective may well meet with destruction (1:28; 3:19), possibly contrary to expectations. Safety is not yet achieved for those who desire it. There are only signs of safety (1:28), but it still needs to be brought about (2:12), with the help of Paul (3:1) and a savior (3:20). The line dividing the destructive and safe fates is slim, since the process of working out one's safety is characterized as fearful (2:12).

Because the dissociation of destruction from safety is so stark and of vital importance to the audience, it seems likely that the entire dissociation may be recalled, when only one element has been mentioned in the argumentation (thus the inclusion of 2:12 and 3:1). While stressing the potential urgency of the situation, the invocation of this kind of argument in Philippians has a foreboding quality. If you want to be safe, you should do what this letter says: take on this struggle against "our" opponents (1:28–30), work in obedience and fear (2:12), and adopt a similar state of mind (3:15). Such a rhetorical tact veers close to making threats.[14]

Most of the instructions developing from these dissociations are also organized relative to Paul. Seeking the path of safety will include joining in the same struggle that is Paul's (1:28–30), acting in obedience to him (whether he is present or not, 2:12), and thinking as "we" do (3:15). Responding properly to these arguments, then, would involve joining Paul's perspective (commonality rhetorics), since what appeared to be safe before is not (differentiation rhetorics).

5. Dissociation of Human from Divine

> Christ Jesus . . . being in the form of God . . . emptied himself, taking the form of a slave, becoming in the likeness of humans . . . Therefore God exceedingly exalted him and gave him a name over all names . . . (2:5–11)

See also 1:28 and 2:1

Though less common than the previous dissociations, the dissociation of human from divine plays a role in the argumentation of the letter.[15] In general, reference to the divine strengthens many arguments. In the case of this dissociation, it seems to function to clarify who is in control and, perhaps, who

---

[14] Olbrechts-Tyteca and Perelman write that "[r]ecourse to argumentation assumes the establishment of a community of minds, which, while it lasts, excludes the use of violence." See Olbrechts-Tyteca and Perelman, *The New Rhetoric*, 55. For more on violence and argumentation, see Olbrechts-Tyteca and Perelman, *The New Rhetoric*, 54–59.

[15] For an example of the tradition behind the human/divine dissociation, see Table II in Olbrechts-Tyteca and Perelman, *The New Rhetoric*, 421. See also the argument from authority and the argument from the divine model, below.

has God "on his side." If we see the arguments in this letter as part of an ongoing conversation about what is the proper relationship to this deity, marshalling the divine in a dissociation implies that while all *think* they are in right relationship to the divine, the reality is that some are left only to human devices. Thus, the dissociative arguments in the letter have a collaborative effect, the human/divine and appearance/reality dissociations working together, and being on the wrong side of these matters involves destruction as expressed in the destruction/safety dissociation.

The hymn tells us of Christ taking on the form and likeness of human status (enslaved and inferior, 2:6–7), but in the end showing Christ's true nature as exalted (2:9–11). If Paul's stance is identified with Christ (as the letter tries vigorously to make clear), then there are implications for Paul's status. While the audience or some of "those who stand against you" ("opponents") might see Paul's struggle as a conflict between humans (1:28), the letter claims that the results of this conflict partake of the divine ("from God" and "in Christ"). The one who conveys this message, then, parallels the arc of the hymn.[16] Though appearing inferior, imprisoned, and quite human, Paul's arguments have the force and assurance of the divine.

6. OTHER DISSOCIATIONS: FLESH FROM SPIRIT, LAW FROM FAITH, EARTHLY FROM HEAVENLY, NEED FROM CONTENTMENT

> For we ourselves are the circumcision, those who are serving the spirit of God and boasting in Christ Jesus and not having confidence in the flesh . . . (3:3)

> But whatever gain there was for me, I counted these things as a loss because of Christ Jesus . . . not having my righteousness from the law but because of trust of Christ, the righteousness from God on the basis of trust (3:7–9)

> Their end is destruction, their god is the belly and glory in their shame, having their minds on the earthly things. For our *politeuma* is in heaven, out of which we also wait for a savior, lord Jesus Christ. (3:19–20)

> Not that I speak according to need, for I have learned to be self-sufficient in whatever (state/way) I am. I know how to be humbled, and I know how to be abounding; in every and all things I have been instructed to be filled and to hunger, to be abounding and to be humbled. (4:11–12)

See also 2:12

---

[16] See the analysis of argument from the model of Christ in V.D.2 below.

The remaining arguments by dissociation play comparatively minor roles in the argumentation of Philippians. Since they do not recur as repetitive argumentative techniques, it is difficult to ascertain how the elements in the dissociation are to be re-arranged. The passages where three of these dissociative pairs appear, flesh/spirit, law/faith, and earthly/heavenly, have garnered some attention in the search for Paul's "opponents." Yet, this line of inquiry has been frustrated by these slim references.[17] It is best that such argumentative techniques be read in terms of the repetitive efforts of the letter. Similar to many of the preceding dissociations, these arguments work to establish Paul and those closest to his views of the community ("we, the circumcision," "our *politeuma*," not them, the mutilation) as having the right kind of spirit and attitude, while others do not meet this standard.

The earthly/heavenly dissociation (3:19–20) can be clearly viewed as affiliated with the human/divine dissociation seen elsewhere in the letter. Paul claims "our *politeuma*" comes not from the human or earthly realm, but from the divine or the heavens. Not only does this polity come *out of* the heavenly, but ultimately the polity will also *lead to* heavenly associations for all those included—all the more crucial to "have your mind" on the right things. Through the earthly/heavenly dissociation Paul seeks to show what thinking the right way will gain for the community, separating himself from those who "have their minds" on "earthly" things. Spatially speaking the argumentation here is explicitly hierarchical. The dissociation entails that the people with their minds on "the right things" belong above those dwelling on earthly matters.

These dissociations operate largely in the service of extolling Paul's own status as a model for the community to imitate (see the argument by model below). Paul knows and acts upon what really matters, counts all other things as loss, and can be self-sufficient even in dire situations (see the argument by sacrifice below). The more frequently these various arguments elevate Paul as the model and authority, the more clearly the rhetorics of differentiation come into view.

B. Quasi-Logical Arguments

Olbrechts-Tyteca and Perelman label certain techniques quasi-logical that draw their rhetorical strength from their similarity to well-established modes of

---

[17] The convoluted and much-debated topic of the identity of the "opponents" of Phil 3 is far too large and nuanced to do justice in this discussion. The lack of consensus and multiple suggestions simply do not allow for an easy summary. For a thorough treatment of the issues surrounding opponents in Paul's letters, including at least eighteen different scholarly suggestions as to their identity in Philippians, see John J. Gunther, *St. Paul's Opponents and Their Background: A Study of Apocalyptic and Jewish Sectarian Teachings* (NovTSup 35; Leiden: Brill, 1973).

reasoning like formal proofs.[18] But, unlike formal proofs that operate only when specifically limited conditions of logic apply, quasi-logical arguments more malleably seek to apply logical *relations* to situations not bound in a tightly controlled system.[19] In this sense arguing that two statements contradict each other has rhetorical weight because it corresponds to the logical concept of contradiction, even when the conditions under which the two statements were made do not fit strict rules of logic.

1. RULE OF JUSTICE

> to all the holy ones in Christ Jesus who are in Philippi (1:1)

> I thank my God in every remembrance of you (pl.), always in every entreaty of mine on all of your (pl.) behalf (1:3–4)

> so that it has become known in the whole praetorian guard and all of the rest that my chains are for Christ (1:13)

> Rejoice in the lord always; again I will say, rejoice. Let all people know your (pl.) reasonableness. The lord is near. Be anxious about nothing, but in every entreaty and prayer with thanksgiving let your (pl.) requests become known to God. (4:4–6)

> Not that I speak according to need, for I have learned to be self-sufficient in whatever (state/way) I am. (4:11)

> Greet every holy one in Christ Jesus... All the holy ones greet you (pl.) (4:21–22)

> See also 1:25

The rule of justice applies in argumentation whenever one claims to be applying the same principle or same standard to similar situations. Olbrechts-Tyteca and Perelman note that "the rule of justice requires giving identical treatment to beings or situations of the same kind."[20] Of course, discerning this characteristic of sameness is typically a source of contention, as finding identical conditions or humans is rare, if not impossible. Yet, negotiating potential

---

[18] Olbrechts-Tyteca and Perelman, *The New Rhetoric*, 193–260.
[19] Olbrechts-Tyteca and Perelman, *The New Rhetoric*, 193–195.
[20] Olbrechts-Tyteca and Perelman, *The New Rhetoric*, 218. For more on the rule of justice in argumentation, see Olbrechts-Tyteca and Perelman, *The New Rhetoric*, 218–220.

differences between similar cases requires maintaining that the cases are comparable enough to apply this principle.[21]

The letter seems to be making use of this rule in order to demonstrate how Paul seeks to apply these invocations to *all* of them, not just a few of them. Though the argumentation of the letter as a whole seems to address an audience in a broad and comprehensive sense, the rule of justice is especially stressed in the beginning and end of the letter. Here Paul argues to encourage a sense of commonality in the community receiving the letter. Paul demonstrates that he thinks/feels appropriately about the community as a whole (1:3–4, 25) and despite variation in his condition (4:11). This results in Paul having a similar effect on other groups as a whole (1:13), while representing how *all* with him send greetings to *all* in the community at Philippi (1:1; 4:21–22). If the audience incorporates this argumentative disposition, then, they too will act in similar ways despite differences in condition (4:4–6).

As an argumentative technique the rule of justice is clearly contributing to the letter's rhetorics of commonality. Indeed, such a principle seems to be a good way to emphasize unity and a more communal sense of identity in the audience (as the argument from community benefit also did). Yet, if the members of the community are to apply the rule of justice in their actions, they are told to do so by following the lead of Paul.

2. ARGUMENT BY COMPARISON

> Look out for the dogs, look out for the evil-workers, look out for the mutilation. For we ourselves are the circumcision, those who are serving the spirit of God and boasting in Christ Jesus and not having confidence in the flesh, though I myself have (reason for) confidence in the flesh. If any other supposes s/he has reason to be confident in the flesh, I have more . . . (3:2–4)

Though the argument by comparison might be implicitly working throughout the various sections of the letter, this is the clearest instance of its explicit implementation in Philippians.[22] In fact, this section seems to be initiating a doubled comparison. First, the opening insults against these potential

---

[21] Perelman's work outside of this project was especially focused on these aspects of "formal justice" and the problems of application in the modern world. See, for example, Perelman, *The Idea of Justice and the Problem of Argument* (International Library of Philosophy and Scientific Method; London: Routledge, 1963).

[22] In the previous chapter's evaluation of the letter's evolving rhetoric, it was suggested that 1:3–11 might be operating as an argument by comparison. Though a tentative suggestion, this might have been the case if Paul is attempting to establish why he is a comparably more concerned figure for the community. Since this case is considerably less explicit than 3:2–4, it will not receive full treatment in this section. For more on the argument by comparison, see Olbrechts-Tyteca and Perelman, *The New Rhetoric*, 242–247.

anti-models make clear that, by comparison, "we" are in a far better position. Whether they are perceived as a threat ("look out") or are simply being pointed out as a reference point ("look to"), the first party is described in a triply negative fashion: as dogs, workers of evil, and as those who have mutilated their genitals. Hot on the heels of such strong language, "we" are characterized as the proper kind of circumcision and servants of the divine spirit. The pronouns in this passage that characterize the more favored side of the comparison are emphatic (*hōmeis, egō* twice). Though this favored group has good reason, they do not "have confidence in the flesh." It is at this point that the argumentation makes the distinct shift from comparing a group ("we") to comparing one person (Paul, "I"). Paul is linked to this first favored group since they share the same quality: not having confidence in the flesh. Yet, he stands out by comparison to them (and "anyone" else, *tis* in 3:4), since he has *more* reason to be confident. If the argument by comparison establishes relative positions in a hierarchy, with the "dogs" in a lower place and the "circumcision" in a higher one, then Paul is even higher (than all others) in the hierarchical arrangement.

In just one brief argument we get a good sense for how the letter treads this line between commonality and differentiation rhetorics. By its nature the argument by comparison certainly focuses upon whatever difference one can highlight between two groups. In one sense this particular argument might help to establish how those in the community who are "on the right side" are brought closer together by virtue of the favorable comparison. "We" are pulled together, especially if these "dogs" are a common threat. At the same time that "we" as a group make out well by means of this comparison to this other group (or groups), Paul looks even better. If "we" compare favorably, Paul compares even more (*mallon*, 3:4) favorably. If there is any reason to have confidence in the flesh, Paul has it and, as the list following in 3:5–6 makes clear, has it in spades.

3. ARGUMENT FROM DEFINITION

> Just as it is right for me to think/feel this on behalf of all of you (pl.) because of my having you (pl.) in my heart . . . (1:7)

Definitions should be seen as arguments, since they involve the selection of certain elements in describing or identifying the term defined. "The argumentative character of definitions is clearly apparent when various definitions occur of some term in ordinary language."[23] Like many other characteristics of argumentation, there are always a variety of definitions from

---

[23] Olbrechts-Tyteca and Perelman, *The New Rhetoric*, 212. For more on the role of definition in argumentation, see Olbrechts-Tyteca and Perelman, *The New Rhetoric*, 210–214.

which to choose. By making this choice one engages in an argument. Since definitions are not always self-evident, an argument from definition seeks to clarify the element defined by its presentation. Here, Paul is making a distinct choice in pointing out how he has the right frame of mind when it comes to the community. That Paul is resorting to a defining argument indicates that he is at least concerned with whether the audience sees his leadership as linked to his frame of mind about the community. The passage not only defines that he thinks/feels about all of them (see arguments by the rule of justice above), but that it is also right or just (*dikaion*) for Paul to think or feel this way.

This definition early in the letter's argumentation helps to establish from the outset that an important component of Paul's role as model for the community is having this *correct* frame of mind. Since this definition interacts with the arguments by Paul's model (see below), it is also clarifying what would be the correct frame of mind for the audience to hold. Just as Paul's frame of mind can be defined in terms of its rightness (especially in relation to the community), so the audience's frame of mind should also desire to be characterized as right (especially in relation to Paul). This argument by definition attempts to draw Paul closer to his audience through his display of proper care for them (commonality rhetorics), even as it also seems to be arguing for the audience to adopt Paul's attitude (differentiation rhetorics).

4. ARGUMENT BY TRANSITIVITY

Think/feel this in you (pl.) which is also in Christ Jesus (2:5)

I exhort Euodia and I exhort Syntyche to think/feel the same thing in the lord. (4:2)

See also 1:11

The argument by transitivity draws upon the principles of association in a slightly more expanded fashion. As Olbrechts-Tyteca and Perelman describe it: "Transitivity is a formal property of certain relations which makes it possible to infer that because a relation holds between a and b and between b and c, it therefore holds between a and c."[24] In the instances highlighted above, each infers a particular relationship between people.

The two instances detailed have to do with translating state of mind to members of the community, first in general, and then in particular (to Euodia and Syntyche). In this latter case the previous chapter's examination of evolving rhetorics went into great detail regarding exactly how this argument functioned

---

[24] Olbrechts-Tyteca and Perelman, *The New Rhetoric*, 227. For more on the argument by transitivity, see Olbrechts-Tyteca and Perelman, *The New Rhetoric*, 227–231.

transitively. It was by examining the argument on these rhetorical grounds that this study gained a different perspective from the majority view of this passage's meaning. The focus on thinking certain things (*touto phronein*, 2:5; 4:2) through transitive techniques stresses their importance for Paul's argument. It also demonstrates how Paul views such thinking, that it can be transferred. Not only is he seeking to link the community to him through this relation, but he is also defining the relation between the community and himself in these terms, so that it can be applied to other situations.

5. ARGUMENT BY SACRIFICE

For to me to live is Christ, and to die is gain . . . having a desire to depart and to be with Christ, this being much more preferred. But remaining in the flesh is more necessary because of you . . . I know that I will remain and stay beside all of you (pl.) for your (pl.) progress and joy of trust (1:21–26)

Because it has been given to you (pl.) on behalf of Christ to not only have confidence in him but also suffer on his behalf (1:29)

Christ Jesus . . . being in the form of God . . . emptied himself, taking the form of a slave, becoming in the likeness of humans. And being found in the form as a human, he humbled himself becoming obedient as far as death, death on a cross (2:5–8)

But even if I am poured out as a sacrifice and service of your (pl.) trust, I rejoice and I rejoice with all of you. (2:17)

Since he (Epaphroditus, 2:25) was longing for all of you and was troubled, because you (pl.) heard that he had fallen ill. For he was ill, coming near to death . . . because he came close as far as death because of the work of Christ, risking his soul in order that he might fulfill your (pl.) lack to my service. (2:26–27, 30)

But whatever gain there was for me, I counted these things as a loss because of Christ Jesus . . . because of him I lost all, and I count them as dung, in order that I might gain Christ. (3:7–8)

The final quasi-logical technique, the argument by sacrifice, develops from the same notion as the argument by comparison, since it shows how much one is willing to endure for some end (in comparison to other ends).[25] The argument by sacrifice demonstrates the value of the result since someone is willing to make the sacrifice for its sake.[26] It can also highlight the esteem or prestige of the one willing to undergo the sacrifice since "the meaning of this sacrifice in the eyes of others depends on the esteem enjoyed by the person."[27] The more willing a person is to make a sacrifice (up to and including death), the greater the prestige, and the stronger the argument. The efficacy of an argument by sacrifice is tied, then, both to the sacrificial act and to the one performing the act.

At least half of the above arguments by sacrifice (1:21–26; 2:17; 3:7–8) refer to Paul's own sacrifice. The first two instances show that Paul is willing to sacrifice for the community at Philippi. The last of these three highlights the worth of "gaining Christ," since it is worth losing everything, if one gains Christ. Through these arguments the letter displays Paul as a model in his concern for the community and in his connectedness to Christ. Earlier in the letter (at 1:29) Paul seeks to convince the audience that their belief or conviction will involve suffering. That they should "suffer on his [Christ's] behalf" also shows the value placed on being in this relation to Christ (and in the same fight with Paul, 1:30). Thus, even when not explicitly naming him, this instance of the sacrificial argumentative technique reinforces Paul's authority as model for the community.

Indeed, most of the above arguments by sacrifice work to establish the figure enduring the sacrifice as a model for the community. What is apparent in the case of Paul is also evident in the passages about Christ's and Epaphroditus' sacrifices (2:6–8, 26–27, 30). In both cases these models are so committed to their course of action that they both go "as far as death" (2:8, 27) in their sacrifice. Just as the extent to which the divine is involved in an argument by model increases the status of this argument, the greater the role the divine plays in a sacrifice elevates the argument by sacrifice.[28] Thus, Christ's suffering (as one "in the form of God") demonstrates the extreme importance and quality of his obedience (2:8, 12).

Though at least one of these arguments refers to sacrifice as part of a common struggle (1:29), these instances of the sacrificial technique work largely as part of the letter's rhetorics of differentiation. This is a function of the pattern

---

[25] For more on the argument by sacrifice, see Olbrechts-Tyteca and Perelman, *The New Rhetoric*, 248–255, and for the relation between arguments by comparison and sacrifice, in particular, see Olbrechts-Tyteca and Perelman, *The New Rhetoric*, 248–249.

[26] "The sacrifice is a measure of the value attributed to the thing for which the sacrifice is made." See Olbrechts-Tyteca and Perelman, *The New Rhetoric*, 248.

[27] Olbrechts-Tyteca and Perelman, *The New Rhetoric*, 249.

[28] In the relationship between the prestige of the one sacrificing and the value of the argument by sacrifice, "the sacrifice of the divine being is the extreme case." See Olbrechts-Tyteca and Perelman, *The New Rhetoric*, 249.

of the sacrificial act: the ability or will to suffer a status-endangering episode (2:6–8, 26–27; 3:4–7) leads ultimately to an even greater gain (1:21; 2:9–11, 29–30; 3:8–11). Status is elevated through this descent-ascent pattern. These arguments focus, then, on the increasingly elevated figure of Paul as sacrifice (1:21–26, 29; 2:17; 3:7–8), more than on any other figure, including Christ (2:6–8). Even when Paul's sacrificial model is not explicitly at work, the techniques heighten certain virtues in keeping with differentiation rhetorics. Christ's sacrifice develops the appeal to obedience (2:8, 12), while Epaphroditus' actions display the lengths he went to complete his service (2:30). Both obedience and service are extolled in the letter as actions owed to Paul. To the extent their sacrifices are linked to the letter's calls for imitation, then, the various models function to exhort the audience to sacrifice.

C. ARGUMENTS BASED ON THE STRUCTURE OF REALITY

The following arguments are based on the assumed structure of reality, on "the way things seem to be," rather than from philosophical reasoning or demonstration. These argumentative techniques attempt to link the accepted judgments or perceptions of reality with the position one is trying to promote.[29] These arguments proceed from commonly accepted ideas and if they arouse disagreement, the weight of the argumentative technique is undermined. Thus, implementing an argument based on the structure of reality requires building upon an audience's perception of reality.[30] These argumentative techniques present a "more general kind of deduction" than quasi-logical arguments and include the relations between cause and effect and consistency between a person and their actions.[31]

1. ARGUMENT OF WASTE

on the basis of your (pl.) partnership in the gospel from the first day up to now, being convinced of this very thing, that the one who began the good work in you (pl.) will complete it at the day of Christ Jesus. (1:5–6)

Only live as citizens worthy of the gospel of Christ in order that, whether I come and see you (pl.) or I am away, I might hear concerning you (pl.) that you (pl.) stand in one spirit, contending together with one mind for the trust of the gospel, and not frightened by anything from those who stand against you, this

---

[29] For more on the argument based on the structure of reality, see Olbrechts-Tyteca and Perelman, *The New Rhetoric*, 261–349.
[30] Olbrechts-Tyteca and Perelman, *The New Rhetoric*, 261–263.
[31] For this brief description, see Wire, *The Corinthian Women Prophets*, 7.

is a sign to them of their destruction, and of your (pl.) safety, and this from God. (1:27–28)

Therefore, my beloved, just as you (pl.) have always obeyed, not only as in my presence but also now much more in my absence, bring about your (pl.) own safety with fear and trembling (2:12)

[direct address to audience, you (pl.)] holding onto the word of life, for my boast at the day of Christ, so that I did not run in vain or toil in vain. (2:16)

For where we have reached, stay in line in the same way. (3:16)

See also 1:24–26; 4:5; and 4:14–16

The argument of waste builds off of an already-established state of affairs or relationship.[32] It is wasteful to nullify previous efforts or benefits. Better to simply maintain a status quo: "one should continue in the same direction."[33] This type of argument in particular seems to be active when Paul is trying to strengthen the ties between the community and himself. The argumentation stresses that this bond has some history: "from the first day up to now" (1:5–6), "always" (2:12), and "once and again" (4:14–16). Yet, it is not solely a past affair, since Paul also repeatedly stresses that he is seeking for it to continue into the future (1:24–26, 27–28; 2:12, 16; 3:16; 4:5).

For example, in the exhortation immediately following the Christ hymn (2:6–11), Paul stresses the importance of obedience. He does so by recalling that they have previously been obedient ("just as you (pl.) have always obeyed" 2:12), and exhorts them to continue working toward their "safety" now. The past applies to the present and future (*kathōs pantote*, "just as always," 2:12). A key aspect is the potential loss if one fails to maintain the practice. The argument indicates that their previously persistent obedience would be a waste if it does not continue, since they could potentially lose their "safety." The seriousness of the situation is only underscored by the manner with which they should act: "with fear and trembling" (*meta phobou kai tromou*). Thus, the argument of waste can support a course of action as a reminder of a potential gain (1:5–6, 24–26; 4:5), a feared loss (2:12), or both (1:27–28).

The argument of waste is another occasion for Paul to play the role of model. Though he wishes to die and be with Christ (1:21–23), he remains alive so that the progress of the community is not jeopardized (1:24–26). Paul not

---

[32] The argument of waste seems to be a specific embodiment of the argument of direction, of which the "slippery slope" argument seems to be an example. For the argument of direction, see Olbrechts-Tyteca and Perelman, *The New Rhetoric*, 281–287.

[33] Olbrechts-Tyteca and Perelman, *The New Rhetoric*, 279. For more on the argument of waste, see Olbrechts-Tyteca and Perelman, *The New Rhetoric*, 279–281.

only exhorts the audience to obedience (2:12), but he also presses them to cling to the "word of life" so that his efforts are not "in vain" (*eis kenon*, twice in 2:16). The arguments of waste thus function to keep the community members on a path where *Paul* wishes them to stay ("stay in line," 3:16).

2. ARGUMENT BASED ON THE RELATION BETWEEN A PERSON AND HER/HIS ACTS

> I thank my God in every remembrance of you (pl.), always in every entreaty of mine on all of your (pl.) behalf, making the entreaty with joy, on the basis of your (pl.) partnership in the gospel from the first day up to now, being convinced of this very thing, that the one who began the good work in you (pl.) will complete it at the day of Christ Jesus. Just as it is right for me to think/feel this on behalf of all of you (pl.) because of my having you (pl.) in my heart, for all of you (pl.) are partners of grace with me both in my chains and in my defense and confirmation of the gospel. (1:3–7)

The relation between a person and her/his acts is a core example of the relations of coexistence in Olbrechts-Tyteca and Perelman's arguments based on the structure of reality.[34] The relation between an act and the person acting is not a temporal or sequential one as was the argument of waste above, but it inheres in the character of the person.[35] In this instance, the argument involving the act and the person is closely connected to an argument by definition (see above) and an argument by a model (see below). The argument here expands upon Paul's definition of how it is right for him to think or feel such a way about the community. This section attempts to demonstrate how extensive Paul's concern is. It is regular ("every remembrance . . . always in every entreaty," 1:3–4) and focused upon them as a group (the second plural is used seven times in this brief passage). Paul twice mentions his partnership with them (1:5, 7).

This detailing of Paul's prayers, concerns and actions also accentuate his model status in the letter's argumentation. To some degree, all forms of modeling are dependent upon this interaction between act and person: something that the person does qualifies them as a model to be imitated by those who might perform similar actions. Most points where Paul discusses the character of people's actions are listed in the arguments by model below. However, it is in this early argument that Paul establishes that his actions reflect his attitude, expression, and actions. From this relation between Paul and his actions, Paul wants to demonstrate his concern for the community and how closely allied he is with them.

---

[34] Olbrechts-Tyteca and Perelman, *The New Rhetoric*, 293.
[35] On the relation between "the person and his [sic] acts," see Olbrechts-Tyteca and Perelman, *The New Rhetoric*, 293–305.

3. ARGUMENT BASED ON THE RELATION BETWEEN A GROUP AND ITS MEMBERS

But even if I am poured out as a sacrifice and service of your (pl.) trust, I rejoice and I rejoice with all of you (pl.). But in the same way you (pl.) yourselves should also rejoice and rejoice with me. (2:17–18)

See also 1:13–14

If the relation between a person and her/his act is the prototype for relations of coexistence in arguments based on the structure of reality, then the relation between a group and its members is another instance.[36] Similar assumptions can be made: the actions of a member tell us something about their group (a member is representative). But this relation is more complex, "because a person always belongs to a number of different groups . . . [and] mainly because the notion of a group is vaguer than the notion of person."[37] Paul is certainly arguing for a specific audience and has a specific idea of communal identity in mind, but often the contours of this group are ill-defined.

Paul first uses this argument to demonstrate how his deeds have had an effect on the group (1:13–14). It might also be subtly (or not so subtly) noting how far the message has gone because of his imprisonment. Even members of the praetorian guard are now part of their movement, shifting the perception of what the community is. The second instance of this argument articulates an important part of the commonality rhetorics of the letter (2:17–18). Here Paul makes clear that if he is rejoicing, then the audience should also be rejoicing. Arguments for sharing and unity among the community are regularly embodied by the model member, Paul.

4. ARGUMENT FROM DIVINE AUTHORITY

For God is my witness how I yearned after all of you (pl.) in the affection of Christ Jesus. (1:8)

and not frightened by anything from those who stand against you, this is a sign to them of their destruction, and of your (pl.) safety, and this from God. (1:28)

Christ Jesus . . . being in the form of God . . . Therefore God exceedingly exalted him and gave him a name over all names, in order that in the name of Jesus every knee might bend in heaven and upon the earth and below the earth, and every tongue should confess that Jesus Christ is lord for the glory of God the father. (2:5–6, 9–11)

---

[36] Olbrechts-Tyteca and Perelman, *The New Rhetoric*, 321–327.
[37] Olbrechts-Tyteca and Perelman, *The New Rhetoric*, 322.

For God is the one who is working within you (pl.) both to wish and to work on behalf of (God's) approval. (2:13)

not having my righteousness from the law but through the trust of Christ, the righteousness from God on the basis of trust (3:9)

Therefore those who are mature, let us think this; and if you think anything other, God will also reveal this to you (3:15)

And the peace of God who goes beyond all understanding will guard your (pl.) hearts and your (pl.) minds in Christ Jesus. (4:7)

The things you have learned and received and heard and seen in me, do these things; and God of peace will be with you (pl.). (4:9)

I am able in all things in the one who strengthens me. (4:13)

See also 1:20 and 4:19

When an audience accepts God as a part of their reality, using an authority from the divine realm is a powerful argument from the structure of reality. Many of the previous argumentative techniques have dealt with the issue of esteem or prestige, but in arguments from authority we have "a series of arguments whose whole significance is conditioned by prestige."[38] In most of the verses cited in this category, God is the witness or guarantor of a statement: "God is my witness" (1:8), "and this from God" (1:28), and "God will also reveal this to you" (3:15). Of all authority arguments, the "extreme case is the divine authority which overcomes all obstacles that reason might raise."[39] By arguing from a divine authority, the letter intensifies the claims made by reference to an outside authority. Many of these arguments also limn close to an argument by transitivity (see above). The more closely the divine authority acts in accordance with how Paul states, or how closely the divine authority endorses or rewards those who do as Paul seeks, the more closely affiliated with the divine Paul becomes.

That Paul resorts so frequently to the authority of the divine figure raises some questions about the tenor and force of this letter's argumentation. In some of these arguments, the allusion to the divine authority is paired with a direct or

---

[38] Olbrechts-Tyteca and Perelman, *The New Rhetoric*, 305. For the argument from authority, in general, see Olbrechts-Tyteca and Perelman, *The New Rhetoric*, 305–310.
[39] Olbrechts-Tyteca and Perelman, *The New Rhetoric*, 308. See here also Wire's categorization of the "argument from God's calling" and the "argument from the Lord's command," in Wire, *The Corinthian Women Prophets*, 30–31, 33–35.

veiled reference to violence (*apōleias*, 1:28; *apokalypsei*, 3:15), comments that veer dangerously close to threats. The regularity with which Paul turns to God to endorse or enforce his perspective could be an indication of the less-than-stable grounds upon which Paul's argumentation rests. "For the greater the authority, the more unquestionable does his [sic] pronouncement become."[40] Does Paul need an authority beyond question to make his argument?

5. ARGUMENT FROM CAUSAL LINK

1:9–11; 1:12–14; 1:19–20; 1:21–23; 1:27; 1:28; 2:1–4; 2:12; 2:14–16; 2:19; 2:23; 2:25–26; 2:27–28; 3:10; 3:12–14; 3:15; 4:1; 4:4–7; 4:9; 4:18–19

Since there are up to twenty occurrences of the argument from causal link, it would be cumbersome to cite each of them in their entirety here. As might be expected with such a high number of arguments, there is a fair amount of variety in the use of this argumentative technique. Some of them appear to be merely explaining (why Paul is sending Epaphroditus in 2:25–26) or affirming (the assurance of God's blessings through Paul in 4:4–7; 4:9; 4:18–19), while others seem linked to recurring or central arguments for the letter, such as the argument by model.

Of the arguments based on the structure of reality, the causal link is essential to argue from sequential or cause-effect relations. The succession of events in the causal link can be construed in at least two ways, depending upon the focus. If the focus is on the result or the effect, then the argument involves a means-end relation; whereas, if the emphasis is on the source or cause, the argument articulates a deed-consequence relation.[41] A causal link attempts to demonstrate that one action or frame of mind will necessarily lead to another, whether these elements are preferable or not, assessing the elements in these relations as either positive or negative.

For example, Paul's initial description of his imprisonment (1:12–14), contrary to expectations, has advanced the gospel with several positive effects. This means-end argument shows that the end has been progress after all, Paul's chains being a means to a more important end. Later in that same chapter, the two potential fates of safety (or salvation) and destruction are linked to God as their source in a deed-consequence argument (1:28). Though the consequences are foreboding, the argumentative focus seems to be squarely upon convincing the audience to commit to a particular course of action: living worthily as citizens and not being afraid (*politeuesthe . . . mō ptyromenoi*).

---

[40] Olbrechts-Tyteca and Perelman, *The New Rhetoric*, 308.
[41] Olbrechts-Tyteca and Perelman, *The New Rhetoric*, 270–278.

In addition to these two categories (means-end or deed-consequence), Paul twice makes use of the *hoste* clause and a direct address (2:12; 4:1) in an effort to explain how he wants the audience to understand the preceding statements, calling for a specific course of action, in these cases, being obedient and standing firm. The frequency of the causal link arguments in Philippians suggests how extensively Paul is attempting to re-shape the way members of the community apply these ideas to their lives.

6. ARGUMENT FROM A TRADITION

> Christ Jesus . . . being in the form of God, did not count being equal with God to be grasped, but he emptied himself taking the form of a slave, becoming in the likeness of humans. And being found in the form as a human, he humbled himself becoming obedient as far as death, death on a cross. Therefore God exceedingly exalted him and gave him a name over all names, in order that in the name of Jesus every knee might bend in heaven and upon the earth and below the earth, and every tongue should confess that Jesus Christ is lord for the glory of God the father. (2:5–11)

> Further, brothers/siblings, whatever is true, whatever is solemn, whatever is just, whatever is pure, whatever is dear, whatever is auspicious, if there is any virtue and if there is any praise, take these things into account. (4:8)

According to most scholarship on this letter, in these verses Paul is making use of materials that would already have been familiar to the audience from sources outside of this letter.[42] The first may be one of the oldest examples we have of a hymn about Christ (2:6–11), while the second is a virtue list (4:8). When Paul cites each of these, he explains how they should be used. In the case of the hymn, Paul introduces it with an exhortation to "have this mind" (2:5) and, immediately after the hymn, highlights the model aspect of Christ that Paul wishes the community would adopt: obedience (2:8, 12). The virtue list is recommended to the audience for their consideration and is then linked to their imitation of Paul (4:9). Both of these arguments from tradition, if applied

---

[42] While technically this argumentative technique is not articulated in Olbrechts-Tyteca and Perelman's work, it seems to be a reasonable extension of their description of the argument from authority. Wire's classification of the argumentation in the first letter to the Corinthians includes four sub-categories from "the argument from what is written:" two of which involve quotations of a previous argument, while the other two are particular or general allusions to written traditions. See Wire, *The Corinthian Women Prophets*, 28–30. While this study cannot confidently place either of these passages in any of those four sub-categories, it does seem evident that Paul is referring to a tradition outside of the invention of this letter's argumentation.

correctly, are expected to net positive results for the audience, safety and peace (2:12; 4:9). Paul may differ somehow with the ways these traditions are already being applied in the community. He introduces them in order to clarify how he thinks they should be practiced.

D. ARGUMENTS ESTABLISHING THE STRUCTURE OF REALITY

The last of these four categories of argumentative techniques is the argument establishing the structure of reality. This kind of argument seeks to add something to the beliefs already accepted as the reality in the audience's experience.[43] It seems difficult to discern exactly how a statement is either based on the structure of reality or establishing this structure.[44] In the face of much feminist and liberation scholarship, this differentiation is even further problematized. Since texts are typically kyriocentric, they do not accurately reflect or describe a reality, but prescribe or construct one understanding of the situation.[45] Rhetors and rhetorical acts communicate in order to establish *their* views. The arguments based on the structure of reality are really only making that claim, rather than necessarily reflecting a given reality.

Still, there is a difference (though fine) between these two categories of argumentative techniques. Those arguments based on the structure of reality work explicitly to claim that the argument comes out of something already established, whether we believe it to be so or not. In the case of an argument establishing the structure of reality, it is not claimed that this structure is already established, rather it is claiming to work toward establishing this as an accepted reality for the audience. In addition, this kind of argument "moves from the particular to the general."[46] Rather than basing the argument on relations of sequence or coexistence, arguments establishing the structure of reality take the form of particular examples, models, analogies or illustrations in order to convince about a wider point.

---

[43] Olbrechts-Tyteca and Perelman, *The New Rhetoric*, 350–410.
[44] Olbrechts-Tyteca and Perelman, in fact, admit as much in their introductory comments to these four categories of argumentative techniques: "One must not believe that these classes of argumentative schemes are isolated entities . . . we can even consider an argument belonging to one of the classes of structure as well as to another." See Olbrechts-Tyteca and Perelman, *The New Rhetoric*, 192.
[45] On the hermeutics of suspicion about prescriptive literature, see Elisabeth Schüssler Fiorenza, *Rhetoric and Ethic: The Politics of Biblical Studies* (Minneapolis: Fortress, 1999), 51; *Wisdom Ways: Introducing Feminist Biblical Interpretation* (Maryknoll, N.Y.: Orbis, 2001), 176.
[46] Wire, *The Corinthian Women Prophets*, 7.

PREVAILING RHETORIC 181

1. ARGUMENT BY MODEL (PAUL)

I thank my God in every remembrance of you (pl.), always in every entreaty of mine on all of your (pl.) behalf . . . Just as it is right for me to think/feel this on behalf of all of you (pl.) because of my having you (pl.) in my heart . . . For God is my witness how I yearned after all of you (pl.) in the affection of Christ Jesus. And I pray this, in order that your (pl.) love may abound more and more . . . (1:3–11)

But I want you to know, brothers, that the things concerning me have really happened for the progress of the gospel, so that it has become known in the whole praetorian guard and all of the rest that my chains are for Christ, and most of the brothers have become confident in the lord because of my chains to speak the word with much more boldness, without fear. (1:12–14)

But remaining in the flesh is more necessary because of you (pl.). And being convinced of this, I know that I will remain and stay beside all of you (pl.) for your (pl.) progress and joy of trust, so that your (pl.) boast in me might abound in Christ Jesus because of my coming again to you (pl.). (1:24–26)

[direct address to audience, you (pl.)] holding onto the word of life, for my boast at the day of Christ, so that I did not run in vain or toil in vain. But even if I am poured out as a sacrifice and service of your (pl.) trust, I rejoice and I rejoice with all of you (pl.). But in the same way you (pl.) yourselves should also rejoice and rejoice with me. (2:16–18)

Become co-imitators of me, brothers, and look to those who have thus walked as you have a type/form in us. (3:17)

I exhort Euodia and I exhort Syntyche to think/feel the same thing in the lord. (4:2)

The things you have learned and received and heard and seen in me, do these things; and God of peace will be with you (pl.). (4:9)

See also 1:30; 2:23–24; 2:29; 3:7–11; and 4:11–13

The most common argument seeking to establish the structure of reality in Philippians is the argument by model.[47] It is so common that I divide its analysis

---

[47] Olbrechts-Tyteca and Perelman, *The New Rhetoric*, 362–368. On imitation in Paul's letters in general, see Elizabeth A. Castelli, *Imitating Paul: A Discourse of Power* (Literary Currents in Biblical Interpretation; Louisville, Ky.: Westminster John Knox

according to who is the model (or anti-model). The argument by model is just one kind of argument from a particular case, but it fits the following passages better than the others for one main reason: it advocates imitation.[48] Indeed, if other model figures correlate with the first, it only strengthens the perception of this imitative aspect.[49]

The argument by model runs throughout every major section of Philippians,[50] and most of these seek to establish Paul as the model. The frequency of the argument seems to run counter to the minimizing attempts of those who call Paul "a limited authority figure." The regularity and numerical priority of Paul as model in comparison to other models in the letter (Christ, Timothy and Epaphroditus) show how hard Paul worked to place himself as a model and in how *many* different ways.[51]

In the first instance Paul displays model qualities in having the appropriate attitude toward the community, *all* members of the community (1:3–11). His prayers will have an efficacy for the audience and he is closely tied to the authority of the divine. Paul's actions lead to positive results. The progress of the movement continues at the site of Paul's imprisonment, reaching "the whole praetorian guard and all of the rest" (1:13). Paul's model status is elevated since they "have been made confident by my chains" (1:14). In keeping with the

---

Press, 1991); Benjamin Fiore, "Paul, Exemplification, and Imitation," in *Paul in the Greco-Roman World: A Handbook* (ed. J. Paul Sampley; Harrisburg, Penn.: Trinity Press International, 2003), 228–257. See also Brian J. Dodd, *Paul's Paradigmatic "I": Personal Example as Literary Strategy* (JSNTSup 177; Sheffield: Sheffield Academic Press, 1999), 13–32. Dodd's analysis of Philippians, however, is mostly focused on Paul's self-presentation in Philippians 3. See Dodd, *Paul's Paradigmatic "I"*, 171–195.

[48] For the differences between the arguments by example, illustration, and model, see Olbrechts-Tyteca and Perelman, *The New Rhetoric*, 350–371, but most especially Olbrechts-Tyteca and Perelman, *The New Rhetoric*, 350.

[49] Olbrechts-Tyteca and Perelman, *The New Rhetoric*, 364.

[50] Markus Bockmuehl maintains that "the theme of imitation recurs as an integrating focus in every major section of Philippians." See Bockmuehl, *The Epistle to the Philippians* (BNTC; London: Hendrickson, 1998), 254.

[51] Where admitted in scholarship on the letter, the authority of Paul as a model is often mitigated or qualified, particularly as a "limited authority figure." Timothy C. Geoffrion repeatedly emphasizes this conception of Paul. See Geoffrion, *The Rhetorical Purpose and the Political and Military Character of Philippians: A Call to Stand Firm* (Lewiston, N.Y.: Mellen, 1993), 85, 100–104. For a similarly defensive view of Paul's modeling, see Frederick W. Weidmann, "An (Un)Accomplished Model: Paul and the Rhetorical Strategy of Philippians 3:3–17," in *Putting Body and Soul Together: Essays in Honor of Robin Scroggs* (ed. Virginia Wiles, Alexandra Brown, and Graydon F. Snyder; Valley Forge, Penn.: Trinity Press International, 1997), 245–257; Andrew D. Clarke, "'Be Imitators of Me': Paul's Model of Leadership," *Tyndale Bulletin* 49 (1998): 329–360. Weidmann's article is, in part, in response to Robert T. Fortna, "Philippians: Paul's Most Egocentric Letter," in *The Conversation Continues: Festschrift for J. Louis Martyn* (ed. Robert T. Fortna and Beverly R. Gaventa; Nashville: Abingdon, 1990), 220–234.

letter's dissociation of self-benefit from community-benefit (see above), Paul is presented as the model who will remain in this world for the audience's benefit (1:24–26), rather than his own. The sacrificial aspect of Paul's actions intensifies these arguments by Paul's model by developing *pathos* for the model, even as it provides cover for the power dynamics that inhere in such argumentation.

Several instances of the argument by Paul's model tell the community directly that they should act the same as Paul (1:30; 2:16–18; 3:17; 4:9). As the letter wears on, the calls to imitation become more and more explicit: the audience is exhorted to have the same struggle (1:30), adopt the same mode of joy (2:18), join together in imitation (*symmimōtai*, 3:17) and to do the things that they "have learned and received and heard and seen in me [Paul]" (4:9). Viewed together, it is not clear how this type of argumentation could be characterized as anything other than a comprehensive call to imitate the model they have in Paul. Even when the letter's argumentation turns to other models (Timothy and Epaphroditus), it seems as though Paul cannot resist the opportunity to insert his own model into the mix (2:23–24, 29).

These arguments by the model of Paul also play an important role in the letter's dominant commonality and differentiation rhetorics. References to Paul's model contribute to the establishment of commonality rhetorics in the letter, as Paul demonstrates concern for groups as a whole (1:3–11, 12–14, 24–26; 2:16–18) over his own potential benefit (1:24–26; 2:16–18), while seeking the audience's united action (1:30; 2:16–18, 29; 3:17; 4:2, 9), particularly in joy (1:24–26; 2:16–18, 29). Even as some of these model arguments present attitudes of unity and togetherness, they also differentiate, being expressed first in terms of Paul's own preeminent ability to demonstrate these qualities. Paul is the precedent, the authority, and the model. Indeed, there is something inherently hierarchical about arguing through imitation.[52] Imitation is based on the superiority of the model in the element to be imitated and proceeds from the assumption that the imitators are inferior or somehow lacking the trait or practice the model provides. As a major expression of the Philippians' rhetorics of differentiation, the arguments by model establish whose position is more highly regarded than that of others in the community. By sheer volume this study can with confidence place Paul towards the top of the letter's hierarchy.

---

[52] Elizabeth A. Castelli has considered the ambiguous power dynamics of imitation, in terms of both its emulative and authoritative aspects. On this ambiguity, see Castelli, *Imitating Paul*, 16, 21–22, 30–31, 68–71, 140–141. Even in these tensive qualifications, however, Castelli clearly states the hierarchical element of imitation. See Castelli, *Imitating Paul*, 16, 21–22, 86–87. On the role of imitation in the master-apprentice model of pedagogy, see Schüssler Fiorenza, *Wisdom Ways*, 30.

2. ARGUMENT BY MODEL (CHRIST, 2:5–11) AND BY MODEL (DIVINE MODEL, ESPECIALLY 2:6, 9–11)

> Think/feel this in you (pl.) which is also in Christ Jesus, who being in the form of God, did not count being equal with God to be grasped, but he emptied himself, taking the form of a slave, becoming in the likeness of humans. And being found in the form as a human, he humbled himself becoming obedient as far as death, death on a cross. Therefore God exceedingly exalted him and gave him a name over all names, in order that in the name of Jesus every knee might bend in heaven and upon the earth and below the earth, and every tongue should confess that Jesus Christ is lord for the glory of God the father. (2:5–11)

Since the argument by model in this instance assumes that Christ shares in the divine realm, we will consider the use of the hymn as an argument by Christ as a divine model. That the hymn functions as an argument from a model here is made clear both by the introduction to the hymn, exhorting the audience to adopt the same frame of mind as Christ (2:5), and by the immediately following exhortation to respond in obedience (*hypōkousate*, 2:12), as Christ did (see especially 2:8, *hypōkoos*).[53] To the extent that Christ is depicted as sharing in the divine (*morphō theou*, 2:6; the regal imagery of 2:9–11),[54] the model status and quality intensifies: "The attribution of good qualities to superior beings makes it possible, if it is accepted, to argue from the model."[55] Rather than making the

---

[53] Here Kittredge's argument is clear and decisive about the function of the hymn in extolling obedience. Cynthia Briggs Kittredge, *Community and Authority: The Rhetoric of Obedience in the Pauline Tradition* (HTS 45; Harrisburg, Penn.: Trinity Press International, 1998), 83–86.

[54] It is here that this study parts ways with the analysis of the hymn offered by Kittredge and other feminist scholars. See Kittredge, *Community*, 99–100, 110; Luise Schottroff, *Lydia's Impatient Sisters: A Feminist Social History of Early Christianity* (trans. Barbara and Martin Rumscheidt; Louisville, Ky.: Westminster John Knox, 1995), 43–46. Though the hymn might have offered a pattern of reversal as a hope to those oppressed in various ways by the kyriarchal culture, its imagery and vocabulary are still embedded in this kyriarchal matrix of slave-master (2:7) and subject-ruler (2:9–11). For a similar assertion about the kyriocentric nature of this text, see Sheila Briggs, "Can an Enslaved God Liberate? Hermeneutical Reflections on Philippians 2:6–11," *Semeia* 47 (1989): 137–153. This analysis of the rhetoric also leads to the difference seen in the evaluation of other rhetorics in the letter. While Kittredge sees a "discontinuity between the language of friendship and the language of obedience" (*Community*, 110), this study attempts to demonstrate how the rhetorics of commonality often cross paths and work with the rhetorics of differentiation in the letter.

[55] Olbrechts-Tyteca and Perelman, *The New Rhetoric*, 365. For more on the divine, or the "perfect being," as a model, see Olbrechts-Tyteca and Perelman, *The New Rhetoric*, 368–371.

model inaccessible for imitation, as many modern interpreters take this passage,[56] the conclusion of the hymn elevates the virtue of the model figure Christ, thus stressing the importance of acting with obedience, even if the obedient action will be incomparable to the original.[57]

This argument by Christ's model also highlights the argument by sacrifice (see above). The primary way Christ's obedience is developed is through his apparent willingness to suffer, even to death (2:6–8). The model's emphasis on sacrificial action is linked to the passages that extol Paul as model of one willing to suffer (1:24–26; 2:17; 3:7–11; 4:11–13). In fact, many scholars have compared the arc of the hymn to Paul's self-description in the letter (especially 3:7–11).[58] Thus, these arguments from models work together and reinforce each other. Both Paul and Christ are modeling a concern for the community in these passages (commonality rhetorics), descending in some way in order to suffer for the community's benefit. But, both are also displayed as exceptional in the letter's argumentation (differentiation rhetorics), gaining in prestige for their actions.

Since the argument by Christ's model is developed only once, its functional role in the argumentation is a supporting one. Even if Paul's mindset and/or membership in the community involved significant *theological* elevation of Christ, it is not a central or repetitive *argument* for Philippians. The argument by Christ's model advocates the course of action set out by Paul and presented

---

[56] The long-standing debate about how to interpret the hymn involves whether or not to view the hymn as possible of imitation. Those readings that reject the hymn as a model for the audience to imitate do so primarily on theological, rather than rhetorical grounds. See Ernst Lohmeyer, *Kyrios Jesus: Eine Untersuchung zu Phil. 2, 5–11* (SHAW Philosophisch-historische Klasse. Jahrgang 1927/28; 4. Abhandllung; Darmstadt: Wissenschaftliche Buchgesellschaft, 1961 [1928]); Ernst Käsemann, "A Critical Analysis of Philippians 2:5–11," *JTC* 5 (1968): 45–68. On Lohmeyer and Käsemann, and more recent discussion of the hymn, see *Where Christology Began: Essays on Philippians 2* (ed. Ralph P. Martin and Brian J. Dodd; Louisville, Ky.: Westminster John Knox Press, 1998).

[57] On the impossibility, or deferral, of full replication of the model by the copy in imitation, see Castelli, *Imitating Paul*, 13, 16, 22, 63–65, 68–71, 86. This, in fact, demonstrates the hierarchical aspect of imitation: "that imitation can never absolutely succeed, only underwrites further the asymmetry of the mimetic struggle and its fixation on the privileged and normative status of the model." See Castelli, *Imitating Paul*, 22.

[58] On the parallels between Paul's self-description in 3:4–11 and the Christ hymn in 2:6–11, see T. E. Pollard, "The Integrity of Philippians," *NTS* 13 (1966–1967): 62–65. On the use of terms from the hymn throughout Phil. 3, see R. Alan Culpepper, "Co-Workers in Suffering: Philippians 2:19–30," *Review and Expositor* 77 (1980): 350–351; David E. Garland, "The Composition and Unity of Philippians: Some Neglected Literary Factors," *NovT* 27 (1985): 157, 159. On the similarity in sacrifice, and the focus on Paul throughout the letter, see Fortna, "Philippians," 226–228.

predominantly by Paul's model. The more associated Paul becomes with respected figures in the community, the more his model status is elevated.

3. ARGUMENT BY MODEL (TIMOTHY AND EPAPHRODITUS)

> But I hope in the lord Jesus to send Timothy to you quickly . . . For I have no one of similar mind, who will truly care about the things concerning you (pl.). For all of them seek their own things, not those of Jesus Christ. But you know his worth, that as a child to a father he has served with me in the gospel. Therefore I hope to send him as soon as I have seen to the things concerning me; but I hope in the lord that I myself will also come quickly. (2:19–24)

> But I have thought it necessary to send to you (pl.) Epaphroditus, my brother and co-worker and co-soldier, and your messenger and minister to my need, since he was longing for all of you and was troubled, because you (pl.) heard that he had fallen ill. For he was ill, coming near to death . . . Therefore receive him in the lord with all joy and hold such people as honored, because he came close as far as death because of the work of Christ, risking his soul in order that he might fulfill your (pl.) lack to my service. (2:25–30)

As already mentioned above, the use of further arguments by model can reinforce others, especially when they are compatible with each other. As Olbrechts-Tyteca and Perelman maintain: "[c]lose adherence to a recognized model guarantees the value of the behavior. The person following the model enjoys an enhanced value, and can thus, in turn, serve as model."[59] To the extent to which Timothy and Epaphroditus echo Paul's role as a model, they more clearly come into view as models in their own right, while Paul's model status is cemented. Timothy's model qualities develop out of his relationship to Paul and to the community. First, Timothy is closely tied to Paul: Paul has "no one of similar mind/soul" (2:20) and Timothy has served with him (2:22). Second, Timothy's appropriate frame of mind (shared with Paul) is characterized as one who "will truly care" about the community at Philippi (2:20). The allusion to a vague group of anti-models in this section (2:21, see below) seems to be positioned to show that Timothy does not "seek his own things." Timothy acts as a brief model of how to respond in terms of community benefit.

Yet, even as the virtues of Timothy are extolled, the passage remains focused on Paul's own perspective. Timothy is a model because he is similar to Paul and has served with him. Paul is the actor in this span, twice explaining how he hopes to send Timothy, and noting how he himself (the emphatic *autos*, 2:24) will come too. Furthermore, Timothy is described as subordinate to Paul

---

[59] Olbrechts-Tyteca and Perelman, *The New Rhetoric*, 364.

"as a child to a father" (2:22).[60] These notes serve as reminders of Paul's status and his own efforts on behalf of the community ("I myself will also come quickly," 2:24; see also 1:12–14; 1:24–26; 2:17). The supporting argument by Timothy's model seeks to establish a chain of authority with Paul above Timothy as models for the audience at Philippi.

Following closely upon the section arguing by the model of Timothy (2:19–24), the additional model of Epaphroditus (2:25–30) greatly strengthens these models in Paul's argument. Epaphroditus is also firmly linked with Paul, extensively described as "my brother and co-worker and co-soldier, and your messenger and minister to my need" (2:25). More important to this model argument is Epaphroditus' willingness to suffer, as both Paul and Christ had previously demonstrated (see arguments by model and sacrifice). Twice Paul notes how close Epaphroditus came to dying (2:27, 30), once using the same terms that described Christ in the hymn, coming "as far as death" (*mechri thanatou*, 2:8, 30). Epaphroditus also demonstrates the appropriate concern for the community in his worrying about the news in Philippi of his serious illness (2:26).

Though Epaphroditus is considerably elevated as a model in the argumentation of Philippians, this section again contains signs of Paul's preeminence. It is clear that Epaphroditus should be seen as a model when Paul exhorts the audience to treat "such people as honored" (2:29) that risk their lives to fulfill their duties. What also seems clear, though, is that this fits Paul's own self-description in the letter. Though there is effusive partnership language in this section (2:25), there are also notes of Paul's authority over Epaphroditus. Epaphroditus' sacrifice demonstrates not just the value of his service, but the value of a service to *Paul* (2:25, 30). Like Timothy before him, Epaphroditus can be sent at the word of Paul (2:19, 23, 25, 28). Even Epaphroditus' recovery and return are explained in terms of the stress and relief for Paul (2:27–28). In the argumentation of this letter, then, the models of Timothy and Epaphroditus play supporting roles to the model of Paul.

---

[60] Timothy also functions as a supporting model in the argumentation of 1 Corinthians, where Timothy is also described as a child (*teknon*) to Paul's paternalistic authority and model (1 Corinthians 4:16–17). See Wire, *The Corinthian Women Prophets*, 31–33. The allusion to Timothy "serving" (*edouleusen*, 2:22) with Paul reflects the tension between their similarity and Timothy's apparent subordination. The letter's opening identification of both Paul and Timothy as servants or slaves (*douloi*, 1:1) of Christ Jesus might also be echoed here, suggesting a sacrificial connotation to Timothy's concern for the community's benefit.

4. ARGUMENT BY ANTI-MODEL

> Some preach Christ out of envy and rivalry, but others from good will. These (the second) do so out of love, knowing that I am placed for the defense of the gospel, but those (the first) proclaim Christ out of divisiveness . . . (1:15–17)

> and not frightened by anything from those who stand against you, this is a sign to them of their destruction, and of your (pl.) safety, and this from God. (1:28)

> in order that you might be blameless and pure, children of God without fault in the midst of a crooked and twisted generation, among whom you appear as lights in the world. (2:15)

> For all of them seek their own things, not those of Jesus Christ. (2:21)

> Look out for the dogs, look out for the evil-workers, look out for the mutilation. (3:2)

> For many walk, of whom I have told you (pl.) many times, but now I say crying, as enemies of the cross of Christ. Their end is destruction, their god is the belly and glory in their shame, having their minds on the earthly things. (3:18–19)

Supporting his regular use of model arguments, Paul also implements a number of anti-models in this letter's argumentation.[61] Just as arguments by model function to encourage imitation of a certain behavior or course of action, arguments by anti-model discourage imitation. The strong language used to describe the various figures in these arguments—opponents, crooked and twisted, dogs, mutilation, and enemies—leaves no doubt as to their negative role. These anti-models can act as foils to explicit model arguments, or simply work as deterrents in general.[62] In some cases, the anti-model does not work in a completely analogous fashion to the model, since "in argument by the anti-model one is trying to get others to be different from someone without its being possible always to infer precise positive behavior from the distinction."[63] It is possible that an anti-model will show what not to do, or with whom one should not identify, even as it fails to point out what to do.

With the abundance of model arguments articulated in this letter, though, it seems that the arguments by anti-model and model are interrelated. The frequent allusion to these anti-models raises the stakes for following the appropriate

---

[61] For the use of anti-models with or without the contrasting models in argumentation, see Olbrechts-Tyteca and Perelman, *The New Rhetoric*, 366–368.
[62] Olbrechts-Tyteca and Perelman, *The New Rhetoric*, 366.
[63] Olbrechts-Tyteca and Perelman, *The New Rhetoric*, 367.

models. The vision forwarded by the argumentation of this letter poses two paths: that of Paul and his supporting models or that of these anti-models. The anti-models are deployed to characterize those who do not operate with the proper concern for communal benefit (1:15–17; 2:21), consumed by rivalry (1:15–17) and focused upon the wrong things (2:21; 3:2, 18–19). Unlike those who stay on the path recommended by Paul, these figures and those who follow them will be met with destruction (1:28; 3:18–19).

In order for these arguments to be most effective, the difference between models and anti-models must be strong and distinct. This seems to be especially the case for Philippians, as these arguments are key for Paul's strategy of defining certain views of the community and communal unity. Here Paul seems to be following the trend in model (and anti-model) arguments described by Olbrechts-Tyteca and Perelman: "writers feel the necessity to embellish or blacken reality, to create heroes and monsters, all good or all bad."[64] This black-and-white orientation with regard to models and anti-models feeds Paul's insistence to the audience that there is no middle ground. If one does not display the right kind of communal unity, as defined throughout the letter by Paul and a few supporting models, then one is more like the anti-models. This implies one is outside of the community, since you are not acting in accordance with the correct kind of communal unity. Thus, the arguments by model and anti-model are firmly connected to the letter's task of defining the structure and bounds of the community.

5. THE CASE OF EUODIA AND SYNTYCHE: ARGUMENT BY MODEL OR ANTI-MODEL?

> I exhort Euodia and I exhort Syntyche to think/feel the same thing in the lord. Yes, I also ask you, true yokeperson, to take hold with these [Euodia and Syntyche], who struggled alongside me in the gospel with Clement and the rest of the co-workers, whose names are in the book of life. (4:2–3)

If this section about the role of Euodia and Syntyche is an argument by anti-model, it would be the sole exception to this "all good or all bad" tendency evident above. These two women in the community are described as "co-workers" and "those who have struggled alongside me [Paul] in the gospel" (4:3). On the basis of such characterization, many scholars have argued for Euodia and Syntyche's prominence and possible leadership roles in the community at Philippi.[65] This indeed seems likely. Perhaps this is also the

---

[64] Olbrechts-Tyteca and Perelman, *The New Rhetoric*, 369.
[65] For further considerations of their roles, see Lillian Portefaix, *Sisters Rejoice: Paul's Letter to the Philippians and Luke-Acts As Received by First-Century Philippian Women*

reason why the letter cannot present them strictly in the oppositional style apparent in these arguments by model and anti-model. In all of the aforementioned anti-model arguments, the anti-models are not denounced by name. Here the two women are named, presumably because they are known in the community. Thus, if the argumentation is going to have an appeal to the audience, it cannot simply dismiss their perceptions of Euodia and Syntyche's roles, whatever they might be.

By referring to a specific case, the model is limited by the constraints of the case. However, that does not eliminate the possibility of using these two women as anti-models, as the letter's argumentation seems to do, only it requires nuancing *how* they can function as anti-models. By admitting their positive aspects, Paul can seem reasonable, even as he moves to make further approval a conditional reality. Based on the exhortation to "think the same thing" (4:2) and the call for a "true yokeperson" to help (4:3), how Euodia and Syntyche react to this letter would be indicative of whether they are in the right frame of mind or not (4:2; see also 1:7; 2:2, 5; 3:15, 19). How they react demonstrates where they fit into the all-or-nothing scenario. The oppositional picture of community boundaries remains.

Yet, this is only the vision of community boundaries as constructed by the argumentation of the letter. The picture is still developing, depending upon how the letter is received at Philippi, both by these women and by the community. If the community accepts Paul's particular view of communal unity as embodied in these model and anti-model arguments, and Euodia and Syntyche do not, they are effectively outside of the community. They are anti-models. If the community and these two women accept these arguments, the community is unified, but it is a unity characterized by subordination to Paul, in obedience to his model and authority. If neither the community nor these women accepted these arguments, Paul's arguments for certain community boundaries fail to convince. But, according to the schema established within the argumentation of Philippians, there are only two options. Euodia and Syntyche can become models for how to imitate Paul and accept this particular view of unity, or they can become anti-models demonstrating what happens to those who do not fit these calls for unity through imitation. As specific cases, Euodia and Syntyche can be versions of what could happen to any member of the community, depending upon their reception of the letter to the Philippians.

(ConBNT 20; Stockholm, Almqvist & Wiksell International, 1988), 135–154; Mary Rose D'Angelo, "Women Partners in the New Testament," *JFSR* 6 (1990): 65–86; Wendy Cotter, "Women's Authority Roles in Paul's Churches: Countercultural or Conventional?" *NovT* 36 (1994): 350–72; Nils A. Dahl, "Euodia and Syntyche and Paul's Letter to the Philippians," in *The Social World of the First Christians: Essays in Honor of Wayne A. Meeks* (ed. L. Michael White and O. Larry Yarbrough; Minneapolis: Fortress, 1995), 3–15.

E. Summary, Implications and Suggestions

1. Summary of the Argumentative Techniques in Philippians

Much of the evaluation of Paul's rhetorics in Philippians occurred in the previous chapter's discussion of evolving rhetoric. This chapter's approach to the prevailing rhetoric of the letter provides another vantage point on this argumentation by examining each type of argumentative technique. As these different techniques were divided out from each other, there were frequent occasions to note how they interact with each other. Such notes are in keeping with the second cue developed in this study, that arguments overlap and reinforce each other. But what has this explained? To address this question, I will first note the most prominent arguments from each of the four categories and discuss how their recurrence points to the overarching rhetorical tendencies of the letter. Then, based on these recurring arguments and the principle of rhetoric's adaptation to the audience, I will conclude with some initial suggestions about where the community might be situated in this rhetorical exchange.

Among the arguments by dissociation, the most common pair was the self-benefit/community-benefit dissociation. By factoring in its interaction with the appearance/reality, division/unity, and destruction/safety dissociations, it seems clear that the issue of communal unity and its consequences is a recurring theme for the letter. Thus, the central dissociations articulate Paul's overarching commonality rhetorics. Yet, since dissociative arguments restructure perceptions of the relation between their two elements, they separate those who act with the appropriate kind of communal benefit from others. The fates of these two different groups in the dissociation of destruction and safety also highlight the letter's differentiation rhetorics.

Of the quasi-logical arguments identified in the letter, the rule of justice and the argument by sacrifice were more common than others. The rule of justice worked to display the even-handedness of Paul's approach to the community. He represents all of those with him, while addressing everyone in the community at Philippi. He cares for all of them and, by implication, with an equal amount of affection and mindfulness. These arguments from the rule of justice were among the repeated building blocks of the letter's commonality rhetorics. The arguments by sacrifice, on the other hand, point to the role of an individual (typically Paul) acting with concern for the community to one's own personal detriment. Such arguments subtly convey how the letter's overarching tendencies are interwoven. By sacrificing something for the community, the figure embodies the rhetorics of commonality, even as this figure then is elevated over other people in the argumentation in keeping with the rhetorics of differentiation.

Among the arguments based on the structure of reality, the techniques of argument by causal link, argument by authority, and argument of waste were particularly recurrent. Two of these (causal link and waste) involve sequential relations that do not betray any particular emphasis on either of the letter's two rhetorical tendencies. Both arguments attempt to connect consequences to actions or dispositions, reinforcing both relations of differentiation and commonality. The argument by authority, though, is an explicit move to a hierarchical division. Some authorities are better than others, and Paul calls upon the divine realm moderately frequently to back up his argumentation.

Finally, in the case of the arguments establishing the structure of reality, the only techniques discussed were the arguments by model and anti-model. The instances of these argumentative techniques represent perhaps the most significant portion of the letter's rhetorical strategy. These arguments recur through every major section of the letter, highlighting the pointed exhortations to imitate Paul and a range of supporting models. These arguments from a model are a key implementation of Philippians' commonality rhetorics, since the models display this letter's particular vision of unity. Yet the argumentation highlights the model's elevated status, contributing to the differentiation rhetorics.

2. Implications of This Analysis

By examining Philippians in this manner, we see how commonality and differentiation rhetorics appear not only through the letter's four chapters but also across Olbrechts-Tyteca and Perelman's four major categories of argumentative techniques. Both the evolving and the prevailing rhetorics have shown that the rhetorics of commonality interlock with the rhetorics of differentiation in this letter. The implications of this persistent intersection of rhetorics are three-fold, one each having to do with the rhetor (Paul), the rhetorical act (the letter of Philippians), and the audience (the community at Philippi). Noting the interactivity of these arguments effects an evaluation of how Paul constructs a series of rhetorics in order to address the community at Philippi.

First, the way these differentiation rhetorics are so frequently interwoven with the commonality rhetorics demonstrates something about the work of the rhetor, in this instance, Paul. Even when Paul is making an argument about a potential benefit to the community, he does so in terms of his own model. As the letter argues for the audience to become unified, it is a particular kind of unity described by Paul, one that promotes certain differentiations in keeping with Paul's view of his relationship with the community. The vision of this letter is far from neutral; it shows Paul's position on these matters. Most of the time this vision involves solutions for the community that shore up a position of prominence for Paul. According to this letter's rhetorics, the surest way to gain communal unity is to assent to arrangements of authority in which Paul or those closely associated with him stand in the heightened position. Time and again, the argumentation of this letter demonstrates Paul's tendency to think and argue hierarchically. Paul's rhetorics inscribe certain power relations of authority and obedience, typically first to Paul's own benefit.[66] Throughout this study there has been significant reason and occasion for examining the rhetorics in this fashion.

The second implication of the argumentative interactivity, concerning the rhetorical act of this letter writing, proceeds from this recognition of the hierarchical nature of the power relations Paul constructs in Philippians. Given what can be described about Paul's authoritative role in the argumentation of the letter, we must sharpen our grasp of commonality and differentiation rhetorics. Initially in this study, for ease of reference, these general categories were a great help in identifying two different kinds of arguments. These broad conceptualizations allowed the rhetorics to be "caught" and grouped in a rudimentary fashion, signaling that something repetitive occurs in the letter, even as some basic differences were recognized.

Yet reliance on these too-general groupings could potentially mask the specificity with which most of these arguments are deployed. The letter is not simply building a sense of commonality, but working toward a particular kind of unity. This unity involves getting the audience to hold to the same position. It is not enough to be unified; they must act the same way or think the same thing as Paul (1:7, 30; 2:2–5, 12, 18, 29; 3:1, 15–17; 4:2, 9). The arguments express a common sentiment through the rhetorics of unity and sameness. Furthermore, when the letter differentiates parties or concepts, it does so in precise ways. When differences are named, they are pointed out specifically to highlight the preference for a value or the superiority of a figure. These differentiating arguments are a prominent expression of the hierarchy Paul fosters. Among the argumentative techniques, model and anti-model arguments are so frequent that they characterize the way the letter differentiates between figures. Thus, the differentiation rhetorics might be more properly labeled the rhetorics of hierarchy and modeling. The argumentation of Philippians, then, can be more precisely discussed in terms of the rhetorics of unity and sameness (hereafter, US rhetorics) and the rhetorics of hierarchy and modeling (hereafter, HiM rhetorics). The letter seeks to establish the authority of a series of model figures,

---

[66] Discussion of this first implication, then, might correspond at least initially to the analytic of domination called for in Elisabeth Schüssler Fiorenza's feminist hermeneutical project. See Schüssler Fiorenza, *Rhetoric*, 50, *Wisdom Ways*, 172–175.

especially Paul, while fashioning a vision of the community unified by both their sameness and their subjection in a hierarchical pattern.[67]

The first two implications (with regard to the rhetor and the rhetorical act) contribute to a feminist interpretation of the letter in significant ways. For our contemporary pursuits, it is vital simply to name the potentially oppressive aspects of Paul's rhetorics, as this study has attempted throughout.[68] By specifying that one set of the rhetorics differentiates in hierarchical ways (HiM rhetorics), this analysis stresses that the arguments attempt to inscribe relations of submission to an authority and obedience to those privileged in a hierarchy. In an allied way, since the HiM rhetorics intersect and reinforce the letter's US rhetorics, the calls for unity construct the issue around conformity to one vision of the community, where differences in action and mind-set are reduced and adherence to Paul's view is the norm. Far from presenting a liberating view on the topics of Philippians or offering a more egalitarian kind of leadership, Paul exhibits numerous traits of a kyriarchal world-view. Such observations based on these first two implications are useful to a feminist analysis of the letter to the Philippians.

The third and final implication of Philippians' persistently interactive argumentation focuses our attention on the perspective of the community. Describing the rhetorics in a more fine-tuned way clarifies how specifically Paul conceives of the community. A rhetorical act demonstrates how the rhetor perceives the audience, since the rhetor desires the audience's acceptance of the rhetorical act. The rhetor shapes the message of the rhetorical act so as to appeal to the audience, while still forwarding the arguments s/he seeks to make. It is this principle in argumentation that Olbrechts-Tyteca and Perelman discuss as the "adaptation to the audience."[69] It would be unwise for a rhetor to make arguments that s/he thought would never be accepted. Thus, the argumentation is always affected by the rhetor's estimation of the audience.

By closer examination of the rhetorics of Philippians, then, it seems possible to make some observations about the views of the community at

---

[67] The discussion of this second implication could echo the disposition of the hermeneutics of suspicion and the hermeneutics of ethical evaluation.

[68] This "naming" of the oppressive relations that inhere in the US rhetorics and HiM rhetorics of Philippians is in keeping with the hermeneutics of ethical and theological evaluation. See Schüssler Fiorenza, *Rhetoric*, 51, *Wisdom Ways*, 177–179.

[69] "There is only one rule in this matter: adaptation of the speech to the audience, whatever its nature." See Olbrechts-Tyteca and Perelman, *The New Rhetoric*, 25. On "adaptation to the audience," see Olbrechts-Tyteca and Perelman, *The New Rhetoric*, 14–26. This view of rhetoric is a departure from the dominance of the rhetor (in line with the "great man" theories of history and ideas) and from the view of rhetoric as manipulation by stylistics. This latter view was one of the main reasons for rhetoric's degradation at the hands of philosophy over the centuries. See Wilhelm Wuellner, *Hermeneutics and Rhetorics: From "Truth and Method" to Truth and Power* (Scriptura Special Issue S3; Stellenbosch, RSA: Centre for Hermeneutical Studies, 1989).

Philippi. If Paul is seeking to convince the community to accept some of his ideas, his expression of them should be adapted to the attitude or expectations of his audience. Yet, Philippians' rhetorics are not strictly shaped by this adapting tendency. The rhetor also evaluates the situation in a way distinct from at least some members of the audience. Paul writes the letter because he either thinks differently from members of the community at Philippi or he perceives the situation as one where distinctions between them are significant. If these persistently interactive rhetorics reveal something about the community at Philippi, ascertaining what it divulges must be attempted with caution and care, balancing the consideration of how Paul might be arguing in both an adaptive and a distinctive way. Examining the letter in terms of both its evolving and prevailing rhetoric, as this study has done, will be an aid in just such a consideration.

In the following brief focus upon the potential views of the audience of Philippians, it is important to stress that this study does not seek to make a historically deterministic argument about the value of Philippians or of the feminist interpretive project as a whole. It is not necessary to make the following suggestive notes about the community at Philippi in order to contribute to feminist interpretation of Philippians, as the above observations have made clear. Yet, it still might be an additional contribution to this project. Constructing such suggestions through the study of this letter's rhetorics does have two major benefits for the aim of liberating resistance: it de-centers the authority of Paul by focusing on the perspective of the audience, and at the same time it presents a alternative picture of the community from the vision of Philippians.[70] Though this pursuit will be tentative, it still remains vital to embark upon it so that the analysis of the rhetorics does not re-inscribe the authority of the letter by reflexively reinstalling Paul in the preeminent position that "Christian tradition" eventually gave him. Indeed, doing so would be not only ethically troubling, but also historically problematic.

3. SUGGESTIONS ABOUT THE AUDIENCE: THE COMMUNITY AT PHILIPPI

On the basis of Olbrechts-Tyteca and Perelman's principle of adaptation to the audience, we can proceed through an analysis of the rhetorics of Philippians to make some initial suggestions about the viewpoint of the community at Philippi. This process is tentative because it involves a kind of triangulation with regard to the rhetorics of this letter. We might assume that, if Paul is trying to be an effective rhetor, the rhetorical act will in some way be *adapted* to the audience. Yet, as already mentioned above, the desire to communicate most

---

[70] This process might be an initial contribution to the hermeneutics of remembrance and reconstruction. See Schüssler Fiorenza, *Rhetoric*, 51–52, *Wisdom Ways*, 183–186.

likely also involves Paul perceiving the situation in a way he believes to be *distinct* from the potential audience. A rhetorical analysis that seeks to construct potential views of the audience must attempt to trace out this negotiation between the appeal to the audience and the expression of a distinct perspective. The following reconsideration of Philippians' prevailing rhetoric looks for the perspective of the community by keeping this negotiation in mind.

The argument by dissociation, which occurs in many different forms in the letter, involves the rhetor's perception of the audience. Dissociations seek to modify a previously held idea. Their end is not simply to nullify the relationship between concepts (no connection between appearance and reality); rather, they are concerned with altering expectations about, while rearranging the relationship between, aspects of the philosophical pair.[71] In order to get a sense of how the dissociation works to alter these expectations, one must comprehend the dissociative pair in its rhetorical context. Thus, the more often a dissociative argument is implemented in Philippians, the more likely this study will be able to discern how these elements are being rearranged.

For example, the appearance/reality dissociation that recurs in the argumentation of Philippians (1:12; [1:28]; 2:6–11; 3:4–6) highlights how, in Paul's eyes, the audience is in need of correction about the way they see things. As mentioned in the analysis above, since two of the dissociative arguments are forwarded to instill a particular impression of Paul, it suggests that Paul is unhappy with how he is being perceived in the community (or at least how he perceives they are perceiving him). In a related fashion these arguments also seem to be attempting to re-define what the community should seek to be (1:28; 3:4–6), as it relates to their perception of Paul. Thus, there is an initial suggestion that the community at Philippi does not see Paul in the same way as he sees himself and/or that they may not have related this mind-set to their own actions and attitudes in the way Paul expresses here.

Reading through these rhetorics in general and these dissociative arguments in particular also requires recognizing how these argumentative techniques could be relevant or important for the audience. In the case of the destruction/safety dissociation, it might be safe to posit that the audience would value safety (or salvation) and seek to avoid destruction. Indeed, the regular focus on elements of communal benefit in the letter fits with the appeal of safety to the audience. It is possible that the prevailing rhetoric demonstrates its adaptive tendency here. If Paul is seeking adherence to the positions advocated in Philippians, it does not seem at all unlikely that he would adopt a rationale of "this will be good for you." A rhetorical critic can also see how such an argumentative tendency would have appeal to a potential audience. Yet, it should also be kept in mind that this functions as a dissociative argument because Paul believes the community needs to see these elements arranged

---

[71] Olbrechts-Tyteca and Perelman, *The New Rhetoric*, 411–412.

differently. The implementation of the destruction/safety pair might be disrupting the assumption of safety (or salvation) for all in the audience. Perhaps the community at Philippi had a universal or at least communal view ("we are all safe"). Thus, Paul seeks to build an appeal on grounds adapted to their view, one that is communal or universal. However, he does so in order to argue distinctively that the outcomes of destruction and safety are dependent upon how they react to the letter.

Some of the quasi-logical arguments might give signs of the community to which Philippians is written. For example, definitions are used in argumentation, not because the defined item or quality is already agreed upon, but precisely because there is a potential distinction in how people might define it. Twice in the opening chapter of Philippians, Paul argues by definition about himself (1:7, 12–13). On the first occasion, he explains how his frame of mind with regard to the community is right or just (*dikaion*). On the second, Paul wants to clarify what he worries are the community's views of his work. At the very least, Paul is concerned that some in the community might not see how he has the right frame of mind or how his imprisonment has not been an impediment. Since these "chains" are not a major focus of the letter's rhetorics, it is hard to judge the relative probability of such a view in the community. However, as noted above, frame of mind (*phronein*) does recur in the argumentation of the letter, suggesting its relative importance. At this point in the analysis, it seems best to proceed cautiously before assigning it as primarily part of either the adaptive or distinctive tendency in Paul's relation to the audience.

Since they proceed from commonly accepted ideas, arguments based on the structure of reality might reflect the views of the community in particular ways. Here, an analysis could be able to assess how the letter grapples with and hopefully builds upon the audience's perception of reality.[72] The argumentative techniques of this kind would be undermined if they did not proceed from an agreeable foundation. That Paul makes use of so many causal link arguments, for example, indicates how extensively he works in the letter to reshape the way members of the community connect more accepted grounds to other less-known or accepted perspectives. The frequent appeals to divine authority function similarly, beginning with a more stable ground (God) in an effort to reinforce a point made about or by Paul. For instance, the emphatic "For God is my witness" in 1:8 engages an accepted authority in order to attest "how I yearned after all of you (pl.) in the affection of Christ Jesus." The repeated gesture towards God provokes questions involving the potential audience at Philippi. Are people questioning how much Paul cares about them? Does Paul need an authority beyond question to make his arguments? Is Paul's word or authority not good enough to vouchsafe his arguments in the eyes of the community?

---

[72] Olbrechts-Tyteca and Perelman, *The New Rhetoric*, 261–263.

Along with these authority and causal link techniques, the arguments of waste are among the most common kinds of arguments based on the structure of reality in Philippians. This technique is effective if it can show how a course of action is connected to previous efforts. Thus, not following the argument would be a waste of what has come before. In this letter's argumentation the past is evoked to keep the audience in line with Paul's view. Working with this principle of continuity, then, such arguments might highlight both the adaptive tendency (what Paul and the audience hold in common: a history) and the distinctive perspective (how Paul thinks the audience should keep this status quo). Moving towards suggestions about the audience through the argument of waste could reveal two aspects of the audience at Philippi. First, if Paul is seeking to adapt the argumentation in a way recognizable to the audience, then claims of their long-standing partnership (1:5–6; 2:12; 4:14–16) might also reflect the community's view of their past links to Paul. Second, if Paul is seeking to communicate a new or distinct perspective through the letter's argumentation, we might assume that at least some members of the community do not think this common history with Paul now means obedience (2:12; "just as you (pl.) have always obeyed") or conformity (3:16; "stay in line in the same way"). In this instance, it seems possible that the letter's US rhetorics may not entirely fit with the community members' version of "us."

Of those arguments based on the structure of reality, the arguments from a tradition (2:5–12; 4:8–9) could reveal the most about the views of the community. In both of these cases, it seems Paul is quoting a tradition (the Christ hymn and the virtue list) that he thinks will have some sway over the audience. It is difficult to determine whether the community would have known these immediately or recognized them as traditional only upon hearing them in Paul's argument. Yet, again in both cases, there is a direct application or explanation right after the tradition is cited (2:12; 4:9). Perhaps these applications can be identified with how Paul interprets these traditions in a way distinct from the community at Philippi. Highlighting obedience over other elements of the hymn might be a counter-measure to the way other interpretations of the hymn were active in the community.[73] The emphatic call to imitation of Paul's model after the virtue list could be indicating the lengths to which Paul is arguing to get the audience to accept his model status. These arguments suggest that, though Paul expects the community will accept the traditional materials, they may not have conceived of their relationship with Paul as one of imitation and obedience.

---

[73] For example, Kittredge contends that the community did not focus upon obedience in the hymn, but reflected upon "the rule of the *kyrios* over the powers of the cosmos and the consequent liberation of those who have been enslaved to those powers." See Kittredge, *Community*, 99.

Finally, the arguments establishing the structure of reality might shed some light on Paul's audience at Philippi in their attempts to add perceptions not already accepted but still somehow consistent with the audience's perception of reality.[74] Arguments by model and anti-model are the most common of these argumentative techniques in Philippians. This study has already noted the prominent regularity with which Paul develops these arguments seeking to establish himself as a model. For many interpreters, the frequency of this argument demonstrates that Paul must have already been a model for the community at Philippi. While this is a possibility, there is at least one other strong possibility. Many of these model arguments, as part of the letter's HiM rhetorics, are intertwined with the letter's prevailing US rhetorics. Specifically, many of these arguments claim that the community's benefit is somehow connected to Paul as model (1:3–11; 1:12–14; 1:24–26; 2:16–18; 4:9). Indeed, it is one of the things that connects the model of Paul to the supporting model figures (2:5–11; 2:19–24; 2:25–30). It seems possible, then, that the communal benefit element of these arguments reflects Paul's adaptation to the audience, while the calls to imitation of these models show his own distinct perspective.

As with the arguments of waste above, this could render a two-fold explanation of the views of the audience. First, rather obviously, we might expect that the benefit of the community would be important to the community. Here, Paul could be seeking to appeal to the audience on grounds more palatable to their own tastes. Second, if imitation of the model is Paul's own perspective, then we may surmise that the community was not inclined towards imitating Paul. Any acceptance by the audience of these calls to imitation would only be further put in question if they were at all familiar with the role of unity rhetorics in hierarchical institutions of their time, such as the military, ancient friendship, and civic politics.[75]

The regular pattern of Paul's model could also reflect the argumentative triangulation between Paul's and the audience's perspectives. Just as communal benefit connected Paul's model to other model figures and the letter's overarching US rhetorics, the argument by sacrifice provides another link. The descent-ascent or "suffer to gain" pattern is evident in several sections of the argumentation (1:12–14, 21–26; 2:6–11, 26–30; 3:4–11). But what would a message of "status loss" mean to people if they have minimal status? Paul recites all that he was willing to lose to gain Christ (e.g. 1:21–23; 3:4–7), but it seems unlikely that many members of the Philippian community had similar backgrounds (see Chapter III.D. above). It seems possible that this sacrificial

---

[74] Olbrechts-Tyteca and Perelman, *The New Rhetoric*, 350–410.
[75] For more on the potential obstacles to seeing communal benefit arguments (as part of unity rhetorics) as unproblematically appealing to an ancient audience, see Chapter II and Chapter III above.

aspect represents a perspective distinct from the audience's perception. However, it is probable that the audience already identified some kind of benefit in belonging to the community. Indeed, it would seem to be a precondition for joining the fledgling movement. Thus, by discussing the gains of his sacrificial model, Paul could have adapted the community's perception of gain to his distinct emphasis upon suffering or sacrifice.[76]

Though the argument for the model of Paul seems to be the dominant and most frequent of these arguments, the rhetorical use of the other models in the letter might also provide hints about the views of the audience at Philippi. Paul develops three figures as models in support of his own model: a particular version of Christ, Timothy and Epaphroditus. As mentioned above in the reflections on the arguments by tradition, the Christ hymn (2:6–11) might have already been in use in the community at Philippi. Not only was Christ a known entity for Paul's potential audience, but it also seems that Epaphroditus and perhaps even Timothy were familiar. Epaphroditus is apparently from the community at Philippi, as Paul describes him as "your messenger" (2:25; see also 4:18). Paul also expects that they will know Timothy's worth (2:22). In these references to respected and/or familiar figures for the community, Paul seems to be adapting his argumentation. If this is the case, then the aim of this adaptation could be to aid in putting forth a new perspective with which perhaps even Paul anticipated problems: the centrality of Paul as model.

Anti-model arguments may not have been as helpful as model arguments in establishing what course of action Paul was seeking from the audience, but they could prove useful in developing suggestions about the audience. An anti-model shows what not to do or with whom one should not identify. Since it works as a deterrent, it could reflect possible attitudes or actions of the community, especially where they are distinct from Paul's perspective. The most compelling argument that could be echoing the anti-model is the exhortation to Euodia and Syntyche (4:2–3). The mixed description of these two women made discerning their role as either models or anti-models difficult. However, these same expressions also highlight how Euodia and Syntyche are not simply deployed as hollow foils to the elevated models in Philippians. The letter presumably cannot present them in a strictly oppositional style because they are known and most likely respected in some way in the community.

This may be an instance of Paul adapting to his audience, since he cannot simply dismiss the potential audience's evaluations of Euodia and Syntyche. Thus, by naming them and noting their positive aspects, Paul seems reasonable, setting the stage for communicating his own distinct perspective. The exhortation itself, then, indicates that at least some members are thinking distinctively from Paul. As argued above, because Paul exhorts Euodia and

---

[76] For further reflections on status in Pauline argumentation and the possible role of the audience, see Wire, *The Corinthian Women Prophets*, 62–71.

Syntyche to "think the same thing" in this way, it seems likely that they are not thinking the same thing as Paul. If Euodia and Syntyche were not thinking the same thing, what were they thinking? Here, we could cite any or all of the above instances where Paul has argued distinctively. Paul could be concerned that Euodia and Syntyche are not acting obediently in conformity with any of his views. Euodia and Syntyche could have disagreed with Paul about the role of sacrifice, the potential for safety or destruction, the need to imitate primarily Paul, or his claims to divine authority.

Thus, by examining where the rhetorics of the letter might be adapting to the views of the audience or offering a distinct perspective, this study offers some initial suggestions about the perspectives of the community at Philippi. Paul expects them to care about their own benefit and safety, to recall parts of their relationship with him, to remember tradition materials, and to recognize certain figures (God, Christ, Timothy, Epaphroditus, Euodia and Syntyche). Beginning with these suggestions about how Paul adapts the argumentation to his audience, we can further gauge the potential views of the community by how Paul appears to be arguing distinctively. At the very least the argumentation indicates Paul's concern that the community at Philippi does not see him in the same way as he sees himself. Some members could be questioning his authority or even his motives, as Paul frequently turns to other authorities to shore up his own position. There are considerable signs that the audience may not have shared Paul's view of the appropriate frame of mind for members of the community. At least some seem *not* to be thinking the same thing as Paul, not linking their experiences to the need for imitation of, conformity with, sacrifice like, and/or obedience to Paul.

Clearly, these possibilities are just that: possibilities. Though they are far from conclusive, they are reasonable suggestions, given the examination of the prevailing rhetoric of the letter to the Philippians. Reading the rhetorics while aware of this negotiation between Paul's perspective and the reception of the audience allows for a wider perspective on the meaning of the letter to the Philippians. The letter reflects on more than just Paul's expression of the intertwined US rhetorics and HiM rhetorics. It functions as a reminder that the letter is just one part of an ongoing exchange between Paul and the members of the community at Philippi. No matter how authoritative Paul seeks to be, it is not a final proclamation or a static picture.

Though it is an alternative to an analysis that focuses solely on Paul as authority and arbiter of meaning, this interpretation of Philippians and its potential audience is also not an idealized picture. It is suggestive and incomplete. For a liberating interpretive project, it would be a mistake to invest only positive evaluations with the audience. This seems not only unrealistic, but also possibly ahistorical. If the goal is to interpret biblical literature so as to contribute to feminist transformative action, then here we must acknowledge much of this project's evaluative work on Philippians' argumentation that has preceded this suggestive contribution about the audience at Philippi.[77] I find it difficult to ascribe only positive characteristics to the community, since our access to the views of the community comes through Paul's arguments in the letter to the Philippians. As has been noted throughout this study, these rhetorics are implicated in a troubling hierarchical tendency. Thus, this particular feminist rhetorical analysis of Philippians is not achieved by painting an ideal picture or constructing ancient heroes for our contemporary struggles. Rather, its feminist aims shine through in the recognition and assessment of the dominating rhetorics of the letter as well as in the rhetorical act of destabilizing claims of Pauline authority by focusing on what *can* be suggested about those community members in Philippi. Just as the rhetorical exchange did not end with the reading aloud of Paul's final greetings to this audience, so the feminist rhetorical project of interpreting Philippians is begun but not completed by this analysis.

---

[77] For more on the hermeneutics of ethical evaluation and the hermeneutics of transformative action for change, see Schüssler Fiorenza, *Rhetoric*, 51, 53–54, *Wisdom Ways*, 177–179, 186-189.

Chapter VI

Conclusions

Before proceeding to some conclusions, implications, and suggestions for further directions coming out of this project, it seems relevant to review the territory these previous chapters have traveled. After introducing the approach and scope of this study, the first part of this study sought to locate the analysis of Philippians within the relevant contexts for both contemporary biblical interpretation and the ancient community at Philippi. The second chapter engaged in a critical overview of some of the more recent developments in Philippians' scholarship. Beginning in a rather standard form, this overview did not end with a summary of the high points of current proposals regarding the relevance of military and friendship imagery in the letter. Instead, as a feminist rhetorical analysis it assessed some of the power dynamics that inhere in these images.

Because most previous scholarship on Philippians has not addressed these dynamics, this analysis produced two cues to ensure that this study remained critically attentive. First, the study needs to track the potentially oppressive power relations reflected in the letter, with the help of feminist conceptualizations, such as kyriarchy. Second, the study needs to distinguish the letter's rhetorics in their multiple specificity *and* in their mutually supporting interactivity, especially where they might function in potentially oppressive or even liberating ways. The third chapter furthered the contextual goals of this first part of the project by following these two cues while situating the rhetorics of Philippians through an examination of women's participation in both the major cults and the early Jesus movement(s) at Philippi, the use of unity rhetorics in ancient civic speeches, and the colonial status and military situation at Philippi.

Having set the stage by examining and evaluating the contexts for the letter and its interpretation, the project turned to its second part, a more concentrated analysis of the argumentation of Philippians. With these two cues and Olbrechts-Tyteca and Perelman's theory of argumentation in mind, this study read the rhetorics of Philippians from two different vantage points. In the fourth chapter, the letter was approached in terms of its evolving rhetoric, assessing the argumentative techniques in the order that they appeared in the letter, as they built upon and interacted with each other. This approach had clear resonances with the second cue developed in the first part of the project, but it also facilitated the first cue, since it focused upon the function of the arguments in Paul's rhetorical strategy. The fifth chapter discussed these same arguments in terms of their prevailing rhetoric, evaluating the techniques as they recur throughout the letter. Whereas the previous chapter engaged in a section-by-section analysis of Philippians, this chapter was geared towards demonstrating what was characteristic of Philippians' rhetorics. This difference in approach encouraged attention to the first cue and allowed for some initial suggestions about the significance of this analysis in terms of the rhetor, the rhetorical act, and the possible audience.

While the fifth chapter ended with a few reflections upon the implications of this project and some tentative suggestions about the audience, there are several concluding tasks that remain. The following conclusions focus upon three areas: a.) where this study contributes to a different understanding of the letter to the Philippians, b.) what are the implications of this project's examination and assessment concerning previous scholarship, and c.) how this study could be useful for feminist and allied interpretations for liberation.

A. A DIFFERENT UNDERSTANDING OF THE LETTER TO THE PHILIPPIANS

As it has been clearly shown throughout this analysis of Philippians, especially in the chapters where the focus is most clearly upon the argumentation of the letter, there is much about which to be suspicious. Contrary to a great deal of scholarship on Philippians, this letter cannot be considered "friendly" by a modern audience, and there are further questions raised as to whether the community at Philippi would have been amenable to these rhetorics. Philippians is a letter focused upon issues of authority, arguing for obedience and conformity from the community. On occasion it appears to be doing so with the force of threats, evoking the specter of violence in its arguments. Time and again, the letter demonstrates a tendency towards hierarchical thinking. As long as one desires to remain within the letter's view of community, dissent or disagreement is not a possibility.

More specifically, the letter is Paul's attempt to establish a kyriarchal relationship between the Philippian community and himself. Throughout the argumentation the focus is persistently upon the figure of Paul. Not only does the figure of Paul predominate in the argumentation of Philippians, but Paul works to create for himself a dominant position through these arguments. The rhetorics of the letter present the audience with a series of models, offered on hierarchical terms. Timothy, Epaphroditus, and even Paul's particular version of

Christ operate as supporting models to Paul's own preeminent place as authority. By stressing the sacrificial aspect of his model actions, these arguments provide cover for Paul's claims to authority, developing *pathos* for the one who makes the sacrifice. In terms of the overall rhetoric of the letter, Paul sits atop the resulting power relations at the apex of a hierarchy of models, which he is hoping the community will be convinced to imitate, even as they remain subordinate to Paul and those most closely allied with him.

In terms of this predominant argumentation, the role of Euodia and Syntyche comes most clearly into view. As likely leaders in the community at Philippi, Euodia and Syntyche are a source of concern for Paul. Through these rhetorics Paul hopes to bring them into his vision of the community. Being among the "us" in the letter's US rhetorics (unity and sameness) means being of one mind with Paul, the "him" in the HiM rhetorics (hierarchy and modeling).[1] If they do not learn to "think the same thing" as Paul, he has so presented a view of unity in the community that nonconformity can only be characterized as selfish rivalry, strife, and disunity.

Such an understanding of the letter evolves from an appreciation of exactly how dense the argumentation is. Because of these repetitive and interlocking rhetorics, the letter of Philippians must be analyzed as a whole. This is the benefit of proceeding with a rhetorical analysis according to the perspectives of Lucie Olbrechts-Tyteca and Chaïm Perelman. With their emphasis on the interactivity of argumentation, it became possible to see how the rhetorics of Philippians were most effective when several argumentative techniques were working together, even as they functioned in different ways. Beyond such micro-level, verse by verse observations, this attention to the densely mutual and interlocking argumentation allowed a comprehension of how the overall rhetorical tendencies, the US rhetorics and HiM rhetorics, are implicated within each other and cannot be easily separated. One set of rhetorics cannot be seen positively extolling unity or the common good, while the other is reduced to its problematically hierarchical function. Thus, even though the US rhetorics are less *explicitly* hierarchical than the HiM rhetorics in Philippians, it is clear that the unity for which it argues is not unity solely for unity's sake. The US rhetorics are as much a part of the letter's kyriarchal agenda, since Paul advocates a kind of unity that promotes certain differentiations in keeping with the relationship he wants with the community. The surest way to gain communal unity is to assent to arrangements of authority in which Paul and those closely associated with him stand in the heightened position. Paul's authority remains a central issue through both of these overarching rhetorical tendencies, especially as they relate to the calls for imitation.

---

[1] See the analysis of Chapter V.E. above for these labels.

Articulating Philippians' rhetorics in this manner, as complex, dense, and persistently interlocking, adds yet another strong argument to the case for the literary integrity of this letter. Paul develops these arguments through every major section of the letter and does so in a coherent and cohesive fashion.

B. IMPLICATIONS CONCERNING PREVIOUS SCHOLARSHIP

Many of the above observations about this project's understanding of Philippians differ in significant ways from previous work on Philippians. Indeed, this was the aim and intent of this study, as the initial considerations of its paradigm and approach sought to demonstrate. The development of two cues for proceeding with a feminist rhetorical reading of Philippians was required so that the analysis would remain consistent with the goals of this interpretive project. These two cues developed out of a critical overview of some of the more recent developments in Philippians' scholarship.

Yet, this critical overview was not a debate about whether friendship or military imagery might be relevant for an interpretation of Philippians. Later contextual work also did not question the importance of ancient civic speeches or the colonial status of Philippi. Rather, this project recommends a shift in analysis from asking simply *if* such images and situations apply to the letter's rhetorics to considering both if and *how* these images and situations apply. While the suggestions by scholars interested in military and friendship images were instructive, their interpretations stop short since they do not consider how such imagery is related to an entire thought-world. Most previous scholarship on these images in Philippians does not recognize how these images are a part of a series of kyriarchal systems in Greco-Roman antiquity. Indeed, this is but one way that friendship imagery is connected to military imagery.

Such gaps in the consideration of the imagery in Philippians has limited the interpretation of Philippians in particular ways. Despite the growth of feminist approaches to biblical interpretation in the last few decades, most scholarship on Philippians has not reflected these critical developments. Thus, these approaches were simply not equipped to ask how Philippians' rhetorics function, especially in terms of Paul's attempts to establish certain power dynamics. Any approach that desires to be useful in the cause of liberation must do more than identify aspects of the argumentation; it must develop means for assessing and evaluating these aspects. A feminist rhetorical approach requires that interpreters reconsider their evaluations, which have often gone unexamined and unexplained. This evaluative element highlights that the interpreter is accountable for how s/he grapples with potentially oppressive aspects of a text, especially as the text might be relevant for or have an impact upon today's communities.

This involves restoring the *critical* element to rhetorical criticism. In order to analyze the rhetorics of a letter like Philippians, we must be prepared for critical engagement with the rhetorics. This would involve less focus upon developing apologies for Paul in our interpretation of his letters. It also entails less defensiveness about preserving certain views of the meaning and content of these letters. In order to be open to the impact of Philippians, we need to be able to critically assess our own scholarly assumptions and models. Interpretation can involve a questioning of our attachments and deeper reflection upon our loyalties. Any interpretation that seeks to be allied with feminist goals must also recognize the kyriarchal foundations for all of our fields, whether it is biblical or classical studies, archaeology, rhetoric, or history. Such a recognition need not lead to a fatalistic hermeneutical determinism or a renewed quest for a bias-removing "restoration of objectivity." An honest assessment of the history of academic complicity in dominating forms of thinking attunes us to the need for critical approaches that deal with this fraught history. An interpretative task that holds this critical view at its center seeks to name such problematic rhetorics as part of a productive inquiry.

A feminist rhetorical analysis of Philippians, or any analysis of the letter that seeks to be allied with a liberating aim, needs to be engaged in both identification and evaluation. These two tasks apply not only to the rhetorics of the letter itself but also to the rhetorics of its interpretation.

C. USEFULNESS FOR FEMINIST AND LIBERATION INTERPRETATIONS

Given its communities of accountability, this project has sought to do more than develop a further understanding of Philippians and its interpretation. It is hoped that this study will have import for feminists both within and outside the academy as well as for all people subject to pyramidal forms of domination.

The role of Euodia and Syntyche in the argumentation of Philippians has been an important recurring topic in this analysis of the letter. The specific attention Paul gives to these two women in the community at Philippi demonstrates their prominence in terms of Paul's rhetorics. It seems likely that this reflects the prominence of Euodia and Syntyche in the community. Paul addresses them specifically because he needs to do so. Their possible leadership role has been noted by scholars before, especially given Paul's comments about them as his "co-workers" and those "who struggled with me in the gospel" (4:3). Yet, most traditional interpretations of the letter have held that Paul is encouraging Euodia and Syntyche to "think the same thing" (4:2) *as each other*, presuming that the two women are in some kind of conflict. Given this project's examination of the recurring argumentation of the letter, it is more likely that this exhortation is meant to encourage Euodia and Syntyche to "think the same thing" *as Paul*. This understanding of the passage fits better with the US rhetorics and HiM rhetorics of Philippians, since it shows how Paul is seeking for Euodia and Syntyche to be in conformity with "us" by acting in accordance with him as a model.

This rhetorical examination of the letter and the particular role of Euodia and Syntyche within it enriches the picture of women's roles in the developing communities of the early Jesus movement(s). This project's later suggestions about the potential views of the audience at Philippi add to the complexity of our constructions for the first century C.E. The focus on these two women helps to demonstrate how a Pauline letter is not descriptive, but prescriptive: it represents an attempt to get Euodia, Syntyche, and other community members to think the same thing as Paul. This analysis of Paul's rhetorics indicates that issues of communal authority are not static and definitive by the middle of the first century C.E. Rather, it can be expected that the audience operated in ways distinctive from Paul's hopes. This project suggested that the audience may not have shared Paul's view of the appropriate frame of mind for members of the community. At least some seem *not* to be thinking the same thing as Paul, not linking their experiences to the need for imitation of, conformity with, and/or obedience to Paul. The community is not monolithic and Paul is not yet in the preeminent position that "Christian tradition" will eventually give him. Several of these indications flow out of this study's analysis of Euodia and Syntyche in the argumentation of Philippians, though the analysis assiduously sought not to idealize these women or the potential audience at Philippi.

This project might also be useful for purposes of liberation because it addresses the role of power relations in the letter and in biblical interpretation. As a feminist rhetorical analysis, it hopefully provides another example for practicing the assessment of kyriarchal rhetorics. The reconsideration of scholarly approaches to the imagery in Philippians demonstrates the importance of the imagery's rhetorical context. In the Greco-Roman world friendship, military, and civic images are embedded within a kyriarchal matrix, functioning in an order that oppresses the vast majority of people. This study shows that where these images are evident in Philippians or any other set of arguments, we must examine how they are connected to this kyriarchal order.

Turning to the rhetorical analysis of the letter in this study, there are also some deeply problematic argumentative gestures not immediately connected to previous analysis of Philippians' imagery. Discussions of potential destruction alongside the invocation of divine authority veer quite close to threats. The call for obedience to Paul is central. The letter so constructs the appropriate frame of mind for the community so as to leave little room for views not in conformity with Paul's. Failure to become united with these views means being characterized as enemies, filled with selfishness and strife. There is no room for debate or dissent; Paul's authority is forwarded, while questioning is explicitly dismissed. Paul does not just allude to images from a kyriarchal thought-world, he constructs his own arguments with kyriarchal ends, typically in an effort to create an authoritative position for himself. As a result, any feminist or allied liberation-oriented approach must remain suspicious of these rhetorics. Arguments for unity and the "common good" can be used for oppressive ends, both then and now. Calls to subordinate oneself as a sacrifice for the community in a time of "crisis" can be a rationale to reinscribe dominating power dynamics. Indeed, such arguments, far from running counter to imperial ideology in the first century, reflected and helped to maintain the status quo of the "pax Romana." There must be some doubt as to how they could aid today in the cause of decolonization.

Naming and assessing these rhetorics for their participation in kyriarchal systems and worldviews is hopefully not the only use of this study for the task(s) of feminist interpretation. Recognizing the interlocking US rhetorics and HiM rhetorics in Philippians while examining the rhetoricity of interpretation provides us with an opportunity for intervention. Just as it was likely that there was more than one response by those who first received this letter at Philippi in the mid first century C.E., an understanding of this letter can generate many responses today. Canonization certainly declared this letter and others of Paul's as worthy of measure. Yet, this does not limit our responses to those of acceptance or denial. In fact, given the conditions of these rhetorics, we can afford neither of these responses. To accept the letter is to become implicated in all that is troubling about its argumentation. To deny its relevance is to risk not addressing its power dynamics, both historically and contemporarily.

Thus, it seems necessary to conceive of multiple ways to respond to the results of this project. Interpreting the letter in creative resistance can still be useful as a practice for feminist and other liberation-oriented approaches. It is hoped that this project's analysis can be a resource for a series of responses.[2]

For example, further feminist inquiries might focus on the issue of imitation in the letter. Since Paul exerts so much rhetorical energy in order to convince the members of the community to imitate him, we can imagine that he is attempting to dissuade them from imitating someone else. Membership and participation in the developing communities of the early Jesus movement(s) might practically involve some level of imitation. Given what seems to be the prominent role of women in these communities, both in Philippi and elsewhere, does this suggest that women were being imitated? Here, some of the background on women's participation in cults at Philippi could be useful. It seems possible that Paul's

---

[2] The rationale for a series of responses can be linked to a different conception of the power of a rhetorical act. In keeping with Michel Foucault's formulation of power/knowledge (*pouvoir/savoir*), power is not simply an exercise of power over something, but power produces a whole series of relations, an entire body of effects. These effects are multiple, diffuse, and ambiguous. In fact, the operation of power can run counter to what is expected. See, for example, Foucault, *Power/Knowledge: Selected Interviews and Other Writing 1972–1977* (ed. Colin Gordon; trans. C. Gordon, Leo Marshall, John Mepham, and Kate Soper; New York: Pantheon Books, 1980).

directed exhortation to Euodia and Syntyche was meant to convince people to stop imitating these two leaders. Further, if the results of imitating Paul were meant to be distinctive from the results of imitating others, different power dynamics might have been reflected in the choice of other models.

The letter's persistent focus on unity in terms of conformity and sameness, is also worthy of further examination and response. Such a rhetorical strategy functions as an attempt to erase difference. How have unity rhetorics been a prominent part of scholarly and activist assumptions about the uniformity and stability of such critical concepts as "experience" or "identity?" What role do claims to universality play in the suppression of the multiple particularity of one's identity? Questions like these have been raised before by scholars interpreting as womanists,[3] as *mujeristas*,[4] or as a part of *minjung*.[5] Any activist or scholar attempting to understand the multiple and interlocking forms of oppression evident in both ancient and contemporary societies would do well to attend to these kinds of critical issues.[6]

The colonial context for the production of Paul's letter to the Philippians also requires further examination and responses. The unique history of Philippi as both a significant site for military conflict and then a colony in the Roman empire presents a number of questions about this letter and its impact. Paul's use of imperial imagery in the letter is particularly relevant. Some scholars have suggested that where Paul makes use of such imagery, it is part of a counter-

---

[3] Renita J. Weems, *Just a Sister Away: A Womanist Vision of Women's Relationships in the Bible* (San Diego: LuraMedia, 1988); "Reading *Her Way* through the Struggle: African American Women and the Bible," in *Stony the Road We Trod: African-American Biblical Interpretation* (ed. Cain Hope Felder; Minneapolis: Fortress, 1991), 57–77, esp. 64–70, 75–77; Jacquelyn Grant, *White Women's Christ and Black Women's Jesus: Feminist Christology and Womanist Resonse* (American Academy of Religion Academy Series 64; Atlanta: Scholars Press, 1989), esp. 3–7, 195–222; Katie Geneva Cannon, *Katie's Canon: Womanism and the Soul of the Black Community* (New York: Continuum, 1995).
[4] Ada María Isasi-Díaz, *En la Lucha/In the Struggle: An Hispanic Women's Theology* (Minneapolis: Fortress Press, 1993); "*La Palabra de Dios en Nosotras*—The Word of God in Us," in *Searching the Scriptures: A Feminist Introduction*, Volume One (ed. Elisabeth Schüssler Fiorenza; New York: Crossroad, 1993), 86–97; *Mujerista Theology* (Maryknoll, NY: Orbis Books, 1996).
[5] Chung Hyun Kyung, *Struggle to Be Sun Again: Introducing Asian Women's Theology* (Maryknoll, N.Y.: Orbis Books, 1990); *Minjung Theology: People as the Subjects of History* (ed. Kim Yong Bock; Singapore: Commission on Theological Concerns, Christian Conference of Asia, 1981); Kwok Pui-lan, *Discovering the Bible in the Non-Biblical World* (Bible & Liberation Series; Maryknoll, N.Y.: Orbis Books, 1995), esp. 15–19, 66–70.
[6] For an interesting engagement with issues of universalism and particularity in both Pauline letters and rabbinic works, with reflections on contemporary racisms, see Daniel Boyarin, *A Radical Jew: Paul and the Politics of Identity* (Contraversions 1; Berkeley: University of California Press, 1994), esp. 228–260.

imperial agenda. According to this view the content of Philippians is somehow seditious for its mid first century C.E. context. Yet, according to this study's analysis Paul's rhetorical strategy seems to accommodate itself to the Roman imperial order. How can we imagine the colonized community that received this letter? How could have the reception of the letter been affected by the conditions in this *colonia*? Some of these issues have been pursued in the interpretation of Pauline letters, in general, but there have been few reflections on such topics in Philippians' scholarship.[7] These kinds of questions would be especially relevant for a postcolonial analysis of Philippians, as a way to grapple with both the ancient Greco-Roman context and the role of biblical rhetorics in modern colonialism and neocolonialism. In fact, postcolonial theory's examination of mimicry as an elusive colonizing strategy could be a provocative aid to the analysis of imitation in Philippians and other Pauline letters.[8]

Just as the previous range of questions circled the study back to the role of imitation in Philippians' argumentation, it might be fruitful to return yet again to an analysis of unity rhetorics. Queer theory, for example, has highlighted the hegemony of certain constructions of normativity, especially with regard to gender and sexuality. The letter's US rhetorics have similar cultural effects, in terms of pressing a singular normative expression for the community members. Paul works persistently for this sameness. Is it coincidental that the ties between Paul and his supporting models are expressed in terms of some affectionate intimacy and intensity? Significantly, the models in the letter's HiM rhetorics are exclusively male, while Paul reserves strong condemnations and echoes of violence for those who do not fit these models. In light of these and other questions, the reason for Euodia and Syntyche's pairing resurfaces.[9] What variety of arrangements might explain the bonds between members of these communities?[10]

---

[7] See, for example, the entries in *Paul and Empire: Religion and Power in Roman Imperial Society* (ed. Richard A. Horsley; Harrisburg, Penn.: Trinity Press International, 1997); *Paul and Politics: Ekklesia, Israel, Imperium, Interpretation* (ed. Horsley; Harrisburg, Penn.: Trinity Press International, 2000). In terms of a postcolonial analysis of Philippians, this lack is soon to be corrected by Efrain Agosto's entry on Philippians in *A Postcolonial Commentary on the New Testament* (ed. Fernando F. Segovia and R. S. Sugirtharajah; Sheffield: Sheffield Academic Press, forthcoming).

[8] For mimicry in postcolonial work, see Homi K. Bhabha, *The Location of Culture* (London: Routledge, 1994); Rey Chow, *The Protestant Ethnic and the Spirit of Capitalism* (New York: Columbia University Press, 2002). For an initial exploration of mimicry's import for biblical interpretation, see Tat-siong Benny Liew, "Tyranny, Boundary, and Might: Colonial Mimicry in Mark's Gospel," *JSNT* 73 (1999): 7–31.

[9] See the suggestions in Mary Rose D'Angelo, "Women Partners in the New Testament" *JFSR* 6 (1990): 65–86.

[10] For more on the significance of the study of homoeroticism and queer theory for Pauline interpretation, see Bernadette J. Brooten, *Love Between Women: Early Christian*

Though addressed in turn, these critical interventions into the interpretation of Philippians cannot always be neatly divided into separate fields of inquiry. In fact, such a division is often neither desirable nor possible, especially if an analysis seeks to grapple honestly with interlocking forms of domination. These are but a few of the many possibilities for a further analysis of Paul's rhetorics. In most cases they represent paths not yet taken in the interpretation of Philippians. Yet, as this project has attempted to demonstrate, the rhetorical exchange did not end in the middle of the first century, nor will it likely end here at the beginning of the twenty-first.

Responses to Female Homoeroticism (Chicago: University of Chicago Press, 1996), esp. 189–302; Stephen D. Moore, *God's Beauty Parlor: And Other Queer Spaces in and around the Bible* (Contraversions; Stanford: Stanford University Press, 2001), esp. 133–172.

Appendix: Outline of Argumentative Techniques in Philippians

The layout of this appendix is meant to more visually demonstrate the function of the arguments in each section of Philippians. If a technique is indented from the rest of the list, it is seen as secondary or complementary to the previous technique. When an argument is listed in brackets [ ], it is an indication of less certainty about this type of argument, though we have reasons to surmise that it could be functioning in the letter. Finally, the parenthetical notes are simply elaborations upon arguments such as dissociation, arguments by authority, or argument by model, in order to specify the terms of these arguments.

    1:1–11. Outline of argumentative techniques
       1:1 rule of justice
       1:3–4 rule of justice
       1:5–6 argument of waste
           [1:3–11 argument by comparison]
       1:7 definition
       1:3–11 argument by model (Paul)
           1:3–7 argument based on the relation between person and her/his acts
           1:8 argument from authority (divine authority)
       1:9–11 arguments by causal link
       1:11 argument by transitivity

    1:12–26. Outline of argumentative techniques
       1:12 dissociation (appearance/reality)
       1:12–14 arguments by causal link
       1:13 dissociative definition
       1:13 rule of justice
           [1:13–14 argument based on the relationship between a group and its members]
       1:12–14 argument by model (Paul)

214 HIERARCHY, UNITY, AND IMITATION

1:15–17 dissociation (division/unity and sameness)
1:15–17 argument by anti-model
1:19–20 arguments by causal link
    [1:20 argument by authority]
1:21 dissociative definition: dissociation (this life/death)
1:21–23 arguments by causal link
1:24–25 dissociation (self-benefit/community-benefit)
1:24–26 argument by model (Paul)
    [1:25 rule of justice]
1:21–26 argument by sacrifice
    [1:24–26 argument by waste]

1:27–2:4. Outline of argumentative techniques
    1:27 argument by causal link (covering 1:27–30)
    1:28 dissociation (destruction/safety or salvation)
        1:28 argument by causal link
    1:28 argument by anti-model
        [1:28 dissociation (human/divine) and/or (appearance/reality)]
        1:28 argument from authority (divine authority)
    1:27–28 argument of waste
    1:29 argument by sacrifice
        [1:30 argument by model (Paul)]
    2:1–4 arguments by causal link
        [2:1 dissociation (human/divine)]
    2:1–3 dissociation (division/unity and sameness)
    2:3–4 dissociation (self-benefit/community-benefit)

2:5–18. Outline of argumentative techniques
    2:5–11 argument by model (Christ)
        2:5 argument by transitivity
    2:6–11 argument from a tradition
    2:6–11 dissociations (human/divine) and (appearance/reality)
    2:6–8 argument by sacrifice
    2:6, 9–11 argument by model (divine model)
        2:6, 9–11 argument by authority (divine authority)
    2:12 argument by causal link (application of argument by model, 2:5–11)
    2:12 argument of waste
        2:12 dissociation (destruction/safety or salvation)
        [2:12 dissociation (slavery/freedom)]
    2:13 argument by authority (divine authority)
    2:14–16 arguments by causal link
    2:15 argument by anti-model

2:16–18 argument by model (Paul)
    2:16 argument of waste
    2:17 argument by sacrifice
    2:17 dissociation (self-benefit/community-benefit)
2:17–18 argument based on the relationship between a group and its members

2:19–30. Outline of argumentative techniques
    2:19–24 argument by model (Timothy)
    2:19 argument by causal link
    2:20–21 dissociation (self-benefit/community-benefit)
        2:21 argument by anti-model
    2:23 argument by causal link
        [2:23–24 argument by model (Paul)]
    2:25–30 argument by model (Epaphroditus)
    2:25–26 arguments by causal link
    2:26 dissociation (self-benefit/community-benefit)
    2:26–27, 30 argument by sacrifice
    2:27–28 arguments by causal link
        [2:29 argument by model (Paul)]

3:1–11. Outline of the argumentative techniques
    3:1 dissociation (self-benefit/community-benefit)
        [3:1 dissociation (destruction/safety or salvation)]
    3:2–4 argument by comparison
    3:2 argument by anti-model
        3:3 dissociation (flesh/spirit)
    3:4–6 dissociation (appearance/reality)
    3:7–9 dissociation (law/faith)
    3:7–8 argument by sacrifice
    3:9 argument by authority (divine authority)
    3:10 argument by causal link
        [3:7–11 argument by model (Paul)]

3:12–21. Outline of the argumentative techniques
    3:12–14 arguments by causal link
    3:15 argument by causal link
    3:15 dissociation (division and difference/unity and sameness)
        3:15 argument by authority (divine authority)
        [3:15 dissociation (destruction/safety or salvation)]
    3:16 argument of waste
    3:17 argument by model (Paul)

3:18–19 argument by anti-model
3:19–21 dissociation (earthly/heavenly)
    3:19–20 dissociation (destruction/safety or salvation)

4:1–9. Outline of argumentative techniques
    4:1 argument by causal link
    4:2 argument by transitivity
        4:2 argument by model (Paul)
        [4:2–3 argument by anti-model]
    4:4–6 rule of justice
        [4:5 argument of waste]
    4:4–7 argument by causal link
        4:7 argument by authority (divine authority)
    4:8 argument from a tradition
    4:9 argument by model (Paul)
        4:9 argument by causal link
        4:9 argument by authority (divine authority)

4:10–23. Outline of argumentative techniques
        [4:10 dissociation (self-benefit/community-benefit)]
    4:11 rule of justice
    4:11–12 dissociation (need/contentment)
    4:13 argument by authority (divine authority)
        [4:11–13 argument by model (Paul)]
    [4:14–16 argument of waste]
    4:17 dissociation (self-benefit/community-benefit)
    4:18–19 arguments by causal link
        [4:19 argument from authority (divine authority)]
    4:21–22 rule of justice

Bibliography

PRIMARY SOURCES

Aelius Aristides. *The Complete Works.* Translated by Charles A. Behr. 2 vols. Leiden: Brill, 1981–1986.
Appian. *Historia romana.* Translated by Horace White. 4 vols. Loeb Classical Library. Cambridge, Mass.: Harvard University Press, 1972–1979.
Aristotle. *Ethica nichomachea.* Translated by Harris Rackham. Loeb Classical Library. Rev. ed. Cambridge, Mass.: Harvard University Press, 1982.
———. *Politica.* Translated by Harris Rackham. Loeb Classical Library. Cambridge, Mass.: Harvard University Press, 1977.
Cicero. *De officiis.* Translated by Walter Miller. Loeb Classical Library. Cambridge, Mass.: Harvard University Press, 1975.
———. *De senectute; De amicitia; De divinatoine.* Translated by William Armistead Falconer. Loeb Classical Library. Cambridge, Mass.: Harvard University Press, 1979.
———. *Epistulae ad familiars.* Edited and Translated by D R. Shackleton-Bailey. Loeb Classical Library. Cambridge, Mass.: Harvard University Press, 2001.
———. *In Verrem.* Translated by L. H. G. Greenwood. 2 vols. Loeb Classical Library. Cambridge, Mass.: Harvard University Press, 1976.
———. *Philippicae.* Translated by Walter C. A. Ker. Loeb Classical Library. Cambridge, Mass.: Harvard University Press, 1926.
———. *Pro lege Manilia; Pro Caecina; Pro Cluentio; Pro Rabirio Perduellionis.* Translated by H. Grose Hodge. Loeb Classical Library. Cambridge, Mass.: Harvard University Press, 1979.
Dio Chrysostom. Translated by James W. Cohoon and H. Lamar Crosby. 5 vols. Loeb Classical Library. Cambridge, Mass.: Harvard University Press, 1932–1951.
Diodorus Siculus. Translated by Charles H. Oldfather. 12 vols. Loeb Classical Library. Cambridge, Mass.: Harvard University Press, 1933–1967.
Diogenes Laertius. *Lives of Eminent Philosophers.* Translated by Robert D. Hicks. 2 vols. Loeb Classical Library. Cambridge, Mass.: Harvard University Press, 1972.
Dionysius of Halicarnassus. *Antiquitates romanae.* Translated by Earnest Cary. 7 vols. Loeb Classical Library. Cambridge, Mass.: Harvard University Press, 1947–1960.
Hennecke, Edgar and Wilhelm Schneemelcher, eds. *New Testament Apocyrpha; Volume II: Writing Related to the Apostles, Apocalypses and Related Subjects.* Translated by R. McL. Wilson. Cambridge: James Clarke & Co.: 1992.

Herodotus. *Historiae.* Translated by Alfred D. Godley. Rev ed. 4 vols. Loeb Classical Library. Cambridge, Mass.: Harvard University Press, 1926.

Homer. *Iliad.* Translated by Augustus T. Murray. 2nd ed. Revised by William F. Wyatt. 2 vols. Loeb Classical Library. Cambridge, Mass.: Harvard University Press, 1999.

———. *The Odyssey.* Translated by Augustus T. Murray. 2nd ed. Revised by George E. Dimock. 2 vols. Loeb Classical Library. Cambridge, Mass.: Harvard University Press, 1998.

Isocrates. Translated by George Norlin and LaRue Van Hook. 3 vols. Loeb Classical Library. Cambridge, Mass.: Harvard University Press, 1966–1968.

Livy. Translated by B. O. Foster. 14 vols. Loeb Classical Library. Cambridge, Mass.: Harvard University Press, 1970–1989.

Lucian. Translated by Austin M. Harmon. 8 vols. Loeb Classical Library. Cambridge, Mass.: Harvard University Press, 1959–1967.

Ovid. *The Art of Love, and Other Poems.* Translated by John H. Mozley. Rev. ed. Loeb Classical Library. Cambridge, Mass.: Harvard University Press, 1939.

Plato. *Charmides, Alcibiades I and II, Hipparchus, The Lovers, Theages, Minos, Epinomis.* Translated by W. R. M. Lamb. Loeb Classical Library. Cambridge, Mass.: Harvard University Press, 1979.

———. *Respublica.* Translated by Paul Shorey. 2 vols. Loeb Classical Library. Cambridge, Mass.: Harvard University Press, 1982–1987.

———. *Timaeus, Critias, Cleitophon, Menexenus, Epistles.* Translated by R. G. Bury. Loeb Classical Library. Cambridge, Mass.: Harvard University Press, 1975.

Plautus. Translated by Paul Nixon. 5 vols. Loeb Classical Library. Cambridge, Mass.: Harvard University Press, 1966–1984.

Pliny the Elder. *Naturalis historia.* Translated by Harris Rackham. 10 vols. Loeb Classical Library. Cambridge, Mass.: Harvard University Press, 1938–1963.

Plutarch. *Lives.* Translated by Bernadotte Perrin. 11 vols. Loeb Classical Library. Cambridge, Mass.: Harvard University Press, 1982–1990.

Polybius *Historiae.* Translated by William R. Paton. 6 vols. Loeb Classical Library. Cambridge, Mass.: Harvard University Press, 1922–1927.

Porphyry. *Vita Pythagorae; Ad Marcellam.* Translated by Edouard des Places. Paris: Societe d'edition, 1982.

Reardon, Bryan P., ed. *Collected Ancient Greek Novels.* Berkeley: University of California Press, 1989.

Richardson, Cyril C., ed. *Early Christian Fathers.* Library of Christian Classics 1. New York: MacMillan, 1978.

Strabo. *Geographica.* Translated by Horace Leonard Jones. 8 vols. Loeb Classical Library. Cambridge, Mass.: Harvard University Press, 1982–1989.

Suetonius. Translated by John C. Rolfe. Rev. ed. 2 vols. Loeb Classical Library. Cambridge, Mass.: Harvard University Press, 1997–1998.

Theophrastus of Eresus: Sources for His Life, Writings, Thought and Influence. Edited and Translated by William W. Fortenbaugh, Andrew D. Barker, R. W.

Sharples, and Pamela M. Huby, 4 vols. Philosophia antiqua; Leiden: Brill, 1992.
Thesleff, Holger. *The Pythagorean Texts of the Hellenistic Period.* Acta Academiae Aboensis. Ser. 1, Humaniora 30:1. Åbo: Åbo Akademi, 1965.
Vegetius, Renatus Flavius. *Epitoma rei militaris.* Translated by Leo F. Stelten. New York: Lang, 1990.
Virgil. Translated by H. Rushton Fairclough. Revised by G. P. Goold. 2 vols. Loeb Classical Library. Cambridge, Mass.: Harvard University Press, 1999.
Xenophon. Translated by Carleton L. Brownson, Edgar C. Marchant, O. J. Todd, Walter Miller, and G. W. Bowerstock. 7 vols. Loeb Classical Library. Cambridge, Mass.: Harvard University Press, 1979–1986.

SECONDARY SOURCES

Abrahamsen, Valerie. "Women at Philippi: The Pagan and Christian Evidence." *Journal of Feminist Studies in Religion* 3 (1987): 17–30.
———. "Christianity and the Rock Reliefs at Philippi." *Biblical Archaeologist* 51 (1988): 46–56.
———. *Women and Worship at Philippi: Diana/Artemis and Other Cults in the Early Christian Era.* Portland, Maine: Astarte Shell Press, 1995.
Adam, A. K. M., ed. *Handbook of Postmodern Biblical Interpretation.* St. Louis: Chalice Press, 2000.
Adkins, A. W. H. "'Friendship' and 'Self-Sufficiency' in Homer and Aristotle." *Classical Quarterly* 13 (1963): 30–45.
Agosto, Efrain. "Paul vs. Empire: A Postcolonial and Latino Reading of Philippians." *Perspectivas: Occasional Papers* 6 (Fall 2002): 37–56.
Alcock, Susan E. *Graecia Capta: The Landscapes of Roman Greece.* Cambridge: Cambridge University Press, 1993.
Alexander, Loveday. "Hellenistic Letter-Forms and the Structure of Philippians." *Journal for the Study of the New Testament* 37 (1989): 87–101.
Amador, J. David Hester. *Academic Constraints in Rhetorical Criticism of the New Testament: An Introduction to a Rhetoric of Power.* Journal for the Study of the New Testament: Supplement Series 174. Sheffield: Sheffield Academic Press, 1999.
———. "Re-discovering/Reinventing Rhetoric." *Scriptura* 50 (1994): 1–22.
Anderson, R. Dean. *Ancient Rhetorical Theory and Paul.* Contributions to Biblical Exegesis and Theology 18. Revised ed. Leuven: Peeters, 1999.
Ando, Clifford. *Imperial Ideology and Provincial Loyalty in the Roman Empire.* Classics and Contemporary Thought 6. Berkeley: University of California Press, 2000.
Badian, Ernst. *Foreign Clientelae. 264–70 B.C.* Oxford: Oxford University Press, 1958.
———. *Roman Imperialism in the Late Republic.* Ithaca, N.Y.: Cornell University Press, 1968.

Bakirtzis, Charalambos, and Helmut Koester, eds. *Philippi at the Time of Paul and After His Death.* Harrisburg, Penn.: Trinity Press International, 1998.

Balch, David L. "Political Friendship in the Historian Dionysius of Halicarnassus, *Roman Antiquities.*" Pages 123–144 in *Greco-Roman Perspectives on Friendship.* Edited by John T. Fitzgerald. Resources for Biblical Study 34. Atlanta: Scholars Press, 1997.

Basevi, Claudio, and Juan Chapa. "Philippians 2:6–11: The Rhetorical Function of a Pauline 'Hymn.'" Pages 338–356 in *Rhetoric and the New Testament: Essays from the 1992 Heidelberg Conference.* Edited by Stanley E. Porter and Thomas H. Olbricht. Journal for the Study of the New Testament: Supplement Series 90. Sheffield: Sheffield Academic Press, 1993.

Baumgardner, Jennifer, and Amy Richards. *Manifesta: Young Women, Feminism, and the Future.* New York: Farrar, Straus and Giroux, 2000.

Benoît, Pierre. *Les épîtres de saint Paul aux Philippiens, aux Colossiens, à Philémon, aux Ephésiens.* Sainte Bible; Paris: Cerf, 1959.

Berry, Ken L. "The Function of Friendship Language in Philippians 4:10–20." Pages 107–124 in *Friendship, Flattery and Frankness of Speech: Studies on Friendship in the New Testament World.* Edited by John T. Fitzgerald. Supplements to Novum Testamentum 82. Leiden: Brill, 1996.

Betz, Hans D. *2 Corinthians 8 and 9: A Commentary on Two Administrative Letters of the Apostle Paul.* Hermeneia. Philadelphia: Fortress Press, 1985.

———. *Galatians: A Commentary on Paul's Letters to the Churches in Galatia.* Hermeneia. Philadelphia: Fortress Press, 1979.

———. "The Literary Composition and Function of Paul's Letter to the Galatians." *New Testament Studies* 21 (1975): 353–379.

Bhabha, Homi K. *The Location of Culture.* London: Routledge, 1994.

Bird, Phyllis A., ed. *Reading the Bible as Women: Perspectives from Africa, Asia, and Latin America. Semeia* 78. Guest editors Katherine Doob Sakenfeld and Sharon H. Ringe. 1997.

———. "What Makes a Feminist Reading Feminist? A Qualified Answer." Pages 124–131 in *Escaping Eden: New Feminist Perspectives on the Bible.* Edited by Harold C. Washington, Susan Lochrie Graham, and Pamela Thimmes. New York: New York University Press, 1999.

Bizzell, Patricia, and Bruce Herzberg, eds. *The Rhetorical Tradition: Readings from Classical Times to the Present.* Boston: Bedford Books of St. Martin's Press, 1990.

Blair, Carole, Julie R. Brown, and Leslie A. Baxter, "Disciplining the Feminine." Pages 563–590 in *Contemporary Rhetorical Theory: A Reader.* Edited by. John Louis Lucaites, Celeste Michelle Condit, and Sally Caudill. Revisioning Rhetoric. New York: The Guilford Press, 1999.

Bloomquist, L. Gregory. *The Function of Suffering in Philippians.* Journal for the Study of the New Testament: Supplement Series 78. Sheffield: JSOT Press, 1993.

Blumenfeld, Bruno. *The Political Paul: Justice, Democracy and Kingship in a Hellenistic Framework.* Journal for the Study of the New Testament: Supplement Series 210. London: Sheffield Academic Press, 2001.
Blümner, Hugo. *Die römischen Privataltertümer.* Handbuch der klassischen Altertums-Wissenschaft. 4. Bd. 2. Abt. 2. T. München, Beck, 1911.
Blundell, Mary Whitlock. *Helping Friends and Harming Enemies: A Study in Sophocles and Greek Ethics.* Cambridge: Cambridge University Press, 1989.
Bockmuehl, Markus. *The Epistle to the Philippians.* Black's New Testament Commentary. London: Hendrickson, 1998.
Bormann, Lukas. *Philippi: Stadt und Christengemeinde zur Zeit des Paulus.* Supplements to Novum Testamentum 78. Leiden: Brill, 1995.
Bornhäuser, D. Karl. *Jesus imperator mundi. Phil 3, 17–21 u. 2, 5–12.* Gütersloh: Bertelsmann, 1938.
Bowersock, G. W. *Augustus and the Greek World.* Oxford: Clarendon Press, 1965.
Boyarin, Daniel. *A Radical Jew: Paul and the Politics of Identity.* Contraversions 1. Berkeley: University of California Press, 1994.
Braund, David. "Function and Dysfunction: Personal Patronage in Roman Imperialism." Pages 137–152 in *Patronage in Ancient Society.* Edited by Andrew Wallace-Hadrill. Leicester-Nottingham Studies in Ancient Society 1. London: Routledge, 1989.
———. "Piracy under the Principate and the Ideology of Imperial Eradication." Pages 195–212 in *War and Society in the Roman World.* Edited by John Rich and Graham Shipley. Leicester-Nottingham Studies in Ancient Society 5. London: Routledge, 1993.
Brewer, R. R. "The Meaning of *politeuesthe* in Phil. 1:27." *Journal of Biblical Literature* 73 (1954): 76–83.
Briggs, Sheila. "Can an Enslaved God Liberate? Hermeneutical Reflection on Philippians 2:6–11." *Semeia* 47 (1989): 137–53.
Brooten, Bernadette J. *Love Between Women: Early Christian Responses to Female Homoeroticism.* Chicago: University of Chicago Press, 1996.
———. *Women Leaders in the Ancient Synagogue.* Brown Judaic Studies 36. Atlanta: Scholars Press, 1982.
Brown, Cheryl Ann. *No Longer Be Silent: First Century Jewish Portraits of Biblical Women.* Gender and the Biblical Tradition. Louisville, Ky.: Westminster John Knox Press, 1992.
Brunt, Peter A. *Italian Manpower, 225 B.C.–A.D. 14.* Oxford: Oxford Unversity Press, 1971.
———. *The Fall of the Roman Republic and Related Essays.* Oxford: Clarendon Press, 1988.
———. *Roman Imperial Themes.* Oxford: Clarendon Press, 1990.
Burke, Kenneth. *A Grammar of Motives.* Berkeley: University of California Press, 1960.
———. *A Rhetoric of Motives.* Berkeley: University of California Press, 1950.

Burrus, Virginia. *Chastity as Autonomy: Women in the Stories of the Apocryphal Acts.* Studies in Women and Religion 23. Lewiston, N.Y.: Edwin Mellen Press, 1987.
Butler, Judith. *Gender Trouble: Feminism and the Subversion of Identity.* Thinking Gender. New York: Routledge, 1990.
Cadoux, C. John. *The Early Christian Attitude to War.* Christian Revolution 3. London, Headley Brothers, 1918.
Cannon, Katie Geneva. *Katie's Canon: Womanism and the Soul of the Black Community.* New York: Continuum, 1995.
Castelli, Elizabeth A. *Imitating Paul: A Discourse of Power.* Literary Currents in Biblical Interpretation; Louisville, Ky.: Westminster/John Knox Press, 1991.
Castelli, Elizabeth A., Stephen Moore, Gary Phillips, and Regina Schwartz, eds. *The Postmodern Bible.* New Haven: Yale University Press, 1995.
Castelli, Elizabeth A., and Rosamond C. Rodman, eds. *Women Gender Religion: A Reader.* New York: Palgrave Press, 2001.
Chow, Rey. *The Protestant Ethnic and the Spirit of Capitalism.* New York: Columbia University Press, 2002.
Christou, Panayotis. "*ISOPSYCHOS*, Phil 2:20." *Journal of Biblical Literature* 70 (1951): 293–296.
Chung Hyun Kyung. *Struggle to Be Sun Again: Introducing Asian Women's Theology.* Maryknoll, N.Y.: Orbis Books, 1990.
Clarke, Andrew D. "'Be Imitators of Me': Paul's Model of Leadership." *Tyndale Bulletin* 49 (1998): 329–60.
Collange, Jean-François. *The Epistle of Saint Paul to the Philippians.* Translated by A. W. Heathcote. London: Epworth Press, 1979.
Collart, Paul. "Philippes." *Dictionnaire d'archéologie chrétienne.* Vol. 14. (1939) 712–742.
———. *Philippes: Ville de Macédoine depuis ses origins jusqu'à la fin de l'époque romaine.* Paris: École Française d'Athènes, 1937.
———. "Le sanctuaire des dieux égyptiens à Philippes." *Bulletin de correspondance hellénique* 53 (1929): 69–100.
Collart, Paul, and Pierre Ducrey. *Philippes I: Les reliefs rupestres. Bulletin de correspondance hellénique Supplément* 2. Athens: École Française d'Athènes, 1975.
Collins, Adela Yarbo, ed. *Feminist Perspectives on Biblical Scholarship.* Biblical Scholarship in North America 10. Atlanta: Scholars Press, 1985.
Conley, Thomas H. *Rhetoric in the European Tradition.* Chicago: University of Chicago Press, 1990.
Cotter, Wendy. "Our *Politeuma* Is In Heaven: The Meaning of Philippians 3.17–21." Pages 92–104 in *Origins and Method: Towards a New Understanding of Judaism and Christianity.* Edited by Bradley H. McLean. Journal for the Study of the New Testament: Supplement Series 86. Sheffield: Sheffield Academic Press, 1993.

———. "Women's Authority Roles in Paul's Churches: Countercultural or Conventional?" *Novum Testamentum* 36 (1994): 350–72.
Countryman, L. William. *Dirt, Greed, and Sex: Sexual Ethics in the New Testament and Their Implications for Today*. Philadelphia: Fortress, 1988.
Culpepper, R. Alan. "Co-Workers in Suffering: Philippians 2:19–30." *Review & Expositor* 77. 1980): 349–358.
Cunningham, David S. "Rhetoric." Pages 220–226 in *Handbook of Postmodern Biblical Interpretation*. Edited by A. K. M. Adam. St. Louis: Chalice Press, 2000.
Dahl, Nils A. "Euodia and Syntyche and Paul's Letter to the Philippians." Pages 3–15 in *The Social World of the First Christians: Essays in Honor of Wayne A. Meeks*. Edited by L. Michael White and O. Larry Yarbrough. Minneapolis: Fortress, 1995.
D'Angelo, Mary R. "Women Partners in the New Testament." *Journal of Feminist Studies in Religion* 6 (1990): 65–86.
Davies, Roy W. *Service in the Roman Army*. Edited by David Breeze and Valerie A. Maxfield. New York: Columbia University Press, 1989.
Davies, Stevan. *The Revolt of the Widows: The Social World of the Apocryphal Acts*. Carbondale: Southern Illinois University Press, 1980.
Davis, Casey Wayne. *Oral Biblical Criticism: The Influence of the Principles of Orality on the Literary Structure of Paul's Epistle to the Philippians*. Journal for the Study of the New Testament: Supplement Series 172. Sheffield: Sheffield Academic Press, 1999.
Dearin, Ray D., ed. *The New Rhetoric of Chaim Perelman: Statement and Response* Lanham, Md.: University Press of America, 1989.
Delatte, Armand. *La vie de Pythagore de Diogène Laërce*. Brussels: Lamerton, 1922.
DeSilva, David A. *The Hope of Glory: Honor Discourse and New Testament Interpretation*. Collegeville, Minn.: Liturgical Press, 1999.
———. *Perseverance in Gratitude: A Socio-Rhetorical Commentary on the Epistle to the Hebrews*. Grand Rapids, Mich.: Eerdmans, 2000.
De Ste. Croix, G. E. M. *The Class Struggle in the Ancient Greek World: From the Archaic Age to the Arab Conquests*. Ithaca, N.Y.: Cornell University Press, 1981.
De Vos, Craig S. *Church and Community Conflicts: The Relationship of the Thessalonian, Corinthian, and Philippian Churches with Their Wider Civic Communities*. Society of Biblical Literature Dissertation Series 168. Atlanta: Scholars Press, 1999.
Dibelius, Martin. *An die Thessalonischer I–II; An die Philipper*. Handbuch zum Neuen Testament 11. Tübingen: Mohr Siebeck, 1925.
Dixon, Suzanne. *Reading Roman Women: Sources, Genres, and Real Life*. London: Duckworth, 2001.

Dodd, Brian J. *Paul's Paradigmatic "I": Personal Example as Literary Strategy.* Journal for the Study of the New Testament: Supplement Series 177. Sheffield: Sheffield Academic Press, 1999.
Donaldson, Laura E., and Kwok Pui-lan, eds. *Postcolonialism, Feminism and Religious Discourse.* New York: Routledge, 2001.
Dormeyer, Detlev. "The Implicit and Explicit Readers and the Genre of Philippians 3:2–4:3, 8–9: Response to the Commentary of Wolfgang Schenk." *Semeia* 48 (1989): 147–59.
Drerup, Heinrich. "Totenmaske und Ahnenbild bei den Römern." *Mitteilungen des Instituts für Orientforschung Roemische Abteilung* 87 (1980): 81–129.
Dube, Musa W. ed. *Other Ways of Reading: African Women and the Bible.* Global Perspectives on Biblical Scholarship 2. Atlanta: Society of Biblical Literature: 2001.
———. *Postcolonialist Feminist Interpretation of the Bible.* St. Louis: Chalice Press, 2000.
Dube Shomanah, Musa W. "Post-Colonial Biblical Interpretation." Pages 299–303 in *Dictionary of Biblical Interpretation, Volume 2.* Edited by John H. Hayes. Nashville: Abingdon Press, 1999.
Ebner, Martin. *Leidenslisten und Apostelbrief: Untersuchungen zu Form, Motivik und Funktion der Peristasenkataloge bei Paulus.* Forschung zur Bibel 66. Würzburg: Echter, 1991.
Elliott, Neil. *Liberating Paul: The Justice of God and the Politics of the Apostle.* The Bible & Liberation. Maryknoll, N.Y.: Orbis, 1994.
Engberg-Pedersen, Troels. "Stoicism in Philippians." Pages 256–290 in *Paul in His Hellenistic Context.* Edited by T. Engberg-Pedersen. Edinburgh: T & T Clark, 1994.
Enos, Theresa, and Richard McNabb, eds. *Making and Unmaking the Prospects for Rhetoric.* Mahwah, N.J.: Lawrence Erlbaum, 1997.
Eriksson, Anders, Thomas H. Olbricht, and Walter Übelacker, eds. *Rhetorical Argumentation in Biblical Texts: Essays from the Lund 2000 Conference.* Emory Studies in Early Christianity 8. Harrisburg, Penn.: Trinity Press International, 2002.
Erskine, Andrew. *The Hellenistic Stoa: Political Thought and Action.* Ithaca, N.Y.: Cornell University Press, 1990.
Evans, John K. *War, Women and Children in Ancient Rome.* London: Routledge, 1991.
Fabella, Virginia, and Mercy Amba Oduyoye, eds. *With Passion and Compassion: Third World Women Doing Theology.* Maryknoll, N.Y.: Orbis, 1988.
Fee, Gordon D. *Paul's Letter to the Philippians.* New International Commentary on the New Testament. Grand Rapids, Mich.: Eerdmans, 1995.
———. *Philippians.* Intervarsity Press New Testament Commentary Series 11. Downers Grove, Ill.: Intervarsity Press, 1999.
Felder, Cain Hope, ed. *Stony the Road We Trod: African-American Biblical Interpretation.* Minneapolis: Fortress, 1991.

Ferguson, John. *Moral Values in the Ancient World.* London: Methuen, 1958.
Finley, Moses I. *The Ancient Economy.* 2nd ed. Sather Classical Lectures 43. Berkeley: University of California Press, 1985.
Fiore, Benjamin. "Paul, Exemplification, and Imitation." Pages 228–257 in *Paul in the Greco-Roman World: A Handbook.* Edited by J. Paul Sampley. Harrisburg, Penn.: Trinity Press International, 2003.
———. "The Theory and Practice of Friendship in Cicero." Pages 59–76 in *Greco-Roman Perspectives on Friendship.* Edited by John T. Fitzgerald. Resources for Biblical Study 34. Atlanta: Scholars Press Press, 1997.
Fitzgerald, John T., ed. *Friendship, Flattery and Frankness of Speech: Studies on Friendship in the New Testament World.* Supplements to Novum Testamentum 82. Leiden: Brill, 1996.
———. "Friendship in the Greek World Prior to Aristotle." Pages 13–34 in *Greco-Roman Perspectives on Friendship.* Edited by John T. Fitzgerald; Resources for Biblical Study 34. Atlanta: Scholars Press, 1997.
———. ed., *Greco-Roman Perspectives on Friendship.* Resources for Biblical Study 34. Atlanta: Scholars Press, 1997.
———. "Paul and Friendship." Pages 319–343 in *Paul in the Greco-Roman World: A Handbook.* Edited by J. Paul Sampley. Harrisburg, Penn.: Trinity Press International, 2003.
———. "Philippians, Epistle to the." *Anchor Bible Dictionary.* Edited by David N. Freedman. New York, 1992. Vol. V: 318–326.
———. "Philippians in the Light of Some Ancient Discussions of Friendship." Pages 141–160 in *Friendship, Flattery and Frankness of Speech: Studies on Friendship in the New Testament World.* Edited by John T. Fitzgerald; Supplements to Novum Testamentum 82. Leiden: Brill, 1996.
Fortna, Robert T. "Philippians: Paul's Most Egocentric Letter." Pages 220–234 in *The Conversation Continues: Festschrift for J. Louis Martyn.* Edited by Robert T. Fortna and Beverly R. Gaventa. Nashville: Abingdon, 1990.
Foss, Karen A., and Sonja K. Foss. *Women Speak: The Eloquence of Women's Lives.* Prospect Heights, Ill.: Waveland, 1991.
Foss, Sonja K., Karen A. Foss, and Cindy L. Griffin. *Feminist Rhetorical Theories.* Thousand Oaks, Calif.: Sage, 1999.
Foss, Sonja K., Karen A. Foss, and Robert Trapp. *Contemporary Perspectives on Rhetoric.* 3rd ed. Prospect Heights, Ill.: Waveland, 2002.
Foss, Sonja K., and Cindy L. Griffin. "Beyond Persuasion: A Proposal for an Invitational Rhetoric." *Communication Monographs* 62 (March 1995): 2–18.
———. "A Feminist Perspective on Rhetorical Theory: Toward a Clarification of Boundaries." *Western Journal of Communication* 56 (1992): 330–49.
Foss, Sonja K., Cindy L. Griffin, and Karen A. Foss. "Transforming Rhetoric Through Feminist Reconstruction: A Response to the Gender Diversity Perspective." *Women's Studies in Communication* 20:2 (1997): 117–135.

Foucault, Michel. *Power/Knowledge: Selected Interviews & Other Writings 1972–1977.* Edited by Colin Gordon. Translated by Colin Gordon, Leo Marshall, John Mepham, Kate Soper. New York: Pantheon, 1980.
Fraisse, Jean Claude. *Philia: La notion d'Amitié dans la philosophie antique.* Bibliothèque d'histoire de la philosophie. Paris: J. Vrin, 1974.
Freire, Paulo. *Pedagogy of the Oppressed.* Translated by Myra Bergman Ramos. New revised ed. New York: Continuum, 2000.
Fuchs, Esther. "Men in Biblical Feminist Scholarship." *Journal of Feminist Studies in Religion* 19:2 (2003): 93–114.
Galinsky, Karl, *Augustan Culture: An Interpretive Introduction.* Princeton, N.J.: Princeton University Press, 1996.
Garland, David E. "The Composition and Unity of Philippians." *Novum Testamentum* 26 (1985): 141–73.
Garnsey, Peter, and Richard Saller. *The Early Principate: Augustus to Trajan.* Greece & Rome: New Surveys in the Classics 15. Oxford: Clarendon Press, 1982.
Geoffrion, Timothy C. *The Rhetorical Purpose and the Political and Military Character of Philippians: A Call to Stand Firm.* Lewiston, N.Y.: Mellen, 1993.
Georgi, Dieter, "God Turned Upside Down." Pages 148–157 in *Paul and Empire: Religion and Power in Roman Imperial Society.* Edited by Richard A. Horsley. Harrisburg, Penn.: Trinity Press International, 1997.
Gilman, F. M. "Early Christian Women at Philippi." *Journal of Gender in World Religions* 1 (1990): 59–79.
Gitay, Yehoshua. *Isaiah and His Audience: The Structure and Meaning of Isaiah 1–12.* Studia semitica neerlandica 30. Assen, The Netherlands: Van Gorcum, 1991.
———. *Prophecy and Persuasion: A Study of Isaiah 40–48.* Forum theologiae linguisticae 14. Bonn: Linguistica Biblica Bonn, 1981.
Given, Mark D. *Paul's True Rhetoric: Ambiguity, Cunning, and Deception in Greece and Rome.* Emory Studies in Early Christianity. Harrisburg, Penn.: Trinity Press International, 2001.
Glenn, Cheryl. *Rhetoric Retold: Regendering the Tradition from Antiquity through the Renaissance.* Carbondale: Southern Illinois University Press, 1997.
Gnilka, Joachim. *Der Philipperbrief.* Herders theologischer Kommentar zum Neuen Testament 10.3. Freiburg: Herder, 1968.
Gold, Barbara K. *Literary Patronage in Greece and Rome.* Chapel Hill: University of North Carolina Press, 1987.
Golden, James L, and Joseph J. Pilotta, eds. *Practical Reasoning in Human Affairs: Studies in Honor of Chaim Perelman.* Synthese Library 183. Dordrecht; Boston: D. Reidel Publishing Company, 1986.
Goldhill, Simon D. *Reading Greek Tragedy.* Cambridge: Cambridge University Press, 1986.
Goodwin, Jean. "Perelman, Adhering, and Conviction." *Philosophy and Rhetoric* 28 (1995): 215–33.

Goss, Robert E., and Mona West, eds. *Take Back the Word: A Queer Reading of the Bible*. Cleveland: Pilgrim, 2000.
Gowler, David, L. Gregory Bloomquist, and Duane Watson, eds. *Fabrics of Discourse: Essays in Honor of Vernon K. Robbins*. Harrisburg, Penn.: Trinity Press International, 2003.
Grant, Jacquelyn. *White Women's Christ and Black Women's Jesus: Feminist Christology and Womanist Resonse*. American Academy of Religion Academy Series 64. Atlanta: Scholars Press, 1989.
Grether, G. "Livia and the Roman Imperial Cult." *American Journal of Philology* 47 (1946): 222–252.
Gross, Alan. "Rhetoric as a Technique and a Mode of Truth: Reflections on Chaim Perelman." *Philosophy and Rhetoric* 33 (2000): 319–35.
Gruen, Erich S. *Studies in Greek Culture and Roman Policy*. Berkeley: University of California Press, 1996.
Gunther, John J. *St. Paul's Opponents and Their Background: A Study of Apocalyptic and Jewish Sectarian Teachings*. Supplements to Novum Testamentum 35. Leiden: Brill, 1973.
Hallett, Judith P. *Fathers and Daughters in Roman Society: Women and the Elite Family*. Princeton, N.J.: Princeton University Press, 1984.
Handelman, Susan. "Facing the Other: Levinas, Perelman, and Rosenzweig." *Religion and Literature* 22 (1990): 61–84.
Hardie, William F. R. *Aristotle's Ethical Theory*. 2nd ed. Oxford: Clarendon Press, 1980.
Hawthorne, Gerald F. *Philippians*. Word Biblical Commentary 43. Waco, Tex.: Word Books, 1983.
Hayes, John H., ed. *Dictionary of Biblical Intepretation*. 2 vols. Nashville: Abingdon Press, 1999.
Hearon, Holly E., ed. *Distant Voices Drawing Near: Essays in Honor of Antoinette Clark Wire*. Collegeville, Minn.: Liturgical Press, 2004.
Hendricks, Osayande Obery. "Guerilla Exegesis: 'Struggle' as A Scholarly Vocation: A Postmodern Approach to African-American Interpretation." *Semeia* 72 (1995): 73–90.
Hendrix, Holland L. "Philippi." *Anchor Bible Dictionary*. Edited by David N. Freedman. New York, 1992. V. 313–317.
Hennessy, Rosemary. *Materialist Feminism and the Politics of Discourse*. Thinking Gender. New York: Routledge Press, 1993.
Hester, James D. and J. David Hester, eds. *Rhetorics and Hermeneutics: Wilhelm Wuellner and His Influence*. Emory Studies in Early Christianity 9. New York: T & T Clark International, 2004.
Heuzey, Leon A. and H. Daumet. *Mission archéologique de Macédoine*. Paris: Librarie de Firmin-Didot et Cie, 1876.

Heyob, Sharon K. *The Cult of Isis among Women in the Graeco-Roman World*. Etudes preliminaries aux religions orientales dans l'empire romain 51. Leiden: Brill, 1975.

Hock, Ronald F. "An Extraordinary Friend in Chariton's *Callirhoe*: The Importance of Friendship in the Greek Romances." Pages 145–162 in *Greco-Roman Perspectives on Friendship*. Edited by John T. Fitzgerald. Resources for Biblical Study 34. Atlanta: Scholars Press, 1997.

Hock, Ronald F., and Edward N. O'Neil. *The Chreia in Ancient Rhetoric. Volume I. The Progymnasmata*. Texts and Translations 27. Texts and Translations: Greco-Roman Religion Series 9. Atlanta: Scholars Press, 1986.

Hoddinott, Ralph F. *The Thracians*. Ancient Peoples and Places 98. New York: Thames and Hudson, 1981.

Holloway, Paul A. *Consolation in Philippians: Philosophical Sources and Rhetorical Strategy*. Society for New Testament Studies Monograph Series 112. Cambridge: Cambridge University Press, 2001.

hooks, bell. *Feminism Is For Everybody: Passionate Politics*. Cambridge, Mass.: South End Press, 2000.

———. *Feminist Theory: From Margin to Center*. 2nd ed.; South End Press Classics; Cambridge, Mass.: South End Press, 2000.

———. *Teaching to Transgress: Education as the Practice of Freedom*. New York: Routledge, 1994.

Hornus, Jean-Michel. *It Is Not Lawful for Me to Fight: Early Christian Attitudes Toward War, Violence, and the State*. Translated by Alan Kreider and Oliver Coburn. A Christian Peace Shelf Selection. Scottsdale, Penn.: Herald Press, 1980.

Horsley, Richard A., ed. *Paul and Empire: Religion and Power in Roman Imperial Society*. Harrisburg, Penn.: Trinity Press International, 1997.

———. ed. *Paul and Politics: Ekklesia, Israel, Imperium, Interpretation*. Harrisburg, Penn.: Trinity Press International, 2000.

———. "Paul's Counter-Imperial Gospel: An Introduction." Pages 140–147 in *Paul and Empire: Religion and Power in Roman Imperial Society*. Edited by R. Horsley; Harrisburg, Penn.: Trinity Press International, 1997.

Horsley, Richard A., and Neil Asher Silberman. *The Message and the Kingdom: How Jesus and Paul Ignited a Revolution and Transformed the Ancient World*. New York: Grosset/Putnam, 1997.

Hubbell, Harry Mortimer. *The Influence of Isocrates on Cicero, Dionysius and Aristides*. New Haven: Yale University Press, 1913.

Hurtado, Larry W. "Jesus as Lordly Example in Philippians 2.5–11." Pages 113–126 in *From Jesus to Paul: Studies in Honour of Francis Wright Beare*. Edited by Peter Richardson and John C. Hurd. Waterloo, Ont.: Wilfrid Laurier University Press, 1984.

Hutter, Horst. *Politics as Friendship: The Origins of Classical Notions of Politics in the Theory and Practice of Friendship*. Waterloo, Ont.: Wilfrid Laurier University Press, 1978.

Ilan, Tal. *Integrating Women into Second Temple History.* Texte und Studien zum antiken Judentum 76. Tübingen: Mohr Siebeck, 1999.

———. *Jewish Women in Greco-Roman Palestine.* Texte und Studien zum antiken Judentum 44. Peabody, Mass.: Hendrickson, 1995.

———. *Mine and Yours Are Hers: Retrieving Wo/men's History from Rabbinic Literature.* Arbeiten zur Geschichte des antiken Judentums und des Urchristentums 41. Leiden: Brill, 1997.

Isasi-Díaz, Ada María. *En la Lucha/In the Struggle: An Hispanic Women's Theology.* Minneapolis: Fortress Press, 1993.

———. "*La Palabra de Dios en Nosotras*—The Word of God in Us." Pages 86–97 in *Searching the Scriptures: A Feminist Introduction*, Volume One. Edited by Elisabeth Schüssler Fiorenza. New York: Crossroad, 1993.

———. *Mujerista Theology.* Maryknoll, N.Y.: Orbis Books, 1996.

———. *Women of God, Women of the People: Four Biblical Meditations.* St. Louis: Chalice, 1995.

Jaeger, Werner. *Paideia: The Ideals of Greek Culture*, Volume 3: *The Conflict of Cultural Ideals in the Age of Plato.* Translated by Gilbert Highet. Oxford: Basil Blackwell, 1961.

Jaquette, James L. "A Not-So-Noble Death: Figured Speech, Friendship and Suicide in Philippians 1:21–26." *Neotestamentica* 28:1 (1994): 177–192.

———. "Life and Death, Adiaphora, and Paul's Rhetorical Strategies." *Novum Testamentum* 38 (1996): 30–54.

Jarratt, Susan C. *Rereading the Sophists: Classical Rhetoric Refigured.* Carbondale: Southern Illinois University Press, 1991.

Jasper, David. "Reflections on the London Conference on the Rhetorical Analysis of Scripture." Pages 476–482 in *The Rhetorical Analysis of Scripture: Essays from the 1995 London Conference.* Edited by Stanley Porter and Thomas Olbricht. Journal for the Study of the New Testament: Supplement Series 146. Sheffield: Sheffield Academic Press, 1997.

Jewett, Robert. "Conflicting Movements in the Early Church as Reflected in Philippians." *Novum Testamentum* 12 (1970): 362–90.

———. "The Epistolary Thanksgiving and the Integrity of Philippians." *Novum Testamentum* 12 (1970): 40–53.

Johnson, Luke Timothy. *The Writings of the New Testament: An Interpretation.* Philadelphia: Fortress, 1986.

Johnstone, Christopher Lyle, ed. *Theory Text Context: Issues in Greek Rhetoric and Oratory.* SUNY Series in Speech Communication. Albany: State University of New York Press, 1996.

Jones, A. H. M., ed., *A History of Rome Through the Fifth Century. Volume I: The Republic.* Documentary History of Western Civilization. New York: Harper & Row, 1968.

———. *Later Roman Empire.* Oxford: Oxford University Press, 1964.

Joshel, Sandra R., and Sheila Murnaghan, eds. *Women and Slaves in Greco-Roman Culture: Differential Equations*. London: Routledge, 1998.
Jost, Walter, and Michael J. Hyde, eds. *Rhetoric and Hermeneutics in Our Time: A Reader*. Yale Studies in Hermeneutics. New Haven: Yale University Press, 1997.
Käsemann, Ernst. "A Critical Analysis of Philippians 2:5–11." *Journal for Theology and the Church* 5 (1968): 45–88.
Kazarow, Gawril. *Grabstele von Mesembria*. Jahreshefte des Österreichischen Archaeoloigschen Institutes Bd. XXVI. 1930.
Keller, Marie Noël. "Choosing What Is Best: Paul, Roman Society and Philippians." Th.D. diss., Lutheran School of Theology at Chicago, 1995.
Kennedy, George A. *A New History of Classical Rhetoric*. Princeton, N.J.: Princeton University Press, 1994.
———. *Classical Rhetoric and Its Christian and Secular Tradition from Ancient to Modern Times*. 2nd ed. Revised. Chapel Hill: University of North Carolina Press, 1999.
———. *Greek Rhetoric under Christian Emperors*. A History of Rhetoric 3. Princeton, N.J.: Princeton University Press, 1983.
———. *New Testament Interpretation through Rhetorical Criticism*. Studies in Religion. Chapel Hill: University of North Carolina, 1984.
———. *The Art of Persuasion in Greece*. Princeton, N.J.: Princeton University Press, 1963.
———. *The Art of Rhetoric in the Roman World*. A History of Rhetoric 2. Princeton, N.J.: Princeton University Press, 1963.
Keppie, Lawrence. *Colonisation and Veteran Settlement in Italy: 47–14 B.C.* London: British School at Rome, 1983.
———. *The Making of the Roman Army: From Republic to Empire*. London: BT Batsford, 1984.
Kim, Yong Bock, ed. *Minjung Theology: People as the Subjects of History*. Singapore: Commission on Theological Concerns, Christian Conference of Asia, 1981.
Kittredge, Cynthia Briggs. *Community and Authority: The Rhetoric of Obedience in the Pauline Tradition*. Harvard Theological Studies 45; Harrisburg, Penn.: Trinity Press International, 1998.
———. "Corinthian Women Prophets and Paul's Argumentation in 1 Corinthians." Pages 103–109 in *Paul and Politics: Ekklesia, Israel, Imperium, Interpretation*. Edited by Richard A. Horsley; Harrisburg, Penn.: Trinity Press International, 2000.
Klijn, A. F. J. "Paul's Opponents in Phil.3." *Novum Testamentum* 7 (1964–65): 278–84.
Koester, Helmut. "The Purpose of a Pauline Fragment. Philippians III." *New Testament Studies* 8 (1961/62): 317–32.
Konstan, David. *Friendship in the Classical World*. Key Themes in Ancient History. Cambridge: Cambridge University Press, 1997.

Koperski, Veronica. *The Knowledge of Christ Jesus My Lord: The High Christology of Philippians 3:7–11*. Contributions to Biblical Exegesis and Theology 1. Kampen, The Netherlands: Kok Pharos, 1996.

Koskenniemi, Heikki. *Studien zur Idee und Phraeseologie des griechischen Briefes bis 400 n. Chr.*. Suomalaisen Tiedeakatemian toimituksia Sarja B. 102, 2. Helsinki: Suomalainen Tiedeakatemia, 1956.

Koukouli-Chrysantaki, Chaido. "Colonia Iulia Augusta Philippensis." Pages 5–35 in *Philippi at the Time of Paul and After His Death*. Edited by Charalambos Bakirtzis and Helmut Koester. Harrisburg, Penn.: Trinity Press International, 1998.

Kraemer, Ross Shepard. *Her Share of the Blessings: Women's Religions Among Pagans, Jews and Christians in the Greco-Roman World*. New York: Oxford University Press, 1992.

Kraemer, Ross Shepard, and Mary R. D'Angelo, eds. *Women & Christian Origins*. New York: Oxford University Press, 1999.

Kraftchick, Steven J. "A Necessary Detour: Paul's Metaphorical Understanding of the Philippians Hymn." *Horizons in Biblical Theology* 15 (1993): 1–37.

———. "Why Do the Rhetoricians Rage?" Pages 55–79 in *Text and Logos: The Humanistic Interpretation of the New Testament*. Edited by Theodore W. Jennings, Jr. Homage Series 16. Atlanta: Scholars Press, 1990.

Krentz, Edgar. "De Caesare et Christo." *Currents in Theology and Mission* 28 (2001): 341–345.

———. "Military Language and Metaphors in Philippians." Pages 105–127 in *Origins and Method: Towards a New Understanding of Judaism and Christianity*. Edited by Bradley H. McLean. Journal for the Study of the New Testament: Supplement Series 86. Sheffield: Sheffield Academic, 1993.

———. "Paul, Games, and the Military." Pages 344–383 in *Paul in the Greco-Roman World: A Handbook*. Edited by J. Paul Sampley. Harrisburg, Penn.: Trinity Press International, 2003.

Kroll, Wilhelm. *Kultur der ciceronischen Zeit*. Vol. I. Leipzig: Dieterich, 1933.

Kurz, William S. "Kenotic Imitation of Paul and of Christ in Philippians 2 and 3." Pages 103–126 in *Discipleship in the New Testament*. Edited by Fernando F. Segovia; Philadelphia: Fortress Press, 1985.

Kwok Pui-lan. *Discovering the Bible in the Non-Biblical World*. Bible & Liberation Series. Maryknoll, N.Y.: Orbis Books, 1995.

Langer, Susanne K. *Philosophy in a New Key: A Study in the Symbolism of Reason, Rite, and Art*. 3rd ed. Cambridge, Mass.: Harvard University Press, 1979.

Larsen, Jakob A. O. *Greek Federal States*. Oxford: Oxford University Press, 1968.

———. "Roman Greece." Pages 259–498 in *An Economic Survey of Ancient Rome*. Volume IV. Edited by Tenney Frank. Baltimore: Johns Hopkins Press, 1938.

Lausberg, Heinrich. *Handbuch der literarischen Rhetorik*. 2 vols. repr. Stuttgart: Franz Steiner, 1990.

Lazarides, Demetrios. "Philippi." Pages 704–705 in *Princeton Encyclopedia of Classical Sites*. Edited by Richard Stillwell. Princeton, N. J.: Princeton University Press, 1976.

Lefkowitz, Mary R., and Maureen B. Fant. *Women's Life in Greece and Rome: A Source Book in Translation*. 2nd ed. Baltimore: John Hopkins University Press, 1992.

Lemerle, Paul. *Philippes et la Macédoine Orientale à l'époque chrétienne et byzantine: Recherches d'histoire et d'archéologie*. Bibliothèque des Ecoles françaises d'Athènes et de Rome 158. Paris: Boccard, 1945.

Levick, Barbara, ed. *The Government of the Roman Empire: A Sourcebook*. London: Croom Helm, 1988.

Levine, Amy-Jill, ed. *"Women Like This": New Perspectives on Jewish Women in the Greco-Roman World*. Early Judaism and Its Literature 1. Atlanta: Scholars Press, 1991.

Liew, Tat-siong Benny. "Tyranny, Boundary, and Might: Colonial Mimicry in Mark's Gospel." *Journal for the Study of the New Testament* 73 (1999): 7–31.

Lightstone, Jack N. *Mishnah and the Social Formation of the Early Rabbinic Guild: A Socio-Rhetorical Approach*. Studies in Christianity and Judaism/Études sur le christianisme et le judaïsme 11. Waterloo, Ont.: Wilfrid Laurier University Press, 2002.

Lintott, Andrew. *Imperium Romanum: Politics and Administration*. London: Routledge, 1993.

Lohmeyer, Ernst. *Die Briefe an die Philipper, an die Kolosser und an Philemon*. Kritisch-exegetischer Kommentar über das Neue Testament 9. Göttingen: Vandenhoeck & Ruprecht, 1964 [1930].

———. *Kyrios Jesus: Eine Untersuchung zu Phil. 2, 5–11*. Sitzungen der heidelberger Akademie der Wissenschaften Philosophisch-historische Klasse. Jahrgang 1927/28. 4. Abhandllung. Darmstadt: Wissenschaftliche Buchgesellschaft, 1961 [1928].

Lucaites, John Louis, Celeste Michelle Condit, and Sally Caudill, eds. *Contemporary Rhetorical Theory: A Reader*. Revisioning Rhetoric. New York: Guilford Press, 1999.

Luck, Georg. *Hexen und Zauberei in der römischen Dichtung*. Lebendige Antike. Zurich: Artemis, 1962.

Lunsford, Andrea A., ed. *Reclaiming Rhetorica: Women in the Rhetorical Tradition*. Pittsburgh Series in Composition, Literacy, and Culture. Pittsburgh: University of Pittsburgh Press, 1995.

Luter, A. Boyd, and Michelle V. Lee. "Philippians as Chiasmus: Key to the Structure, Unity and Theme Questions." *New Testament Studies* 41 (1995): 89–101.

Luttwak, Edward N. *The Grand Strategy of the Roman Empire: From the First Century A.D. to the Third*. Baltimore: Johns Hopkins University Press, 1976.

Lyon, Arabella. "Susanne K. Langer: Mother and Midwife at the Rebirth of Rhetoric." Pages 265–284 in *Reclaiming Rhetorica: Women in the Rhetorical Tradition*.

Pittsburgh Series in Composition, Literacy, and Culture. Pittsburgh: University of Pittsburgh Press, 1995.
MacDonald, Dennis R. *The Legend and the Apostle: The Battle for Paul in Story and Canon*. Philadelphia: Westminster, 1983.
Mack, Burton. *Rhetoric and the New Testament*. Guides to Biblical Scholarship New Testament Series. Minneapolis: Fortress Press, 1990.
MacMullen, Ramsay. *Enemies of the Roman Order: Treason, Unrest, and Alienation in the Empire*. Cambridge, Mass.: Harvard University Press, 1966.
Mailloux, Steven. *Rhetorical Power*. Ithaca, N.Y.: Cornell University Press, 1989.
Malherbe, Abraham J. *Ancient Epistolary Theorists*. Sources for Biblical Study 19. Atlanta: Scholars Press, 1988.
———. *Moral Exhortation: A Greco-Roman Sourcebook*. Library of Early Christianity 4. Philadelphia: Westminster, 1986.
———. *Paul and the Popular Philosophers*. Minneapolis: Fortress, 1989.
———. *Paul and the Thessalonians*. Philadelphia: Fortress, 1987.
———. "Paul's Self-Sufficiency. Philippians 4:11." Pages 125–139 in *Friendship, Flattery and Frankness of Speech: Studies on Friendship in the New Testament World*. Edited by John T. Fitzgerald. Supplements to Novum Testamentum 82. Leiden: Brill, 1996.
Malina, Bruce J. "Rhetorical Criticism and Social-Scientific Criticism: Why Won't Romanticism Leave Us Alone?" Pages 72–101 in *Rhetoric, Scripture, and Theology: Essays from the 1994 Pretoria Conference*. Edited by Stanley E. Porter and Thomas H. Olbricht. Journal for the Study of the New Testament: Supplement Series 131. Sheffield: Sheffield University Press, 1996.
Malina, Bruce J., and Jerome H. Neyrey. *Portraits of Paul: An Archaeology of Ancient Personality*. Louisville, Ky.: Westminster John Knox, 1996.
Maneli, Mieczyslaw. *Perelman's New Rhetoric as Philosophy and Methodology for the Next Century*. Library of Rhetorics 1. Dordrecht; Boston: Kluwer Academic Press, 1994.
Mann, John C. *Legionary Recruitment and Veteran Settlement*. Occasional Publication 7. London: Institute of Archaeology, University of London, 1983.
Marchal, Joseph A. "Military Images in Philippians 1-2: A Feminist Analysis of the Rhetorics of Scholarship, Philippians, and Current Contexts." Pages 265–286 in *Her Master's Tools? Feminist and Postcolonial Engagements of Historical-Critical Discourse*. Edited by Caroline Vander Stichele and Todd Penner. Global Perspectives on Biblical Scholarship 9; Atlanta: Society of Biblical Literature, 2005.
Marshall, Howard. *The Epistle to the Philippians*. Epworth Commentaries. London: Epworth Press, 1992.
Marshall, John W. "Paul's Ethical Appeal in Philippians." Pages 357–372 in *Rhetoric and the New Testament: Essays from the 1992 Heidelberg Conference*. Edited

by Stanley E. Porter and Thomas H. Olbricht. Journal for the Study of the New Testament: Supplement Series 90. Sheffield: JSOT Press, 1993.

Marshall, Peter. *Enmity in Corinth: Social Conventions in Paul's Relations with the Corinthians.* Wissenschaftliche Untersuchungen zum Neuen Testament 2. Reihe. 23. Tübingen: Mohr, 1987.

Martin, Clarice J. "Acts of the Apostles." Pages 763–799 in *Searching the Scriptures: A Feminist Commentary.* Volume 2. Edited by Elisabeth Schüssler Fiorenza. New York: Crossroad, 1994.

Martin, Dale B. *The Corinthian Body.* New Haven: Yale University Press, 1995.

———. *Slavery as Salvation: The Metaphor of Slavery in Pauline Christianity.* New Haven: Yale University Press, 1990.

Martin, Ralph P. *Carmen Christi: Philippians 2:5–11 in Recent Interpretation and the Setting of Early Christian Worship.* Society for New Testament Studies Monograph Series 4. Cambridge: Cambridge University Press, 1967.

Martin, Ralph P., and Brian J. Dodd, eds. *Where Christology Began: Essays on Philippians 2.* Louisville, Ky.: Westminster John Knox Press, 1998.

Martínez-Vázquez, Hjamil A. "Postcolonial Criticism in Biblical Interpretation: A Response to Efrain Agosto." *Perspectivas: Occasional Papers* 6 (Fall 2002): 57–63.

Mattern, Susan P. *Rome and the Enemy: Imperial Strategy in the Principate.* Berkeley: University of California Press, 1999.

Matthews, Shelly. *First Converts: Rich Pagan Women and the Rhetoric of Mission in Early Judaism and Christianity.* Contraversions. Stanford: Stanford University Press, 2001.

Matthews, Shelly, Cynthia Briggs Kittredge, and Melanie Johnson-DeBaufre, eds. *Walk in the Ways of Wisdom: Essays in Honor of Elisabeth Schüssler Fiorenza.* Harrisburg, Penn.: Trinity Press International, 2003.

Mattingly, David J., ed. *Dialogues in Roman Imperialism: Power, Discourse, and Discrepant Experience in the Roman Empire.* Journal of Roman Archaeology Supplementary Series. International Roman Archaeology Conference Series 23. Portsmouth, R.I.: Journal of Roman Archaeology, British Academy, 1997.

McKerrow, Rayme. "Critical Rhetoric: Theory and Practice." Pages 441–463 in *Contemporary Rhetorical Theory: A Reader.* Edited by John Louis Lucaites, Celeste Michelle Condit, and Sally Caudill. Revisioning Rhetoric. New York: Guilford Press, 1999.

Meeks, Wayne. *The First Urban Christians: The Social World of the Apostle Paul.* New Haven: Yale University Press, 1983.

———. "Man from Heaven in Paul's Letter to the Philippians." in *The Future of Early Christianity: Essays in Honor of Helmut Koester.* Edited by Birger A. Pearson. Minneapolis: Fortress, 1991.

Meggitt, Justin J. *Paul, Poverty and Survival.* Studies of the New Testament and Its World. Edinburgh: T & T Clark, 1998.

Meyers, Carol, Toni Craven, and Ross Shepard Kraemer, eds. *Women in Scripture: A Dictionary of Named and Unnamed Women in the Hebrew Bible, the Apocryphal/Deuterocanonical Books, and the New Testament.* Grand Rapids, Mich.: Eerdmans, 2000.

Minear, Paul S. "Singing and Suffering in Philippi." Pages 202–219 in *The Conversation Continues.* Edited by Robert T. Fortna and Beverly R. Gaventa; Nashville: Abingdon Press, 1990.

Mitchell, Alan C. "'Greet the Friends by Name': New Testament Evidence for the Greco-Roman *Topos* on Friendship." Pages 225–262 in *Greco-Roman Perspectives on Friendship.* Edited by John T. Fitzgerald. Resources for Biblical Study 34. Atlanta: Scholars Press, 1997.

Mitchell, Margaret M. *Paul and the Rhetoric of Reconciliation: An Exegetical Investigation of the Language and Composition of 1 Corinthians.* Hermeneutische Untersuchungen zur Theologie 28. Tübingen: Mohr-Siebeck, 1991.

———. *The Heavenly Trumpet: John Chrysostom and the Art of Pauline Interpretation.* Hermeneutische Untersuchungen zur Theologie 40. Tübingen: Mohr Siebeck, 2000.

Moore, Stephen D. *God's Beauty Parlor: And Other Queer Spaces in and around the Bible.* Contraversions. Stanford: Stanford University Press, 2001.

———. *God's Gym: Divine Male Bodies of the Bible.* New York: Routledge, 1996.

Muilenberg, James. "After Form Criticism What?" *Journal of Biblical Literature* 88 (1969): 1–18.

Müller, Ulrich B. *Der Brief des Paulus an die Philipper.* Theologischer Handkommentar zum Neuen Testament 11:1. Leipzig: Evangelische Verlagsanstalt, 1993.

Müller-Bardorff, Johannes. "Zur Frage der literarischen Einheit des Philipperbriefes." *Wissenschaftliche Zeitschrift der Universität Jena* 7 (1957–58): 591–604.

Nelson, John S., Allan Megill, and Donald N. McCloskey, eds. *The Rhetoric of the Human Sciences: Language and Argument in Scholarship and Public Affairs.* Rhetoric of the Human Sciences. Madison: University of Wisconsin Press, 1987.

Newsom, Carol A., and Sharon H. Ringe, eds. *The Women's Bible Commentary.* Louisville, Ky.: Westminster/John Knox, 1992.

Neyrey, Jerome H. *Honor and Shame in the Gospel of Matthew.* Louisville, Ky.: Westminster John Knox, 1998.

Nicholson, Linda, ed. *The Second Wave: A Reader in Feminist Theory.* New York: Routledge, 1997.

Nicolet, Claude. *Space, Geography, and Politics in the Early Roman Empire.* Jerome Lectures 19. Ann Arbor: The University of Michigan Press, 1991.

Nissinen, Martti. *Homoeroticism in the Biblical World: A Historical Perspective.* Translated by Kirsi Stjerna. Minneapolis: Fortress, 1998.

Oakes, Peter S. *Philippians: From People to Letter*. Society for New Testament Studies Monograph Series 110. Cambridge: Cambridge University Press, 2001.
Oakman, Douglas E. "The Countryside in Luke-Acts." in *The Social World of Luke-Acts: Models for Interpretation*. Edited by Jerome H. Neyrey. Peabody, Mass.: Hendrickson, 1991.
O'Brien, Peter T. *Commentary on Philippians*. New International Greek Testament Commentary. Grand Rapids, Mich.: Eerdmans, 1991.
Olbrechts-Tyteca, Lucie. *Le Comique du discours*. Bruxelles: Editions de l'Université de Bruxelles, 1974.
———. "Les Couples philosophiques: Une nouvelle approche." *Revue internationale de philosophie* 33 (1979): 81–98.
Olbrechts-Tyteca, Lucie, and Chaïm L. Perelman. *The New Rhetoric: A Treatise on Argumentation*. Translated by John Wilkinson and Purcell Weaver. Notre Dame, Ind.: University of Notre Dame Press, 1969.
Olbricht, Thomas H., "Introduction." Pages 1–6 in *Rhetorical Argumentation in Biblical Texts: Essays from the Lund 2000 Conference*. Edited by Anders Eriksson, Thomas H. Olbricht, and Walter Übelacker. Emory Studies in Early Christianity 8. Harrisburg, Penn.: Trinity Press International, 2002.
Olbricht, Thomas H., and Jerry L. Sumney. *Paul and Pathos*. Society of Biblical Literature Symposium Series 16. Atlanta: Society of Biblical Literature, 2001.
O'Neil, Edward N. "Plutarch on Friendship." Pages 105–122 in *Greco-Roman Perspectives on Friendship*. Edited by John T. Fitzgerald. Resources for Biblical Study 34. Atlanta: Scholars Press, 1997.
Onwu, Nlenanya. "Mimetes Hypothesis: A Key to the Understanding of Pauline Parenesis." *African Journal of Biblical Studies* [Nigeria] 2 (1986): 95–112.
Osiek, Carolyn. *Philippians, Philemon*. Abingdon New Testament Commentaries. Nashville: Abingdon, 2000.
———. "Philippians." Pages 237–249 in *Searching the Scriptures: A Feminist Commentary*. Volume 2. Edited by Elisabeth Schüssler Fiorenza. New York: Crossroad, 1994.
Papazoglou, Fanoula. *Les Villes de Macédoine à l'époque Romaine. Bulletin de correspondance hellénique* Supplement 16. Paris: École Française d'Athènes, 1988.
Patrick, Dale, and Allen Scult. *Rhetoric and Biblical Interpretation*. Bible and Literature Series 26. Journal for the Study of the Old Testament: Supplement Series 82. Sheffield: Almond Press, 1990.
Patte, Daniel. *The Ethics of Biblical Interpretation: A Reevaluation*. Louisville, Ky.: Westminster John Knox, 1995.
Patterson, John. "Military Organization and Social Change in the Later Roman Republic." Pages 92–112 in *War and Society in the Roman World*. Edited by John Rich and Graham Shipley. Leicester-Nottingham Studies in Ancient Society 5. London: Routledge, 1993.

Perelman, Chaïm L. *The Idea of Justice and the Problem of Argument*. International Library of Philosophy and Scientific Method London: Routledge, 1963.

———. *The New Rhetoric and the Humanities: Essays on Rhetoric and Its Applications*. Translated by William Kluback. Synthese Library 140. Dordrecht; Boston: D. Reidel Publishing Company, 1979.

———. *The Realm of Rhetoric*. Translated by William Kluback. Notre Dame, Ind.: University of Notre Dame Press, 1982.

———. "The Rhetorical Point of View in Ethics: A Program." *Communications* 5 (1981): 315–20.

Perkins, Pheme. "Christology, Friendship and Status: The Rhetoric of Philippians." *SBL 1987 Seminar Papers* (1987): 509–520.

———. "Philippians: Theology for the Heavenly Politeuma." in *Pauline Theology*, Vol. 1: *Thessalonians, Philippians, Galatians, Philemon*. Edited by Jouette M. Bassler; Minneapolis: Augsburg Fortress Press, 1991.

Pervo, Richard I. "With Lucian: Who Needs Friends? Friendship in the *Toxaris*." Pages 163–180 in *Greco-Roman Perspectives on Friendship*. Edited by John T. Fitzgerald. Resources for Biblical Study 34. Atlanta: Scholars Press, 1997.

Peskowitz, Miriam B. *Spinning Fantasies: Rabbis, Gender, and History*. Contraversions 9. Berkeley: University of California Press, 1997.

Peterlin, Davorin. *Paul's Letter to the Philippians in the Light of Disunity in the Church*. Supplements to Novum Testamentum 79. Leiden: Brill, 1995.

Peterman, G. W. *Paul's Gift from Philippi: Conventions of Gift Exchange and Christian Giving*. Society for New Testament Studies Monograph Series 92. Cambridge: Cambridge University Press, 1997.

Pilhofer, Peter. *Philippi I: Die erste christliche Gemeinde Europas*. Wissenschaftliche Untersuchungen zum Neuen Testament 87. Tübingen: J. C. B. Mohr, 1995.

———. *Philippi II: Katalog der Inschriften von Philippi*. Wissenschaftliche Untersuchungen zum Neuen Testament 119. Tübingen: Mohr Siebeck, 2000.

Plaskow, Judith. *Standing Again at Sinai: Judaism from a Feminist Perspective*. San Francisco: Harper & Row, 1990.

Pollard, T. E. "The Integrity of Philippians." *New Testament Studies* 13 (1966–1967): 57–66.

Pomeroy, Sarah B. *Goddesses, Whores, Wives, and Slaves: Women in Classical Antiquity*. New York: Schocken Books, 1975.

Portefaix, Lilian. *Sisters Rejoice: Paul's Letter to the Philippians and Luke-Acts as Received by First-Century Philippian Women*. Coniectanea biblica: New Testament Series 20; Stockholm: Almqvist & Wiksell, 1988.

Porter, James E. *Rhetorical Ethics and Internetworked Writing*. New Directions in Computers and Composition Studies. Greenwich, Conn.: Ablex Publishing, 1998.

Porter, Stanley E., ed. *Handbook of Classical Rhetoric in the Hellenistic Period (330 B.C.–A.D. 400)*. Leiden: Brill, 1997.

Porter, Stanley E., and Thomas H. Olbricht, eds. *Rhetoric and the New Testament: Essays from the 1992 Heidelberg Conference*. Journal for the Study of the New Testament: Supplement Series 90. Sheffield: Sheffield Academic Press, 1993.

———. *The Rhetorical Analysis of Scripture: Essays from the 1995 London Conference*. Journal for the Study of the New Testament: Supplement Series 146. Sheffield: Sheffield Academic Press, 1997.

———. *Rhetoric, Scripture, and Theology: Essays from the 1994 Pretoria Conference*. Journal for the Study of the New Testament: Supplement Series 131. Sheffield: Sheffield University Press, 1996.

Porter, Stanley E., and Jeffrey T. Reed. "Philippians as a Macro-Chiasm and Its Exegetical Significance." *New Testament Studies* 44 (1998): 213–31.

Porter, Stanley E., and Dennis L. Stamps, eds. *Rhetorical Criticism and the Bible*. Journal for the Study of the New Testament: Supplement Series 195. London: Sheffield Academic Press, 2002.

———. *Rhetorical Interpretation of Scripture: Essays from the 1996 Malibu Conference*. Journal for the Study of the New Testament: Supplement Series 180. Sheffield: Sheffield Academic Press, 1999.

Rabinowitz, Nancy Sorkin, and Amy Richlin, eds. *Feminist Theory and the Classics*. Thinking Gender. New York: Routledge, 1993.

Rahtjen, B. D. "The Three Letters Of Paul to the Philippians." *New Testament Studies* 6 (1959–60): 167–173.

Rawson, Beryl, ed. *The Family in Ancient Rome: New Perspectives*. Ithaca, N.Y.: Cornell University Press, 1986.

———. *Marriage, Divorce and Children in Ancient Rome*. Oxford: Oxford University Press, 1991.

Reed, Jeffrey T. *A Discourse Analysis of Philippians: Method and Rhetoric in the Debate over Literary Integrity*. Journal for the Study of the New Testament: Supplement Series 136. Sheffield: Sheffield Academic Press, 1997.

Reimer, Ivoni Richter. *Women in the Acts of the Apostles: A Feminist Liberation Perspective*. Translated by Linda M. Maloney. Minneapolis: Fortress, 1995.

Reimer, Raymond Hubert. "'Our Citizenship Is in Heaven': Philippians 1:27–30 and 3:20–21 As Part of the Apostle Paul's Political Theology." Ph.D. diss., Princeton Theological Seminary, 1997.

Reumann, John. "Contributions of the Philippian Community to Paul and to Earliest Christianity." *New Testament Studies* 39 (1993): 438–57.

———. "Justification and the Imitatio Motif in Philippians." Pages 17–29, 92–99 in *Promoting Unity: Themes in Lutheran-Catholic Dialogue*. Edited by H. George Anderson and James R. Crumley, Jr. Minneapolis: Fortress Press, 1989.

———. "Philippians, Especially Chapter 4, as a 'Letter of Friendship': Observations on a Checkered History of Scholarship." Pages 83–106 in *Friendship, Flattery and Frankness of Speech: Studies on Friendship in the New Testament World*. Edited by John T. Fitzgerald. Supplements to Novum Testamentum 82. Leiden: Brill, 1996.

———. "Theologies of 1 Thessalonians and Philippians: Contents, Comparison, and Composite." *SBL Seminar Papers* 26 (1987): 521–536.
Rich, John. "Patronage and International Relations in the Roman Republic." Pages 117–135 in *Patronage in Ancient Society*. Edited by Andrew Wallace-Hadrill. Leicester-Nottingham Studies in Ancient Society 1. London: Routledge, 1989.
Rich, John, and Graham Shipley, eds. *War and Society in the Roman World*. Leicester-Nottingham Studies in Ancient Society 5. London: Routledge, 1993.
Robbins, Charles J. "Rhetorical Structure of Philippians 2:6–11." *Catholic Biblical Quarterly* 42 (1980): 73–82.
Robbins, Vernon K. "Argumentative Textures in Socio-Rhetorical Interpretation." Pages 27–65 in *Rhetorical Argumentation in Biblical Texts: Essays from the Lund 2000 Conference*. Edited by Anders Eriksson, Thomas H. Olbricht, and Walter Überlacker. Emory Studies in Early Christianity 8. Harrisburg, Penn.: Trinity Press International, 2002.
———. *Exploring the Texture of Texts: A Guide to Socio-Rhetorical Interpretation*. Harrisburg, Penn.: Trinity Press International, 1996.
———. "The Rhetorical Full-Turn in Biblical Interpretation: Reconfiguring Rhetorical-Political Analysis." Pages 48–60 in *Rhetorical Criticism and the Bible*. Edited by Stanley E. Porter and Dennis L. Stamps. Journal for the Study of the New Testament: Supplement Series 195. London: Sheffield Academic Press, 2002.
Roberts, Richard H., and James M. M. Good, eds. *The Recovery of Rhetoric: Persuasive Discourse and Disciplinarity in the Human Sciences*. Knowledge, Disciplinarity and Beyond. Charlottesville: University Press of Virginia, 1993.
Rossing, Barbara R. *The Choice Between Two Cities: Whore, Bride, and Empire in the Apocalypse*. Harvard Theological Studies 48. Harrisburg, Penn.: Trinity Press International, 1999.
Russell, Letty, ed. *Feminist Interpretation of the Bible*. Philadelphia: Westminster, 1985.
Sakellariou, Michael B., ed. *Macedonia: 4000 Years of Greek History and Civilization*. Greek Lands in History. Athens: Ekdotike Athenon, 1994.
Saller, Richard P. "Dowries and Daughters in Rome." Pages 204–224 in *Patriarchy, Property and Death in the Roman Family*. Cambridge Studies in Population, Economy, and Society in Past Time 25. Cambridge: Cambridge University Press, 1994.
———. *Patriarchy, Property and Death in the Roman Family*. Cambridge Studies in Population, Economy, and Society in Past Time 25. Cambridge: Cambridge University Press, 1994.
———. "Patronage and Friendship in Early Imperial Rome: Drawing the Distinction." Pages 49–62 in *Patronage in Ancient Society*. Edited by Andrew Wallace-Hadrill. Leicester-Nottingham Studies in Ancient Society 1. London: Routledge, 1989.
———. *Personal Patronage Under the Early Empire*. Cambridge: Cambridge University Press, 1982.

Salmon, E. T. *Roman Colonization Under the Republic*. Aspects of Greek and Roman Life. Ithaca, N.Y.: Cornell University Press, 1970.
Salviat, François. "Une nouvelle loi thasienne." *Bulletin de correspondance hellénique* 82 (1958): 193–267.
Salyer, Gary. *Vain Rhetoric: Private Insight and Public Debate in the Book of Ecclesiastes*. Journal for the Study of the Old Testament: Supplement Series 327. Sheffield: Sheffield Academic Press, 2001.
Sampley, J. Paul, ed. *Paul in the Greco-Roman World: A Handbook*. Harrisburg, Penn.: Trinity Press International, 2003.
―――. *Pauline Partnership in Christ*. Philadelphia: Fortress, 1980.
Santosuosso, Antonio. *Storming the Heavens: Soldiers, Emperors, and Civilians in the Roman Empire*. History and Warfare. Boulder, Colo.: Westview Press, 2001.
Sarikakēs, Theodoros Ch. "Des Soldats Macedoniens dans l'armée romaine." Pages 431–464 in *Ancient Macedonia II: anakoinēseis kata to Deutero Diethues Symposio, Thessalonikē, 19–24 Augoustou 1973*. Thessaloniki: Institute for Balkan Studies, 1977).
Schaberg, Jane, Alice Bach, and Esther Fuchs, eds. *On the Cutting Edge: The Study of Women in Biblical Worlds: Essays in Honor of Elisabeth Schüssler Fiorenza*. New York: Continuum, 2003.
Schenk, Wolfgang. *Die Philipperbriefe des Paulus*. Stuttgart: Kohlhammer, 1984.
Schmithals, Walter. "Die Irrlehrer des Philipperbriefes." *Zeitschrift für Theologie und Kirche* 54 (1957): 297–341.
Schollmeier, Paul. *Other Selves: Aristotle on Personal and Political Friendship*. SUNY Series in Ethical Theory. Albany: State University of New York Press, 1994.
Schottroff, Luise. *Let the Oppressed Go Free: Feminist Perspective on the New Testament*. Translated by Annemarie S. Kidder. Gender and the Biblical Tradition. Louisville, Ky.: Westminster/John Knox, 1991.
―――. *Lydia's Impatient Sisters: A Feminist Social History of Early Christianity*. Translated by Barbara and Martin Rumscheidt. Louisville, Ky.: Westminster John Knox, 1995.
Schottroff, Luise, Silvia Schroer, and Marie Therese Wacker. *Feminist Interpretation: The Bible in Women's Perspective*. Minneapolis: Fortress, 1998.
Schroeder, Frederic M. "Friendship in Aristotle and Some Peripatetic Philosophers." Pages 35–58 in *Greco-Roman Perspectives on Friendship*. Edited by John T. Fitzgerald. Resources for Biblical Study 34. Atlanta; Scholars Press, 1997.
Schuster, John Paul. "Rhetorical Situation and Historical Reconstruction in Philippians." Ph.D. diss., The Southern Baptist Theological Seminary, 1997.
Schüssler Fiorenza, Elisabeth. *Bread Not Stone: The Challenge of Feminist Biblical Interpretation*. Revised ed. Boston: Beacon Press, 1995.
―――. *But She Said: Feminist Practices of Biblical Interpretation*. Boston: Beacon Press, 1992.
―――. "Challenging the Rhetorical Half-Turn: Feminist and Rhetorical Biblical Criticism." Pages 28–53 in *Rhetoric, Scripture, and Theology: Essays from the*

1994 Pretoria Conference. Edited by Stanley E. Porter and Thomas H. Olbricht. Journal for the Study of the New Testament: Supplement Series 131. Sheffield: Sheffield University Press, 1996.

———. "The Ethics of Biblical Interpretation: Decentering Biblical Scholarship." *Journal of Biblical Literature* 107:1 (1988): 3–17

———. *In Memory of Her: A Feminist Theological Reconstruction of Christian Origins*. 10th anniversary ed. New York: Crossroad, 1994.

———. *Jesus and the Politics of Interpretation*. New York: Continuum, 2000.

———. *Rhetoric and Ethic: The Politics of Biblical Studies*. Minneapolis: Fortress, 1999.

———. "Rhetorical Situation and Historical Reconstruction in 1 Corinthians." *New Testament Studies* 33 (1987): 386–403.

———. "The Rhetoricity of Historical Knowledge: Pauline Discourse and Its Contextualizations." Pages 443–470 in *Religious Propagana and Missionary Competition in the New Testament World: Essays Honoring Dieter Georgi*. Edited by Lukas Bormann, Kelly Del Tredici, Angela Standhartinger. Leiden: Brill, 1994.

———. ed. *Searching the Scriptures*. 2 vols. New York: Crossroad, 1993-1994.

———. *Wisdom Ways: Introducing Feminist Biblical Interpretation*. Maryknoll, N.Y.: Orbis, 2001.

Scott, Sarah, and Jane Webster, eds. *Roman Imperialism and Provincial Art*. Cambridge: Cambridge University Press, 2003.

Searle, John R. *Intentionality: An Essay on the Philosophy of Mind*. New York: Cambridge University Press, 1983.

Segovia, Fernando F. *Decolonizing Biblical Studies: A View from the Margins*. Maryknoll, N.Y.: Orbis, 2000.

———. ed. *Toward A New Heaven and A New Earth: Essays in Honor of Elisabeth Schüssler Fiorenza*. Maryknoll, N.Y.: Orbis Books, 2003.

Segovia, Fernando F., and Mary Ann Tolbert, eds., *Reading from This Place*. 2 vols. Minneapolis: Fortress, 1995.

Seim, Turid Karlsen. *The Double Message: Patterns of Gender in Luke & Acts*. Nashville: Abingdon, 1994.

Sellew, Phillip. "*Laodiceans* and the Philippians Fragment Hypothesis." *Harvard Theological Review* 87 (1994): 17–28.

Sève, Michel, and Patrick Weber. "Un monument honorifique au forum de Philippes." *Bulletin de correspondance hellénique* 112 (1988): 467–479.

Shapiro, Susan. "Rhetoric as Ideology Critique: The Gadamer-Habermas Debate Reinvented." *Journal of the American Academy of Religion* 62 (1994): 123–50.

Sheppard, A. R. R. "*Homonoia* in the Greek Cities of the Roman Empire." *Ancient Society* 15–17 (1984–1986): 229–252.

Sherwin-White, Adrian N. *The Roman Citizenship*. 2nd ed. Oxford: Clarendon, 1973.

———. *Roman Foreign Policy in the East: 168 B.C. to A.D. 1*. London: Duckworth, 1984.

Siegert, Folker. *Argumentation bei Paulus, gezeigt an Römer 9–11*. Wissenschaftliche Untersuchungen zum Neuen Testament 34. Tübingen: J. C. B. Mohr/Paul Siebeck, 1985.
Simons, Herbert W., ed. *Rhetoric in the Human Sciences*. Inquiries in Social Construction Series. Newbury Park, Calif.: Sage, 1989.
Snyman, A. H. "Persuasion in Philippians 4:1–20." Pages 325–337 in *Rhetoric and the New Testament: Essays from the 1992 Heidelberg Conference*. Edited by Stanley E. Porter and Thomas H. Olbricht. Journal for the Study of the New Testament: Supplement Series 90. Sheffield: JSOT Press, 1993.
Stendahl, Krister. *Paul Among Jews and Gentiles And Other Essays*. Philadelphia: Fortress, 1976.
Stowers, Stanley K. *The Diatribe and Paul's Letter to the Romans*. Society of Biblical Literature Dissertation Series 57. Chico, Calif.: Scholars Press, 1981.
———. "Friends and Enemies in the Politics of Heaven: Reading Theology in Philippians." Pages 105–121 in *Pauline Theology*, Vol. 1: *Thessalonians, Philippians, Galatians, Philemon*. Edited by Jouette M. Bassler. Minneapolis: Augsburg Fortress Press, 1991.
———. *Letter Writing in Greco-Roman Antiquity*. Library of Early Christianity 5. Philadelphia: Westminster, 1986.
———. *A Rereading of Romans: Justice, Jews, and Gentiles*. New Haven: Yale University Press, 1994.
Sugirtharajah, R. S. *Postcolonial Criticism and Biblical Interpretation*. Oxford: Oxford University Press, 2002.
———. ed. *Voices From the Margin: Interpreting the Bible in the Third World*. 2nd ed. Maryknoll, N.Y.: Orbis, 1995.
Sutherland, Christine Mason, and Rebecca Sutcliffe, eds. *The Changing Tradition: Women in the History of Rhetoric*. Calgary: University of Calgary Press, 1999.
Swearingen, C. Jan. "Ethos: Imitation, Impersonation and Voice." Pages 115–148 in *Ethos: New Essays in Rhetorical and Critical Theory*. Edited by James S. Baumlin and Tita French Baumlin. SMU Studies in Composition and Rhetoric. Dallas: Southern Methodist University Press, 1993.
———. "Originality, Authenticity, Imitation and Plagiarism: Augustine's Chinese Cousins." Pages 19–30 in *Perspectives on Plagiarism and Intellectual Property in a Postmodern World*. Edited by Lise Buranen and Alice M. Roy. Albany: State University of New York Press, 1999.
———. "Plato's Feminine: Appropriation, Impersonation, and Metaphorical Polemic." *Rhetoric Society Quarterly* 22. 1992. *Special Issue: Feminist Rereadings in the History of Rhetoric*. 109–23.
———. *Rhetoric and Irony: Western Literacy and Western Lies*. New York: Oxford University Press, 1991.
Tamez, Elsa. *Bible of the Oppressed*. Translated by Matthew J. O'Connell. Maryknoll, N.Y.: Orbis, 1982.

Tarn, W. W. *Alexander the Great,* Vol. II: *Sources and Studies.* Cambridge: Cambridge University Press, 1948.

Taylor, Lily Ross. *Party Politics in the Age of Caesar.* Sather Classical Lectures 22. Berkeley: University of California Press, 1949.

Tellbe, Mikael. "The Sociological Factors Behind Philippians 3.1–11 and the Conflict at Philippi." *Journal for the Study of the New Testament* 55 (1994): 97–121.

Theissen, Gerd. *Social Setting of Pauline Christianity: Essays on Corinth.* Edited, translated, with an introduction by John H. Schütz. Philadelphia: Fortress, 1982.

Thimmes, Pamela. "What Makes a Feminist Reading Feminist? Another Perspective," Pages 132–140 in *Escaping Eden: New Feminist Perspectives on the Bible.* Edited by Harold C. Washington, Susan Lochrie Graham, and Pamela Thimmes. New York: New York University Press, 1999.

Thom, Johan C. "'Harmonious Equality': The *Topos* of Friendship in Neopythagorean Writings." Pages 77–104 in *Greco-Roman Perspectives on Friendship.* Edited by John T. Fitzgerald. Resources for Biblical Study 34. Atlanta; Scholars Press, 1997.

Thraede, Klaus. *Grundzüge griechisch-römischer Brieftopic.* Zetemata 48 Munich: Beck, 1970.

Tolbert, Mary Ann, ed. *The Bible and Feminist Hermeneutics; Semeia* 28. 1983.

———. "Defining the Problem: The Bible and Feminist Hermeneutics." *Semeia* 28 (1983): 113–126.

———. "Social, Sociological, and Anthropological Methods" Pages 255–271 in *Searching the Scriptures: A Feminist Introduction* Vol. 1. Edited by Elisabeth Schüssler Fiorenza. New York: Crossroad, 1993.

———. *Sowing the Gospel: Mark's World in Literary-Historical Perspective.* Minneapolis: Fortress Press, 1989.

Toulmin, Stephen. *The Uses of Argument.* Cambridge: Cambridge University Press, 1958.

Treggiari, Susan. *Roman Marriage: 'Iusti Coniuges' from the Time of Cicero to the Time of Ulpian.* Oxford: Oxford University Press, 1991.

Trible, Phyllis. *God and the Rhetoric of Sexuality.* Overtures to Biblical Theology. Philadelphia: Fortress Press, 1978.

———. *Rhetorical Criticism: Context, Method, and the Book of Jonah.* Guides to Biblical Scholarship Old Testament Series. Minneapolis: Fortress Press, 1994.

———. *Texts of Terror: Literary-Feminist Readings of Biblical Narratives.* Overtures to Biblical Theology 13. Philadelphia: Fortress Press, 1984.

Trinh T. Minh-ha. *Woman Native Other: Writing Postcoloniality and Feminism.* Bloomington, Ind.: Indiana University Press, 1989.

Van Der Horst, Pieter W. *Aelius Aristides and the New Testament.* Studia ad corpus hellenisticum Novi Testamenti 6. Leiden: Brill, 1980.

Vermeule, Cornelius C. *Roman Imperial Art in Greece and Asia Minor*. Cambridge, Mass.: Belknap Press, 1968.

Vickers, Brian. *In Defense of Rhetoric*. Oxford: Clarendon, 1988.

———. ed. *Rhetoric Revalued: Papers from the International Society for the History of Rhetoric*. Medieval and Renaissance Texts and Studies 19 Binghampton, N.Y.: Center for Medieval and Renaissance Studies, 1982.

Vollenweider, Samuel. "Der 'Raub' der Gottgleichheit: Ein religionsgeschichtlicher Vorschlag zu Phil 2.6(–11)." *New Testament Studies* 45 (1999): 413–33.

Von Harnack, Adolf. *Militia Christi: The Christian Religion and the Military in the First Three Centuries*. Translated with an introduction by David McInnes Gracie. Philadelphia: Fortress, 1981.

Wachob, Wesley H. *The Voice of Jesus in the Social Rhetoric of James*. Society for New Testament Studies Monograph Series 106. Cambridge: Cambridge University Press, 2000.

Wallace-Hadrill, Andrew. "Introduction." Pages 1–13 in *Patronage in Ancient Society*. Edited by A. Wallace-Hadrill. Leicester-Nottingham Studies in Ancient Society 1. London; Routledge, 1989.

———. ed. *Patronage in Ancient Society*. Leicester-Nottingham Studies in Ancient Society 1. London: Routledge, 1989.

———. "Patronage in Roman Society: From Republic to Empire." Pages 63–87 in *Patronage in Ancient Society*. Edited by A. Wallace-Hadrill. Leicester-Nottingham Studies in Ancient Society 1. London: Routledge, 1989.

Walter, Nikolaus. "Die Philipper und das Leiden, aus den Anfangen einer heidenchristlichen Gemeinde." Pages 417–433 in *Die Kirche des Anfangs: Festschrift für Heinz Schürmann*. Edited by Rudolf Schnackenburg, Joseph Ernst, and Joachim Wanke. Erfurter theologische Studien 38. Freiburg: Herder, 1978.

Walter, Nikolaus, Eckart Reinmuth, and Peter Lampe. *Die Briefe an die Philipper, Thessalonicher und an Philemon: Übersetzt und erklart*. Gottingen: Vandenhoeck and Ruprecht, 1998.

Wansink, Craig S. *Chained in Christ: The Experience and Rhetoric of Paul's Imprisonment*. Journal for the Study of the New Testament: Supplement Series 130. Sheffield: Sheffield Academic Press, 1996.

Warnick, Barbara. "Lucie Olbrechts-Tyteca's Contribution to *The New Rhetoric*." Pages 69–85 in *Listening to Their Voices: The Rhetorical Activities of Historical Women*. Edited by Molly Meijer Wertheimer. Studies in Rhetoric/Communication. Columbia: University of South Carolina Press, 1997.

Washington, Harold C., Susan Lochrie Graham, and Pamela Thimmes, eds. *Escaping Eden: New Feminist Perspectives on the Bible*. New York: New York University Press, 1999.

Watson, Duane F. "1 Corinthians 10:23–11:1 in the Light of Greco-Roman Rhetoric: The Role of Rhetorical Questions." *Journal of Biblical Literature* 108 (1989): 301–318.

———. "A Rhetorical Analysis of Philippians and Its Implications for the Unity Question." *Novum Testamentum* 30:1 (1988): 57–88.

———. *Invention, Arrangement, and Style: Rhetorical Criticism of Jude and 2 Peter.* Society of Biblical Literature Dissertation Series 104 Atlanta: Scholars Press, 1988.

———. "The Integration of Epistolary and Rhetorical Analysis of Philippians." in *The Rhetorical Analysis of Scripture: Essays from the 1995 London Conference.* Edited by Stanley E. Porter and Thomas H. Olbricht. Journal for the Study of the New Testament: Supplement Series 146. Sheffield: Sheffield Academic Press, 1997.

———. "Rhetorical Criticism, New Testament." Pages 399–402 in vol. 2 of *Dictionary of Biblical Interpretation.* Edited by John H. Hayes. 2 vols. Nashville: Abingdon Press, 1999.

———. "Why We Need Socio-Rhetorical Commentary and What It Might Look Like." Pages 129–157 in *Rhetorical Criticism and the Bible.* Edited by Stanley E. Porter and Dennis L. Stamps. Journal for the Study of the New Testament: Supplement Series 195. London: Sheffield Academic Press, 2002.

Watson, Duane F., and Alan J. Hauser. *Rhetorical Criticism of the Bible: A Comprehensive Bibliography with Notes on History and Method.* Biblical Interpretation Series 4. Leiden: Brill, 1994.

Webster, Graham. *The Roman Imperial Army of the First and Second Centuries A. D.* London: Adam & Charles Black, 1969.

Webster, Jane, and Nicholas J. Cooper, eds. *Roman Imperialism: Post-colonial perspectives.* Leicester Archaeology Monographs 3. Leicester: School of Archaeological Studies, 1996.

Weems, Renita J. *Just a Sister Away: A Womanist Vision of Women's Relationships in the Bible.* San Diego: LuraMedia, 1988.

———. "Reading *Her Way* through the Struggle: African American Women and the Bible." Pages 57–77 in *Stony the Road We Trod: African-American Biblical Interpretation.* Edited by Cain Hope Felder. Minneapolis: Fortress, 1991.

Wegner, Judith Romney. *Chattel or Person? The Status of Women in the Mishnah.* New York: Oxford University Press, 1988.

Weidmann, Frederick W. "An (Un)Accomplished Model: Paul and the Rhetorical Strategy of Philippians 3:3–17." Pages 245–257 in *Putting Body and Soul Together: Essays in Honor of Robin Scroggs.* Edited by Virginia Wiles, Alexandra Brown, and Graydon F. Snyder. Valley Forge, Penn.: Trinity Press International, 1997.

Welborn, L. L. *Politics and Rhetoric in the Corinthian Epistles.* Macon, Ga.: Mercer University Press, 1997.

Wertheimer, Molly Meijer, ed. *Listening to Their Voices: The Rhetorical Activities of Historical Women.* Studies in Rhetoric/Communication. Columbia: University of South Carolina Press, 1997.

West, Gerald O. *The Academy of the Poor: Towards a Dialogical Reading of the Bible.* Sheffield: Sheffield Academic Press, 1999.

White, L. Michael. "Morality Between Two Worlds: A Paradigm of Friendship in Philippians." Pages 201–215 in *Greeks, Romans and Christians: Essays in Honor of Abraham J. Malherbe.* Edited by David L. Balch, Everett Ferguson and Wayne A. Meeks. Minneapolis: Fortress Press, 1990.

Williams, Demetrius K. "'Enemies of the Cross of Christ': A Rhetorical Analysis of the 'Theology of the Cross' in Conflict in Paul's Philippians Correspondence." Th.D. diss., Harvard University, 1997.

———. *Enemies of the Cross of Christ: The Terminology of the Cross and Conflict in Philippians.* Journal for the Study of the New Testament: Supplement Series 223. London: Sheffield Academic Press, 2002.

Wimbush, Vincent L., and Rosamond C. Rodman, eds. *African Americans and the Bible: Sacred Texts and Social Textures.* New York: Continuum, 2000.

Wire, Antoinette Clark. *The Corinthian Women Prophets: A Reconstruction Through Paul's Rhetoric.* Minneapolis: Fortress, 1990.

———. "Response: The Politics of the Assembly in Corinth." Pages 124–129 in *Paul and Politics: Ekklesia, Israel, Imperium, Interpretation.* Edited by Richard A. Horsley. Harrisburg, Penn.: Trinity Press International, 2000.

Witherington, Ben, III. *Friendship and Finances in Philippi: The Letter of Paul to the Philippians.* The New Testament in Context. Valley Forge, Penn.: Trinity Press International, 1994.

Witt, Rex. "The Egyptian Cults in Ancient Macedonia." in *Ancient Macedonia.* Edited by B. Laourdas. Thessaloniki: Institute for Balkan Studies, 1970.

Wood, Neal. *Cicero's Social and Political Thought.* Berkeley: University of California Press, 1988.

Wood, Sheila. "Is Philippians 2:5–11 Incompatible with Feminist Concerns?" *Pro Ecclesia* 6 (1997): 172–83.

Woolf, Greg. "Roman Peace." Pages 171–194 in *War and Society in the Roman World.* Edited by John Rich and Graham Shipley. Leicester-Nottingham Studies in Ancient Society 5. London: Routledge, 1993.

Wrede, Henning *Das Mausoleum der Claudia Semne und die bürgerliche Plastik der Kaiserzeit.* Mitteilungen des Deutschen Archaeologischen Instituts, Roemische Abteilung, Bd. 78, 1971.

Wuellner, Wilhelm. "Biblical Exegesis in the Light of the History and Historicity of Rhetoric and the Nature of the Rhetoric of Religion." Pages 492–512 in *Rhetoric and the New Testament: Essays from the 1992 Heidelberg Conference.* Edited by Stanley E. Porter and Thomas H. Olbricht. Journal for the Study of the New Testament: Supplement Series 90. Sheffield: Sheffield Academic Press, 1993.

———. "Greek Rhetoric and Pauline Argumentation." Pages 177–188 in *Early Christian Literature and the Classical Intellectual Tradition: In Honorem Robert M.*

Grant. Edited by William R. Schoedel and Robert L. Wilkin. Théologique historique 53. Paris: Beauchesne, 1979.

———. *Hermeneutics and Rhetorics: From "Truth and Method" to Truth and Power.* Scriptura Special Issue S3. Stellenbosch, RSA: Centre for Hermeneutical Studies, 1989.

———. "Rhetorical Criticism in Biblical Studies." *Jian Dao: A Journal of Bible and Theology* 4 (1995): 73–96.

———. "Reading Romans in Context." Paper presented at the annual meeting of the Society for New Testament Studies. Gottingen, August 25–27, 1987.

———. "Paul's Rhetoric of Argumentation in Romans: An Alternative to the Donfried-Karris Debate over Romans." *Catholic Biblical Quarterly* 38 (1976): 330–351.

———. "Where Is Rhetorical Criticism Taking Us?" *Catholic Biblical Quarterly* 49 (1987): 448–463.

Wuellner, Wilhelm, and the Bible and Culture Collective. "Rhetorical Criticism." Pages 149–186 in *The Postmodern Bible*. Edited by Elizabeth Castelli, Stephen Moore, Gary Phillips and Regina Schwartz. New Haven: Yale University Press, 1995.

Zanker, Paul. *The Power of Images in the Age of Augustus*. Translated by Alan Shapiro. Jerome Lectures 16. Ann Arbor: The University of Michigan Press, 1988.

Index of Ancient Sources

Aelius Aristides
Or.
23	91
23.8–12	96
23.29	93
23.31	92, 93
23.34	94
23.35	93
23.42	92, 93
23.43	92, 93
23.78	92, 94
24	91
24.5	92, 127, 162
24.20	96
24.29	92, 93
24.31	96
24.32	96-97
24.32–33	92
24.37	92
24.51	93
26.60	96
26.65	97
27.39	93
27.40–41	95

Appian
Bell. civ.
2.47	58
2.93	58
2.140	102
3.42	67
4.105	99, 100
4.105–138	101
5.13	58
5.128	58

Hist. rom.
61.14.84	66

Aristotle
Eth. nic.
8.1.4	95
8.1.1155	38
8.9.1160	65
8.10.1161	40
9.8.2	26, 27

Pol.
3.1280	95

Chariton
Chaer.
8.2.10	65

Cicero
Amic.
15	26
51	35, 43

Caecin.
14	45

Fam.
1.20	42
2.1.28	42
2.5–6	42
5.8.1–2	95
5.8.5	42
7.29	42
8.9.4	42
13.65	42

Off.
1.5.1   26

Phil.
2.5–6   43
4.3   67

Planc.
2.5   26

Verr.
2.4.25   42

Dio Chrysostom
Apam.
41   91
41.12   95
41.13   93, 95
41.26   58

Borsyth.
36.21   95

Conc. Apam.
40   91

Diod.
51.4.6   104

Gen.
25.2   94

In cont.
48.3.2   58
48.15   93

Nicaeen.
39   91

Nicom.
38   91
38.15   94–95, 97
38.33   93
38.34   96
38.43   93

Rec. mag.
49.3   96
49.13   58

2 Tars.
34.19   92, 127, 162
34.20   26
34.22   92, 127, 162

Diodorus Siculus
9.6   100
11.70.5   100
12.68.1–3   100
16.3.7   100
16.8.6–7   100

Diogenes Laertius
5.20   27
8.10   37

Dionysus of Halicarnassus
Ant. rom.
3   46

Herodotus
Hist.
3.80–82   40
7.112   99

Homer
Il.
4.360–361   36
15.710   36
16.219   36
17.267   36
21.489–496   75
22.262–265   36

Od.
6.102   75
6.180–185   36

Isocrates
De pace
8   91
8.2   94
8.36–37   92

Paneg.
4   91, 94, 96
4.168   93

Phil.
5	91, 96
5.16	95
5.113	92
5.113–114	92
5.114	92

Josephus
B.J.
3.72–76	52

Livy
45.29.5–9	100
45.44	67

Lucian
Tox.
10	37, 65
29–34	27

Ovid
Am.
1.720–722	45

Plato
Alc.
126–127	26

Ly.
207	26

Resp.
449	26
450	26

Plautus
Bacch.
193	45

Curc.
593	45

Epid.
702	45

Pliny the Elder
Nat.
4.42	101

Plutarch
Amic. mult.
93.20	37, 65
96	27

Ant.
55	56, 104

Pel.
18	65

Polybius
31.29	100

Porphyry
Vit. Pyth.
59–61	38

Strabo
Geogr.
7	99
7.331	101

Suetonius
Aug.
24.1	59
24.2	57

Tacitus
Ann.
1.35	57

Theophrastus of Eresus
2.360	38

Vegetius, Renatus Flavius
Epi. rei mil.
1.11–14	52
1.27	52
3.4	52

Virgil
Aen.
1.496–504	75
7.812–817	75

Xenophon			16:36	88
Mem.			16:37	88
2.2.2	66		16:38	88
3.7.9	66		16:40	86, 87
3.11	45			
			Rom	
BIBLICAL LITERATURE			16:1–2	88
			16:7	88
Exod				
32:32	150		**1 Cor,**	91, 115, 146, 157, 160, 179
Ps			1:10	92, 127
69:28	150		3:3	127
			4:16–17	187
Isa			12:28–30	97
4:3	150		16:15–16	97
Ezek			**2 Cor**	91
13:9	150			
			Gal	
Dan			6:3	160
12:1	150			
			Phil	
1 En.			1:1	26, 93, 119, 120,
47:3	150			139, 167, 168, 187
			1:1–11	119–123
Luke			1:2	26, 93, 120
10:20	150		1:3	26, 93
			1:3–4	120, 167, 168, 175
Acts			1:3–7	121, 148, 175
10:1–43	87		1:3–11	119, 154, 168, 181,
16	86, 87, 88, 89			182, 183, 199
16:9	86		1:4	26, 93, 121
16:11–40	86		1:5	26, 32, 93, 120, 175
16:12	88		1:5–6	173, 174, 198
16:13	86		1:6	121, 152
16:13–15	86		1:7	26, 32, 93, 94, 120,
16:14	86			121, 122, 132, 133,
16:15	87			139, 144, 145, 148,
16:16	87			169, 175, 190, 193,
16:16–18	86			197
16:17	87		1:7–8	25, 122
16:18	87		1:8	26, 93, 122, 148,
16:19–23	87			176, 177, 197
16:20	88		1:9	26, 93, 122
16:23–36	86		1:9–10a	123
16:26	87		1:9–11	122, 178
16:27	87		1:10	122, 123, 152
16:33	87		1:11	123, 137
16:34	87			

INDICES

1:12	32, 93, 94, 124, 159, 160, 196	1:27–2:4	128–132
1:12–13	197	1:28	32, 94, 130, 131, 136, 139, 141, 144, 145, 151, 159, 160, 163, 164, 165, 176, 177, 178, 188, 189, 196
1:12–14	88, 128, 133, 139, 144, 148, 154, 160, 178, 181, 183, 187, 199		
1:12–26	123–128	1:28–30	132, 164
1:13	26, 30, 93, 124, 125, 148, 154, 167, 168, 182	1:29	32, 131, 171, 172, 173
		1:29–30	27, 131
1:13–14	124, 176	1:30	32, 129, 131, 132, 172, 181, 183, 193
1:14	124, 132, 182		
1:15	93, 125, 128, 161	2:1	131, 164
1:15–16	125	2:1–2	132
1:15–17	94, 126, 139, 144, 148, 160, 161, 188, 189	2:1–3	160, 161
		2:1–4	131, 178
		2:1–5	139, 144, 145, 148
1:15–18	27, 132	2:2	26, 27, 93, 131, 132, 133, 144, 153, 190
1:17	93, 94, 125, 132		
1:17–18	125		
1:18	26, 32, 93, 125, 126, 161	2:2–4	131
		2:2–5	193
1:19	126	2:3	93, 132
1:19–20	178	2:3–4	132, 138, 139, 140, 162, 163
1:19–26	25		
1:20	26, 93, 126, 177	2:4	132
1:20–26	140, 143	2:5	93, 132, 133, 134, 144, 148, 153, 170, 171, 179, 184, 190
1:21	126–127, 173		
1:21–23	127, 148, 174, 178, 199		
		2:5–6	176
1:21–26	27, 128, 133, 135, 138, 139, 140, 171, 172, 173, 199	2:5–8	171
		2:5–11	120, 133, 135, 148, 155, 159, 164, 179, 184, 185, 199
1:23	26, 93		
1:24	127	2:5–12	198
1:24–25	32, 161, 162, 163	2:5–18	133–138
1:24–26	131, 132, 139, 144, 148, 154, 174, 181, 183, 185, 187, 199	2:6	134, 135, 184
		2:6–7	165
		2:6–8	134, 172, 173, 185
1:25	26, 28, 32, 93, 127, 128, 167	2:6–11	17–18, 27, 133, 134, 135, 142, 143, 146, 174, 179, 184, 185, 196, 199, 200
1:25–26	138		
1:27	25, 26, 27, 30, 31, 33, 93, 129, 130, 139, 178	2:7	120, 134, 135, 137, 139, 184
1:27–28	131, 146, 148, 173–174	2:7–8	33, 94, 160
1:27–30	29, 30, 33, 99, 124, 129, 130, 144, 148		

Phil, continued
2:8	134, 135, 137, 138, 140, 141, 143, 146, 172, 173, 179, 184, 187	2:23–24	181, 183
		2:24	25, 186, 187
		2:25	26, 30, 31, 33, 93, 140, 141, 148, 171, 187, 200
2:9	26, 93, 134, 146	2:25–26	178
2:9–11	134, 135, 165, 173, 176, 184	2:25–30	148, 155, 186, 187, 199
2:10	26, 93, 134, 146	2:26	26, 93, 139, 162, 163, 187
2:11	26, 93, 134, 137, 146, 160	2:26–27	139, 171, 172, 173
2:12	25, 26, 33, 93, 94, 136, 137, 138, 141, 151, 163, 164, 165, 172, 173, 174, 175, 178, 179, 180, 184, 193, 198	2:26–30	94, 199
		2:27	140, 172, 187
		2:27–28	178, 187
		2:28	26, 31, 93, 140, 141, 187
		2:29	26, 93, 140, 181, 183, 187, 193
2:12–18	154		
2:13	137, 177	2:29–30	173
2:14	26, 33, 93, 137	2:30	139, 140, 171, 172, 173, 187
2:14–16	138, 139, 148, 178		
2:14–18	27	3	18, 27-28, 141, 166
2:15	94, 137, 138, 188	3:1	26, 93, 94, 141, 144, 148, 162, 163, 164, 193
2:16	67, 137, 138, 152, 174, 175		
2:16–17	94, 148	3:1–11	141–143
2:16-18	140, 181, 183, 199	3:2	141, 188, 189
2:17	26, 93 138, 139, 140, 143, 162, 163, 171, 172, 173, 185, 187	3:2–3	94
		3:2–4	148, 168
		3:3	141, 142, 148, 165
		3:3–17	64, 136, 182
2:17–18	139, 144, 148, 176	3:4	144, 160, 169
2:18	26, 93, 138, 148, 183, 193	3:4–6	142, 143, 159, 160, 196
2:19	138, 140, 141, 178, 187	3:4–7	173, 199
		3:4–8	148
2:19–24	27, 148, 155, 186, 187, 199	3:4–11	142, 185, 199
		3:5–6	142, 169
2:19–30	26, 138-141, 142, 185	3:7	142
		3:7–8	142, 171, 172, 173
2:20	27, 33, 93, 139, 140, 148, 186	3:7–9	165
		3:7–11	143, 148, 155, 181, 185
2:20–21	162, 163		
2:20–22	148	3:8	26, 93, 148, 155
2:21	26, 93, 94, 139, 186, 188, 189	3:8–10	94
		3:9	142, 143, 177
2:22	26, 93, 120, 139, 186, 187, 200	3:10	26, 32, 93, 142, 143, 146, 150, 178
2:23	139, 140, 141, 178, 187	3:10–11	143, 148
		3:11	143

3:12	143	4:9	28, 33, 152, 154, 155, 177, 178, 179, 180, 181, 183, 193, 198, 199
3:12–14	143, 144, 152, 178		
3:12–21	143–147		
3:13–15	148		
3:14	143	4:10	26, 28, 93, 152, 153, 162
3:15	93, 144, 145, 148, 149, 152, 155, 160, 161, 163, 164, 177, 178, 190, 193		
		4:10–20	18, 28, 122, 153
		4:10–23	152–154
		4:11	153, 167, 168
3:16	144, 174, 175, 198	4:11–12	153, 165
3:17	26, 33, 93, 94, 144, 145, 148, 149, 152, 155, 181, 183	4:11–13	153, 155, 181, 185
		4:12	26, 93
		4:13	26, 93, 153, 177
3:17–4:3	31	4:14	26, 32, 93, 153
3:18	28, 33, 51, 94, 145	4:14–16	174, 198
3:18–19	94, 148, 188, 189	4:15	26, 32, 93
3:18–21	147	4:15–16	153
3:19	94, 145, 148, 149, 151, 153, 164, 190	4:17	28, 153, 162
		4:18	26, 93, 153, 154, 200
3:19–20	94, 152, 163, 165, 166		
		4:18–19	178
3:19–21	145, 147, 149, 151	4:19	26, 93, 154, 177
3:20	93, 145, 146, 164	4:21	26, 93, 154
3:20–21	30, 145, 146	4:21–22	167, 168
3:21	26, 93, 146, 150	4:22	26, 88, 93, 154
4	18, 89	4:23	26, 93
4:1	25, 26, 67, 93, 147, 178, 179		
		1 Thess	
4:1–9	147–152	2:1–2	88
4:2	26, 28, 93, 147, 148, 149, 150, 153, 155, 170, 171, 181, 183, 190, 193, 207		
		Heb	
		12:23	150
4:2–3	28, 33, 85, 152, 155, 189, 200	**Rev**	87
		3:5	150
4:3	26, 33, 64, 85, 88, 93, 148, 149, 150, 151, 189, 190, 207	13:8	150
		17:8	150
		20:12	150
4:4	26, 93, 151	20:15	150
4:4–6	151, 167, 168	21:27	150
4:4–7	178		
4:5	26, 93, 151, 152, 174	*Acts Paul*	
		41–42	89
4:6	26, 93, 151		
4:7	26, 33, 93, 152, 154, 177	*Pol. Phil*	
		4.2	89
4:8	28, 152, 179	5.1–3	89
4:8–9	33, 152, 198	5.3	89
		6.3–7.2	89

Index of Modern Authors

Abrahamsen, Valerie, 64, 74–82, 85, 89–90, 108
Adam, A. K. M., 3
Adkins, A. W. H., 37
Agosto, Efrain, 50, 211
Alexander, Loveday, 24
Amador, J. David Hester, 3–10, 118

Bach, Alice, 16
Badian, Ernst, 47, 55, 61, 103
Bakirtzis, Charalambos, 76
Balch, David L., 25, 46, 122
Baxter, Leslie A., 12
Berry, Ken L., 26, 28–29, 122, 153
Betz, Hans D., 4–5, 8
Bhabha, Homi K., 211
Bird, Phyllis A., 11,
Bizzell, Patricia, 3, 11, 116
Blair, Carole, 12
Bloomquist, L. Gregory, 6, 7, 18, 24, 26, 27, 119, 128, 133
Blumenfeld, Bruno, 91–97, 129
Blümner, Hugo, 80
Blundell, Mary Whitlock, 27
Bockmuehl, Markus, 16, 19, 121, 126, 127, 148, 182

Bormann, Lukas, 9, 29, 99–102, 104, 110
Bornhäuser, D. Karl, 110–111
Bowerstock, G. W., 56, 104
Boyarin, Daniel, 210
Braund, David, 42, 47–48, 57, 67
Brewer, R. R., 30, 102
Briggs, Sheila, 135, 184
Brooten, Bernadette J., 86, 211–212
Brown, Julie R., 12
Brunt, Peter A., 41, 59, 101–102, 104
Burke, Kenneth, 10, 11, 116
Burrus, Virginia, 89

Cadoux, C. John, 52
Cannon, Katie Geneva, 210
Castelli, Elizabeth A., 9, 12–13, 70, 82, 85, 121–122, 137, 145, 181–183, 185
Caudill, Sally, 12
Chow, Rey, 211
Christou, Panayotis, 33
Chung Hyun Kyung, 210
Clarke, Andrew D., 64, 136–137, 182
Collange, Jean-François, 23
Collart, Paul, 29, 74–75, 77–79, 99–102

Collins, Adela Yarbro, 83
Condit, Celeste Michelle, 10, 12
Conley, Thomas, 3, 11, 116
Cooper, Nicholas J., 49
Cotter, Wendy, 18, 148, 190
Craven, Toni, 83–84
Culpepper, R. Alan, 26, 142, 146, 185
Cunningham, David S., 3–5

Dahl, Nils A., 19, 148, 151, 190
D'Angelo, Mary R., 83, 85, 148, 190, 211
Daumet, H., 79
Davies, Roy W., 52–53, 57, 59
Davies, Stevan, 89
Dearin, Ray D., 116
Delatte, Armand, 38
DeSilva, David A., 6
De Ste. Croix, G. E. M., 57–58, 64, 105
De Vos, Craig S., 29–33, 51, 69, 99–103, 105–111, 129, 135
Dibelius, Martin, 32
Dodd, Brian J., 18, 121, 132, 140, 142, 182, 185
Drerup, Heinrich, 82
Dube, Musa W., 50–51
Ducrey, Pierre, 74–75

Ebner, Martin, 28, 153
Engberg-Pedersen, Troels, 153
Eriksson, Anders, 7,
Erskine, Andrew, 39

Fant, Maureen B., 74, 109–110
Fee, Gordon D., 16, 25, 36, 131, 148
Felder, Cain Hope, 210
Ferguson, John, 96
Finley, Moses I., 39, 61–62, 103
Fiore, Benjamin, 43–44, 68, 121, 182
Fitzgerald, John T., 25–29, 36–37, 41, 65, 122, 125–126, 129, 132, 136, 139, 148, 152–153

Fortna, Robert T., 64, 137, 142, 182, 185
Foss, Karen A., 3, 11–12
Foss, Sonja K., 3, 11–12
Foucault, Michel, 209
Fraisse, Jean Claude, 39
Fuchs, Esther, 7, 16, 84

Garland, David E., 26, 142, 146, 185
Garnsey, Peter, 57, 62, 102
Geoffrion, Timothy C., 23, 30–34, 50, 64, 94, 102, 124, 126, 128–129, 133, 135–136, 144, 150, 182
Georgi, Dieter, 9, 146
Gitay, Yehoshua, 118
Given, Mark D., 8
Glenn, Cheryl, 12
Gnilka, Joachim, 28, 153
Gold, Barbara K. 42
Golden, James L., 116
Goldhill, Simon D., 39
Good, James M. M., 10
Gowler, David, 6–7
Grant, Jacquelyn, 210
Grether, G., 79
Griffin, Cindy L., 12
Gunther, John J., 141, 166

Hardie, William F. R., 37,
Hauser, Alan J., 3–5, 8–10
Hawthorne, Gerald F., 23, 31
Hayes, John H., 3, 51
Hearon, Holly E., 14
Hendrix, Holland L., 77, 99–101, 106
Herzberg, Bruce, 3, 11, 116
Hester, James D., 8
Heuzey, Leon A., 79
Heyob, Sharon K., 78
Hock, Ronald F., 39, 65–66
Hoddinott, Ralph F., 76
Holloway, Paul A., 16, 19, 25–26, 123, 148

INDICES 259

Hornus, Jean-Michel, 52
Horsley, Richard A., 51, 146, 211
Hubbell, Harry Mortimer, 91
Hutter, Horst, 38–43, 45, 47–48, 65–66, 68

Isasi-Díaz, Ada María, 210

Jaeger, Werner, 94,
Jaquette, James L., 26–27, 35, 128, 135
Jarratt, Susan C., 12
Jasper, David, 5
Jewett, Robert, 26
Johnson, Luke Timothy, 26
Johnson-DeBaufre, Melanie, 16
Jones, A. H. M., 59, 102

Käsemann, Ernst, 18, 133, 185
Kazarow, Gawril, 75
Kennedy, George A., 3–4
Keppie, Lawrence, 54–62, 67, 103–106
Kim, Yong Bock, 210
Kittredge, Cynthia Briggs, 16–17, 19, 70, 85, 119, 134–136, 146, 148, 155–156, 184, 198
Koester, Helmut, 76
Konstan, David, 37, 39–43, 45–46, 65–66, 68
Koperski, Veronica, 143
Koskenniemi, Heikki, 24
Koukouli-Chrysantaki, Chaido, 75–77, 79, 99–101
Kraemer, Ross Shepard, 83–85
Kraftchick, Steven J., 118
Krentz, Edgar, 29–34, 50, 102, 124, 129, 135, 150, 152
Kroll, Wilhelm, 41
Kwok Pui-lan, 50, 210

Langer, Susanne K., 11
Larsen, Jakob A. O., 93, 102–103, 107
Lausberg, Heinrich, 8
Lazarides, Demetrios, 76

Lefkowitz, Mary R., 74, 109–110
Lemerle, Paul, 90
Levick, Barbara, 51, 102
Liew, Tat-siong Benny, 211
Lightstone, Jack N., 6
Lintott, Andrew, 48
Lohmeyer, Ernst, 18, 24, 133, 135, 185
Lucaites, John Louis, 12
Luck, Georg, 80
Lunsford, Andrea A., 10, 12
Luttwak, Edward N., 46, 53, 60
Lyon, Arabella, 11

MacDonald, Dennis R., 89
Mack, Burton, 6
Malherbe, Abraham J., 24–28, 35, 44, 93, 129, 132
Malina, Bruce J., 6
Mann, John C., 56
Marchal, Joseph A., 29
Marshall, John W., 18
Marshall, Peter, 35
Martin, Clarice J., 86–88
Martin, Dale B., 91–93, 95–98, 127, 129, 147, 162
Martin, Ralph B., 18, 133, 135, 185
Mattern, Susan P., 41, 53, 57–59
Matthews, Shelly, 16, 86–89
Mattingly, David J., 49
McCloskey, Donald N., 12
McKerrow, Rayme, 13
Meeks, Wayne, 18–19, 25, 34, 122, 136
Megill, Alan, 13
Meggitt, Justin J., 111
Meyers, Carol, 83–84
Mitchell, Alan C., 25
Mitchell, Margaret M., 5, 8–9, 91–98, 127, 162
Moore, Stephen D., 147, 212
Muilenberg, James, 4, 9
Müller, Ulrich B., 18

Nelson, John S., 12

Newsom, Carol A., 83, 85
Neyrey, Jerome H., 6, 105

Oakes, Peter S., 19, 29, 69, 99–102, 105–108, 110–111, 128, 148
Oakman, Douglas E., 105
Olbrechts-Tyteca, Lucie, 10–11, 13, 115–125, 127–128, 130, 133–135, 137–139, 142, 145, 154–155, 157–159, 161, 164, 166–170, 172–182, 184, 186, 188–189, 192, 194–197, 199, 203–205
Olbricht, Thomas H., 4–8, 18
O'Neil, Edward N., 37, 40
Osiek, Carolyn, 16–17, 63, 85, 137–138, 144, 148

Papazoglou, Fanoula, 99
Patte, Daniel, 119
Patterson, John, 57, 59
Perelman, Chaïm L., 10–11, 13, 115–125, 127–128, 130, 133–135, 137–139, 142, 145, 154–155, 157–159, 161, 164, 166–170, 172–182, 184, 186, 188–189, 192, 194–197, 199, 203–205
Perkins, Pheme, 25
Pervo, Richard I., 66
Peterlin, Davorin, 19, 30, 33, 86, 110, 120, 148
Peterman, G. W., 153
Pilhofer, Peter, 29, 99–102, 107
Pilotta, Joseph J., 116
Pollard, T. E., 23–24, 26, 142, 185
Pomeroy, Sarah B., 74, 109
Portefaix, Lilian, 29–33, 64, 74–75, 77–82, 85–86, 88, 99–101, 108–109, 124, 129, 148, 150, 189
Porter, Stanley E., 4–7, 18

Rabinowitz, Nancy Sorkin, 74

Rawson, Beryl, 109
Reed, Jeffrey T., 18
Reimer, Ivoni Richter, 86–88
Reimer, Raymond Hubert, 30–33, 99–102, 124–125, 128–129, 135, 150, 152
Reumann, John, 18, 25
Rich, John, 47–48, 57, 67
Richlin, Amy, 74
Ringe, Sharon H., 83, 85
Robbins, Charles J., 135
Robbins, Vernon K., 6–7, 13
Roberts, Richard H., 10
Rossing, Barbara R., 87
Russell, Letty, 83

Saller, Richard P., 42, 44, 57, 62, 102, 109
Salviat, François, 76
Salyer, Gary, 118
Sampley, J. Paul, 25–26, 32, 36, 121–122, 182
Santosuosso, Antonio, 52–55, 57, 59, 62, 106
Sarikakēs, Theodoros Ch., 30
Schaberg, Jane, 16
Schenk, Wolgang, 28, 122
Schollmeier, Paul, 36–38, 40, 65
Schottroff, Luise, 86–87, 135, 184
Schroeder, Frederic M., 38, 66
Schuster, John Paul, 30–32, 63, 124–125, 128–129
Schüssler Fiorenza, Elisabeth, 3, 5–9, 11–17, 35, 69, 83–86, 88, 97, 147, 180, 183, 193–195, 202, 210
Scott, Sarah, 49
Segovia, Fernando F., 16, 50, 211
Seim, Turid Karlsen, 86–88
Sellew, Phillip, 18
Sève, Michel, 79
Sheppard, A. R. R., 91–92, 94–98
Sherwin-White, Adrian N., 51, 102

Shipley, Graham, 57
Siegert, Folker, 118
Simons, Herbert W., 12
Snyman, A. H., 18–19, 33
Stamps, Dennis L., 6
Stowers, Stanley K., 8, 25–29, 35, 39, 122, 125, 129, 135–136, 153
Sugirtharajah, R. S., 50, 211
Sumney, Jerry L., 7–8
Sutcliffe, Rebecca, 12
Sutherland, Christine Mason, 12

Tarn, W. W., 96
Taylor, Lily Ross, 42
Theissen, Gerd, 97, 147
Thimmes, Pamela, 11
Thom, Johan C., 38
Thraede, Klaus, 24
Tolbert, Mary Ann, 2, 5, 7, 11, 83, 158
Toulmin, Stephen, 10–11, 116
Trapp, Robert, 3, 11
Treggiari, Susan, 109
Trible, Phyllis, 9, 12

Übelacker, Walter, 7

Van Der Horst, Pieter W., 91
Vickers, Brian, 10
Von Harnack, Adolf, 30–31, 124

Wachob, Wesley H., 6-7
Wallace-Hadrill, Andrew, 42, 44–48, 67
Walter, Nikolaus, 128
Wansink, Craig S., 19, 128
Warnick, Barbara, 116–117
Washington, Harold C., 11
Watson, Duane F., 3–6, 8–10, 26–27, 30, 129, 133
Weber, Patrick, 79
Webster, Graham, 53, 57
Webster, Jane, 49
Weems, Renita J., 210

Weidmann, Frederick W., 64, 136–137, 182
Welborn, L. L., 91–96, 129
Wertheimer, Molly Meijer, 12, 116
White, L. Michael, 19, 25–29, 122, 129, 135, 148, 152, 190
Williams, Demetrius K., 19, 145
Wire, Antoinette Clark, 3–6, 8–10, 12–14, 84, 115, 118–119, 127, 133, 137, 146, 157, 160, 162, 173, 177, 179–180, 187, 200
Witherington, Ben, III., 17, 19, 25, 63, 91, 131
Witt, Rex, 77-78
Wood, Neal, 44
Woolf, Greg, 57
Wrede, Henning, 75
Wuellner, Wilhelm, 3–4, 8, 10, 116, 194

www.ingramcontent.com/pod-product-compliance
Lightning Source LLC
Chambersburg PA
CBHW020645300426
44112CB00007B/241